WORKFLOW PATTERNS

Information Systems

Eric Yu, Florian Matthes, Michael P. Papazoglou, editors

WORKFLOW PATTERNS
The Definitive Guide

Nick Russell
Wil M.P. van der Aalst
Arthur H.M. ter Hofstede

The MIT Press
Cambridge, Massachusetts
London, England

For information about special quantity discounts, please email special sales@mitpress.mit.edu.

This book was set in Times Roman using LATEX 2_ε by the authors.

Printed and bound in the United States of America.

Library of Congress Cataloging-in-Publication Data

Russell, Nick, 1967–
Workflow patterns : the definitive guide / Nick Russell, Wil M.P. van der Aalst, and Arthur H.M. ter Hofstede.
p. cm
Includes bibliographical references and index.
ISBN 978-0-262-02982-7 (hardcover : alk. paper)
1. Workflow—Data processing. 2. Industrial management—Data processing. I. Aalst, Wil M.P. van der. II. Ter Hofstede, Arthur H.M., 1966– III. Title.
HD62.17.R87 2016
658.5'3—dc23

2015011429

10 9 8 7 6 5 4

Excerpts from previously published workflow patterns papers are included with kind permission from Springer Science+Business Media:

Proceedings of the 24th International Conference on Conceptual Modeling (ER 2005), Workflow data patterns: Identification, representation and tool support, volume 3716 of Lecture Notes in Computer Science, 2005, pages 353–368, N. Russell, A.H.M. ter Hofstede, D. Edmond, and W.M.P. van der Aalst, figures 3, 4, © Springer-Verlag, Berlin, Heidelberg, 2005.

Proceedings of the 17th Conference on Advanced Information Systems Engineering (CAiSE'05), Workflow resource patterns: Identification, representation and tool support, volume 3520 of Lecture Notes in Computer Science, 2005, pages 216–232, N. Russell, W.M.P. van der Aalst, A.H.M. ter Hofstede, and D. Edmond, figures 2, 3,4, © Springer-Verlag, Berlin, Heidelberg, 2005.

Proceedings of the 18th International Conference on Advanced Information Systems Engineering (CAiSE'06), Workflow exception patterns, volume 4001 of Lecture Notes in Computer Science, 2006, pages 288–302, N. Russell, W.M.P. van der Aalst, and A.H.M. ter Hofstede, figures 1, 2, 3, 5, © Springer-Verlag, Berlin, Heidelberg, 2006.

Modern Business Process Automation: YAWL and Its Support Environment, A.H.M. ter Hofstede, W.M.P. van der Aalst, M. Adams, and N. Russell (eds.), figures 2.1, 2.13, 2.14, 2.16, table 2.3, © Springer-Verlag, Berlin, Heidelberg, 2010.

Process-Aware Information Systems: Bridging People and Software Through Process Technology, M. Dumas, W.M.P. van der Aalst, and A.H.M. ter Hofstede, figure 1.4, © 2005 by John Wiley & Sons, Inc. All rights reserved.

For Carol and Hugo, who lived the journey and made it all worthwhile — Nick

For Petia — Arthur

Contents

Preface

This book is the culmination of more than a decade of research in the area of workflow patterns. The *Workflow Patterns Initiative*, as it is now known, started in 1999, with the development of a collection of control-flow patterns. This was followed by the development of other pattern collections, notably for the data and resource perspectives, and a revision of the original control-flow patterns. These pattern collections are described in a number of academic publications and there is also a dedicated web site (www.workflowpatterns.com).

This book aims to be a comprehensive reference text for those interested in the workflow patterns, bringing together and revising material from a number of sources. The primary audience for this book is intended to be practitioners in the field of Business Process Management (BPM), particularly those with an interest in Business Process Automation (BPA). However, we also hope that this book will be of interest to academics and students in the field of BPM.

We have tried to make the book self-contained as much as possible. Therefore, we have explained a number of basic techniques and tools in some depth, before the detailed discussion of the various patterns. The patterns themselves are, by their very nature, language-independent and should provide the reader with a profound insight into essential process modelling requirements and solutions. This knowledge can prove to be invaluable during process model construction, tool selection, and language/tool development.

We would like to acknowledge the help that we have received from a wide range of vendors and industry sources during the course of the Workflow Patterns Initiative, Oracle Corp and Pallas Athena/Perceptive Software merit particular mention in this regard.

A number of people have been involved, in one way or another, in the Workflow Patterns Initiative over the years and we are grateful for their participation and their contributions. Some of these contributors played a significant role in the development of the patterns and/or in the conduct of patterns-based evaluations: Alistair Barros, Marlon Dumas, David Edmond, Bartek Kiepuszewski, Nataliya Mulyar, and Petia Wohed. We consider ourselves fortunate to have had the opportunity to collaborate with them.

Nick Russell, Brisbane, Australia,
Wil M.P. van der Aalst, Eindhoven, the Netherlands
Arthur H.M. ter Hofstede, Brisbane, Australia

List of Figures

List of Tables

Contributors

Nick Russell
Principal Research Fellow, Information Systems School, Queensland University of Technology

Wil M.P. van der Aalst
Distinguished University Professor and Chair, Architecture of Information Systems Group, Eindhoven University of Technology

Arthur H.M. ter Hofstede
Professor and Head of the Business Process Management Discipline, Information Systems School, Queensland University of Technology

I INTRODUCTION

1 Introduction

In recent years, the importance of the business process has come to the fore in many organizations. It is increasingly recognized that successful businesses are defined by the maturity and effectiveness of their business processes. These processes provide a means of ensuring that the core objectives and values of the business are embodied in the day-to-day business activities conducted on its behalf. Moreover, they also provide a means of guiding and focusing the efforts of individual resources that form part of the organization.

The advent of the business process can be traced back to the Industrial Revolution. Up until that time, people were largely responsible for their own subsistence requirements, and most processes were conducted under the auspices of a single individual. The establishment of factories and the large-scale automation of production activities led to a change in the notion of production where groups of individual workers became responsible for conducting individual activities that formed part of an overall process on a repetitive basis rather than undertaking the entire process themselves. Major innovations were proposed by people such as Adam Smith, Frederick Taylor, and Henry Ford. Smith (1723-1790) showed the advantages of the division of labor. Taylor (1856-1915) introduced the initial principles of scientific management. Ford (1863-1947) introduced the production line for the mass production of "black T-Fords." As a result of these innovations, workers changed from being generalists to specialists, and the process itself, rather than an individual resource, became the means of coordinating the series of work activities leading to the desired production outcome.

Although originally conceived as a means of coordinating activities associated with large-scale industrial production, over time the notion of the process has also been recognized as a useful approach to coordinating complex service- and knowledge-based activities. It is now generally accepted that modern organizations are underpinned by a series of business processes that describe their core activities. The increasing complexity and variability associated with these processes has seen an increased reliance on technological support to guide their definition and enactment, and the importance of the area has led to the establishment of the field of *Business Process Management (BPM)*, an area focused on "supporting business processes using methods, techniques, and software to design, enact, control, and analyze operational processes involving humans, organizations, applications, documents and other sources of information" [42].

The emergence of the BPM domain has garnered significant interest both from *Information Technology (IT)* practitioners and academics alike. It is frequently cited as one of the major challenges that corporate IT departments are facing and has led to a series of conferences in both the commercial and academic arenas. There are probably two major reasons for the rapid rise to prominence of the BPM domain. First, the notion of the business process is *pervasive*. It is a fundamental building block of the modern organization, and it is recognized that much of the value of an organization can be attributed to the effectiveness of its business processes. As such, the business processes that underpin an organization have an intrinsic financial value and need to be managed in the same way as other corporate assets. Second, the BPM field recognizes that this management process is *holistic* and extends not just to the design or development of business processes but also needs to consider how their operation and refinement will be managed in an ongoing sense.

Although the value proposition that the BPM field offers is compelling, it is important to consider a salient point in regard to the business process itself: *there is no commonly agreed notion of what constitutes a business process.* Traditional approaches to modeling business processes have attempted to do so from a single viewpoint. One stream of research thinking has focused on the data requirements of processes and developed diagrammatic notations for capturing the data elements and the relationships between them, leading to the production of data models and data dictionaries. Another has looked at the dynamics of the process as a sequence of activities resulting in a variety of modeling techniques that capture the constraints and causal dependencies that exist between these activities. A third line of investigation has proposed modeling the business as a whole rather than its individual processes and has focused on capturing its strategy, intentions, goals, and so on. A myriad of other approaches have also been proposed. However, none of them has resulted in an integrated notion of a business process. Moreover, attempts by both industry bodies and standards organizations to introduce some commonality in the areas of business process modeling and enactment have proven to be similarly unsuccessful. (The problem is not a lack of standards but rather an abundance of immature, industry-driven standards.) Consequently, the BPM field is currently characterized by a broad range of approaches to representing and enacting business processes and lacks both a core conceptual foundation and common vocabulary.

In effect, the current state of the BPM field is analogous to the confusion of languages that mythically occurred at the Tower of Babel. There are a series of distinct approaches all of which attempt to model and enact business processes in different ways and each of which has a different conceptual underpinning. This raises the question of how their fundamental characteristics might be identified and defined in a way that is sufficiently generic that it applies to the BPM domain more generally. An approach that has proven successful in other fields for addressing this sort of problem is the use of *patterns*.

First identified by Christopher Alexander in his seminal book *A Pattern Language* [25], which attempts to provide a means of gathering useful recurrent concepts in the architectural domain, patterns provide an extremely effective means of recognizing and delineating common constructs in a particular subject area. They do this by characterizing them in the form of problems and solutions to those problems. In recent years, patterns have been used in a number of different domains, but they have enjoyed the most success in the IT field, where the dialectic approach that they engender to problem solving has proven useful for identifying common approaches to resolving issues occurring in areas such as software design, enterprise application integration, data modeling, and user interface design [53, 54, 65].

In this book, we apply the pattern metaphor to the business process domain as a means of empirically deriving the core constructs that are desirable in a business process. The derivation activity is based on a broad survey of contemporary commercial BPM offerings, research prototypes, and modeling formalisms together with a systematic review of the BPM literature. Later in this introduction, we will discuss the approach taken to identifying patterns, but first we turn our attention to the notion of a business process, in particular, what should it contain and how can it be represented.

1.1 What is a business process?

Although there is no commonly agreed definition, a good description of a business process is provided by Pall [100], who defines it as "the logical organization of people, materials, energy, equipment, and procedures into work activities designed to produce a specified end result (work product)." Implicit in this definition is the notion that a business process incorporates a number of distinct dimensions. In other words, capturing a comprehensive view of a business process requires consideration of several distinct viewpoints. There are several distinct research fields that give guidance as to the range of viewpoints that should be considered. Table 1.1 gives an indication of four significant modeling frameworks from the enterprise modeling, enterprise architecture and workflow modeling fields, and the main modeling viewpoints that they each delineate.

Table 1.1

The viewpoints included in significant business/enterprise modeling frameworks. The viewpoints are grouped in three main areas: Control-flow, Data, and Resources.

	Zachmann [150]	ARIS [120]	CIMOSA [129]	MOBILE [68]
Control-flow	Function Schedule	Function Control	Function	Function Operation Behavior
Data	Data	Data	Information	Information
Resource	Organization Network Strategy	Organization	Resource Organization	Organization

Not surprisingly, it is immediately evident that there is a great deal of commonality among the conceptual viewpoints encompassed by each of them. Moreover, the terminology is almost identical in many cases. Therefore, we can usefully group these viewpoints into three main areas:

- **Control-flow,** which describes the set of tasks that make up a business process and the way in which the thread of execution is routed between them. This encompasses the Function viewpoint, which describes the activities making up a business process, the Control viewpoint, which describes how execution is routed between these activities (i.e., the order in which they are executed), and the Behavior viewpoint, which describes how individual activities are actually facilitated.
- **Data,** which captures the information that is required during the execution of a business process (i.e., "working data") and also that which is retained on a more permanent basis and corresponds to the Data and Information viewpoints.
- **Resource,** which identifies the people and facilities that actually carry out the business process, the organizational context in which they operate, and the various relationships between them. This encompasses the Resource and Organization viewpoints, which describe the human and physical resources utilized to accomplish a business process and the relationships between them, respectively. It also incorporates some elements of the Network and Strategy viewpoints in terms of the geographic relationship between resources and the rationale with which they select and undertake tasks associated with a business process.

These three areas form the basis for describing the dominant *perspectives* of a business process, and we will adopt them as the major dimensions for business process definition throughout this book. It is interesting to observe that although the enterprise modeling frameworks detailed above seek to provide a comprehensive description of a business process from multiple perspectives, the actual models for each of these perspectives are largely independent of each other and typically utilize distinct modeling notations. Table 1.2 gives an indication of the wide range of modeling approaches that are commonly used in each of these perspectives.

Table 1.2

Common modeling techniques grouped by the three dominant business process perspectives.

Control-flow perspective	Data perspective	Resource perspective
BPMN	UML class diagrams	Use cases
UML Activity Diagrams	ER diagrams	Role-activity diagrams
Petri nets	Object-role models	Organizational charts
State charts		X.500
EPCs		

One of the difficulties that arises when trying to provide a comprehensive view of a business process from multiple perspectives is in interrelating the information contained in the various underlying models. Because it is likely that distinct perspectives are documented using differing techniques, presenting a coherent view of the "big picture" is not easily achieved. Moreover, there is significant variation in the modeling constructs supported by individual techniques and the extent of information that they are able to capture. The challenges experienced in modeling business processes are complex and merit further discussion.

1.2 What are the challenges in modeling them?

There are a wide range of considerations that individual modeling techniques must address to effectively capture the information in a given domain and enable it to be interpreted and reused on a more general basis (cf. [61]). The same challenges apply to the modeling of business processes. To be effective as a vehicle for capturing and communicating business processes, a modeling formalism needs to demonstrate a number of qualities:

- **Expressiveness** It needs to be able to capture the complete range of concepts that occur in the domain of interest.
- **Suitability** The range of modeling constructs that are available should mirror the concepts and needs that arise in practice.
- **Sufficiency** There should not be an excess of modeling constructs, such that the same underlying concept can be represented in many different ways.
- **Precision** It needs to be able to capture concepts occurring in the domain in a precise and unambiguous way.
- **Enactability** There should be sufficient detail to allow the business process to be directly enacted without requiring the elicitation of any further information from users.
- **Comprehensibility** It needs to present the details of the business process being captured in a form that is intuitive to users. The captured process model should retain a resemblance to the operational process as it exists in practice.
- **Analyzability** It should facilitate further analysis of the business process both to establish its static design-time correctness as well as allowing for monitoring of its operation at run-time.
- **Independence** The formalism should not rely on any specific technological foundation.

Thus far, we did not show any concrete process models. To make the above discussion clearer, consider figure 1.1, which depicts a simple process. Business Process Model and Notation (BPMN) is used to describe the first part of a fictitious car rental process. Only the control-flow perspective is modeled. The process starts when the customer books a car. Insurance may be added or not. Then the check-in process is initiated. Then there are three

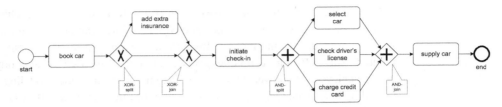

Figure 1.1

Business Process Model and Notation (BPMN) diagram describing a simple process allowing for 12 scenarios.

activities that can be executed in any order: selecting the car, checking the driver's licence, and charging the credit card. Finally, the car is supplied to the customer. BPMN does not show states explicitly: it just specifies possible orderings of activities. The model in figure 1.1 allows for $2 \times 3 = 12$ possible *scenarios*, also referred to as *traces* or *execution sequences*. One of these scenarios is *book car*, *initiate check-in*, *check driver's license*, *charge credit card*, *select car*, and *supply car*.

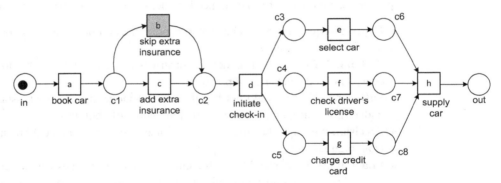

Figure 1.2

Workflow net (particular type of Petri net) allowing for the same 12 scenarios.

Figure 1.2 shows a so-called *workflow net*. This model is behaviorally equivalent to the BPMN model. Workflow nets are a subclass of Petri nets tailored toward the modeling of business processes. In this model, states are represented explicitly. The distribution of tokens (represented using "black dots") over places (represented as circles) determines the state of a particular case (process instance). In a workflow net, cases start with one token in the source place *in* and (hopefully) complete with one token on the sink place *out*. Transitions (the squares) consume and produce tokens depending on their input and output arcs (details will be given later).

Figure 1.3 shows another workflow net that can be viewed as an extension of figure 1.2. In comparison to the initial model, the process model has been modified to allow for adding

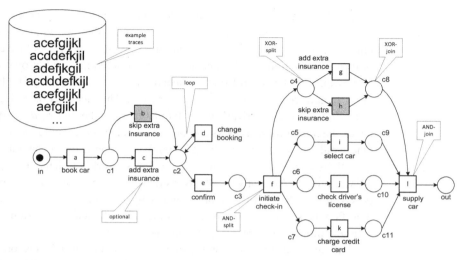

Figure 1.3
Workflow net allowing for infinitely many scenarios, some of which are shown (based on [4]).

insurance at a later stage. The *add extra insurance* activity can happen at two positions in the process as is shown by the two transitions *c* and *g*. The *skip extra insurance* activity can also happen at two positions in the process, as is shown by transitions *b* and *h*. These transitions are "invisible" (i.e., they cannot be observed because they do not correspond to real activities). Transitions *b* and *h* are merely added for routing purposes (like the AND/XOR-splits/joins in the BPMN model). Moreover, the booking can be changed (transition *d*) before the new confirmation activity (transition *e*). Multiple changes to the booking are possible, and a loop construct is used to model this. The resulting process has finitely many states but allows for infinitely many scenarios. Figure 1.3 shows some example traces. Note that the skip transitions are not recorded.

Using the aforementioned BPMN model and the two workflow nets, we now reflect on the qualities mentioned earlier (expressiveness, suitability, sufficiency, precision, enactability, comprehensibility, analyzability, and independence). The formalism used determines *expressiveness*. For example, classical Petri nets (or workflow nets) cannot be used (in general) to model priorities and cancelation. Expressiveness is different from *suitability*. For example, the "invisible" transitions in figure 1.3 can be used to model the skipping of activities. However, if this construction is needed frequently, then perhaps it is better to add it as a special construct. In some cases, cancelation can be modeled by enumerating all possibilities, but clearly such a solution is not suitable. However, there is a trade-off here. There should not be an excess of modeling constructs that can all be used to express the same behavior. Figure 1.3 is *precise*: it allows people to reason about what behaviors are possible according to the model. Not all notations have such clear semantics (i.e., some notations are deliberately vague or have semantics that are intuitively clear in most cases, but not if they are used in an atypical manner) (see e.g., the inclusive OR-join). Because of its precision, figure 1.3 can be enacted without requiring additional information (at least with respect to the control-flow perspective). Comprehensibility is a bit subjective. Is figure 1.1 more comprehensible than figure 1.2? This depends on training, experience, and taste. To use models actively, it is vital that they can be *analyzed* easily. One would like to check the model for deadlocks and other anomalies. One would like to predict bottlenecks. One would also like to "confront" models with the actual behavior observed (i.e., show deviations and observed bottlenecks). Clearly, workflow nets are easier to analyze than BPMN models. To analyze BPMN models, we often need to convert the model to Petri nets or some other formalism providing analysis techniques. Both formalisms (BPMN and workflow nets) do not rely on any specific technological foundation and are supported by a variety of tools. Hence, *independence* is ensured.

Challenges related to expressiveness, suitability, sufficiency, precision, enactability, comprehensibility, analyzability, and independence point to the need for a comprehensive modeling formalism for business processes that facilitates the capture of details from multiple perspectives in an integrated way. This is a challenge that has not yet been met. To achieve this aim, there is a fundamental need to establish an agreed vocabulary of elementary BPM concepts. One approach to developing this vocabulary is to pursue its development based on the identification of recurrent *patterns* that occur in BPM modeling.

1.3   How are process models being used?

After providing some examples of process models and discussing the core qualities of the formalism used to model, we now summarize "how, where, and when" BPM techniques can be used. We do this by briefly discussing the twenty *BPM use cases* presented in [4]. These use cases capture essential BPM activities and illustrate typical application scenarios using process models. The spectrum of process model usage is quite broad and ranges from creating handmade models to sophisticated types of analysis and enactment.

Figure 1.4 shows graphical representations for all twenty use cases. Models are depicted as pentagons marked with the letter "*M*." A model may be descriptive (*D*), normative (*N*), and/or executable (*E*). A "*D|N|E*" tag inside a pentagon means that the corresponding model is descriptive, normative, or executable. Tag "*E*" means that the model is executable. Configurable models are depicted as pentagons marked with "*CM*." Event data (e.g., an event log) are denoted by a disk symbol (cylinder shape) marked with the letter "*E*." Information systems used to support processes at runtime are depicted as squares with rounded corners and marked with the letter "*S*." Diagnostic information is denoted by a star shape marked with the letter "*D*." We distinguish between conformance-related diagnostics (star shape marked with "*CD*") and performance-related diagnostics (star shape marked with "*PD*"). The twenty atomic use cases can be chained together in so-called *composite* use cases. These composite cases correspond to realistic BPM scenarios.

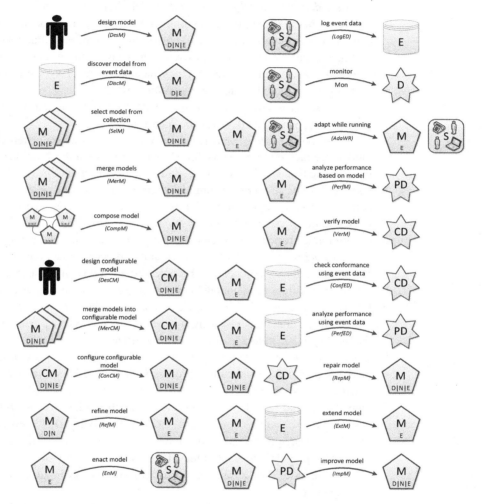

Figure 1.4
Twenty BPM use cases (from [4]).

We now briefly describe the twenty BPM use cases (see [4] for details):

1. Use case *design model* (DesM) refers to the creation of a process model from scratch by a human. This is still the most common way to create models. The hand-made model may be descriptive, normative, or executable. Descriptive models are made to describe

the as-is or to-be situation. If the model only describes the desired behavior, then it is called normative. An executable model can be interpreted unambiguously by software (e.g., to enact or verify a process).

2. Use case *discover model from event data* (DiscM) refers to the automated generation of a process model using process mining techniques [3]. The goal of process mining is to extract knowledge about a particular (operational) process from event logs (i.e., process mining describes a family of *a posteriori* analysis techniques exploiting the information recorded in audit trails, transaction logs, databases, etc). The (semi-)automated construction of process models is an alternative for DesM.

3. Use case *select model from collection* (SelM) refers to the retrieval of existing process models (e.g., based on keywords or process structures).

4. Use case *merge models* (MerM) refers to the scenario where different parts of different models are merged into one model. Unlike classical composition, the original parts may be indistinguishable (i.e., a completely new model is created).

5. Use case *compose model* (CompM) refers. to the situation where different models are combined into a larger model. Unlike the use case MerM, the different parts can be related to the original models used in the composition.

6. Configurable process models can be created from scratch as shown by the use case *design configurable model* (DesCM). A configurable process model represents a *family of process models*, that is, a model that through configuration can be customized for a particular setting. Sometimes such a model is referred to as a *reference model*.

7. Use case *merge models into configurable model* (MerCM) refers to approaches that obtain a configurable model by merging example members of a process family into a model that is able to generate a least the example variants.

8. Use case *configure configurable model* (ConCM) refers to the scenario where a concrete model is obtained by selecting a process variant (i.e., from a family of process variants one member is selected).

9. Only executable models can be enacted. Therefore, the use case *refine model* (RefM) describes the scenario of converting a model tagged with "*D|N*" into a model tagged with "*E*" (i.e., a descriptive or normative model is refined into a model that is also executable).

10. Executable models can be interpreted by BPM systems and used to support the execution of concrete cases. Use case *enact model* (EnM) takes as input a model and as output a running system.

11. Use case *log event data* (LogED) refers to the recording of event data, often referred to as *event logs*. Such event logs are used as input for various data-driven analysis techniques.

12. Use case *monitor* (Mon) refers to all measurements done at runtime without actively creating or using a model.

13. Use case *adapt while running* (AdaWR) refers to the situation where the model is adapted at runtime. The adapted model may be used by selected cases (ad-hoc change) or by all new cases (evolutionary change).

14. Executable process models can be used to analyze the expected performance in terms of response times, waiting times, flow times, utilization, costs, and so on. Use case *analyze performance based on model* (PerfM) refers to such analyzes. Simulation is the most widely applied analysis technique in BPM because of its flexibility.

15. Before a process model is put into production, one would like to get assurance that the model is correct. Use case *verify model* (VerM) refers to the analysis of such properties using techniques such as model checking.

16. Use case *check conformance using event data* (ConfED) refers to all kinds of analysis aiming at uncovering discrepancies between modeled and observed behavior. Conformance checking may be done for auditing purposes (e.g., to uncover fraud or malpractices).

17. Event data often contain timing information (i.e., events have timestamps that can be used for performance analysis). Use case *analyze performance using event data* (PerfED) refers to the combined use of models and timed event data. By replaying an event log with timestamps on a model, one can measure delays (e.g., the time in between two subsequent activities).

18. Use case ConfED can be used to see where reality and model deviate. The corresponding diagnostics can be used as input for use case *repair model* (RepM) (i.e., the model is adapted to better match reality).

19. Event logs refer to activities being executed, and events may be annotated with additional information such as the person/resource executing or initiating the activity, the timestamp of the event, or data elements recorded with the event. Use case *extend model* (ExtM) refers to the use of such additional information to enrich the process model. For example, timestamps of events may be used to add delay distributions to the model.

20. Performance-related diagnostics obtained through use case PerfED can be used to generate alternative process designs aiming at process improvements (e.g., to reduce costs or response times). Use case *improve model* (ImpM) refers to functionality helping organizations to improve processes by suggesting alternative process models. These models can be used to do "what-if" analysis. Note that unlike RepM, the focus of ImpM is on improving the process itself.

Clearly, some use cases have received more attention than others. In [4], BPM literature is analyzed to identify trends. The focus of this book is mostly on modeling and enactment (i.e., use cases DesM and EnM). However, one should not forget that the ultimate goal of process models is to improve the process themselves. In other words, the model is not the goal but improvements in terms of conformance and performance.

1.4 What are patterns?

The notion of patterns as a means of categorizing recurring *problems* and *solutions* in a particular domain is generally attributed to Christopher Alexander. He first proposed their use in the architectural domain as a means of organizing accumulated knowledge relating to building design practices. To characterize this knowledge, he proposed the notion of a pattern for capturing recurring concepts where a pattern is a descriptive construct with three parts: a *context*, which defines the situation in which the pattern applies, a set of *forces*, which arise repeatedly within a domain and characterize the problem being encountered, and a *solution*, which provides a means of resolving the problem and reconciling the forces being experienced. An intrinsic part of Alexander's approach was to describe different patterns in the same way, thus forming the basis for a *pattern language* in which the patterns serve as a vocabulary for the core concepts in the domain.

The original patterns work centered on the field of architecture; however, it was soon recognized to have more general applicability. The pattern concept has subsequently been used in a number of different fields. It has had most impact, however, in the field of IT where patterns have been used to categorize the major concepts in a number of areas including system design, business analysis, business process design, software architecture, and enterprise application integration. Perhaps the most significant patterns initiative in the IT domain is the *Design Patterns* initiative of Gamma, Helm, Johnson, and Vlissides (commonly referred to as the *Gang of Four*), in which they define a collection of common issues encountered in object-oriented software design [54]. They document these issues in the form of patterns based on a template that includes not only the *motivation* for the pattern and definition of its area of *applicability* but also a consideration of the *consequences* of its use, issues associated with its *implementation*, and even excerpts of *sample code*.

The *Gang of Four* approach to pattern definition has been extremely influential and has resulted in a more practical, solutions-oriented approach to the patterns catalogues developed in the IT community than has been the case in other disciplines such as architecture, which have remained closer in form to Alexander's original work. Indeed the use of patterns has become increasingly pervasive, not only as a means of defining and standardizing the terminology used in particular application areas, but also providing a source book of potential solutions to common issues that are able to be directly utilized in practice. There are dozens of patterns collections in the IT domain (e.g., the enterprise integration patterns by Hohpe and Woolf [65] and the analysis patterns by Fowler [53]).

Workflow, PAIS, BPM, or BPMS Patterns?

Both the terminology and the functionality of systems to support and automate processes have changed markedly since the first office information system emerged in the 1970s. In the 1990s the term Workflow Management (WFM) was hyped, and hundreds of commercial Workflow Process Management Systems (WFMS) emerged. The Workflow Patterns Initiative started in the late 1990s and was inspired by the differences in functionality of WFM products. The focus of classical WFMSs was on process automation, and the workflow patterns focused on the control-flow perspective. Over time, WFM technology was embedded in a variety of larger systems. For example, Enterprise Resource Planning (ERP) systems like SAP embed one or more workflow engines, most document management systems embed a WFM system, and the Windows Workflow Foundation (WF) adds WFM functionality to the .NET framework. The term Process-Aware Information Systems (PAIS) was introduced to signify that process support is not limited to pure-play WFMSs. Moreover, over time, vendors and analysts started to refer to WFMSs as Business Process Management Systems (BPMS). The term BPMS illustrates that the scope of most systems has broadened from process automation to process management, support, and analysis. In parallel, the scope of the initial workflow patterns collection was extended to include different BPM perspectives. Although the patterns described in this book are still called workflow patterns, they can also be viewed as PAIS patterns, BPM patterns, BPMS patterns, or process patterns.

1.5   What are workflow patterns?

There have been rapid advances in the technologies available for supporting the design and enactment of business processes over the past decade. As a consequence, there are now a wide range of systems that are driven by implicit or explicit business process models. This range of systems is collectively known as *Process-Aware Information Systems* (PAIS) and includes offerings as diverse as Workflow Management (WFM), Enterprise Resource Planning (ERP), and Customer Relationship Management (CRM) systems. These technologies are increasingly being used by organizations to underpin complex, mission-critical business processes. Yet despite the plethora of systems in both the commercial and research domains, there is a notable absence of commonly agreed concepts that individual offerings could be expected to support or that could be used as a basis for comparison. This absence differs markedly from other areas of information systems such as database design or transaction management, which are based on formal conceptual foundations that have effectively become de facto standards.

In an effort to gain a better understanding of the fundamental concepts underpinning business processes, the *Workflow Patterns Initiative* was conceived in the late 1990s with the goal of identifying the core conceptual constructs inherent in workflow technology. The original objective was to delineate the fundamental requirements that arise during business process modeling on a recurring basis and describe them in an imperative way. A patterns-based approach was taken to describe these requirements as it offered both a language-independent and technology-independent means of expressing their core characteristics in a form that was sufficiently generic to have broad relevance. As a result, the patterns can be applied to a wide variety of offerings.

One of the drivers for this research was the observation that although many workflow systems were based on similar conceptual underpinnings, they differed markedly in the range of concepts that they were able to capture with relative ease. Indeed, these differences were so significant that it raised the question of how the *suitability* of specific tools for specific purposes might be evaluated.

As an example, consider the difference between the *Deferred choice* pattern and the *Exclusive choice* pattern (both described in chapter 4). The *Exclusive choice* represents the divergence of a branch into two or more branches, such that when the incoming branch is enabled, the thread of control is immediately passed to precisely one of the outgoing branches. Such a choice is typically based an data. The *Deferred choice* is markedly different. Again one of several branches is chosen but now based on interaction with the operating environment. There is a "race" between different branches, only one of which can ultimately be chosen. After the decision is made, the execution alternatives in branches other than the one selected are withdrawn. The *Deferred choice* is different from the *Exclusive choice* in two respects:

- The decision is *not* based on evaluating a data-based condition; instead, it is based on interaction (e.g., an external message).
- The *moment of choice* is different. In an *Exclusive choice*, the decision is made immediately (i.e., the moment the choice is reached, the condition is evaluated). In a *Deferred choice*, the decision is left open. At the moment the choice is reached, it may be impossible to make a decision immediately because it may depend on a race between two triggers that is resolved much later.

Obviously, any reactive process requires a *Deferred choice* notion. However, before the workflow patterns were commonly accepted, most stakeholders were unable to distinguish both. In fact, checklists would mention AND-splits and XOR-splits as requirements without distinguishing the many variants. As we will show later, these differences are crucial.

Despite the plethora of workflow systems in the late 1990s (in both the commercial and research domains), there was a notable absence of core foundational concepts that individual offerings could be expected to support or that could be used as a basis for comparison. The *Workflow Patterns Initiative* aimed to address this shortcoming.

In line with the traditional patterns approaches used by Alexander and the "Gang of Four," which are based on a broad survey of existing problems and practices within a particular domain, the initial work (see the Workflow Patterns website[1] for further details) conducted as part of the *Workflow Patterns Initiative* identified twenty control-flow patterns through a comprehensive evaluation of workflow systems [14]. These patterns described a series of constructs that are embodied in existing offerings and offer solutions to problems commonly encountered in practice. The objective approach employed in their description ensured that their intent and function were clearly presented without mandating a specific implementation technology. An overriding objective was that they described control-flow characteristics that are *desirable* to support in a given offering.

Over time, different paradigms emerged on the basis of which languages were developed for the specification of workflows. Examples of such paradigms are the artifact-centric approach [6, 35], the object-centric approach, case handling [21], and the declarative approach [17]. Some of these paradigms are centered around a perspective other than the control-flow perspective, whereas the declarative modeling approach has a different and less prescriptive view on control-flow modeling (tending to focus on what is not allowed rather than on what is).

Initially, the focus was on control-flow only. This changed around 2004, when we started adding patterns for other core perspectives such as the workflow resource patterns, the workflow data patterns, and the exception handling patterns. Later, patterns related to service interaction and flexibility were also added. Whereas the control-flow patterns could be used to evaluate a language or notation, for the other patterns, it made more sense

---

1 http://www.workflowpatterns.com

to consider them in the context of a WFM/BPM system. In 2006, the original set of 20 control-flow patterns was revisited with the goal to provide a more precise description of each of the patterns and also to identify any potential gaps in the original set of patterns. As a result, the number roughly doubled (see chapter 4).

1.6   How do they help describe business processes?

The publication of the original 20 patterns in 2000 had a galvanizing effect on the BPM community. It provided clarity to concepts that were not previously well defined and provided a basis for comparative discussion of the capabilities of individual BPM offerings. Among some vendors, the extent of patterns support became a basis for product differentiation and promotion. Although initially focused on workflow systems, it soon became clear that the patterns were applicable in a much broader sense, and they were used to examine the capabilities of business process modeling languages such as BPMN, XPDL, UML Activity Diagrams and EPCs, web service composition languages such as WSCI, and business process execution languages such as BPML and BPEL.

The original workflow patterns focused on the control-flow perspective; however, a comprehensive description of a business process also requires consideration of the data and resource perspectives. With this requirement in mind, the *Workflow Patterns Initiative* was subsequently extended to include 40 data patterns [116] and 43 resource patterns [113]. Later research [89, 111] has also investigated relationships between these perspectives and proposed patterns-based approaches to workflow exception handling, process flexibility, and process interaction. Most recently, a comprehensive review of the control-flow patterns reorganized their classification and extended their scope to encompass 43 patterns describing control-flow characteristics of business processes [115].

The original workflow patterns provided the conceptual basis for the YAWL language and subsequent workflow system (see [12] for more details). YAWL is an acronym for "*Yet Another Workflow Language,*" an initiative that aims to provide both a workflow language that is based on the workflow patterns and an open-source reference implementation that demonstrates the manner in which these constructs can co-exist and interoperate. This work has been subsequently extended to encompass the data and resource perspectives and forms the basis for *new*YAWL [111], a reference language for workflow systems that has influenced subsequent development of the data and resource capabilities in the YAWL System.

The main article on the original control-flow patterns published in Distributed and Parallel Databases in 2003 has attracted a significant number of citations over the years, so much so in fact that it has become one of the most cited articles in the workflow area. The article's analysis of contemporary commercial tools and research prototypes showed lacunae in their capabilities and as such provided a basis for a roadmap to supporting more functionality. The article also showed how in some instances a lack of direct support for a certain pattern could be overcome through the use of other patterns. In addition, the workflow patterns filled a gap in the literature by providing a concrete framework of reference against which languages and tools, whether established or newly proposed, could be assessed. Over time, a substantial number of languages, standards, and systems were evaluated in terms of their support for the workflow patterns. Furthermore, numerous standards and products were influenced by the workflow patterns. A number of self-evaluations by vendors of their BPM offerings can be found in the "Vendors Corner" of the workflow patterns website. The patterns also played a role in the initial design of BPMN. The BPMN 2.0.2 standard document [97] still makes a number of references to the workflow control-flow patterns identifying correspondences between language constructs and specific patterns.

Seen from the viewpoint of today's systems and languages, it may seem obvious that there is a need for supporting patterns like the *Deferred choice*. However, one should not forget that few systems were able to support this pattern in the late in the late 1990s.

1.7   What is the format of a workflow pattern?

One of the major benefits offered by the workflow patterns is that they provide a common vocabulary for describing concepts arising in business processes without prescribing a specific approach to their implementation. To ensure that they are described in a comparable way, all of the workflow patterns are documented in the same format. This is based on the use of a standard template that contains the following elements:

- **Name:** A few words describing the essence of the pattern.
- **Description:** A summary of its functionality.
- **Synonyms:** Alternative names for the pattern (optional).
- **Examples:** One or more illustrative examples of the pattern's usage.
- **Motivation:** The rationale for the use of the pattern.
- **Operation:** An explanation of the problem the pattern addresses and the manner in which it does so, including details of the pattern operationalization where necessary.
- **Context:** Conditions that must hold in order for the pattern to be used in a process context.
- **Implementation:** How the pattern is typically realized in practice.
- **Issues:** Problems potentially encountered when using or implementing the pattern.
- **Solutions:** How these problems can be overcome.

The use of a standard approach to documenting the workflow patterns is consistent with other pattern catalogues and has a number of advantages. It ensures that all of the patterns are documented in a similar manner and are described at the same level of detail. Additionally, it necessitates that the definition process is rigorous and every pattern is subject to the same degree of scrutiny. Most importantly, the use of a standard format provides the basis for the development of a pattern language in a given domain as all patterns are described in the same manner. This leaves open the way for patterns to be used in a compositional way to describe more complex scenarios that might be encountered in the domain in which the patterns operate.

The approach taken to documenting the workflow patterns seeks to both motivate their need and define how they can be used to resolve common issues encountered in the modeling and enactment of business processes. There is significant emphasis on describing the manner in which they operate from a conceptual standpoint. This approach is consistent with other patterns initiatives, particularly the Gang of Four's Design Patterns, which adopt a dialectic problem/solution approach to describing recurrent design considerations occurring in the architectural and software design and analysis domains.

1.8   How is this book organized?

The aim of this book is to provide a comprehensive guide to the workflow patterns in terms of both their individual operation and their application to business process modeling and enactment issues that arise in practice. *Although possible, the patterns have not been fully formalized, as this would complicate their definition and also introduce a bias toward a particular formalism.* There is a delicate balance between generality and precision. A patterns collection should not impose a particular language. However, when describing a pattern, one often needs to resort to concrete examples. For example, the design patterns book by the "Gang of Four" [54] includes many examples using C++ and Smalltalk. However, these examples should not be confused with the actual patterns. Similarly, the workflow patterns are clarified using small examples, whereas the actual description is kept as general as possible (without losing precision).

The various chapters in the book are organized into four main parts as illustrated in figure 1.5. It is anticipated that the book will be used in one of two ways. For those readers seeking a comprehensive introduction to the workflow patterns material, the various sections are best read sequentially, although readers with a strong background in the BPM area will be able to directly tackle the material in the workflow patterns sections (part III) without difficulty. For those readers who already have some familiarity with the patterns, it is intended that this work can be used as a reference supporting BPM practice. With this aim in mind, the various descriptions of individual patterns are documented such that they do not assume significant knowledge of facilities provided by other patterns, thus ensuring that they can be used independently.

```
┌─────────────────────────────────────────┐
│ I. Introduction                          │
│    1. Introduction                       │
│                                          │
│ II. BPM Fundamentals                     │
│    2. Business process modeling          │
│    3. Business process management        │
│       systems                            │
│                                          │
│ III. Workflow Patterns                   │
│    4. Control-flow patterns              │
│    5. Data patterns                      │
│    6. Resource patterns                  │
│                                          │
│ IV. Conclusion                           │
│    7. Related BPM patterns               │
│       collections                        │
│    8. Epilogue                           │
└─────────────────────────────────────────┘
```

Figure 1.5

Organization of the book.

For illustrative purposes, throughout the book, we have selected three candidate technologies for discussing the issues associated with individual patterns and potential solutions. These technologies include BPMN (version 2.0.2), a widely used business process modeling formalism, BPMone (version 2.2), a leading example of a case management system, and Oracle BPEL, part of Oracle SOA Suite (version 11g release 1), one of the foremost toolsets for service-oriented process enablement.

The workflow patterns are part of a continually expanding field that seeks to provide a comprehensive foundation for process-aware information systems. There are a number of other patterns initiatives — some of which are ongoing — that produced complementary sets of patterns. In part IV, we survey some of the more important efforts in this area and the opportunities that they offer, before concluding the book.

1.9   Further reading

The following books and journal articles provide further background material on the topics introduced in this chapter:

- [25] is the seminal book by Christopher Alexander, in which he proposed the use of patterns languages as a means of capturing and sharing tacit knowledge on recurrent problems in the architectural domain and proven solutions to them. This work is based on his work on architectural patterns in [24]. The patterns concept has subsequently been used as a mechanism for quantifying knowledge in a wide variety of domains and has proven to be particularly successful in the IT field.

- [54] was the first application of the patterns concept in the IT domain. It documented 23 recurrent designs relevant to software development and immediately garnered significant interest in the use of patterns-based approaches for capturing IT knowledge in a generic form that facilitated its reuse on a widespread basis. The format it utilized for documenting patterns has been widely adopted by subsequent patterns initiatives.
- [14] introduces the notion of *workflow patterns*, which constitute desirable features for workflow languages and systems. In this article, 20 control-flow patterns are presented, and their occurrence in a variety of commercial and academic workflow systems is evaluated. Subsequent extensions to this work include:

  — [115], which extends the range of identified control-flow patterns to 43 distinct constructs.
  — [116], which describes a collection of 40 data patterns. These patterns describe BPM functionality for storing, managing, and using data.
  — The resource patterns in [113] also extend the scope of the original workflow patterns. Forty-three patterns describe how work can be distributed and managed in a BPMS.
  — [111] presents the first multiperspective view of the workflow patterns and examines the relationships between these perspectives leading to a formal definition of the workflow patterns.

- [12], introduces YAWL, a workflow language (and subsequently an open-source system) based on the workflow patterns. Its initial focus was on the control-flow perspective as exemplified by the original 20 workflow patterns. Subsequent extensions to the workflow patterns (especially to the data and resource perspectives) led to a comprehensive overhaul — termed *new*YAWL — which accommodates the majority of these patterns and serves as a reference implementation for a workflow language. This is described in detail in [111].
- [64] is the definitive work on YAWL and provides both a comprehensive description of the language and its various features together with two case studies illustrating its operation in practice.
- [42] surveys the definition and automation of business processes based on process-aware technologies. It provides a collection of readings in the area of process-aware information systems.
- [19] describes a Petri-net-based approach to model and analyze business information systems.
- [150] presents the Zachmann framework, a widely cited means of describing the various perspectives that an enterprise architecture should contain and the different levels of information granularity within each perspective.
- [10] uses Petri nets as a means to conceptualize the desired functionality of a workflow management system. It already pointed out the need to distinguish between *Exclusive choice* (called explicit split) and *Deferred choice* (called implicit split).

- [120] describes the ARIS framework for business process modeling and introduces the various modeling formalisms that it encompasses.
- [129] presents the Computer aIded Manufacturing Open Source Architecture (CIMOSA) framework, an enterprise modeling framework specifically developed in the context of a European Union project for the computer manufacturing domain.
- [68] is one of the first books devoted to the area of workflow technology. It presents MOBILE, a prototype workflow architecture that has been influential in defining the various perspectives deemed relevant when modeling and enacting business processes.
- [55] is a seminal paper in the workflow technology area and presents one of the first comprehensive frameworks characterizing the spectrum of technologies falling under the workflow umbrella.
- [143] presents the Workflow Reference Model, a canonical model for workflow technology advanced by the Workflow Management Coalition (WfMC), an industry consortium of workflow tool vendors.
- [4, 45, 103, 136] provide comprehensive surveys of the business process management field.

II BPM FUNDAMENTALS

2 Business Process Modeling

In this chapter, we introduce the area of business process modeling, the practice of capturing the details associated with the operation of business processes in written form. In doing so, we define the fundamental concepts that underpin the act of business process modeling, examine the objectives and history of the field, and outline popular contemporary modeling techniques.

2.1 Fundamental concepts

The genesis of the business process modeling field lies in the areas of *process modeling*, which seeks to describe the dynamic aspects of processes and has its antecedents in the area of mathematics, and *system modeling*, which stems from the need to describe software systems and their intended operation. *Business process modeling* seeks to provide a holistic description of an operational process and considers not only the issues of task coordination and control-flow but also data definition and usage in the context of the process and the organizational environment (organizational structure, resources, reporting lines, etc.) in which it will operate.

A *process* is considered to be a collection of related activities together with associated execution constraints that lead to some anticipated end goal or outcome. Although the notion of a process has general applicability, it is the execution of a process in the context of a given organizational setting — commonly termed a *business process* — that is of most interest for us in this book.

A business process is described by a *business process model*, which defines its means of operation. This may be at an *abstract* level, where there is no consideration of how it will ultimately be effected and the focus is on the type of work activities making up a process and the sequence in which they are undertaken, or at a *concrete* level, where it is described in sufficient detail such that the model can be directly executed by a software system.

Figure 2.1 outlines the various aspects associated with business process design and execution. A dedicated software system called the *business process designer* or *editor* is used to design the business process model. Once this contains sufficient detail, it can be utilized to guide the operation of the *Business Process Management System (BPMS)*. This involves loading the business process model into the BPMS and executing it in conjunction with any other information that is required to facilitate its operation. This may include data associated with resources and the organizational structure from an *organizational repository* (e.g., HR systems, LDAP, or X.500 databases), data from *external databases*, and the results of interactions with *external systems* and *web services*. The interaction of *process*

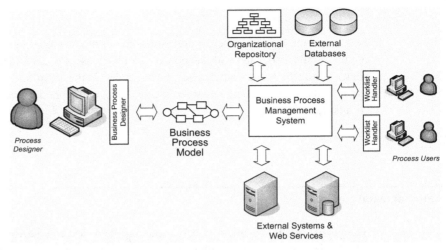

Figure 2.1
Design and execution of a business process.

participants with the business process occurs via individual *worklist handlers*, which display the work allocated to specific users and allow them to signal how they intend to deal with it.

The business process model is typically centered around a description of the control-flow aspects of the process in the form of a directed graph, in which the constituent *tasks*, which describe the individual work activities that comprise the process, are connected by directed arcs indicating the various execution paths through the process. Different forms of gateway constructs (splits and joins) allow alternate execution paths to be taken through the process model. Business process models can be *hierarchical* in nature as the operation of an individual task within a model can be described in terms of a more detailed process specification, a concept commonly known as *decomposition*.

Figure 2.2 outlines the main control-flow and data concepts relating to a business process model in the form of a UML class diagram. A *specification* defines a particular process model within an overall business process. A specification is composed of *tasks*, *gateways*, and *arcs*. As shown by the *contains* relationship, a task appears in precisely one specification. Although not shown, this also holds (implicitly) for gateways and arcs: they are only added to describe the routing of tasks within a specification. Gateways define the various splits and joins that connect (and diverge) branches within process models. Within a given process specification, directed arcs connect tasks and/or gateway nodes and define the execution sequence within the process model. Each arc has precisely one source and one target (task or gateway). In some cases (e.g., the individual output branches from an XOR-split), the triggering of an individual arc is based on the positive evaluation of an associated Boolean *condition*. Similarly, specifications and tasks may have *preconditions* and *postconditions* associated with their execution defining the time at which they are able to be enabled and can complete, respectively.

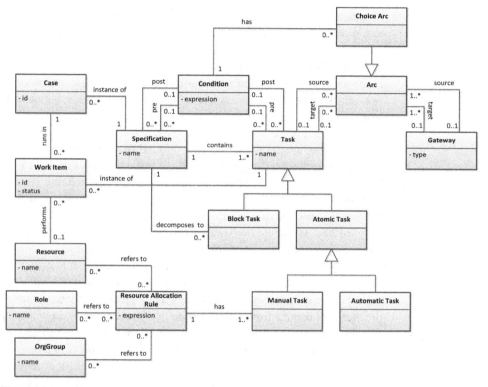

Figure 2.2

UML class diagram of main control-flow and resource concepts.

A *task* corresponds to a single unit of work. An *atomic task* has a simple, self-contained definition (i.e., one that is not described in terms of other tasks). A *block task* (also known as a *composite task*) is a complex activity whose implementation is described in terms of a *subprocess*, which has an associated process specification. As shown by the *decomposes to* relation in figure 2.2, a block task corresponds to precisely one specification, but multiple block tasks may refer to the same specification. When a block task is started, it passes control to the first task(s) in its corresponding subprocess. This subprocess executes to completion, and at its conclusion it passes control back to the composite task.

Tasks can be of two types: *manual* or *automatic*. A *manual task* is allocated to one or more resources (usually human resources) for completion, whereas an *automatic task* can be undertaken without requiring any human input (e.g., by executing a program or invoking a web service). A manual task has an associated *resource allocation rule* that indicates how the corresponding work items will be allocated to resources. The resource allocation rule is an expression that may refer to individual *resources*, *roles*, and *organizational groups*. An example expression is "Task A should be executed by a manager (role) in the sales department (organizational group) or by Pete (resource)." An *organizational group* is formal grouping of resources within an organization, and a role is a set of resources with a common characteristic.

Each invocation of a task is termed a *work item*. Specific invocations are undertaken by at most one resource. Each invocation of a complete business process model is termed a *case*. Each work item executes within the context of a particular case. Usually there is one work item initiated for each task in a given case; however, where a task forms part of a loop, a distinct work item is created for each iteration of the loop (e.g., the task is invoked each time the thread of control cycles around the loop). Similarly multiple instances of a task are created for a designated "multiple instance" task construct when it is initiated.

There may be multiple cases of a particular process running simultaneously; however, each of these is assumed to have an independent existence, and they typically execute without reference to each other. There is usually a unique first node and a unique final node in a process. These are the starting and finishing points for each given process instance. The execution of a case is typically signified by the notion of a *thread of control* (of which there may be several in any given process instance), which indicates the current execution point(s) within the process. The initiation of a case occurs when a new thread of control is placed in the starting node for a process. The execution of the case involves the traversal of the thread of control from the start node to the end node. As a consequence of the presence of split gateway operators in a process, it is possible for the thread of control to be split into several distinct threads of control during execution of a process instance. Similarly, join gateway operators in a process provide a mechanism for execution threads on several incoming branches to be merged into one execution thread on a single outgoing branch.

A desirable quality of a process, however, is that it is *sound* as this excludes some of the basic (but relatively commonplace) process design flaws. Soundness is defined with respect to a start node (initial state) and an end node (desired end state). A process is sound if (1) it is always possible to reach the end state (there is always an option to complete, i.e., no deadlocks or livelocks), (2) upon reaching the end state there should be no other threads of control, and (3) for every task there should be at least one scenario from start to end where it is executed [1, 11].

Just as soundness is one possible property of a process based on its structural characteristics, there are other properties that a process may demonstrate. *Structuredness* refers to a structural property of a process where splits and joins are balanced as illustrated in figures 2.3(a) and (d). In figures 2.3(b) and (c), there are examples of processes that seem to be structured but are not. In figure 2.3(b), the split and join types don't match, and in figure

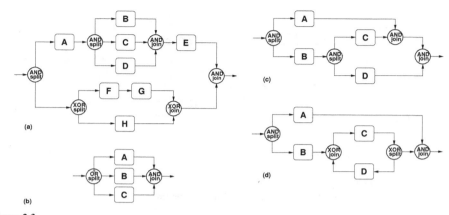

Figure 2.3

The concept of structuredness: illustrative examples.

2.3(c), the splits and joins are balanced but overlap. All of the processes are sound except for that in figure 2.3(b).

One of the desirable characteristics of a structured process model is that it is also *safe*. In an unsafe model, there may be multiple indistinguishable threads of control belonging to the same case concurrently visiting a node in the process. As a result, there may be two indistinguishable task instances.

Traditionally, much of the focus of business process modeling has been on the control-flow aspects; however, there are also other considerations in regard to data and resource handling that are of particular importance when attempting to develop business process definitions that closely mirror real-life scenarios. The representation and usage of data within a process is of fundamental importance as in practice, almost every process involves the coordination of business tasks based on various items of information available both within and outside of the context of the business process. We consider a distinction between two types of data associated with a process model: (1) *model data*, which refer to data elements used in the structural definition of the business process model — these are essentially static in nature for a given process model and do not change once a business process has been defined (i.e., their values are identical for each instance of the process), and (2) *production data*, which relate to actual working data elements that are directly utilized and may change during the operation of the business process (i.e., they are dynamic in nature).

The set of *production data* associated with a given process instance defines its *state* at any given point in time. This takes the form of a series of data elements, which may be simple or structured in form and have a value (or set of values) associated with them. Data elements may be used for a variety of purposes during process execution, including

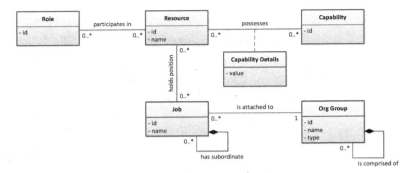

Figure 2.4
UML class diagram of main organizational concepts.

communication of data between task instances and process instances, routing decisions when deciding which branches to take during execution, and when to start and complete a task instance (*preconditions* and *postconditions*).

Each data element has a specific *scope* that defines the region in a given process in which it is available. This may be as broad as every instance of the process, throughout an entire case associated with the process, or as limited as a given task instance. The scope of a data element also determines its lifespan. Case data elements may exist for the entire time that a case executes, whereas a data element whose scope is limited to a specific task may only exist for a given execution instance of the task within a case. Should the task execute more than once, then there may be more than one instance of the data element during the execution of the case. For a given case, the notion of *state* refers to the complete collection of model and production data elements. This collection completely specifies the current execution status of the case.

The other aspect of a business process that merits further discussion relates to *resources* (i.e., the entities that actually undertake the work items in the business process). In general, it is assumed that a business process is defined in the context of an organization and utilizes specific resources within the organization to complete the tasks of which the business process is composed. Hence (other than for fully automated processes), there is usually an *organizational model* associated with each business process that describes the overall structure of the organization in which it operates and captures details of the various resources and the relationships between them that are relevant to the conduct of the business process. Figure 2.4 outlines the main organizational concepts relating to business processes in the form of a UML class diagram.

A resource is considered to be an entity that is capable of doing work. Although resources can be either human or non-human (e.g., plant and equipment), we will focus on human resources. Work is assigned to a resource in the form of work items, and they receive notification of work items distributed to them via a *worklist handler*, a software application that provides them with a view of their work items and supports their interaction with the system managing overall process execution. Depending on the sophistication of this application, users may have one or several work queues assigned to them through which work items are distributed. They may also be provided with a range of facilities for managing work items assigned to them through to completion.

A human resource is assumed to be a member of an *organization*. An organization is a formal grouping of resources that undertake work items pertaining to a common set of business objectives. Resources usually have a specific *job* within that organization, and in general, most organizational characteristics that they possess relate to the position(s) that they occupy rather than directly to the resource themselves. There are two sets of characteristics that are exceptions to this rule, however: *roles* and *capabilities*.

Roles serve as another grouping mechanism for human resources with similar job roles or responsibility levels (e.g., managers, union delegates, etc.). Each resource may have one or more corresponding roles. Individual resources may also possess *capabilities* or attributes that further clarify their suitability for various kinds of work. These may include qualifications and skills as well as other job-related or personal attributes such as specific responsibilities held or previous work experience.

Each *job* is attached to an *organizational group*, which is a permanent group of human resources within the organization that undertake work items relating to a common set of business objectives. Organizational groups may be comprised of other (subordinate) organizational groups and thus form a hierarchy within the organization. Within the organizational hierarchy, each job may have a number of specific *subordinates* for whom they are responsible and to whom each of them reports.

Of particular interest from a resource perspective is the manner in which work items are distributed and ultimately bound to specific resources for execution. Figure 2.5 illustrates the lifecycle of a work item in the form of a state transition diagram from the time that a work item is created through to final completion or failure. It can be seen that there are a series of potential states that comprise this process.

Initially, a work item comes into existence in the *created* state. This indicates that the preconditions required for its enablement have been satisfied, and it is capable of being executed. At this point, however, the work item has not been offered or allocated to a resource for execution, and there are a number of possible paths through these states that the individual work item may take.

Transitions from the *created* state are typically initiated by the system. They center on the activity of making resources aware of work items that require execution. This may occur in one of three distinct ways denoted by the subsequent states. A work item may be *offered to a single resource*, meaning that the system informs exactly one resource about the availability of a work item. It may do this by sending a message to the resource or adding the work item to the list of available work items that the resource can view. Inherent in this

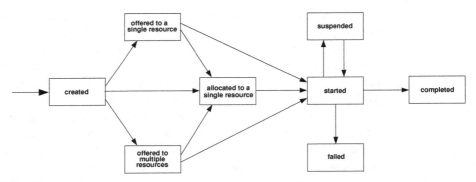

Figure 2.5
Basic work item lifecycle (from [113]).

is the notion of the system selecting a specific resource to which the work item should be advertised. This may occur in a variety of different ways — the process model may include specific directives about the identity of the resource to which a given work item should be directed or it may be based on more general requirements such as utilizing the least busy, cheapest, or most appropriately qualified resource. In each of these situations, there is the need to determine which resources are suitable and available to undertake the work item and then to rank them and select the most appropriate one.

An alternative to this course of action is indicated by the state *offered to multiple resources*, where the system informs multiple resources of the existence of a work item. Again the notion of resource selection applies; however, in this case, the system informs all suitable resources of the work item. It does not attempt to identify which of them should undertake it. This is now left to the resources (i.e., they can "compete" for work or divide the work in an informal manner) (outside of the system).

The *allocated to a single resource* state denotes the state of a work item where a specific resource has committed to its execution at some time in the future. A work item may progress to this state either because the system pre-emptively allocates newly created work items to a resource or because a resource volunteers to undertake a work item that has been offered.

Subsequent states in the work distribution model are *started*, which indicates that a resource has commenced executing the work item, *suspended*, which denotes that the resource has elected to cease execution of the work item for a period but does intend to continue working on it at a later time, *failed*, which identifies that the work item cannot be completed and that the resource will not work on it any further, and *completed*, which identifies a work item that has been successfully executed to completion.

2.2   Objectives of business process modeling

There are a variety of reasons for undertaking business process modeling, and in many cases, the desired outcome is more than just a series of diagrams capturing a business process. In this section, we discuss the motivations for business process modeling in more detail.

2.2.1   Business process definition

One of the major benefits offered by the act of business process modeling is that it provides a guided approach to gaining an understanding of the most important aspects of a business process and documenting them in a form that alleviates any potential for ambiguous interpretation. The notion of modeling the dynamic aspects of processes is not particularly novel and has been undertaken in the software design field for many years; however, it is only with the advent of richer, multiperspective business process modeling techniques that the accurate capture of the broader range of aspects relevant to business processes has been possible in a single model.

2.2.2   Business process enactment

Although in some cases business process modeling may be an objective in its own right, more generally, the development of such models is an intermediate step to their ultimate automation using some form of BPMS. As such, the business process model serves as a design blueprint for the subsequent software development and deployment activity. It may also serve as a means of identifying the most appropriate enactment technology.

2.2.3   Business process communication

The use of business process models provides an effective means of communicating their intention and operation in an unambiguous way to the various parties involved in their operation. As the underlying technology matures and the ambition level associated with business process automation initiatives increases, this becomes increasingly important as often the parties involved are not located within a single department or at a single operating location within a single organization but increasingly are located across a variety of different geographic locations and may even be members of different organizations (e.g., upstream suppliers or downstream customers). Business processes increasingly span organizational boundaries, and cross-organizational business process automation offers opportunities for enhancing and optimizing these processes in ways that were previously not possible. As the various parties to such a process will frequently utilize differing enabling technologies, business process models provide a way of communicating the operational expectations associated with these processes in an organizationally and technologically independent way.

2.2.4 Business process analysis

Business process models provide a good starting point for all kinds of analyses. For example, there are striking similarities between simulation models and the models used to enact processes using a WFM or BPM system. In the context of business process modeling, the two main types of analysis are *verification* and *performance analysis*.

The goal of verification is to find errors in systems or procedures (potential deadlocks, livelocks, etc.) in an early stage (i.e., before enactment). *Model checking* can be used to verify that the modeled system exhibits a set of desirable properties. Unfortunately, despite the availability of powerful analysis techniques and tools, few organizations apply verification techniques. This is unfortunate because empirical research shows that modelers tend to make many errors. For example, in [81], it is shown that more than 20 percent of the process models in the SAP reference model contain serious flaws (deadlocks, livelocks, etc.). Such models are not aligned with reality and introduce errors when used to configure the system. Unreliable and low-quality models provide little value for their end users.

Performance analysis aims to analyze processes with respect to key performance indicators such as throughput, response times, waiting times, and utilization. Techniques like *simulation* can be used to better understand the factors influencing these performance indicators Moreover, "what-if" scenarios can be analyzed and compared. This helps managers to improve and manage processes.

Verification and performance analysis are typically model-driven (i.e., the modeled reality is analyzed rather than reality itself). However, information systems are becoming more and more intertwined with the operational processes they support. As a result, a multitude of events are recorded by today's information systems. Reality can be observed by inspecting such event data. The goal of *process mining* is to use this data to extract process-related information (e.g., to automatically *discover* a process model by observing events recorded by some enterprise system) [3]. By linking business process models and historic and current data in the information system, new types of analyses come into reach. For example, process mining can reveal factual bottlenecks and quantify conformance.

2.2.5 Business process compliance

Many organizations have deployed automated business processes in recent years; however, changing business conditions and the relative inflexibility of the enabling technologies often means that the actual business process enacted by members of an organization on a day-to-day basis does not necessarily match that described in the original or intended business process model. Nonetheless, many corporate quality and risk management systems assume adherence to a given set of operating norms, which are often based on process models. Indeed, recent legislation such as the Sarbanes-Oxley Act [118] requires that U.S. organizations demonstrate compliance with a set of standard business processes in order to mitigate potential business risk.

Although country-specific, there is a large degree of commonality among Sarbanes-Oxley (US), Basel II/III (EU), J-SOX (Japan), C-SOX (Canada), 8th EU Directive (EURO-SOX), BilMoG (Germany), MiFID (EU), Law 262/05 (Italy), Code Lippens (Belgium), Code Tabaksblat (The Netherlands), and others [3]. These regulations require companies to identify the financial and operational risks inherent to their business processes and establish the appropriate controls to address them. Although the focus of these regulations is on financial aspects, they illustrate the desire to make processes transparent and auditable. The ISO 9000 family of standards is another illustration of this trend. For instance, ISO 9001:2008 requires organizations to model their operational processes. Currently, these standards do not force organizations to check conformance at the event level. For example, the real business process may be very different from the modeled business process.

An increasing area of focus for organizations deploying automated process solutions is the comparison of recorded execution history with standard corporate processes to assess the degree of compliance. To ensure that this activity is effective, precise business process models are a necessity. *Conformance checking* techniques [3, 5, 39] compare modeled behavior with observed behavior. These techniques basically try to replay reality on the modeled process. If there are deviations, then these are recorded, and the most similar path through the model is chosen.

Whereas conformance checking techniques compare observed event sequences with execution paths of the model, other business process compliance approaches compare different models (where models can also be just rules). For example, in [59], process models are compared with contracts. In other approaches, the specification model is compared with the implementation model (e.g., using refinement or inheritance notions) [7].

2.3   History of process modeling

The notion of process modeling has existed in various forms for several decades, and its specific application to business processes has been a particular objective for much of this time. The timeline shown in Figure 2.6 illustrates various techniques that have achieved some degree of popular use over the past 70 years and their relationship with other similarly founded techniques. As part of this analysis, we also give a relative evaluation of the *expressiveness* of each technique, by which we refer to the ability of the technique to capture the various aspects associated with a business process in a precise and holistic manner. These techniques fall into three main groups: software design methods, formal techniques, and dedicated BPM techniques. We discuss each in turn.

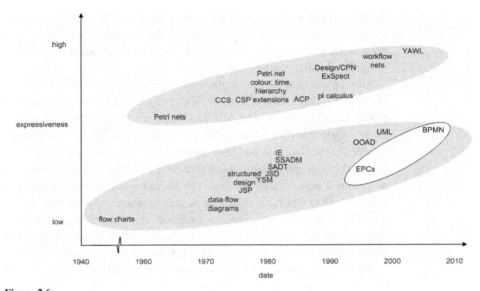

Figure 2.6

Timeline of process modeling techniques. Three main groups can be identified: software design methods (e.g., UML), formal techniques (e.g., Petri nets), and dedicated BPM techniques (e.g., BPMN).

2.3.1   Software design methods

Software design methods stem from the field of computing and aim to provide mechanisms for describing the dynamic aspects of processes. Much of the focus of these methods is on providing design-time support for the capture of processes with the intention of subsequently automating them using various forms of computing technology. With the advent of mechanized process support in the 1940s, it was soon apparent that a means of describing the structure of and execution flow through computer programs was required. Although there is some debate as to who was responsible for recognizing their applicability, it is clear that the flow process chart pioneered by Gilbreth in 1921 was introduced to the computing field in the period 1944–1947. Commonly known as flowcharts, the technique provides a graphical means of representing the set of steps in a process or algorithm as boxes connected by lines denoting the flow of control between them together with decision nodes identifying points in the process whether control-flow might take alternate paths on the basis of a specific decision.

Perhaps the next significant advance in the development of BPM techniques was the development of the Data Flow Diagram (DFD) in 1974, where a software system was viewed as a sequence of data transformations and individual programs effectively operated as functions on the data elements that flowed between them. The implicit notions behind

DFDs — that program units should be based on groups of tightly related functions, that the dependencies between them should be minimized, and that their coupling should be precisely defined — quickly led to the establishment of the structured design field for defining software systems and spawned techniques such as Jackson Structured Programming (JSP) as a means of describing software programs.

The initial successes associated with the structured design field subsequently led to the establishment of the notion of structured analysis, which proposed that an entire software system should be viewed in terms of the data flowing through it. It introduced additional modeling notations such as structure charts and context diagrams to show the manner in which program functionality was decomposed into individual functions and how they were assigned to available processing resources. In addition to the original proposal, this design philosophy also led to a plethora of related techniques, including Jackson Structured Design (JSD), Yourdon Structured Method (YSM), Structured Analysis and Design Technique (SADT), Structured System Analysis and Design Method (SSADM), and Information Engineering (IE).

The next significant advance in the software design field was the rise of Object-Oriented Analysis and Design (OOAD) methodologies, where the design of a software system was conceptualized in terms of tightly bound functional units known as classes and the interaction between individual instances of these classes known as objects. The major proponents of these techniques included Booch, Rumbaugh, and Jacobson, who devised their own OOAD technique, complete with various new ways of describing both the static and dynamic aspects of system operation. In 1997, the most significant aspects of the three techniques were merged into the Unified Modeling Language (UML), a methodology for describing software systems comprising 13 distinct modeling notations. Of these, the activity diagram notation is the most useful for modeling business processes.

2.3.2 Formal techniques

One of the criticisms associated with the use of many of the software design techniques described in the previous section is that they are informally defined; as a consequence, there is the potential for ambiguities and inconsistencies to arise where they are used for modeling business processes. To remedy this, a number of formal process modeling techniques have been developed in recent years, which have a fully defined operational semantics ensuring there is no potential for ambiguity to arise in their usage.

Perhaps the most well-known formal technique for process modeling is that of Petri nets devised by Carl Adam Petri in 1962. Petri nets have been widely used in a number of domains for modeling and analyzing concurrent systems and, more recently, for capturing dynamic aspects of business processes. One of the drawbacks with the original definition of Petri nets was that it lacked data concepts requiring that any notions of data manipulation be explicitly represented in the model. Another difficulty stemmed from the absence of the notion of hierarchy, allowing a model to be neatly decomposed into submodels with defined interfaces. There was also no notion of time in the original modeling formalism. High-level Petri nets, developed during the 1970s, added the notions of color (data support), hierarchy, and time to the original definition and addressed these deficiencies. The precise operational foundation associated with Petri nets and their graphical nature makes them an effective technique for modeling and evaluating process models, and several design and simulation tools have been developed for both basic Petri nets and variants of them. Two widely used tools supporting modeling and simulation of Colored Petri nets are Design/Colored Petri Nets (CPN) (1989) and ExSpect (early 1990s). Later Design/CPN was replaced by CPN Tools, providing enhanced support for simulation, animation, and analysis of models. Petri nets triggered the development of workflow nets — a variant of standard Petri nets suited to the specification of workflow processes — and also motivated the creation of YAWL (Yet Another Workflow Language), a multiperspective workflow modeling language and reference workflow management system implementation.

Process algebra techniques provide another stream of formal methods that have proven useful for modeling dynamic processes. Although they lack the intuitive graphical form of Petri nets, process algebras offer a powerful technique for modeling and analyzing concurrent systems and more recently have proven useful in capturing mobile processes. Significant process algebra initiatives include Calculus of Communicating Systems (CCS) during the period from 1973 to 1980, Communicating Sequential Processes (CSP) developed in 1978, and the Algebra of Communicating Processes (ACP) established in 1982. Most recently, the π-calculus, a successor to CCS, has been advocated as a suitable basis for modeling business processes, particularly mobile processes, which involve changing communication links between active process elements during execution.

2.3.3   Dedicated BPM techniques

The increasing interest in BPM in recent years and the growing use of business process automation tools such as workflow systems have led to several modeling techniques specifically developed for capturing business processes. In the early 1990s, Event-Driven Process Chains (EPCs) were developed at the University of Saarland as a means of modeling business processes in terms of functions and events. EPCs have been widely used as the modeling basis in a number of commercial tools such as the popular ARIS Toolset.

In 2003, the Business Process Modeling Initiative (BPMI), an industry consortium, proposed the Business Process Modeling Notation (BPMN), the first attempt at a standard for capturing business processes. In its original form, BPMN was a graphical representation for specifying business processes and was intended as a notation capable of specifying complex processes in a form that is intuitive to both technical and business users. The BPMN standard proposed a mapping to the WS-BPEL execution language for enactment purposes, although this was not complete. The latest release of BPMN (version 2.0.2, now titled Business Process Model and Notation) extends the original modeling notation with a more comprehensive underlying metamodel, which enables all aspects of a business process to be specified. Where there is sufficient detail captured for a given model, the BPMN metamodel provides the ability for it to be directly executed. A number of current BPMS offerings, including the Oracle BPM Suite examined in this book, provide for the direct execution of a BPMN process model without the need for the process designer to map it to an intermediate execution model such as WS-BPEL, as has previously been the case. The BPMN standard is currently managed under the auspices of OMG.

2.4   Overview of popular techniques

As can be seen from the preceding section, over time, a variety of techniques have been proposed for business process modeling. Many of these did not achieve any degree of prominence or are no longer in popular usage. However, the increased focus on the area in recent years has seen a convergence on five specific approaches for modeling business processes. In this section, we introduce each of these techniques and discuss their capabilities and shortcomings.

2.4.1   Petri nets

Petri nets were developed by Carl Adam Petri as part of his doctoral thesis in 1962 [102]. He proposed them as a means of describing the operation of discrete distributed systems. Petri nets (which are also known as place/transition nets [P/T] nets) are a particularly useful means of describing the dynamics of processes. One of their attractions is that they have a simple graphical format together with precise operational semantics that provide an intuitive way of modeling both the static and dynamic aspects of processes.

Figure 2.7 illustrates the language constructs for Petri nets. A Petri net takes the form of a directed bipartite graph where the nodes are either *transitions* or *places*. Places represent intermediate stages that exist during the operation of a process, and transitions correspond to the activities or events of which the process is made up. *Arcs* connect places and transitions in such a way that places can only be connected to transitions and vice versa. It is not permissible for places to be connected to places or for transitions to be connected to other transitions (i.e., places and transitions alternate along any path in the graph). A directed arc from a place to a transition indicates an input place to a transition, and a directed arc from a transition to a place indicates an output place from a transition. These places play an important role in the overall operational semantics of Petri nets.

The operational semantics of a Petri net are described in terms of *tokens*, which signify a thread of control flowing through a process. Places in a Petri net can contain any number of tokens. The distribution of tokens across all of the places in a net is called a *marking*

Figure 2.7
Petri net constructs (from [64]).

and signifies the overall state of the Petri net. A transition in a Petri net can "fire" whenever there is one or more tokens in each of its input places. When it fires, it consumes a token from each input place and adds a token to each output place. Figures 2.8(a) – (e) illustrate the act of firing for various Petri net configurations. It is assumed that the firing of a transition is an atomic action that occurs instantaneously and cannot be interrupted.

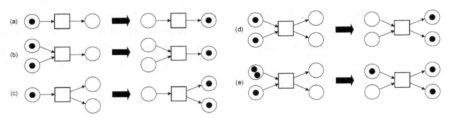

Figure 2.8
Petri net operational semantics (from [64]).

The manner in which a Petri net executes is deliberately intended to be non-deterministic. Hence, when multiple transitions in a Petri net are enabled, any one of them may fire, although it is not possible for two transitions to fire simultaneously as firing is considered atomic (assuming interleaving semantics). Furthermore, a distinction is drawn between a transition being able to fire and it actually firing, and one of the salient features of Petri nets is that an enabled transition is not obliged to fire immediately but can do so at a time of its choosing. These features make Petri nets particularly suitable for modeling concurrent process executions such as those that occur in business processes.

Figure 2.9 depicts a licence application process in the form of Petri net. In this process, an applicant lodges an *application* for a new license, which then triggers two distinct lines of activity: (1) a testing sequence, which consists first of a *written test* and then a *practical test* within a given timeframe otherwise a *timeout* occurs, and (2) determination of whether any *special requirements* apply to the license. If they do, then there is an iterative process to *investigate* each requirement and *assess* whether it should apply to the license. When the testing and special requirements sequences have been completed, a *recommendation* is made regarding the application, and on the basis of a *positive decision*, a *pass* action occurs for the license or, alternatively, on the basis of a *negative decision*, a *fail* action occurs. Regardless of the outcome of the application, at the conclusion of each case, the application is subject to *archive*.

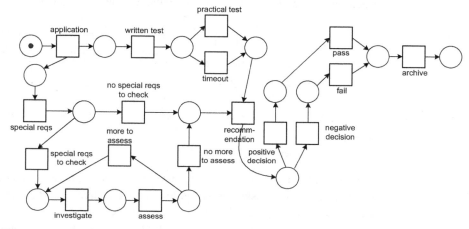

Figure 2.9
License application process: Petri net.

Despite its relative simplicity, this process model gives an insight into the use of Petri nets for modeling business processes. As a means of comparison with other modeling techniques, the same process model will be used for illustrative purposes throughout this chapter.

2.4.2   Workflow nets

Workflow nets were developed by Wil van der Aalst as a means of describing workflow processes in a precise way, making them amenable to subsequent analysis at both design-time and runtime [1]. Workflow nets are based on Petri nets with some additional constraints:

1. A workflow net has a single start place and a single end place; and
2. Every transition in the workflow net is on a path from the start place to the end place.

It is also desirable that a workflow net is sound; hence, a *sound workflow net* has the additional property that for any case, the procedure can always eventually terminate. At the moment of termination, there will be precisely one token in the end place, and all other places in the workflow net will be empty. Moreover, there should be no dead transitions — for any arbitrary transition in the net, there should be a scenario in which this transition can be executed by following an appropriate route through the net.

The format of workflow nets is essentially the same as for Petri nets, although some specific operators encompass the particular sorts of operations that arise in workflow systems. These operators can be seen as "syntactic sugar" and provide a shorthand notation for common constructs. Figure 2.10 illustrates the range of workflow net constructs. Transitions as they arise in Petri nets are replaced with the task construct; however, the essential structural form of a workflow net is largely the same as for a Petri net.

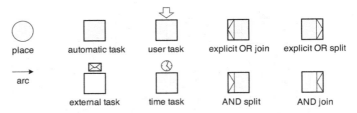

Figure 2.10
Workflow net constructs (from [64]).

Tasks can be initiated in one of four ways: (1) *automatic* tasks execute as soon as they are enabled, (2) *user* tasks are passed to human resources for execution once enabled, (3) *external* tasks only proceed once they are enabled and a required message or signal is received from the operating environment, and (4) *time* tasks only proceed once they are enabled and a specified (time-based) deadline occurs. It is also possible for split and join behavior to be associated with individual tasks.

As an illustration of the form that a workflow net takes, figure 2.11 shows the earlier license application example in the form of a workflow net. It has a similar format to the Petri net shown in figure 2.9. However, AND/XOR splits/joins are represented explicitly, and the diagram also shows the way in which tasks are initiated (i.e., either by users or on the basis of a time-based trigger).

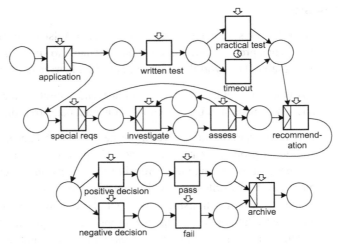

Figure 2.11
License application process: workflow net.

2.4.3 EPCs

Event-driven process chains (EPCs) were developed by August-Wilhelm Scheer as part of the ARIS framework at the University of Saarland in Germany in the early 1990s. Figure 2.12 illustrates the main EPC constructs. Essentially, an EPC model describes a business process in terms of a series of function-based transformations between a set of input events and a set of output events. An EPC model takes the form of a directed graph, which always starts and ends with events. The set of constructs that make up an EPC model is shown in figure 2.12. The AND, OR, and XOR constructs can be utilized as either join or split operators.

Figure 2.12
EPC constructs.

Within the model, events correspond to potential states that may exist within a process, and functions essentially describe actions that are undertaken to transform one state (or set of states) to another. Hence, a function is always preceded and followed by an event. It is not permissible for an event to be linked either directly (or indirectly through a join or split construct) to another event, nor for a function to be linked to another function (i.e., events and functions alternate along any path in the graph). Where several events precede or follow a function (i.e., events and functions alternate along any path in a model), one of the AND, OR, or XOR constructs can be used to define the intended split or join behavior between the event and function nodes. Figure 2.13 illustrates the range of allowable and invalid split and join configurations between events and functions. It is important to note that the use of OR-split and XOR-split constructs immediately after an event (or directly preceding a function) is not allowed under the EPC modeling formalism.

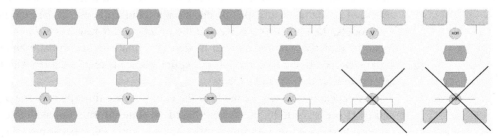

Figure 2.13
EPCs: Allowable and invalid join and split combinations.

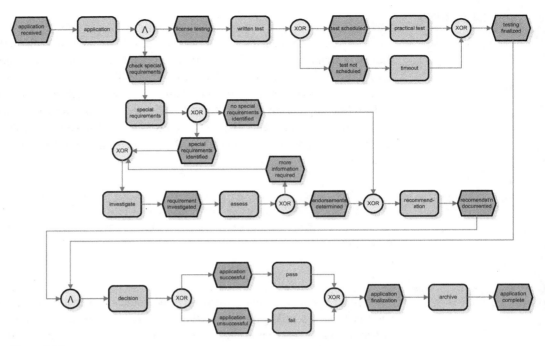

Figure 2.14
License application process: Event-driven process chain.

Figure 2.14 shows an example of an event-driven process chain. In this case, it depicts the license application process, which has also been shown earlier as a Petri net and a workflow net. This figure mirrors the process depicted in the Petri net and workflow net models in figures 2.9 and 2.11 with one minor exception: EPCs lack the ability to model a situation where a user- or environment-initiated action makes an explicit choice as to the course of action taken at a specific decision point in a process. In the Petri net and workflow net models, the ability to specify that the *practical test* task has a *timeout* associated with it can be directly captured as both modeling formalisms incorporate an explicit notion of state; however, in the EPC model, an explicit choice is required as to whether the *practical test* or *timeout* task should execute.

This decision can only be made at the expiry of the timespan for the *practical test* task and in effect is made by the system based on state information available to it rather than as a result of a specific user intervention. Hence, the EPC process model is subtly different from the earlier models, although in most practical situations the outcome will ultimately be the same.

2.4.4   BPMN

Business Process Model and Notation (BPMN) is an XML-based language for defining business processes with a formal meta-model and an associated graphical notation. In its current incarnation (version 2.0.2), it is designed to be utilized at one of three levels:

- as a high-level, graphical, business modeling language (with a limited range of modeling constructs);
- as a detailed graphical modeling language (with a comprehensive range of modeling constructs); and
- as an executable business process language, capturing sufficient details about the control-flow, data, and resource aspects of a business process that it can be directly executed by a business process engine.

The initial version of BPMN (then termed Business Process Modeling Notation) was proposed by the Business Process Modeling Institute (BPMI), an industry consortium, in 2002 as a graphical modeling language. It was informally defined and intended primarily for high-level modeling of business processes.

Since 2005, it has been under the auspices of the Object Management Group (OMG), when it merged with BPMI. Its focus has now broadened from business process modeling to offering a range of techniques supporting all aspects of business process capture, from high-level, abstract modeling through to detailed business process definition capable of direct execution. All of these techniques co-exist within the same meta-model, thus ensuring that the semantics of the various levels are consistent.

For this discussion, we will focus on the graphical modeling notation as it is the aspect of the BPMN that is most widely used for high-level modeling of business processes. As with other business process modeling notations, it depicts a process in the form of a directed graph that connects a series of *flow objects* (essentially events, activities, joins, and splits) and *data objects* (which identify data resources and the way in which they are utilized in the process) using various types of *connecting objects* (arcs that identify different types of object flowing through the process). *Swimlanes* are used to organize the various parts of the process into parts, which are undertaken by the same class of resource. *Artifacts* allow additional details to be added to the process. Figure 2.15 illustrates the main graphical constructs in BPMN 2.0.2. These divide into five main categories.[1]

---

1 Note that when referring to BPMN artifacts in the text, they are identified as proper nouns and hence capitalized, e.g., Task, Pool, etc.

Flow objects

Flow objects describe the main active elements in a process: in particular, *events* that signal that nominated start, intermediate, and end parts of the process have been reached, *activities* that correspond to the actual conduct of work in a process, and *gateways* that indicate the various types of split and join constructs within a process.

Data

Data denote individual information objects and collections that exist within the context of a process. *Data objects* identify data elements that are consumed and produced by activities within the process. *Data inputs* and *data outputs* identify formal parameters to processes and subprocesses. *Data stores* denote permanent repositories of data that exist beyond the life of individual process instances.

Connecting objects

Connecting objects describe the various flows within a process. *Sequence* flow connects activities and indicates the order in which they will be done. *Message* flow depicts the flow of messages between two participants in a process. It typically connects two separate pools. One end connects to a pool boundary and the other to a flow object within a pool boundary. The direction of the message flow indicates the initiating and receiving participant for the message. *Conditional* flow corresponds to a sequence flow between activities that has a condition associated with it, which is evaluated at runtime to determine whether the flow will be used (i.e., whether control-flow will pass along it). *Default* flow identifies a path from a decision construct (i.e., a *data-based exclusive gateway* or *inclusive gateway*) that is selected if all other conditional flows are not chosen (because conditions associated with them evaluate to false). *Associations* are used to link information with flow objects. *Data Associations* identify mappings between data objects and an activity or event in a process. The data association may indicate the direction of data flow or it may be unidirectional in the situation where it is linked to a sequence flow (in which case it assumes the direction of the sequence of the sequence flow). *Exception flow* occurs outside normal flow and identifies how an activity deals with a particular type of event that arises during its execution. *Compensation Association* also occurs outside normal flow and indicates how the failure of a transaction or the occurrence of a compensation event within an activity are dealt with and compensated for.

Swimlanes

Swimlanes provide a means of grouping elements within a process. A *pool* identifies a participant in a collaboration and provides a means of partitioning specific activities from other pools. Pools may be *white-box*, in which case they contain flow elements and are labeled with the process to which they correspond, or they may be *black-box*, in which case they have no internal details and are labeled with the role or business entity to which they correspond. A *lane* is a subpartition within a pool that is used to categorize and organize activities within it. They can be used for a variety of types of categorization (e.g., to indicate activities undertaken by a specific actor, role, or organizational group or even to partition activities on a specific basis, e.g., chargeable vs non-chargeable).

Artifacts

Artifacts provide additional information about a process. Two distinct types of artifact are denoted: *groups* provide a visual mechanism for grouping related activities, and *text annotations* provide a means of adding additional information to a process model.

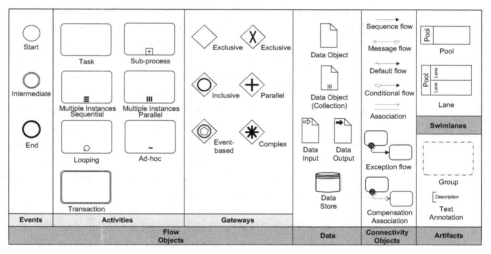

Figure 2.15
BPMN constructs.

Event handling

An important aspect of BPMN is that it provides support for modeling exception flow as part of the business process. This is done using events that can be included in the sequence flow within a process or can be attached to either individual activities or subprocesses. Each event is of a specific type, indicating what form of exception is being handled. The actual definition of the handling strategy for a given event can be specified in one of two ways: (1) a path from the event construct to the specific sequence of activities that can deal with the event is specified and the thread of control is passed to this branch when the event arises, or (2) if there is not a specific handling strategy specified, the thread of control is instead passed to an appropriate handler in the surrounding block (or if this is already the outermost block, then the process instance is terminated).

For events that form part of sequence flow, they may either be *catching* events, meaning that they are triggered when the execution thread has arrived at the event and a specific type of trigger signal is received, or they may be *throwing* events, which generate a specific type of signal when the execution thread reaches the throwing event during normal execution.

Events that are attached to the boundary of an activity or a subprocess denote boundary events that are listened for during the execution of the activity (or subprocess) and where the nominated trigger signal is received cause the exception flow from the event to be triggered. There are two types of boundary event distinguished by different event notations: *interrupting*, which causes the execution of activity to cease on receipt of the trigger signal and the exception flow to be triggered, and *non-interrupting*, which immediately trigger the exception flow on receipt of the trigger signal but also allow the activity to continue and for normal sequence flow to be triggered from the activity when it completes.

Figure 2.16(a) shows how an exception handler can be specified to handle errors encountered in the *book ticket* activity. In figure 2.16(b), a timer event is attached to the *finalize booking* subprocess, allowing it to be terminated if it is not completed by a specified deadline. Figure 2.16(c) illustrates the use of inline throwing and catching events. In this case, an interaction occurs with an external *Customer* participant involving message events to confirm acceptance of charges. Figure 2.16(d) illustrates the range of events that are recognized within BPMN. Event detection and handling can be associated with start, intermediate, and end activities depending on whether the event is signaled from outside the process or detected inside during its operation and whether it can be handled within the process during the course of its operation, such that execution can continue or whether it results in the process instance terminating.

As a comparative illustration, figure 2.17 shows the license application process in the form of a BPMN model. Of particular interest are (1) the specific exception construct associated with the *practical test* activity to handle the timeout if it is not completed within a required timeframe, and (2) the relatively complex gateway structure required to handle the optional *investigate – assess* task cycle, which comprises part of the *special requirements* branch within the process.

2.4.5   UML activity diagrams

UML activity diagrams are part of the UML modeling framework that provide a means of describing the operation of a process. Although originally intended for describing software processes, they have also shown themselves to be useful for describing business processes. Like BPMN, UML is managed under the auspices of OMG. The current version of the UML standard (2.5) was finalized by the OMG in 2015. Figure 2.18 gives an overview of the main UML constructs. These are divided into four groups.

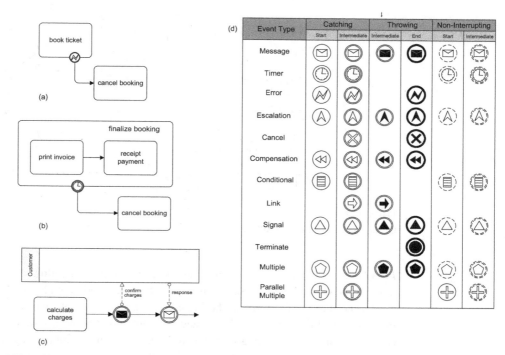

Figure 2.16
Event handling in BPMN.

Actions

An *Action* corresponds to a single step within an activity in a business process. It can be either atomic and self-contained in terms of its definition or in the case of a *Call Behavior Action*, it may involve a call to another activity. An *Action* can have preconditions and postconditions associated with its execution, which can be graphically depicted. The *AcceptEventAction* waits for the occurrence of an event meeting a specified condition. This event may be triggered from within the process instance via a *SendSignalAction* or it may be a time-based event (in which case the receiving *AcceptEventAction* is denoted by a different symbol).

Nodes

Nodes are constructs that interlink actions in a process and further clarify the specific details associated with control and data flow. An *InitialNode* marks the starting point for a process. A process may be terminated by either an *ActivityFinal* node, which immediately causes the process instance to terminate when the first execution thread reaches it, or a

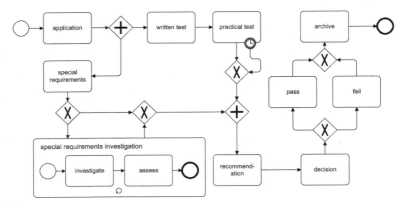

Figure 2.17
License application process: BPMN.

FlowFinal node, which simply consumes execution threads but allows the process instance to continue until all active execution threads have reached an end node. A *DecisionNode* allows the thread of control in the incoming branch to be split into one or more outgoing branches on a conditional basis, and the corresponding *MergeNode* allows threads of control in multiple incoming branches to be merged into a single outgoing branch on an unconditional basis. The *ForkNode* provides the ability to split the thread of control in an incoming branch into several outgoing branches, and the corresponding *JoinNode* supports the synchronization of the execution threads in multiple incoming branches, only allowing

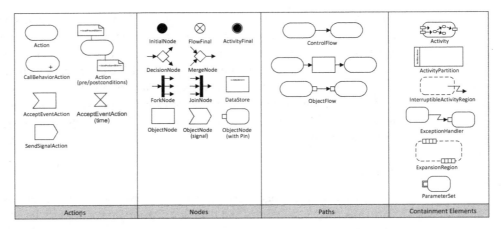

Figure 2.18
UML 2.5 activity diagram constructs.

the outgoing branch to be triggered when all incoming branches have been triggered. The *DataStore* node denotes a persistent store of data within a process. Three types of *ObjectNode* identify abstract activity nodes that are part of the object flow in an activity. These may correspond to data elements and signals used within a process and may include *Pins*, which denote input and output data values.

Paths

There are two types of paths identifying flows within a UML 2.5 activity diagram: *ControlFlow* identifies how the thread of control is passed between nodes in a process, and *ObjectFlow* signifies the flow of objects, data elements, tokens and signals in a process.

Containment elements

Containment elements provide various mechanisms for grouping nodes within a process model for specific purposes. *Activity* elements serve as a means of grouping related individual actions into a single step in a process. There is provision for passing parameters to and from individual activities. An *ActivityPartition* provides a means of grouping actions that are performed by the same organizational enitity. An *InterruptibleActivityRegion* is a means of grouping related activity nodes that have the same exception handling behavior. The various steps that make up a given approach to handling a specific exception are characterized by an *ExceptionHandler* node. An *ExpansionRegion* is a structured activity region that executes multiple times on the basis of the parameters passed to it. A *ParameterSet* denotes a complete set of inputs or outputs to an *activity*.

Figure 2.19 illustrates the use of UML 2.5 activity diagrams for modeling business processes using the license application example discussed earlier.

2.5 Analysis of process models

Process models can be used to analyze the correctness and performance of business processes. Moreover, as more and more event data is stored in enterprise information systems, processes can be analyzed easily using factual data. First, we summarize two mainstream approaches for model-based analysis: *verification* and *performance analysis*. Verification is concerned with the correctness of a system or process. Performance analysis focuses on flow times, waiting times, utilization, and service levels. After discussing these two types of model-based analysis, we focus on techniques that exploit event data when analyzing processes and their models.

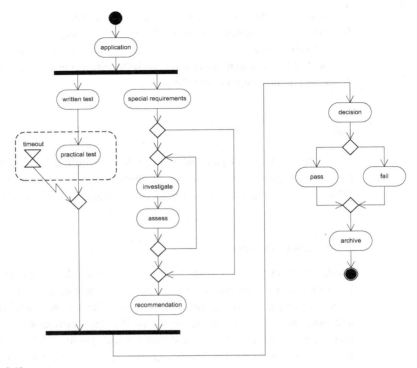

Figure 2.19
License application process: UML 2.5 activity diagram.

2.5.1 Verification

When modeling a process, it is easy to make design errors. Consider, for example, the process shown in figure 2.20. The model will always deadlock just before reaching task *archive*. This tasks wants to synchronize two flows, but only one of them will be activated after task *recommendation*.

The workflow net shown in figure 2.20 is *not sound*. As described earlier, a workflow net is sound if and only if (a) "proper completion" is guaranteed (i.e., when the unique end place is reached all other places should be empty), (b) the process always has the "option to complete" (i.e., no matter what path is chosen, it is always possible to reach the end of the process), and the workflow net contains no "dead parts" (i.e., in principle all tasks are reachable) [1]. The workflow net of figure 2.20 does not have the "option to complete" as it gets stuck before task *archive*. The notion of soundness can easily be adapted for other languages such as YAWL, EPCs, and BPMN.

Soundness is a generic property. Sometimes a more specific property needs to be investigated (e.g., "there should be a practical test for all failed applications"). Such properties

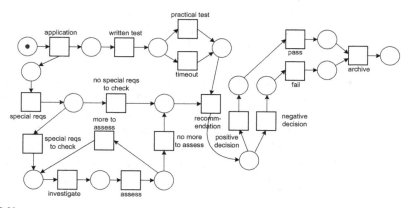

Figure 2.20

A workflow net that is not sound.

can be expressed in *temporal logic* [34]. *Linear Temporal Logic* (LTL) is an example of a temporal logic, which in addition to classical logical operators uses temporal operators such as always ($\Box$), eventually ($\Diamond$), until ($\sqcup$), weak until (*W*), and next time ($\bigcirc$). The expression $(\Diamond x) \implies (\Diamond y)$ means that for all cases where *x* is executed, *y* is also executed. Another example is $\Box(x \implies \Diamond y)$, which states that any occurrence of *x* will be followed by *y*. *Model checking* techniques can be used to check such properties [34].

Another verification task is related to the comparison of two models. For example, the implementation of a process needs to be compared to the high-level specification of the process. Different equivalence notions exist (e.g., trace equivalence and branching bisimilarity) that can be checked automatically.

There are various tools to verify process models. A classic example is Woflan, which is tailored toward checking soundness [127]. Also workflow systems such as YAWL provide verification capabilities [64].

2.5.2   Performance analysis

The performance of a process or organization can be defined in different ways. Typically, three dimensions of performance are identified: *time*, *cost*, and *quality*. For each of these performance dimensions, different *key performance indicators* can be defined. When looking at the *time dimension*, the following performance indicators can be distinguished:

- The *lead time* (also referred to as flow time) is the total time from the creation of the case to the completion of the case. In terms of a workflow net, this is the time it takes to go from the start place to the end place. One can measure the average lead time over all cases. However, the degree of variance may also be important (i.e., it makes a difference whether all cases take more or less two weeks of if some take just a few hours while others take more than one month). The *service level* is the percentage of cases having a lead time lower than some threshold value (e.g., the percentage of cases handled within two weeks).

- The *service time* is the time actually worked on a case. One can measure the service time per activity (e.g., the average time needed to make a decision is 35 minutes) or for the entire case. Note that in case of concurrency, the overall service time (i.e., summing up the time spent on the various activities) may be more than the lead time. However, typically, the service time is just a fraction of the lead time (minutes versus weeks).

- The *waiting time* is the time a case is waiting for a resource to become available. This time can be measured per activity or for the case as a whole. An example is the waiting time for a customer wanting to talk to a sales representative. Another example is the time a patient needs to wait before getting a knee operation. Again one can be interested in the average or variance of waiting times. It is also possible to focus on a service level (e.g., the percentage of patients that has a knee operation within three weeks after the initial diagnosis).

- The *synchronization time* is the time an activity is not yet fully enabled and waiting for an external trigger or another parallel branch. Unlike waiting time, the activity is not fully enabled yet (i.e., the case is waiting for synchronization rather than a resource).

Performance indicators can also be defined for the *cost dimension*. Different costing models can be used (e.g., Activity Based Costing (ABC), Resource Consumption Accounting (RCA), etc). The cost of executing an activity may be fixed or depend on the type of resource used, its utilization, and/or the duration of the activity. Cost may depend on the utilization of resources. A key performance indicator in most processes is the *average utilization* of resources over a given period (e.g., an operating room in a hospital has been used 85% of the time over the last two months). A detailed discussion of the various costing models is outside of the scope of this book. The *quality dimension* typically focuses on the "product" or "service" delivered to the customer. Like cost, this can be measured in different ways. One example is customer satisfaction measured through questionnaires. Another example is the average number of complaints per case or the number of product defects.

Whereas verification focuses on the logical correctness of the modeled process, performance analysis aims at improving processes with respect to time, cost, and/or quality. Within the context of operations management, many analysis techniques have been developed. Some of these techniques "optimize" the model given a particular performance indicator. For example, integer programming or Markov decision problems can be used to find optimal policies. Analytical models typically require many assumptions and can only be used to answer particular questions. Therefore, one often needs to resort to *simulation*. Most BPM tools provide simulation capabilities.

Although many organizations have tried to use simulation to analyze their business processes at some stage, *few are using simulation in a structured and effective manner.* This may be caused by a lack of training and limitations of existing tools. However, there are also several additional and more fundamental problems. First of all, simulation models tend to *oversimplify* things. In particular, the behavior of resources is often modeled in a rather naive manner. People do not work at constant speeds and need to distribute their attention over multiple processes. This can have dramatic effects on the performance of a process [2], and therefore such aspects should not be "abstracted away." Second, various *artifacts available are not used as input for simulation.* Modern organizations store events in logs, and some may have accurate process models stored in their BPM/WFM systems. Also note that in many organizations, the state of the information system accurately reflects the state of the business processes supported by these systems because of the tight coupling between both. Today, such information (i.e., event logs and status data) is rarely used for simulation or a lot of manual work is needed to feed this information into the model. Fortunately, process mining can assist in extracting such information and use this to realize performance improvements. Third, the focus of simulation is mainly on "design" while managers would also like to use simulation for *"operational decision making"* (solving the concrete problem at hand rather than some abstract future problem). Fortunately, *short-term simulation* [110] can provide answers for questions related to "here and now." The key idea is to start all simulation runs from the current state and focus on the analysis of the transient behavior. This way a "fast-forward button" into the future is provided.

2.5.3 Process mining

Process mining is a relative young research discipline that sits between machine learning and data mining, on the one hand, and process modeling and analysis, on the other hand [3]. The idea of process mining is to discover, monitor, and improve real processes (i.e., not assumed processes) by extracting knowledge from event logs readily available in today's systems.

Figure 2.21 shows that process mining establishes links between the actual processes and their data, on the one hand, and process models, on the other. Today's information systems log enormous amounts of events. Classical WFM systems (e.g., Staffware and COSA), BPM systems (e.g., BPMone by Pallas Athena, SmartBPM by Pegasystems, FileNet, Global 360, YAWL, and Teamwork by Lombardi Software), ERP systems (e.g., SAP R/3, Oracle E-Business Suite, and Microsoft Dynamics NAV), PDM systems (e.g., Windchill), CRM systems (e.g., Microsoft Dynamics CRM and SalesForce), middleware (e.g., IBM's WebSphere and Cordys Business Operations Platform), hospital information systems (e.g., Chipsoft and Siemens Soarian), and so on provide detailed information about the activities that have been executed. Figure 2.21 refers to such data as *event logs*. Most of the process-aware information systems just mentioned directly provide such

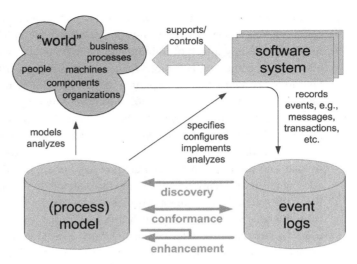

Figure 2.21

Positioning of the three main types of process mining: *discovery*, *conformance* and *enhancement*.

event logs. However, most information systems store information in less structured form (e.g., event data is scattered over many tables or needs to be tapped off from subsystems exchanging messages). In such cases, the event data exists, but some effort is needed to extract it. Data extraction is an integral part of any process mining effort.

Event logs can be used to conduct three types of process mining as shown in figure 2.21. The first type of process mining is *discovery*. A discovery technique takes an event log and produces a model without using any a priori information. An example is the α-algorithm [20]. This algorithm takes an event log and produces a Petri net. For example, given sufficient example executions of the process shown in figure 2.9, the α-algorithm is able to automatically construct the Petri net without using any additional knowledge. If the event log contains information about resources, then one can also discover resource-related models (e.g., a social network showing how people work together in an organization).

The second type of process mining is *conformance*. Here an existing model is compared with an event log of the same process. Conformance checking can be used to check whether reality, as recorded in the log, conforms to the model and vice versa. For example, there may be a process model indicating that purchase orders of more than one million Euro require two checks. Analysis of the event log will show whether this rule is followed. Another example is the checking of the so-called "four-eyes" principle, stating that particular activities should not be executed by one and the same person. By scanning the event log using a model specifying these requirements, one can discover potential cases of fraud. Hence, conformance checking may be used to detect, locate, and explain deviations and to measure the severity of these deviations. An example is the conformance checking algorithm described in [110]. Given the model shown in figure 2.9 and a corresponding event log, this algorithm can quantify and diagnose deviations.

The third type of process mining is *enhancement*. Here the idea is to extend or improve an existing process model using information about the actual process recorded in some event log. While conformance checking measures the alignment between model and reality, this third type of process mining aims at changing or extending the a priori model. One type of enhancement is *repair* (i.e., modifying the model to better reflect reality). For example, if two activities are modeled sequentially but in reality can happen in any order, then the model may be corrected to reflect this. Another type of enhancement is *extension* (i.e., adding a new perspective to the process model by cross-correlating it with the log). An example is the extension of a process model with performance data. For example, by using timestamps in the event log, one can report on bottlenecks, service levels, throughput times, and frequencies. Similarly, process models can be extended with information about resources, decision rules, quality metrics, and so on based on event data in the system's logs.

2.6   Further reading

Suggested further readings relevant to the material presented in this chapter include:

- Standard readings on Petri net theory are [40] and [101]. The issue of structured process modeling is considered at length in [74] and [72].
- [10] presents a comprehensive overview of the use of Petri nets and workflow nets for business process modeling. The application of Petri nets to WFM was first discussed in [1]. In [11], various notions of soundness are defined and corresponding analysis techniques are discussed.
- The current version of the BPMN standard is available in [97]. A high-level introduction to the use of BPMN for business process modeling is presented in [138]. A more comprehensive recent work is [123].
- The UML standard is contained in [96], and within this document, there is a comprehensive overview of activity diagrams. [51] and [80] provide an introduction to the use of various UML techniques, including activity diagrams for business modeling purposes.
- The original EPC proposal [71] is only available in German; however, the two books [119, 120] give a good introduction to EPCs and the ARIS modeling framework more generally.
- A general introduction to business process modeling is available in [63] and [136].
- For more information about the analysis of business process models, see [69]
- For more information about modeling business processes using colored Petri nets, see [70] and [19].

Business Process Management Systems

In this chapter, we examine the use of Business Process Management Systems (BPMSs) as a means of operationalizing business processes. In recent years, BPMSs have emerged as a generic means of supporting business processes and allow for processes in a wide variety of application areas to be automated using standard "off-the-shelf" technology. The rise of BPMS technology is consistent with trends in other areas of software engineering where generic application functionality is developed on a specialist basis and made available for reuse in the context of large software development initiatives. As a consequence, application developers are increasingly able to access high-quality software components for particular areas of functionality, thus alleviating the need to develop these components.

Figure 3.1 illustrates the evolution of supporting technology for business processes over the past five decades. In the 1960s, almost all applications were developed completely from scratch, and the available technology of the day generally resulted in the creation of monolithic applications, each fulfilling a specific purpose.

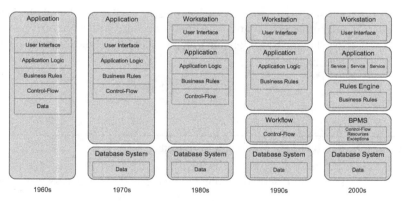

Figure 3.1
Evolution of BPM technology (from [64]).

In the 1970s, database technology became available as a generic piece of application technology, and in the 1980s, PCs, GUIs, and networking technology meant that richer user interfaces were able to be provided for software applications. The core of application functionality, however, including the majority of the associated business logic, was still coalesced in a single software module. This situation began to change in the 1990s when generic workflow technology started to become available. It provided a means of coordinating the functionality contained in a given application on the basis of a process model that was independent of the actual application. For the first time, it was possible to decouple the control-flow aspects of an application from the actual business functionality. The development of BPM technology continued to evolve in the 2000s, with rules engine technology becoming available to handle the business rules associated with an application on an independent basis. Perhaps the most significant of recent developments in the BPM area (and the IT field more generally) is the establishment of the service-orientation paradigm as the dominant means of application construction. Service-oriented architectures (SOAs) are now the predominant means of software design and construction.

For BPM offerings, SOAs are a fundamental means of coupling the various parts of business logic within an application and also for integrating the various functional areas (UI, data, etc.) that it comprises. Moreover, the various components of a BPM application are now engineered in a more "open" way, with an increased expectation that they will need to co-exist with a wide range of third-party offerings and evolving technologies.

As workflow technology has continued to mature, it is now increasingly able to offer a broader range of facilities with which to design, deploy, and analyze business processes. In the following sections of this chapter, we will examine BPM technology in more detail, looking at how it has evolved, what form it takes, and how it aims to provide the flexibility and agility required by today's business processes. We examine three BPMS technologies — XPDL, BPEL, and case handling — as an indication of the range of BPMS solutions that are currently available, and finally we close with a brief overview of the current challenges faced in the BPM domain. First, we will look at the issues associated with business process automation.

3.1   Introduction to business process automation

In common with many other software artifacts, business processes have a distinct lifecycle associated with them. This lifecycle is shown in figure 3.2 and consists of four distinct phases. The overall lifecycle for a business process is cyclic in form, and in much the same way as the spiral model applies to the software development process, it provides the basis for the continuous improvement of a business process during its operational lifetime.

The first stage in the business process lifecycle is *process design*, during which a candidate business process is first designed or redesigned based on previous incarnations. This typically involves capturing the operational details of the process using some form of modeling notation. Ideally sufficient details of the process are recorded to facilitate its direct enactment; however, this relies on the use of an executable modeling formalism, such as that provided by a workflow offering. Generally, the design is captured using notations such as BPMN, EPCs, or UML activity diagrams, and it takes the form of a conceptual process model. Further detail (which is often added subsequently) is generally required to enable it to be executed.

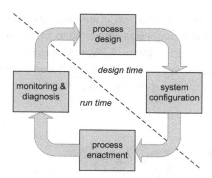

Figure 3.2
Business process lifecycle.

The second stage in automating a business process is *system configuration*. In contrast to traditional software development activities, the deployment of a business process is generally based on the configuration of BPMS software and usually only involves minimal amounts of direct programming effort. This is a consequence of some assumptions about the approach to process deployment that are embodied in the BPMS software. Typically the configuration process is done using facilities provided by the BPMS tool and involves activities such as importing or creating the candidate process model using some form of graphical editor, defining data objects and their interrelationship with the control-flow aspects of the process model, and defining resources and the distribution of work within the process to those resources. Figure 3.3 outlines the standard architecture for a BPMS. It consists of two main parts:

- a *BPMS engine*, which handles the execution of a business process on a centralized basis and manages current process state, working data, work distribution, and so on for each process instance that is initiated; and
- a *worklist handler* for each user who is involved in a process, which advises them of the work that needs to be undertaken and provides them with the opportunity to interact with the BPMS engine to advise of their work preferences and manage the scheduling and completion of work to which they have committed.

Process design and system configuration are *design-time* activities that involve the development of a process model that has sufficient detail to allow it to be directly executed. In contrast, the next two stages in the lifecycle are *runtime* activities, which occur once the model of the business process that has been developed is actually under execution. Traditionally, in many systems, there was a distinction between the design-time and runtime process models, and they were handled by distinct components of the BPMS software. The design-time process model was used to facilitate the overall definition and capture of the business process and was often undertaken using a graphical design tool or editor. Once finalized, the model was converted to a runtime process model that was used as the basis of process execution by the BPMS. More recently, with the increased use of executable process models such as BPMN, this is becoming less of an issue, and design time and runtime models are effectively one and the same.

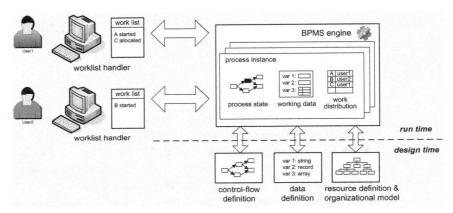

Figure 3.3
Overview of an operational BPMS.

The next stage in the business process lifecycle is *process enactment*. This involves the actual execution of the candidate process model and the routing of associated work items to users. This is done in accordance with a defined control-flow model in conjunction with data and resource definitions and an associated organizational model, although the specific details of how this is done vary on a system-by-system basis.

The final phase in the business process lifecycle is *monitoring & diagnosis*, in which the operation of the process is tracked and the resultant information is used as the basis for further refinements to the business process model. These may be dynamic changes intended to improve performance or may be more pervasive in nature and focus on adapting the process to changes that have been identified in the operational environment, providing support for new (sub-)processes or leveraging new technologies that have become available.

In this section, we have overviewed the main characteristics of the business process lifecycle and the way in which they are supported in a BPMS. The structure of WFM systems and BPMSs has been discussed in detail, and in the next section, we look at these architectural considerations in more depth.

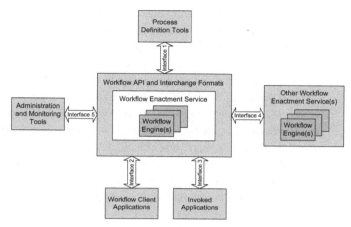

Figure 3.4
Workflow reference model (from [143]).

3.2 Architectural considerations

In an attempt to provide some direction and standardization to the workflow area, the Workflow Management Coalition (WfMC), a loose consortium of vendors, research organizations, and workflow users, was formed in 1993. In 1995, it introduced the Workflow Reference Model illustrated in figure 3.4 in an effort to align terminology in the area and define a series of interfaces for various aspects of workflow systems that vendors could adopt, thus promoting the opportunity for interoperability between distinct offerings.

The workflow reference model defined five key interfaces for workflow systems:

- *Interface 1* (Process definition tools), which details a generic process definition language (Workflow Process Definition Language (WPDL)) that describes common workflow elements and their interrelationships;
- *Interface 2* (Workflow client applications), which describes the interactions between a workflow engine and a client application (e.g., a worklist handler);
- *Interface 3* (Invoked applications), which defines an interface for invoking remote applications;
- *Interface 4* (Other workflow enactment services), which provides an interface for distinct workflow systems to interact with each other; and
- *Interface 5* (Administration and monitoring tools), which focuses on the specification of the format and interpretation of the audit trail details associated with workflow execution.

Although it met with varying degrees of criticism and vendor support among the workflow community, the workflow reference model had a significant impact on the overall technological foundations of workflow, and for many years it remained the only "standard" in the area with any degree of broad acceptance. More significantly, it reinforced the notion of what constituted the architecture for a workflow system. The workflow systems that came to market in the 1990s for the most part operated as standalone applications, with the workflow application providing all of the process enablement and user interface functionality other than data persistence, which was typically provided by distinct database system software. In recent years, however, there has been a trend away from "closed" workflow applications to a new generation of more "open" BPMSs, which incorporate workflow technology and position themselves more as solutions for embedding process support in an organizational environment. Figure 3.5 illustrates the broad range of potential integration options offered by this technology. In essence, it focuses on providing coordination of process state and allows all other aspects of business process operation to be delivered by other software applications.

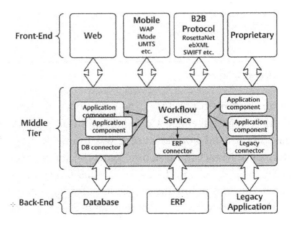

Figure 3.5

Embedded workflow as an integration technology (from [88]).

3.3   A brief history of BPMS technology

In this section, we provide a brief overview of the history of BPMS technology. This starts with early work in the area of office information systems and, through workflow systems, takes us to contemporary BPM systems. Figure 3.6 illustrates this timeline, showing the main technology streams and some prominent examples of actual systems in each of these areas.

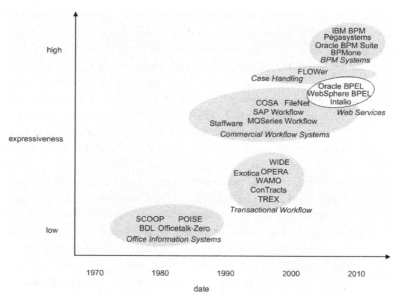

Figure 3.6
BPM technology timeline.

3.3.1 Office information systems

The antecedents of the BPMS research area lie in the field of office information systems. The promise of automating aspects of the office function (such as document and work distribution, communication and retention of work-related information, etc.) triggered several independent research initiatives into the formal definition of office procedures. Zisman [151], Holt [66], and Ellis [62] all proposed state-based models of office information systems based on Petri nets. Gibbs and Tsichritzis [56] documented a data model for capturing the "structure and semantics of office objects." There were also several prototype systems developed, including SCOOP [151], POISE [36], BDL [62], and Officetalk-Zero [50], although none of these progressed into more widespread usage. A variety of reasons are cited for their ultimate failure [42, 49], including the inherent rigidity of the resultant systems interfering with rather than expediting work processes, the inability of the process modeling formalisms to deal with changes in the application domain, the lack of comprehensive modeling techniques, and more generally the relative immaturity of the hardware and networking infrastructure available to support them.

3.3.2 Transactional workflow

One of the first attempts to establish generalizable workflow facilities was based on the notion of "transactional workflow," which sought to extend database technology to support the notion of long-duration transactions. This approach to workflow was based on the idea that real-life processes were composed of activities that could best be enacted using related sequences of transactions. Although few of these offerings in this area progressed beyond the research stage, they had a significant impact on the architecture of later workflow systems, particularly in the area of exception handling. Notable contributions included WAMO [47], which provided the ability to specify transactional properties for tasks that identified how failures should be dealt with; ConTracts [105], which proposed a coordinated, nested transaction model for workflow execution allowing for forward, backward, and partial recovery in the event of failure; and Exotica [26], which provided a mechanism for incorporating Sagas and Flexible transactions in the commercial Flow-Mark workflow product. TREX [124] proposed a transaction model that involves treating all types of workflow failures as exceptions. OPERA [60] was one of the first initiatives to extend the transaction paradigm to incorporate language primitives for exception handling in a workflow system, and it also allowed exception handling strategies to be modeled in the same notation as that used for representing workflow processes. WIDE [33] incorporated transactional primitives in the workflow language and developed a comprehensive language — Chimera-Exc — for specifying exception handling strategies in the form of Event-Condition-Action (ECA) rules. METEOR [122] is a CORBA-based WFM system supporting transactions. MOBILE [68] is another example of a prototype WFM system that influenced later commercial WFM systems.

3.3.3 Commercial workflow systems

Commercial workflow technology evolved without such a tight emphasis on transactional aspects and consequently met with greater success. It soon achieved the aim of providing a general purpose enactment vehicle for processes. Initially focused on specific domains such as document routing, image management (especially in the medical diagnostics area), and advanced email applications for supporting group work, these offerings became increasingly configurable and domain independent and led to an explosion of offerings in the commercial and research spheres. Indeed by 1997, it was estimated that there were more than 200 commercial workflow systems in existence [8]. As a software domain, it was an extremely volatile area, and many offerings failed to achieve the critical mass required for long-term survival and either disappeared from the market or were merged into competitive products. Increasingly, it became clear that those offerings that were successful in achieving long-term viability were those that specialized in a particular area or demonstrated a unique capability. Staffware achieved success through its ability to facilitate rapid deployment of workflow solutions, SAP Workflow was an early example of a workflow offering that effectively coordinated the operations of other complex software offerings (in this case, the SAP R/3 offering) and integrated closely with other third-party offerings, COSA demonstrated the viability of a deterministic workflow offering based on formal foundations (in this case, Petri nets), and MQSeries Workflow/WebSphere provided an industrial strength workflow solution capable of scaling to meet the needs of enterprise users.

The range of offerings that can be classified as workflow systems is extremely broad. Georgakopoulos et al. [55] offered a characterization of the area as a "workflow umbrella," in which workflow technology can be viewed as a continuum ranging from human-oriented workflow, which supports humans coordinating and collaborating on tasks that they are ultimately responsible for undertaking, through to system workflow, which undertakes computationally intensive tasks on a largely automated basis. Along this spectrum are a variety of forms of workflow technology, including Computer Supported Cooperative Work (CSCW) or groupware, commercial WFM systems, and commercial Transaction Processing (TP) systems. Another perspective is offered in figure 3.7, which classifies process-enabling technologies on the basis of whether they tightly adhere to a process model (tightly framed) or not (unframed) and what the automation intent of the system is (e.g., P2P: person-to-person, P2A: person-to-application, or A2A: application-to-application). This delineates a range of distinct technology groupings, including various types of workflow technology.

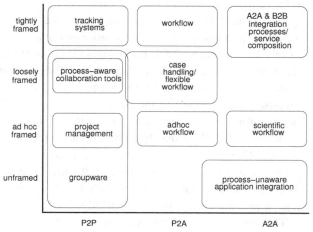

Figure 3.7

Classes of business process technologies (from [42]).

3.3.4   Case handling

Around the same time as the explosion of commercial workflow technology, the case handling paradigm was also established [21]. This specific approach to business process enactment is based on the idea that processes are driven by data-flow rather than control-flow. This approach to process enablement is particularly suited to processes that are highly data intensive, execute over a long duration, and are largely under the auspices of a single individual or group, such as the evaluation of an insurance claim or the registration of a newborn child. The leading offering in this area is the BPMone product from Perceptive Software. The specifics of this offering are discussed in more detail in section 3.4.3. Case handling is one of several approaches to make WFM/BPM technology more flexible. Examples of WFM systems providing innovative flexibility support are ADEPT and Declare (see section 3.5).

3.3.5   Web services

Web services composition languages have been an area of significant research over the past few years as more flexible and lightweight means were sought for providing business process support, particularly where these processes involve distributed participants or services provided by distinct vendors. Increasingly, the focus of these languages has moved beyond the traditional focus of the workflow system to the broader class of execution environments referred to as Business Process Management Systems (BPMSs).

One of the foci of standards initiatives in the business process area has been to define a modeling language for business processes that contains sufficient detail for it to ultimately be enacted. In 2002, the Business Process Management Institute (BPMI) released the Business Process Modeling Language (BPML), a standard for describing business processes and their constituent activities at varying levels of abstraction. Accompanying this proposal in draft form was the Business Process Modeling Notation (BPMN), a graphical notation for expressing business processes (see chapter 2 for more details on BPMN).

Although BPMI ultimately withdrew support for BPML, the graphical modeling notation BPMN received widespread attention, and despite its initial focus on the control-flow perspective of business processes, its influence has extended to the WfMC standards, and Interface 1 is now implemented as XPDL 2.2, which is essentially an XML-based serialization and interchange format for BPMN 2.0.2.

The most pervasive initiative in this area has been BPEL, a workflow-based web service composition language that has a broader range of capabilities in comparison to other initiatives in this area. A particular feature of BPEL is that it is designed to allow for the specification of both abstract and executable processes. Although mainly focused on the control-flow perspective, it also incorporates concepts from other perspectives such as data-passing, event and exception handling, messaging, and constraint enforcement.

Two of the most significant offerings in this area are Oracle BPEL Process Manager and WebSphere Process Server. Oracle BPEL Process Manager and WebSphere Process Server are enterprise-grade offerings that form part of the Oracle SOA Suite and WebSphere Process Server suites, respectively. Both offerings are designed to co-exist with the wide range of other development tools (database, application, webserver technology, etc.) that fall under these umbrellas, thus enabling workflow technology to be integrated with other corporate applications. In an attempt to better support human interactions within the BPEL framework, the BPEL4People extension has been proposed and is supported in commercial offerings such as Oracle SOA Suite and BPM Suite.

3.3.6   Business process management systems

As business process technology continues to mature, there is an increasing trend for offerings to provide support for all aspects of the BPM lifecycle. Whereas early workflow offerings simply provided a process design tool (generally with some form of graphical interface) and a process execution environment, recent BPMS offerings are also including support for various forms of process analytics (including process monitoring and business activity monitoring), content management, business rule support, and collaboration tools. In effect, a BPMS offering provides total support for the design, deployment, monitoring, and ongoing enhancement of business processes.

Pegasystems SmartBPM Suite, IBM Business Process Manager, Oracle SOA Suite and Oracle BPM Suite are leading offerings in this area. Oracle is particularly comprehensive in its process modeling and enactment capabilities supporting process specification in both BPEL and BPMN in an integrated application infrastructure together with integrated support for human processes as described in the BPEL4People and WS-HumanTask proposals, and business rules and business activity monitoring (BAM) functionality

BPMone is capable of supporting both workflow-style processes as well as its unique case handling approach. It incorporates a range of process management facilities relevant to the lifecycle of business processes, including simulation, process mining, and visual analytics.

3.4   Overview of popular techniques

Multitudes of business process definition languages have been proposed over recent years. In this section, we look at three significant initiatives that focus on the definition of business processes in sufficient detail that they can be directly executed. XPDL and BPEL are language initiatives operating under the auspices of the WfMC and OASIS industry bodies, respectively. Case handling is an alternative approach to business process enablement, which performs well in data-intensive business processes. For each of these three techniques, we look at a candidate offering and examine the capabilities it provides for business process enablement.

3.4.1   XPDL

XML Process Definition Language (XPDL) is a process definition language developed by the WfMC. It grew out of the Workflow Process Definition Language (WPDL) effort, which aimed to provide a standard for the interchange of process definitions, thus fulfilling the requirements for Interface 1 of the Workflow Reference Model. The first release of XPDL was finalized in 2002 and received significant industry focus; however, although many vendors claimed to provide support for the language, few actually made any serious efforts to achieve compliance. As a consequence, the language remained largely dormant and had little impact on industry trends.

This situation changed in 2004 when the WfMC formally adopted BPMN (up until that point perceived as a competing initiative for representing business processes) as the graphical formalism it would use for standardizing the visualization of business processes. As part of this effort, it made the decision to extend XPDL to allow it to represent all of the concepts contained in BPMN, including not only the semantic content of the BPMN model but also any relevant graphical layout information. The latest revision — XPDL 2.2 — was finalized in 2012 and caters to the wide range of concepts embodied in the BPMN 2.0.2 modeling standard.

XPDL uses an XML-based syntax based on XML Schema, and consequently process definitions are captured in a textual format. The emphasis of the current version is to provide a serialization of the BPMN modeling language that enables BPMN models to be exchanged between distinct BPM modeling tools, a concept that falls outside the purvue of the BPMN specification. One of the issues that comes to the fore when attempting to support the portability of process definitions is dealing with the additional executable details that specific vendors allow to be added to a BPMN model in order for it to be able to be directly executed by their toolset. Obviously, these extensions are vendor specific and do not form part of the "abstract" BPMN model that is able to be exchanged, and for this reason, in the most recent XPDL revision, considerable effort has been put into delineating the range of abstract concepts that are intended to be portable from the executable details that are not. XPDL 2.2 includes the notion of *Portability Conformance Classes* describing the various abstract concepts that are able to be shared and defines three distinct portability levels: *simple*, *standard*, and *complete*, which enable a specific modeling tool to assert the extent of model interoperability that it is able to support.

A significant debate in recent years has centered on the ability of a BPMN model to be executed. Two distinct viewpoints have formed on the matter: those who believe that a

BPMN model is intended as a purely abstract modeling notion and those who believe that the modeling formalism can be made more precise and enhanced to the point where it is able to be directly executed. Despite this debate, the use of executable BPMN is now becoming widely adopted as the standard business process modeling and execution language in commercial offerings. Because the focus of XPDL is now essentially to provide a serialization of BPMN, it does little more than reflect the concepts agreed on and embodied in BPMN, and hence XPDL is beginning to wane in attractiveness as an execution language. In the following section, we introduce the first significant attempt at standardizing a BPM execution language: BPEL.

3.4.2 BPEL

Web Services Business Process Execution Language (BPEL) is an executable language for describing web service interactions. It has its genesis in the WSFL and XLANG initiatives championed by Microsoft and IBM, respectively, who recognized the need for such a language and, faced with the increasing prominence of another initiative in the area (BPML), decided to amalgamate their efforts. The result was BPEL4WS, which was first released in 2003 and has met with broad support from vendors. Soon after, in conjunction with a group of vendors, the BPEL proposal was submitted to OASIS as part of a formal standardization effort, and they have overseen its development from this point. The current release is termed WS-BPEL 2.0, in line with other web services standards that OASIS administers.

BPEL is intended as an orchestration language, and consequently it describes web service interactions from the viewpoint of a single business process. It can be used at two distinct levels, allowing for the specification of either *abstract* or *executable* business processes depending on the level of detail that is captured about a candidate process.

Unlike earlier attempts at defining web services, which were limited to stateless interactions, BPEL is deliberately intended as a means of describing stateful, conversation-oriented business processes that are based on web services. A BPEL process is described in terms of XML. The high-level structure of a BPEL process is illustrated in Listing 3.1. It contains a number of language elements prior to the definition of the activity section, which describe the actual mechanics of the business process.

The purpose of each of these elements is as follows:

- `<extensions>` describe language extensions used in the context of the BPEL process. These may range from new types or elements through to new activity definitions and provide a mechanism for restricting or further extending current runtime behavior. Each `<extension>` element identifies the namespace in which the extension is located.
- `<import>` provides a means for a BPEL process to include any externally defined XML Schema or WSDL definitions on which it relies. These may include partner link types (the notion of partner links is described below), variable properties, and property aliases described elsewhere.

```
<process>
  <extensions> </extensions>
  <import> </import>
  <partnerLinks> </partnerLinks>
  <messageExchanges> </messageExchanges>
  <variables> </variables>
  <correlationSets> </correlationSets>
  <faultHandlers>? </faultHandlers>
  <eventHandlers> </eventHandlers>

  activity

</process>
```

Listing 3.1: BPEL process definition structure.

- `<partnerLinks>` are a key feature of a BPEL process. They describe the individual conversational links that a process has with various external partner services during its operation. The services fulfill specific functional requirements that are required during process execution. Each link identifies the service interaction(s) that occur between the process and its partner and the role that each of them is expected to perform during the course of an interaction.
- `<messageExchanges>` are used to distinguish between distinct conversational interactions that an instance of a BPEL process may have with a partner service. Because all conversations are based on incoming message receival activities and corresponding reply activities within a BPEL process, and it is possible for distinct conversations to occur with the same partner simultaneously, individual `<messageExchange>` constructs facilitate the pairing of receival and reply activities, thus enabling distinct conversations to be disambiguated.
- `<variables>` provide the containers for storing the state information relevant to a process. This can be messages received from or intended for transmittal to a partner or it can be data elements used during the execution of a business process.
- `<correlationSets>` provide a means of tying related incoming and outgoing messages from a business process to a given partner service into a conversation. A `<correlationSet>` consists of a list of message properties that remain fixed during the course of a given conversation and can therefore be used for correlation purposes. When the first message in a conversation is sent, the values of the message properties are fixed. By including these properties in subsequent message interactions, the correlation of messages into a conversation by both the BPEL process and the partner service is possible.
- `<faultHandlers>` provides a means of associating error handling strategies with a BPEL process. Termed fault handlers, these strategies may apply to a specific scope within a process or to the entire process. They can respond to nominated faults generated

by the execution of the BPEL engine or raised during the execution of activities within the process. When a fault is detected during the execution of a process, execution is suspended within the scope of the process to which the fault handler corresponds and control passes to the relevant fault handler. Once invoked, fault handlers have a range of options at their disposal for dealing with a detected fault: they can handle it themselves and then resume execution, they can invoke a compensation handler to try and mitigate the effects of the fault, they can trigger a fault at a higher level in the process, or they can cause execution of the associated scope or even the entire process to be halted.

- `<eventHandlers>` are analogous to fault handlers; however, they have a distinct purpose and consequently operate in a different manner. Event handlers provide a means of responding to events arising during the operation of a BPEL process that need to be dealt with but are not necessarily error-related (e.g., a timeout occurring). Event handlers can be associated with either a specific scope within a process or the entire process. They can be triggered by either the receipt of a specific message type or the occurrence of a nominated event, such as an alarm. When invoked, event handlers run concurrently with the process. They can deal with the detected event in a number of ways, including resolving the issue themselves, canceling execution in the associated scope, propagating the detected event to a higher level in the process, or terminating the process.

As shown in Listing 3.1, the final part of a BPEL process definition is the activity. At the top level, a BPEL process consists of a single activity; however, this can contain an arbitrary number of nested subactivities. Activities can be either *basic* or *structured*. Basic activities correspond to the fundamental actions undertaken during process execution. The following basic activities are supported by BPEL:

- `<invoke>` provides a means of invoking a partner service.
- `<receive>` allows an inbound message to be received for processing.
- `<reply>` enables a response to an inbound message to be sent to a partner service.
- `<assign>` enables data to be copied from one variable to another.
- `<wait>` causes execution to be delayed until a nominated timeframe has expired.
- `<empty>` corresponds to the "do nothing" activity.
- `<extensionActivity>` allows a task implementation to be extended by some form of new technology.
- `<exit>` causes the process to terminate immediately.
- `<throw>` generates a fault during process execution.
- `<rethrow>` enables a fault to be redirected to another fault handler.
- `<compensate>` initiates compensation handling for all inner scopes.
- `<compensateScope>` initiates compensation handling for a nominated (inner) scope.
- `<validate>` supports the validation of the values of variables against their data types.

Structured activities capture control-flow logic and may also include other basic and/or structured activities. The following structured activities are supported:

- <sequence> provides a means of indicating that a group of enclosed activities should be executed sequentially.
- <if>, <elseif>, <else> provides a mechanism for denoting that activities should be executed on a conditional basis.
- <while> provides a means of executing an enclosed activity on a conditional (pretested) basis zero or more times.
- <repeatUntil> provides a means of executing an enclosed activity on a conditional (posttested) basis one or more times.
- <forEach> provides a means of executing an enclosed activity a specified number of times either sequentially or concurrently.
- <pick> allows one out of several specified activities to be executed depending on which of a group of associated events occurs first.
- <flow> enables one or more specified activities to be executed concurrently.
- <scope> provides a means of defining a nested activity that is able to be compensated independently of other activities.

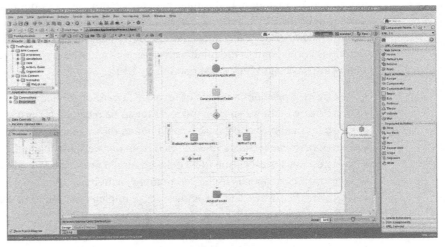

Figure 3.8
jDeveloper: the graphical editor used with Oracle BPEL.

A number of BPEL engines are available in the marketplace, ranging from open-source initiatives through to commercial engines intended for production usage. In this book, we will examine Oracle BPEL Process Manager, a widely used offering that is effectively integrated with the broader Oracle SOA Suite (a range of software incorporating products in the database, middleware, and BPM areas). An innovative feature of the Oracle SOA Suite offering is the jDeveloper graphical editor; it provides for the specification of business processes. Figure 3.9 shows the main screen for the editor, which provides an interactive graphical means of specifying BPEL processes and all of their associated elements and linkages with other partner services. It significantly reduces the effort associated with the specification of a BPEL process by providing a series of palettes of process constructs that can be used in the design of BPEL processes as shown in figure 3.9.

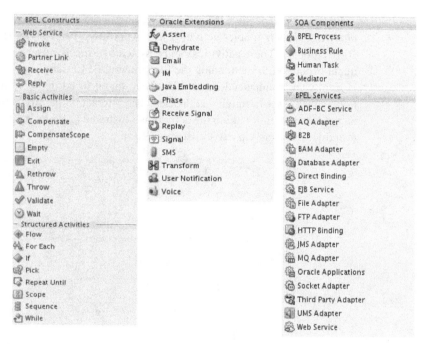

Figure 3.9
Process construct palette in jDeveloper.

Four main palettes are available for use in developing BPEL processes:

- *BPEL Constructs*, which correspond to language constructs in the current BPEL version.
- *Oracle Extensions*, which provide a series of additional (Oracle specific) constructs that can be incorporated directly in BPEL processes to enable features such as specification of assertions, external notification of events via various communication technologies (email, fax, IM, voice, etc.), supporting persistent storage of the state of long-duration processes, embedding Java code in a process, re-executing activities, and supporting coordination between master and detail processes.

- *SOA Components*, which provide four additional (Oracle-specific) service components enabling BPEL processes to interact with other distinct BPEL processes, utilize business rule functionality, support human interaction with processes, and incorporate mediation facilities for managing data interactions with other components in a composite application.
- *BPEL Services*, which provide facilities for BPEL processes to communicate and interact with other web-based services and applications via a range of distinct adapters and binding mechanisms.

From our perspective, the most interesting of the extensions to Oracle BPEL is the *Human Task*, which enables activities with workflow-like behavior to be embedded within a BPEL process. These activities can be routed to a specific user or group of users for subsequent execution. By extending the fundamental BPEL language in this way, its usefulness is significantly enhanced, and the criticism that it faced in regard to its lack of support for human processes is suitably addressed. The interaction facility between the BPEL process and the person undertaking the activity is illustrated in figure 3.10. Activities are presented to individual users via a worklist application.

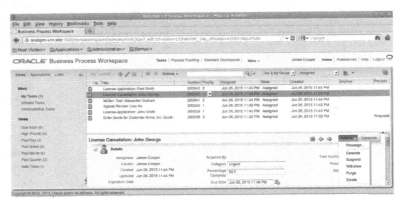

Figure 3.10
Oracle Business Process worklist.

The worklist serves as the interface between the human user and the executing process. It allows tasks to be routed to specific users and their execution to be managed through to conclusion. Once triggered, each human task in an Oracle BPEL process transitions through a sequence of states as illustrated in figure 3.11 as its execution progresses to a successful conclusion or some other final state. Tasks may be routed directly to one or more individual users, groups, or roles. The identity of these participants may be statically specified in the process model or determined dynamically based on business rules or some other form of programmatic assignment. It is even possible to utilize the services of an external routing service for this purpose. A number of distinct task assignment approaches

— known as participant types — are supported in order to cater for the range of ways in which individual tasks are assigned and undertaken by process participants:

- *Single approver* allows a task to be routed to a single user, group, or role; however, it assumes the task will be claimed and completed by a single user. Once claimed, it is withdrawn from the task list of other users to whom it may have also been routed.
- *Parallel* enables a task to be routed to and worked on by several users simultaneously. Task completion is determined on the basis of a group vote. Various voting configurations are supported.
- *Serial* allows a task to be routed sequentially to a set of users, each of whom may work on it in turn. This approach caters to approval policies such as management chain, where a number of users in an organizational hierarchy each undertake and confirm parts of a task.
- *FYI (For Your Information)* differs from the previous participant types in that it supports users receiving notifications about a task and being able to contribute to its information content (e.g., by adding comments or attachments) but does not involve the task being actually routed to the user for execution nor can the user have any impact on the overall progress of the task.

Where tasks are routed to the worklists of multiple users (e.g., by a group or role allocation), they must subsequently be claimed by individual users before they can be completed. As soon as they are assigned, tasks are assumed to be active (i.e., there is not a distinct start action). However, there is a distinct completion action, and this can be configured in a number of ways for each task depending on the specific routing approach that has been selected.

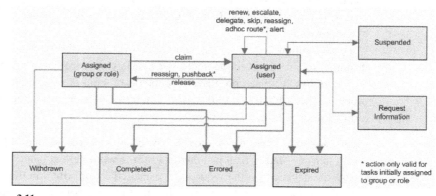

Figure 3.11

Task lifecycle in Oracle BPEL.

As can be seen, Oracle BPEL provides a broad range of facilities for configuring the routing of tasks and the range of task support facilities available to users. Furthermore, all of these features can be programmatically extended to further refine their capabilities and applicability to the wide range of situations in which process support may be required. The following three chapters discuss the various features and capabilities of Oracle BPEL in greater detail in the context of the control-flow, data, and resource patterns.

3.4.3   Case handling

One of the frequent criticisms of classical WFM/BPM technology is its focus on routing as the main means of driving work through a process model. The execution of a given case is based on the traversal of the thread of control though a process model using a predefined set of rules and constraints. Tasks in the process are only triggered when they receive the thread of control. There is no direct consideration of other important workflow factors such as the availability of data or resources when determining the execution sequence for activities in a given case, a phenomenon known as *context tunneling*. The emphasis that traditional workflow places on breaking down processes into a set of activities that can be routed to users for execution also has other difficulties as often there is a discrepancy between the way in which work activities are described by the process and the way in which users actually perceive and execute them. Typically users undertake work at varying levels of granularity. The classical process model breaks down work into fixed chunks, whereas users tend to dynamically compose activities from lower level actions.

In a workflow system, work is typically routed to users by the system on a preemptive basis, and users are not empowered to choose what they would like to do from work that needs to be done. Moreover, the routing of work serves two distinct functions: *distribution* and *authorization*. Individual workers only see the work that they are authorized to undertake. It is not possible for them to gain a broader view of their part in the conduct of the overall process.

These limitations seriously constrain the overall flexibility of workflow technology and its ability to effectively implement a wide variety of processes. As a remedy to these issues, *case handling* has been proposed as a means of supporting knowledge-intensive business processes [21]. Case handling has a number of core features that alleviate many of the aforementioned issues. In particular, it seeks to:

- avoid context tunneling by providing workers with access to all of the information relevant to a case rather than just the data for the work item at hand;
- base the decision on the work to be executed on information that is currently available within the case rather than on which activities have completed execution;
- impose a distinction between the act of work distribution and the concept of authorization; and
- allow users to access and amend data elements before or after the tasks to which they correspond have been executed.

Case handling is based on the fundamental notion that the *case* is the most important aspect of process execution, not the individual tasks that make up a process or the way in which work associated with it is distributed. As in a traditional workflow, a process is assumed to be made up of tasks, and there are directed arcs between them indicating precedence relations. However, unlike traditional workflows, the precedence relationship does not dictate the order of execution or the way in which tasks will be routed; it only provides a guide as to the dependencies that exist in the ordering of tasks in the process. Later tasks typically have some sort of execution dependency on or information requirement from earlier tasks. Moreover, the existence and value of data elements influence the sequence of tasks undertaken in a specific case. In contrast to other traditional BPM systems, users can also partially execute tasks or undertake them on an incremental basis.

BPMone is an integrated business process management environment that supports the full business process lifecycle. It includes support for process design, execution, analysis, and enhancement and has a particular focus on case handling as a means of conducting individual process instances. It integrates a number of tools that previously had an independent existence and area of focus, including Protos (process design and analysis), Activate (workflow), and FLOWer (case handling). BPMone also provides simulation facilities and supports process mining both during the early design stages and while controlling processes. Moreover, cases executed by the system can be analyzed using visual analytics. A key characteristic of the BPMone product is the way in which it integrates the process, data, and resource aspects of business processes. It supports processes definitions at two levels: (1) higher level business processes that can be used for process analysis and workflow-style process execution, and (2) more detailed business processes that contain sufficient detail for their execution to be undertaken on a case handling basis and support a greater range of options for adapting the specific process actions undertaken for individual cases.

Figure 3.12 illustrates the higher level BPMone process for the license application process discussed in chapter 2. It shows the way in which the BPMone design environment integrates the various aspects of the process from the control-flow, data, and resource perspectives. In general, the semantics of the model are much the same as the Petri net process model illustrated in figure 2.9. BPMone is able to handle both a deferred choice (i.e., a choice made in the operating environment of the process) and an explicit choice (i.e., a choice made by a user) between specific paths in the process as illustrated by the branches after the *Practical test pending* and *Make recommendation* nodes, respectively.

The higher level process models in the BPMone environment can be used directly for process analysis and execution but assume a more traditional workflow-style approach to process execution, where a case proceeds basically in terms of the task sequence in the associated process model. The more detailed process models supported by BPMone (known as *case type* models) support the full range of case handling options when dealing with the tasks associated with a given case.

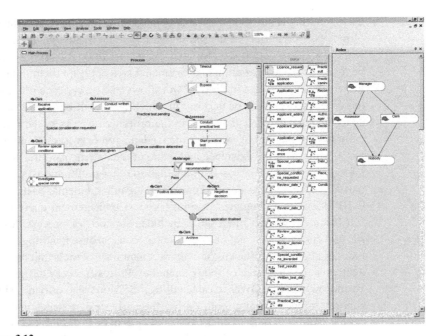

Figure 3.12
Process design using BPMone.

Case-type models in BPMone are comprised of a series of elements connected by directed arcs in a hierarchical graph structure as with other process modeling formalisms. Figure 3.13 illustrates the various constructs that make up a BPMone process model. Note that BPMone uses the term *plan* to refer to an individual process model and *step* to refer to an individual task or activity within a plan. The function of each of these constructs is as follows:

Figure 3.13
Language elements in BPMone case-type process models.

- the *Plan* construct corresponds to a subprocess embedded within a process model. A plan may have several distinct forms depending on whether it executes once, a number of times concurrently, or sequentially, or whether it contains alternate decision paths that may be selected by a user or the system at runtime;

- the *Plan Element* construct defines a step within a process;
- the *Form* construct identifies a form that is used for interacting with process participants during execution. This may be for gathering data or to display information relevant to case execution. An example of the forms supported within BPMone is shown in figure 3.15;
- the *Formfill Action* construct defines a step where part or all of a form is filled out;
- the *Milestone* construct defines a step within a plan that corresponds to a waiting moment where execution is delayed pending data availability or some other form of event;
- the *Standard Letter* construct defines a form letter that can be populated with data during execution. Letters provide a means of interacting with users in regard to more complex data conditions or where the user is not able to interact directly with the system;
- the *Branch* construct defines a decision point in a process;
- the *Standard Letter Action* construct describes a step where a standard letter is actually generated;
- the *Action Action* construct describes the action taken when a button on a form is selected;
- the *Operation Action* construct describes a step that is based on the execution of a module function within the BPMone system or an external function residing on the same server;
- the *Automatic Action* construct describes a step that is based on the automatic start and execution of a module function within the BPMone system or an external function residing on the same server;
- the *Mapping* construct identifies data retrieved from or stored in a database during execution;
- the *Action* construct defines a function in a module, an application or a rule that is utilized during execution;
- the *Database* construct defines an internal or external database in which information is stored or retrieved from during execution;
- the *Expression* construct defines a parameter or expression used during execution;
- the *Role* construct identifies a role for a user utilized within the process model. Roles form a hierarchy (as can be seen in figure 3.12) and define the basis for various privileges during execution (e.g., completing, redoing or skipping a step); and
- the *Comment Note* construct, which provides a means of annotating a process model.

Although there is generally a correspondence between the high-level BPMone model and the case-type model for a given process (and indeed there is a function within the tool to convert the former to the latter), the latter typically includes a great deal more information in regard to the way that individual process steps should be managed. They also include comprehensive support for forms and external application and database linkage. Figure 3.14 illustrates the case-type model corresponding to the license application process. A number of variations are evident when compared with the high-level model in figure 3.12.

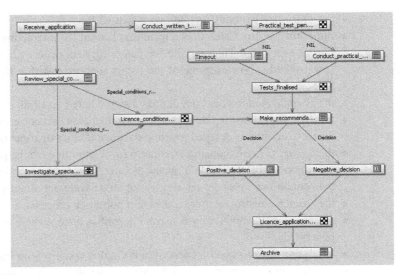

Figure 3.14
Case-type model of the license application process.

Data objects have a preeminent role during the execution of a case and, unlike traditional workflows, determine the manner in which case execution occurs. Data objects are attached to a process and correspond to a piece of information that may or may not be present. Where a data object is present, it has a value recorded for it. Data objects can be either *free*, meaning they can be amended at any time during case execution and are not explicitly linked to a specific task in the process, or *mandatory* and/or *restricted*, in which case they are linked to one or more specific tasks. A mandatory data object means that its value must be recorded before the task to which it is attached can complete. It may be provided ahead of the time that the task is executed or during its execution, but either way it must be available at task completion. In contrast, a restricted data object can only have its value recorded during the execution of the task(s) with which it is associated.

The resources that undertake the tasks in a case are termed *actors*. They are organized in terms of *roles* that group actors with similar responsibilities or capabilities. An actor may be a member of more than one role. Roles are specific to a given process and can be linked together via *is_a* relationships to illustrate the relationship between them. Actors that are members of a superior role in the overall hierarchy are automatically members of any of its subordinate roles.

Three types of roles can be specified for each process and activity:

- the *execute* role indicates which actors can execute a task or start a process instance.
- the *redo* role indicates which actors can undo a task reverting the state of the case to that before the task executed. Undoing a task also undoes the effects of all subsequent

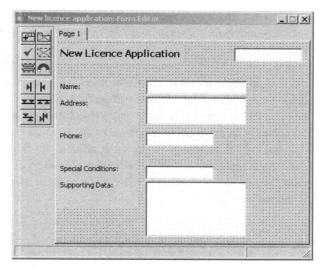

Figure 3.15
Form definition in BPMone.

activities. (Of course it is impossible to undo externally visible actions, e.g., a payment. In such cases, a compensating action is needed.)

- the *skip* role indicates which actors can skip over the execution of a task.

There is a significant difference in the way that work is distributed when using a case handling approach. Unlike traditional workflow systems, which rely on the use of an in-tray or worklist client to indicate which tasks an actor must undertake, case handling relies on the use of case queries that are more flexible in form and allow an actor to search for any tasks that may need attention in order to complete a case. It does not require that these tasks be distributed to the actor in order to undertake them.

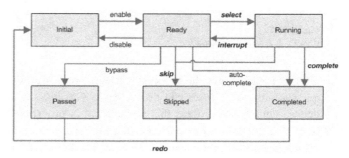

Figure 3.16
Task lifecycle in BPMone.

The lifecycle for each step in BPMone is illustrated in figure 3.16. User-initiated actions via the worklist are shown in bold. Once created at case initialization, steps become enabled when any precursing data constraints have been met. Once in a *ready* state, they can be commenced (and enter a *running* state) when selected by a user. The user can interrupt them at any time by returning to the worklist (causing a transition to a running state) or can complete them, causing a transition to a *completed* state. A *ready* or *running* step can be skipped by a user at any time, triggering a change to a *skipped* state. Where configured accordingly in the process model, a *ready* step can transition automatically to a *passed* or *completed* state where qualifying conditions for this event are met. Finally, a user can trigger the repetition of a step in the *passed*, *skipped*, or *completed* state via an explicit redo request in the worklist handler. Each of these states has a distinct annotation in the BPMone worklist.

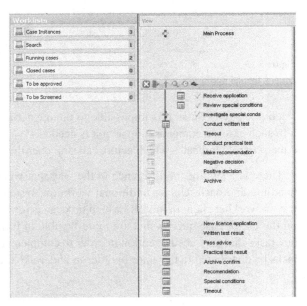

Figure 3.17
Worklist operation in BPMone.

Figure 3.17 shows the worklist interface for a user. On the left are the standard work queues into which cases can be retrieved. The right-hand side shows an instance of the license application process that is currently in progress. The top part of this frame indicates that the "Main Process" (i.e., the top-level process) is active at present. The middle frame shows the current state of the case. The bottom frame shows the forms that make up the process. The vertical blue line in the middle frame is known as the *wavefront*, and it indicates which steps are currently active. Anything to the right of the wavefront has been completed or is no longer active (i.e., the *Receive application* and *Review special conditions* steps are complete as indicated by the green tick). The *Investigate special conds* step has also been completed but is currently back on the wavefront as a user has requested it be redone. The *Conduct written* test step is also currently active. Anything to the left of the wavefront is not yet active. However, unlike traditional workflow tools, in BPMone, a user can elect to *execute*, *skip*, or *redo* any step at any time. There is no prescribed ordering for the process, only a suggested sequence based on interdependencies between steps. Where a step is done outside of the recommended sequence and changes are made to associated data elements, any subsequent steps depending on the step are also redone.

The case handling paradigm makes a significant contribution to the BPM landscape and provides a valuable alternative approach to executing business processes. It especially highlights the need for flexible business processes that are better able to accommodate special operational requirements and deviations that may arise during execution. This is a critical issue in today's turbulent business environment. The following section examines these needs in more detail.

3.5   Flexibility

A desirable characteristic for business processes is that they are resilient to changes that may arise in the operational environment. The increased prevalence of automated business process support and the volatile nature of the environments in which they are deployed mean that it is increasingly likely that during their operation, business processes may encounter unusual and/or unanticipated situations that need to be catered for. The ability of a business process to successfully respond to unanticipated events or changes is termed *flexibility* or *agility*.

There are a variety of ways in which business processes can respond to these situations, and these are enumerated in the *Taxonomy of Flexibility* [121], a broad classification of approaches to facilitating process flexibility derived from a comprehensive survey of flexibility support in BPMSs and the BPM literature.

This taxonomy recognizes five distinct approaches to incorporating flexibility in a process, and the relationship between them is shown in figure 3.18. These approaches are as follows:

- *Flexibility by design* involves the explicit incorporation of flexibility mechanisms into a process at design-time using available process modeling constructs such as splits and joins;
- *Flexibility by deviation* involves supporting the ability for individual process instances to temporarily deviate from the prescribed process model in order to accommodate change that may be encountered in the operating environment at runtime;

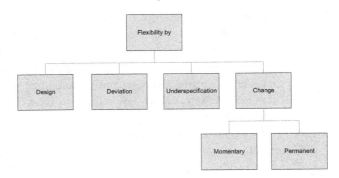

Figure 3.18
Taxonomy of flexibility types.

- *Flexibility by underspecification* is the ability to deliberately underspecify parts of a process model at design-time in anticipation of the fact that the required execution details will become known at some future time. When a process instance encounters an underspecified portion of a process at runtime, the missing part can be instantiated in accordance with the required operational outcomes and then executed; and
- *Flexibility by change* where changes in the operational environment are catered for by actually amending the process model. There are two approaches to this:

  — *Flexibility by momentary change* involves changing the process model corresponding to a specific process instance. Any other process instances are unaffected by the change; and
  — *Flexibility by permanent change* involves changing the process model for all process instances. This may involve migrating any other currently executing instances from the old to the new process model.

Contemporary BPM modeling languages and BPMSs offer varying degrees of support for process flexibility as illustrated in table 3.1. In general, flexibility by design is well supported by most offerings reflecting the common preconception that flexibility can be foreseen and designed into a process. Less well supported are other approaches to flexibility that involve (1) relaxing the strict approaches to process execution at runtime and allowing for deviation from the prescribed execution sequence, (2) allowing process designs to be deliberately underspecified with the expectation that any shortfalls in the precision or clarity of a process can be rectified before or at runtime, or (3) allowing processes to be changed at runtime, for either a single execution instance or all execution instances.

Although BPMone provides a modicum of support for flexibility by deviation as a consequence of the case handling approach it adopts to process execution and Oracle BPEL supports late binding, in general terms, there is minimal support for enabling flexible process behaviors among contemporary BPM languages and systems. However, there are a

Table 3.1

Flexibility type support for BPMN, BPMone. Oracle BPEL, YAWL with worklets, ADEPT1 and Declare : + indicates full support, +/- partial support, and – no support (results for ADEPT1 and Declare from [121]).

Flexibility Type	Realization Option	BPMN	BPMone	Oracle BPEL	YAWL + worklets	ADEPT1	Declare
Flexibility by Design	Parallelism	+	+	+	+	+	+
	Choice	+	+	+	+	+	+
	Iteration	+	+	+	+	+	+
	Interleaving	+	+	+	+	–	+
	Multiple instances	+	+	+	+	–	+
	Cancellation	+	–	+	+	–	+
Flexibility by Deviation	*Imperative languages*						
	Undo	–	+	–	–	–	N/A
	Redo	–	+	–	–	–	N/A
	Skip	+	+	+	–	–	N/A
	Create additional instance	–	+/–	–	–	–	N/A
	Invoke task	+	+	+	–	–	N/A
	Declarative languages						
	Violation of constraints	N/A	N/A	N/A	N/A	N/A	+
Flexibility by Underspecification	*Placeholder enactment*						
	Late binding	+	–	+	+	–	–
	Late modeling	–	–	–	+	–	–
	Moment of realization						
	Static, before placeholder	–	–	–	–	–	–
	Dynamic, before placeholder	–	–	–	–	–	–
	Static, at placeholder	–	–	–	–	–	–
	Dynamic, at placeholder	+	–	+	+	–	–
Flexibility by Change	*Effect of Change*						
	Momentary change	–	–	–	–	+	+
	Evolutionary change	–	–	–	–	–	+
	Moment of allowed change						
	Entry time	–	–	–	–	+	+
	On–the–fly	–	–	–	–	+	+
	Migration strategies for evolutionary change						
	Forward recovery	–	–	–	–	–	–
	Backward recovery	–	–	–	–	–	–
	Proceed	–	–	–	–	–	+
	Transfer	–	–	–	–	–	+

number of approaches utilized within current BPM tools that go some way toward supporting expected and unexpected events that may arise during process execution. Dynamic workflow provides a means of extending processes at runtime to deal with situations not anticipated at design-time. Exception handling provides a means of dealing with undesirable events that arise during process execution. Declarative workflow offers an alternative means of specifying and executing processes that focus on what needs to be achieved rather than how it should be done. Each of these approaches is described in the remainder of this chapter.

3.5.1 Dynamic workflow

Dynamic workflow provides a means of extending and adapting design-time process definitions at runtime to cater to unanticipated changes in either the required process behavior or unexpected events arising in the execution environment. There are two possible approaches to dealing with such scenarios: (1) deliberately underspecify the design-time process model and allow it to be extended when the required process behavior becomes known or unexpected events occur, or (2) provide a range of mechanisms within the workflow environment to allow an executing process to be dynamically changed at runtime to deal with evolving requirements and events occurring in the operational environment that the process must cater to.

An example of *flexibility by underspecification* is provided by the Worklet service in the open-source YAWL workflow engine. The Worklet service provides a repository for a range of *worklets,* each of which corresponds to a group of activities intended to deal with a particular processing requirement. A worklet takes the form of a complete YAWL process. For any given YAWL process, it is permissible to indicate that a given task will be fulfilled by a worklet at runtime. This removes the immediate need to specify all implementation details for the task at design-time and instead passes responsibility for this to the Worklet service. When the task is triggered at runtime, the Worklet service matches the task up with an appropriate worklet based on the current state of the process and its associated data elements. It utilizes a "Ripple Down Rule" (RDR) tree for this purpose. In the event that a suitable worklet cannot be located, it is possible to dynamically add either a new case for the RDR tree or even a complete new worklet. An example of such an RDR tree is shown in figure 3.19 for an order returns processing task. Depending on whether the goods were damaged, the number of returns for the customers this year, the seniority of the staff member handling the return, the value of the return, whether the customer is a staff member, and the status of the customer, one of several distinct worklets is selected as the means by which the task is operationalized at runtime.

The ADEPT/ADEPT2/AristaFlow lineage of workflow engines chart the cutting edge of research into *flexibility by change.* Originally conceived as a research prototype, the AristaFlow BPM Suite is now available as a fully fledged commercial offering. It provides users and process administrators with the ability to intervene in a process where an unexpected situation has arisen. In order to resolve the situation within the context of the process, a range of facilities are provided to allow the process to be dynamically changed to cater to a wide range of exceptions, including the addition or deletion of elements (which may be activities, splits, joins, loops, branches, etc.) in the process, and the addition of, deletion of, or changes to the use of data elements within a process. In order to ensure that the operational integrity of the process is maintained, any changes are subject to a consistency check to ensure they do not invalidate the correctness of the process. Any such changes can be limited to a single process instance or may be propagated to a range of process instances. There is also provision for structural changes to an overall process model and the propagation of these changes to executing process instances. Figure 3.20 illustrates the addition of a *review findings* task to a medical process.

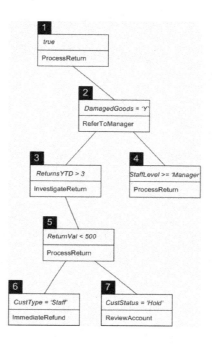

Figure 3.19
RDR tree selection of worklet.

3.5.2 Exception handling

Exception handling is a technique that has been widely used for many years in software development as a means of dealing with the range of scenarios that may occasionally be encountered during the execution of a program that are not specifically catered to as part of its processing logic. The basic premise of exception handling is that a generic strategy is defined that can best deal with the effects of a specific type of error (or indeed all types of unexpected errors) that might arise during execution of a business process. In this section, we will consider two distinct approaches to exception handling that are commonly used in BPM systems.

Exception handlers
Exception handlers have been utilized in the software engineering field for many years as a means of responding to a broad range of unanticipated program errors that might arise at runtime. They typically take the form of a procedure that is associated with a given process or a block within a process that describes the action to be taken when a nominated event occurs. This event can be system-generated (e.g., hardware fault, divide by zero error) or application-generated (e.g., remote service call returns an error). Usually a given handler

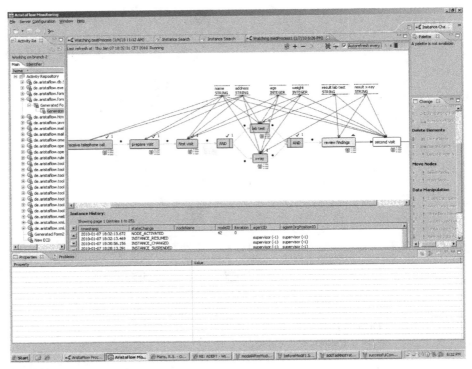

Figure 3.20
Support for *flexibility by change* in AristaFlow.

has a specific exception that it responds to and aims to resolve; however, it is possible to define blanket exception handlers for all detected errors.

When the nominated exception is detected, the execution of the part of the process to which the exception is attached ceases, and the thread of control is passed to the exception handler. The exception handler takes any necessary steps that it can to resolve the exception and then at its conclusion can do one of three things: (1) cease execution and pass the thread of control back to the place in the process instance from which it was invoked, (2) cease execution and trigger no further action, or (3) escalate the detected exception to a higher level by triggering (often termed "throwing") another exception handler possibly in a surrounding program block.

Oracle BPEL provides a range of exception handling capabilities in the form of fault handlers, event handlers, and compensation handlers. The use of these features provides a wide array of options for dealing with undesirable events that may occur during the execution of a process. Depending on the handling option being utilized, these events may be expected or unexpected, the distinction being whether the process definition identifies the potential for the event to arise and how to deal with it or not. In all cases, the use of these features requires the relevant handling behavior to be associated with a specific scope within a process definition.

A *fault handler* reverses the effects of partially complete or unsuccessful work in the scope in which the fault is detected. BPEL identifies two types of faults: (1) *business* faults, which are application-specific and generally relate to *information* being processed; and (2) *runtime* faults, which arise as a consequence of problems in the operating environment. Business faults occur when a process recognizes that an error has occurred and initiates a *throw* activity or when an *invoke* activity generates a fault during its operation. In contrast, runtime faults are triggered by the system when it detects a problem during the execution of a BPEL process (e.g., logic errors, messaging faults). A fault handler takes the form of a sequence of activities or a process that is associated with a specific error type in a given scope. Once a fault is detected, control is passed to the relevant handler in the scope in order to deal with the detected exception. At its conclusion, it may terminate any further execution of the process, resume execution in the scope in which the exception was detected, or escalate the fault by propagating it to the surrounding or parent scope.

In contrast to a fault hander, a *compensation handler* undoes the effect(s) of a successfully completed scope. It can also allow for the undoing of a multi-part or distributed transaction that has partially completed execution. A compensation handler takes the form of a sequence of activities or a process that is associated with a specific scope. It is invoked via the *compensate* activity and can only be triggered in the fault handler or compensation handler of the scope that immediately encloses the scope being compensated. Once the requested compensation has been completed, the thread of control passes to the activity immediately following the compensate activity.

An *event handler* provides a means for a scope to respond to specific events that may arise during its execution that need to be dealt with. In the main, these are timeouts or the receipts of specific types of messages. Similar to fault handlers, event handlers correspond to sequences of activities or processes associated with a scope and have an *OnAlarm* or *OnMessage* event that defines when they are to be invoked. At their conclusion, they can either terminate the process or pass the thread of control back to the scope in which they were triggered. In contrast to fault handlers, which address error situations, event handlers are assumed to form part of the normal processing sequence where some form of asynchronous event needs to be dealt with.

Dynamic process extension

An alternate means of dealing with unanticipated events during process execution is provided by dynamic process extension. This involves extending the process with the necessary tasks to deal with the effects of the detected event at runtime. Typically this approach to exception handling involves manual intervention during process execution when an exception is detected in order to amend the process instance in a way that addresses the issue.

Although this is a novel concept in contemporary BPM offerings, the open-source YAWL workflow engine provides the *Exlet* feature as part of its Worklet service that allows for the runtime adaptation of processes to cater for unanticipated or undesirable events. In much the same way that worklets provide a repertoire of alternate implementation behaviors for an activity, a set of exlets provides the ability to specify a repertoire of exception handling behaviors that can be utilized throughout a process definition. An exlet can be bound to either an individual activity or a process instance within an operational BPM environment. Each exlet has a unique event that causes it to execute. Supported events include pre/postconstraint violations, time outs, external triggers, abort requests, and unavailable resources. An exlet is defined in terms of a sequence of primitives that describe how an unanticipated event should be handled when detected during process execution. In order to provide a rich array of constructs with which to define exception handling strategies, the standard language primitives in YAWL are extended with sixteen additional language elements specifically aimed at exception handling. These are illustrated in figure 3.21.

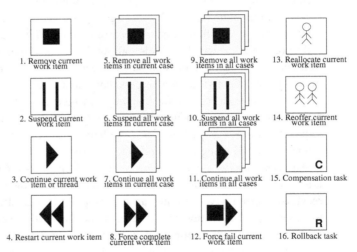

Figure 3.21
Exlet exception handling primitives (from [112]).

An exlet operates in much the same way as a worklet. When the trigger event for a specific exlet is detected during process execution, the relevant exlet is initiated and attempts to resolve the detected event. Depending on the primitives defined for the exlet, further execution of "normal" process related activities may continue or it may be suspended. At its conclusion, the exlet can pass control back to the process, cause the process instance that detected it to terminate, or even cause all related process instances to terminate. Figure 3.22 illustrates the use of exlets to handle exception events detected in the context of a *pack order* task in an order fulfillment process. Three distinct exlets are defined for this activity:

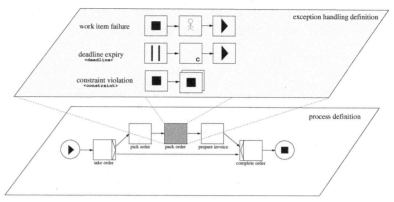

Figure 3.22

Exlet event handing strategy for order process (from [112]).

(1) in the event of the work item associated with the activity failing, it is stopped, manually reassigned to another resource, and continued; (2) in the event of a deadline for the activity being exceeded, it is paused, any necessary compensation is undertaken (e.g., advising the customer of the delay), and then it is continued; and (3) in the event of a constraint associated with the task (e.g., outstanding customer credit) being exceeded, the task is stopped and all other tasks in the current process instance are also stopped.

3.5.3 Declarative workflow

Today's process-aware information systems tend to either support business processes *or* provide flexibility. Classical WFM systems offer good process support as long as the processes are structured and do not require much flexibility. Information systems that allow for flexibility have a tendency to provide little process-related support. When enabling business processes using IT, there is a difficult trade-off to be made. On the one hand, there is a desire to control processes and avoid incorrect or undesirable executions of these processes. On the other hand, users want flexible processes that do not constrain them in their actions. This apparent paradox has limited the application of WFM/BPM technology thus far because, as indicated by many authors, classical systems are too restrictive and have problems when dealing with change. The case-handling paradigm used by BPMone and the worklets/exlets of YAWL aim to address this problem. Another approach to balance between support and flexibility is provided by *Declare* [17].

Traditional approaches tend to use procedural process models to explicitly (i.e., step-by-step) specify the execution procedure. Declarative approaches are based on *constraints* (i.e., anything is possible as long as it is not explicitly forbidden). Constraint-based models, therefore, implicitly specify the execution procedure by means of constraints: any execution that does not violate constraints is possible.

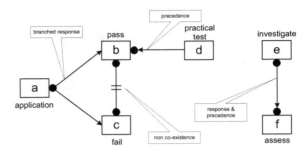

Figure 3.23
Declare specification consisting of five constraints: two precedence constraints, one non-co-existence constraint, one response constraint, and one branched response constraint.

Declare is an example of a declarative constraint-based language (in fact a family of languages). Moreover, Declare is supported by fully functional BPM system [17, 85]. Declare uses a graphical notation and semantics based on Linear Temporal Logic (LTL) [34]. Figure 3.23 shows a Declare specification consisting of four constraints. The construct connecting activities b and c is a so-called *non-co-existence constraint*. In terms of LTL, this constraint means "$!((\Diamond b) \wedge (\Diamond c))$"; $\Diamond b$ and $\Diamond c$ cannot both be true (i.e., it cannot be the case that both b and c happen for the same case). There are two *precedence constraints*. The semantics of the precedence constraint connecting d to b can also be expressed in terms of LTL: "$(!b) \ W \ d$" (i.e., b should not happen before d has happened). Because the weak until (W) is used in "$(!b) \ W \ d$," execution sequences without any b and d activities also satisfy the constraint. The constraint connecting a to b and c is a so-called branched constraint involving three activities. This *response constraint* states that every occurrence of a should eventually be followed by b or c: "$\Box(a \Rightarrow (\Diamond(b \vee c)))$." Note that the latter constraint allows for $\langle a, a, a, b, c, a, a, b \rangle$ but not $\langle a, b, c, a \rangle$. The constraint connecting e to f is a combination of a response and a precedence constraint. The response part states that "$\Box(e \Rightarrow (\Diamond f))$" (i.e., any occurrence of e should eventually be followed by f). The precedence part states that "$(!f) \ W \ e$" (i.e., f should not happen before e has happened). Example traces that satisfy all four constraints are $\langle a, a, d, b \rangle$, $\langle a, a, c, c, c \rangle$, $\langle e, e, f, f \rangle$, $\langle d, d, e, a, e, b, f, b, f \rangle$, and so on.

Procedural languages only allow for activities that are explicitly triggered through control-flow (token semantics). As indicated before, in a declarative language like Declare, "*everything is possible unless explicitly forbidden*." This is illustrated by figure 3.23, which allows for a wide range of behaviors difficult to express in procedural languages.

The Declare language is supported by the Declare system, which is much more flexible than traditional procedural WFM systems [17]. Moreover, it is possible to learn Declare models by analyzing event logs [85]. The graphical constraint language is also suitable for conformance checking (one of the types of process mining introduced before). Given an event log, it is possible to check all constraints. Consider, for example, figure 3.23. Given an event log, one can compute for each constraint the proportion of cases that respects this constraint [17, 85]. In the case of conformance checking, complex time-based constraints may be used (e.g., after every occurrence of activity a for a gold customer, activity b or c should happen within 24 hours).

3.6   Current challenges

This chapter has outlined the development of the BPMS field and the role it has played in automating the operation of business processes. There have been significant developments over the past 30 years, and the available technology now provides an effective means of enacting business processes in an organizational context. Nevertheless, the BPM domain remains in a continual state of flux as it continues to evolve. In this section, we examine some of the current challenges that exist in the BPM arena.

Absence of widely adopted BPM standards

One of the motivations for the establishment of the Workflow Reference Model by the WfMC in 1995 was to establish a common vocabulary for the workflow domain. By doing so, it was anticipated that the foundation would be laid for interchange of process models between the wide variety of technologies falling under the workflow umbrella. In essence, the aim of the WfMC was to promote the use of workflow technology in a consistent way regardless of the underlying formalisms on which it was based. To some degree the effort was successful in establishing a basic vocabulary for common workflow terms, which is relatively widely used in the BPM community. However, attempts at establishing a common reference model for workflow definition and execution were largely ignored by workflow developers particularly because the proposed workflow execution model was not especially powerful, and many did not see any benefit in migrating their proprietary modeling formalisms to a common technique. More recently, BPEL achieved relatively widespread support among vendors as a common format for specifying executable business processes based on web services; however, it suffered from the difficulty that it was only informally defined, leading to varying interpretations of its constructs and operation. Perhaps the most successful initiative in this area to date has been the continued evolution of BPMN. Initially positioned as a modeling formalism and only informally defined, it has now matured into a fully fledged business process modeling and execution language based on a comprehensive meta-model together with an associated graphical modeling notation and an execution semantics defining how BPMN processes should be enacted. It is increasingly being seen as the de facto standard for business process definition and has been adopted by a wide range of vendors.

Disparity between modeling and enactment tools

Traditionally in the BPM domain, distinct formalisms have been used for the modeling of business processes at the conceptual and executable levels. The modeling strategies used at the conceptual level have concentrated on providing a wide range of modeling artifacts without any immediate consideration of how they will be operationalized. Examples of such techniques include EPCs, UML activity diagrams, and BPMN. Techniques used at the executable level focus on the ability to enact the various elements of a process model and consequently are designed with determinism in mind rather than conceptual power. Where a business process is defined in terms of a conceptual modeling notation such as EPCs or UML activity diagrams, there is a consequent mapping activity that is required into an executable format before the process can actually be enacted. The semantic disparity between conceptual and executable modeling notations means that there is generally some form of (manual) remodeling of a process required during this mapping activity, and consequently there is the potential for information loss and misinterpretation of the candidate business process. Two distinct approaches have been proposed to resolving this issue. The first focuses on the development of execution semantics for individual conceptual modeling notations that allows them to be directly enacted without ambiguity. Perhaps the most successful initiative in this area is BPMN 2.0.2, which is now the basis of a number of commercial offerings such as Oracle BPM Suite, which provides direct execution support for process models specified using BPMN.

Incorporating flexibility in business processes

The modern business environment is in a continual state of flux, and it is a desirable property of a business process that it is able to accommodate the various types of changes that might arise during its operational lifetime. Workflow technology has faced significant criticism in recent years in regard to its inflexibility and inability to adapt to changing operational circumstances. Consequently, there is increased focus on incorporating various types of flexibility support into business processes as a means of improving their overall resilience. As indicated in section 3.5, four distinct approaches have been identified to incorporating change support in processes: (1) *flexibility by design*, (2) *flexibility by deviation*, (3) *flexibility by underspecification*, and (4) *flexibility by change*. Individual BPMS offerings are starting to provide various types of flexibility support in specific areas (e.g., BPMone provides a number of deviation facilities); however, widespread flexibility support among BPMS offerings has not yet emerged).

Supporting commercial-scale business processes

The potential benefits of BPM come to the fore when automating large-scale, complex business processes that operate on a "whole-of-organization" basis or between several organizational participants in a business process. Such processes are so broad in form that they do not fall under the auspices of any one individual but instead have specific sections that are managed by distinct groups of resources. It is possible that all of the expertise required to undertake a given process does not lie within the organization and that the business process also needs to integrate external resources and services in order to achieve corporate goals, or indeed that a business process operates between several organizations and coordinates their interactions in an overall business initiative. When automating business processes of this scale, a new range of issues arise that are not evident in smaller processes that involve less complex set of activities or operate over a shorter time horizon, such as handling the evolution of individual sections of the process, versioning of process instances, coordinating resource assignment, managing workload, amending/outsourcing/insourcing task implementation, and monitoring process operation to ensure expected service levels are achieved. The criticality of business processes of this scale means that these issues must be dealt with on a dynamic basis and cannot necessitate the termination or restart of a process. The introduction of service orientation as a means of constructing business processes offers some initial support for dealing with some of these issues; however, there is still significant work required in this area.

Empowering users in the business process

There has been a great deal of work conducted on the optimization of business processes from a global standpoint; however, in many situations, it is actually the individual users who undertake specific activities within a process that are best positioned to identify potential opportunities for improvement. Consequently, there is significant potential in providing users with an insight into the operation of a process instance in which they are involved and the impact that their individual work activities have on it. This information is particularly useful when coupled with a range of alternative options (e.g., start a work item, delegate a work item, escalate a work item, etc.) from which a user can select how they will interact with a process in the most beneficial way. Providing suitable intelligence to users about process performance may take a number of forms. As illustrated in section 2.5, one possible approach involves the use of *process mining*, which seeks to provide users with decision-making information based on the analysis of preceding executions of a process. Although there are a variety of different analysis techniques with which to do this, the most important consideration is ensuring that the necessary information is presented to the user in a meaningful way at the exact time that they require decision support. This approach can be especially powerful when linked with richer worklist visualization facilities, which provide workflow users with a much broader range of information about outstanding work items when making a decision as to which work item to execute next or which work items need prioritizing. The YAWL workflow system has been successfully coupled with the ProM process mining suite as a demonstration of how this may be achieved, and it is anticipated that similar capabilities will find their way into commercial offerings in due course.

Leveraging the knowledge contained in business processes

Achieving best practice in the operation of a given business process is one of the overarching aims of BPM deployment. In doing so, organizations seek to optimize the function of a business process in an effort to maximize both its effectiveness and efficiency. Reference models have long been advocated as a means of distributing knowledge in regard to optimal process designs for a given domain. These typically present standardized processes for common business activities in a form that facilitates their reuse by other organizations that do not have prior experience in their deployment and serve as a guideline for the form that a candidate business process should take. Although the rationale for the use of reference models is sound, in practice, however, it is often found that the specific context in which a reference model can be applied is extremely limited, and large parts of the "standard model" are not generally applicable to organizations seeking to use them. Configurable reference models have been proposed as a solution to this difficulty and offer a means of describing a standard business process along with the various configuration alternatives that might exist for it, thus allowing an organization to tailor it to their specific requirements. The concept has been successfully demonstrated for the EPC and YAWL modeling languages, but in order for it to achieve more widespread usage, it needs to be extended to the wide range of mainstream business process modeling languages, and there needs to be a comprehensive library of standard business processes that is freely available to organizations seeking to use them.

3.7   Further reading

- Full details of the Workflow Reference Model can be found in [143]. A wealth of related workflow material is also available from the website `www.wfmc.org`.
- Widely recognized texts on workflow technology have been written by Van der Aalst and Van Hee [10], Leymann and Roller [79], and Jablonski and Bussler [68].
- The definitive work on Process-Aware Information Systems (PAIS), the broader class of technologies of which BPMSs are a part, is that by Dumas et al. [42].
- The definition for XPDL 2.2 is contained in [145] available from the WfMC website.
- The current version of BPEL (2.0) is defined in [93]. The related BPEL4People and WS-HumanTask specifications are both now at version 1.1, full details are available

in [95] and [94] respectively. Comprehensive documentation on Oracle BPEL is available from the Oracle website at `www.oracle.com/technetwork/middleware/bpel/overview/index.html`.

- A comprehensive overview of case handling can be found in [21]. Further information on the BPMone product is available from Perceptive Software's website at `www.perceptivesoftware.com`.

- An overview of the issues associated with process flexibility can be found in [23] and [104]. The worklets and exlets aspects of the YAWL system (including the use of Ripple-Down Rules) are comprehensively documented in [22]. Further details on YAWL can be found at `www.yawlfoundation.org` and in [64].

- The chronology of the ADEPT/ADEPT2/AristaFlow system is documented in [37]. Further details on the software are available from `www.aristaflow.com`.

- An introduction to the ProM initiative can be found in [18]. The software and comprehensive technical information about the offering are available at `www.processmining.org`.

- The widely recognized standard text on process mining is [3].

- Details on the constraint-based language Declare, the Declare system, and the use of process logs to develop Declare models can be found in [17] and [85].

- The concept of configurable reference model languages is introduced in [109], and details of the implementation of a configurable workflow model (in the context of the YAWL system) is presented in [58]. A comprehensive treatment of process model variability and configuration strategies in contained in [108].

- [103] provides a comprehensive treatment of flexibility and change management issues in the context of BPMSs.

III WORKFLOW PATTERNS

4

As indicated in section 1.1, there are three main perspectives in a business process model: control-flow, data, and resources. The most dominant of these is the control-flow perspective as this "glues" the other perspectives together and is mostly used as a starting point during process design and development. Therefore, we start by describing the patterns for this perspective.

Section 4.1 provides an overview of the control-flow patterns. The *control-flow patterns* can be grouped in *eight categories* of patterns. The *branching patterns* are described in section 4.2. These include patterns such as the AND-split (starting concurrent threads), the XOR-split (selecting a path), and the OR-join (selecting one or more concurrent paths). The *synchronization patterns* in section 4.3 describe the different ways in which the paths meet again (AND-join, XOR-join, OR-join, etc.). The *repetition patterns* described in section 4.4 are concerned with the repeated sequential execution of a task or subprocess for a given process instance (e.g., loops and recursion). The *multiple instances patterns* described in section 4.5 consider multiple, possibly concurrent, instances. For example, given an order composed of 25 order lines, the task "check availability" needs to be performed 25 times, and these checks do not have to be executed in a particular order. Section 4.6 describes the *concurrency patterns*. These patterns aim to control or restrict the concurrent execution of tasks in a particular way. For example, parts of the process may need to be executed sequentially because of data sharing. The *trigger patterns* discussed in section 4.7 describe the interactions of the process with some external environment (e.g., a process may block until a message is received). Section 4.8 describes *cancelation and completion patterns*. For example, due to some failure, it may be necessary to abort all work items in a particular region of the process. The *termination patterns* describe the different ways in which a process may end and are described in section 4.9. Section 4.10 concludes the chapter by pointing out related work.

4.1   Overview of the control-flow patterns

Figure 4.1 gives an example of a number of common control-flow patterns in a BPMN process model. In many cases, the patterns correspond to common process modeling notions, which while seemingly well understood actually lack a precise description.

The *Sequence* is perhaps the simplest (and most frequently occurring) pattern in a process model. It characterizes a sequence of tasks that execute one after the other in a defined order. Often these tasks are connected by directed arcs that indicate the direction of the flow of control (i.e., the sequence in which the tasks execute).

The *Parallel split* pattern corresponds to the notion of a split in the branch of a process into two or more branches that execute in parallel after the split. This situation is

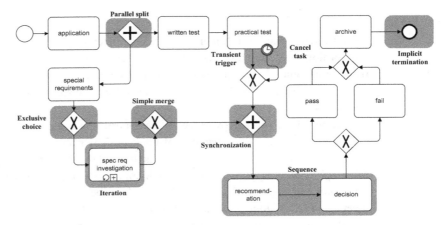

Figure 4.1
Common control-flow patterns in the BPMN License Application process model.

often termed an "AND split." Frequently, the split is represented by a specific construct; in BPMN, the Parallel Fork serves this purpose.

The *Exclusive choice* pattern corresponds to another branching scenario where the thread of control in a branch is passed on a selective basis to one of two (or more) possible branches. A situation that is often termed an "XOR split" is represented by an Exclusive Decision (data-based) in BPMN. The actual choice of the branch is usually based on one or more characteristics of the process instance (e.g., a value of a variable) at the time when the execution reaches the branch in the process.

The merging of two (or more) branches into a single branch, such that any execution threads in preceding branches are passed to the subsequent branch, is captured by the *Simple merge* pattern. This scenario can be represented in a process model by several branches simply joining into one or via a specific construct and is often termed an "XOR-join." In BPMN, the pattern is represented by a Parallel Join, which has several incoming branches. The fact that the same construct can be used in BPMN to implement more than one pattern (i.e., the Exclusive Gateway can represent the *Exclusive choice* or the *Simple merge*) sharply characterizes the importance of patterns as a means of describing different situations during process modeling and execution. Frequently within a given modeling formalism or BPMS, the same graphical construct can operate in a variety of ways each with a distinct outcome and purpose.

An alternative merging of branches is depicted by the *Synchronization* pattern, which captures the notion of an "AND-join" in a process where several branches merge into one and the thread of control only passes on when it has been received on each incoming branch. In BPMN, this corresponds to a Parallel Join with several incoming branches.

Once again we see that the same BPMN symbol can have several means of operation (*Synchronization* vs. *Parallel split*).

Another example of overloading of symbols in BPMN is illustrated by the *practical test* task. It has a timer event associated with it that allows an external event (in this case, a timer event signal) to trigger an alternate course of action in the process. In this case, it is a timeout event if the *practical test* task takes longer than a nominated timeframe to be completed. Should this occur, the execution of the task is canceled, and the thread of control passes to the next part of the process. There are two distinct patterns embodied in this construct: (1) the *Transient trigger* pattern identifies the situation where an external event influences the execution of a process (other common examples include messages and signals), and (2) the *Cancel task* pattern identifies a situation where the execution of a task is canceled.

A final pattern identified in this process model is that of *Implicit termination*. This pattern indicates that the execution of a process instance completes when there is no more work to do (i.e., there are no remaining execution threads in the process instance). In BPMN, the None End Event operates in this way. In addition to denoting the endpoint of a process, it also consumes execution threads as they arrive, and when all active execution threads are complete, the process instance is considered complete.

As this informal introduction to some examples of patterns in a BPMN process model has illustrated, the control-flow patterns provide a useful means of characterizing the common constructs and structures that arise in the control-flow perspective of business processes. They allow for the precise description of the behavior of frequently used constructs and process structures whose actual operation is usually described informally and tends to vary between distinct implementations. As individual patterns are presented in a general sense without reference to any particular implementation approach, they provide an independent means of describing desirable control-flow characteristics that does not rely on a specific conceptual foundation or technology. The patterns can be divided into eight main groups as illustrated in figure 4.2, each of which focuses on distinct aspects of modeling and operationalizing control-flow. These groups include:

- **Branching** patterns, which capture branching scenarios in processes;
- **Synchronization** patterns, which describe synchronization scenarios arising in processes;
- **Repetition** patterns, which describe various ways in which repetition may be specified;
- **Multiple Instances (MI)** patterns, which delineate situations with multiple threads of execution in a process instance all relating to the same activity;
- **Concurrency** patterns, which reflect situations where restrictions are imposed on the extent of concurrent control-flow in a process instance;
- **Trigger** patterns, which catalogue the different triggering mechanisms appearing in a process context;

- **Cancelation and completion** patterns, which categorize the various cancelation and completion scenarios that may be relevant for a process; and
- **Termination** patterns, which address the issue of when the execution of a process instance is considered to be finished.

The pattern groups identify related patterns with a common focus, and we will use these groupings when describing each of the individual patterns. However, the focus in this chapter will remain on the patterns themselves, which will be presented in the standard pattern format described in chapter 1. Our discussion will start with the group that identifies some of the most widely used control-flow structures: branching patterns.

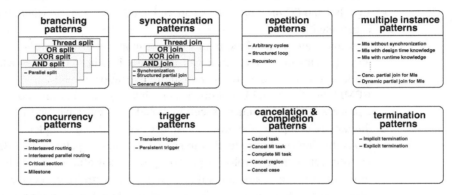

Figure 4.2
Overview of the control-flow patterns.

4.2   Branching patterns

Branching patterns characterize situations where a branch in a process model is split into two or more distinct branches or the thread of control in a branch is split into two or more concurrent execution threads. Depending on the nature of the branching construct employed, when the thread of control reaches the point of divergence, it may be routed into one, several, or all of the subsequent branches.

There are four distinct branching variants that can be identified as illustrated in figure 4.3:

- **AND-split**, where the thread of control in a branch is diverged into concurrent execution threads in each of the subsequent branches. This is illustrated in figure 4.3(a), where after every program is written, both the `unit test` and `inspect code` tasks are run (in any order);

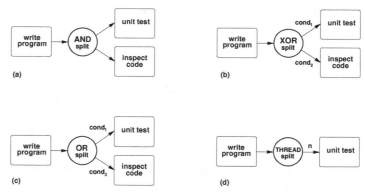

Figure 4.3
Illustrative examples of the various split types.

- **XOR-split**, where the thread of control in a branch is directed into one of the subsequent branches following the split construct. The actual decision as to which of the subsequent branches the thread of execution is passed to is based on the evaluation of conditions associated with each of the outgoing arcs from the XOR-split construct. In the example illustrated in figure 4.3(b), only one of the `unit test` and `inspect code` tasks is run;
- **OR-split**, where the thread of control in a branch is diverged into concurrent execution threads in one or more of the subsequent branches. As for the XOR-split, the actual decision as to which of the subsequent branches the execution thread is passed to is based on the evaluation of conditions associated with each of the outgoing arcs from the OR-split construct. However, unlike the XOR-split, multiple branches may be selected. In the example illustrated in figure 4.3(c), various factors such as the complexity of the program and the availability of staff may be used to determine whether just one or both of the `unit test` and `inspect code` tasks are run; and
- **Thread split**, where the execution thread in a branch is split into two or more concurrent execution threads in the same branch. In the example illustrated in figure 4.3(d), once the program is written, the thread of control is split into multiple independent threads (the actual number of threads initiated is indicated by the value n assigned to the outgoing arc), each of which triggers a concurrent instance of the `unit test` task.

Although each of these branching constructs corresponds to concepts that are common-place in contemporary process models, there are a variety of ways in which each of them can be interpreted and implemented. *Each of these alternative approaches to their config-uration and operation forms the basis for an individual pattern*. In the following sections, the various ways in which each of the branching constructs can potentially be realized are described in detail.

4.2.1 AND-split

The AND-split construct is widely utilized in BPM offerings. The characteristics that are generally ascribed to the AND-split are fully defined by the *Parallel split* pattern.

Parallel split

Description The divergence of a branch into two or more parallel branches, each of which executes concurrently.

Synonyms AND-split, parallel routing, parallel split, fork.

Examples

- After completion of the *capture enrollment* task, run the *create student profile* and *issue enrollment confirmation* tasks simultaneously.
- When an *intrusion alarm* is received, trigger both the *despatch patrol* task and the *inform police* task immediately.
- Once the customer has paid for the goods, pack them and issue a receipt (these two tasks can be done simultaneously or in either order).

Motivation The *Parallel split* pattern allows a single thread of execution to be split into two or more branches, which can execute tasks concurrently, potentially expediting the overall throughput of a process instance. These branches may or may not be resynchronized at some future time.

Operation Figure 4.4 illustrates the operation of the *Parallel split* in the context of an airport arrival process. After clearing customs, three distinct activities — `collect luggage`, `find trolley`, and `change money` — can proceed concurrently.

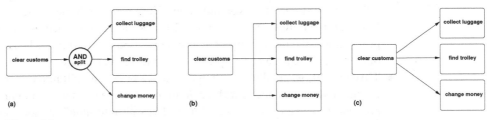

Figure 4.4
Parallel split operation: (a) explicit depiction and (b), (c) implicit depiction.

Context There are no specific context conditions for this pattern.

Implementation The *Parallel split* pattern is implemented by most BPM offerings. It may be depicted either *explicitly* or *implicitly* in process models. Where it is represented explicitly, a specific construct exists for the *Parallel split*, with one incoming edge and two or more outgoing edges. Where it is represented implicitly, this can be done in one of two ways: either (1) the edge representing control-flow can split into two (or more) distinct branches, or (2) the task after which the *Parallel split* occurs has multiple outgoing edges that do not have any conditions associated with them or where it does these conditions always evaluate to true. BPMone represents the pattern implicitly by simply joining two or more subsequent plans in a process to an earlier plan. Both plans are triggered when the earlier plan completes. Oracle BPEL does so explicitly with the Flow activity. BPMN allows it to be represented in both ways either explicitly by the Parallel Fork or implicitly by multiple outgoing arcs from an Activity or by enclosing two Activities within a single parent Activity, causing them to be enabled simultaneously. Figure 4.5 illustrates the configuration of the pattern in the three BPM offerings.

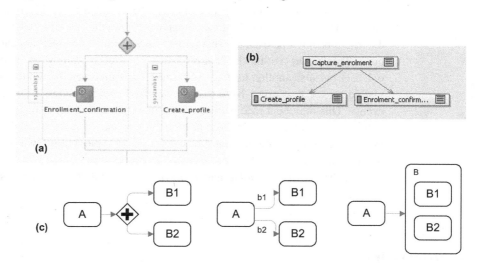

Figure 4.5

Parallel split configuration in (a) Oracle BPEL, (b) BPMone, and (c) BPMN.

4.2.2 XOR-split

The XOR-split construct where the thread of control is passed to precisely one of two or more subsequent branches on a selective basis is embodied in two distinct patterns: the *Exclusive choice* and the *Deferred choice*. The distinction between them is the moment at which the decision is made about which outgoing branch will be pursued. For the *Exclusive choice*, this decision is made prior to or at the time that the decision construct is encountered using information available in the context of the process instance. The *Deferred choice* seeks to delay the moment at which the actual decision is made, such that it occurs after (and possibly a long while after) the decision construct is reached. Additionally, the *Deferred choice* can make use of a wide range of factors in reaching the decision on which branch to take. Most usually, the approach taken to doing this is to allow a user to select which branch should be pursued.

The distinction between these two patterns and the way in which they implement the XOR-split is shown in figure 4.6. In both cases, the thread of execution has just reached the XOR-split construct. In figure 4.6(a), the XOR-split implements the *Exclusive choice* pattern. When the thread of control reaches the XOR-split, there is already sufficient information for the required output branch to be identified. From the user standpoint, they are only presented with a single option in their worklist, being the first task in the branch chosen by the XOR-split. The behavior of the *Deferred choice* pattern differs markedly from this as shown in figure 4.6(b). When the execution point reaches the XOR-split, the user is presented with the option to execute the first task in each of the subsequent branches; however, once the user chooses one of them, the thread of control is routed into this branch, and the ability to execute the tasks in the other branches is withdrawn. Note that in figure 4.6, there is only one user. However, there may be multiple users that can execute different tasks. This means that for the *Deferred choice*, the *book plane* work item can disappear for one user because another user has selected *book train* (even though this work item was not visible for the first user). Note that the deferred choice models a "race" among different events. This may be a race between work items in the worklists of resources. However, a deferred choice may also be used to model a race between an external trigger (e.g., a payment) and a timer to model that the customer should pay within two weeks, otherwise the order is canceled.

Both the *Exclusive choice* and *Deferred choice* patterns are discussed in more detail below.

Exclusive choice

Description The divergence of a branch into two or more branches such that when the incoming branch is enabled, the thread of control is immediately passed to precisely one of the outgoing branches based on a mechanism that can select one of the outgoing branches.
Synonyms XOR-split, exclusive OR-split, conditional routing, switch, decision, case statement.
Examples
- Depending on the volume of earth to be moved, either the *despatch-backhoe*, *despatch-bobcat*, or *despatch-D9-excavator* task is initiated to complete the job.
- After the *review election* task is complete, either the *declare results* or the *recount votes* task is undertaken immediately based on the results received.

Motivation The *Exclusive choice* pattern allows the thread of control to be directed to a specific (subsequent) task depending on the values of specific data elements in the process, the results of an expression evaluation, or some other form of programmatic selection

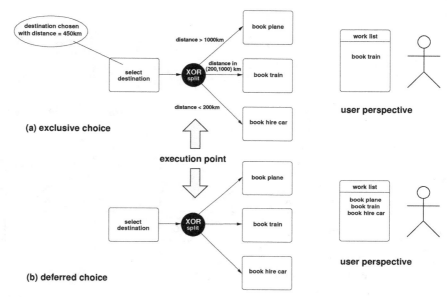

Figure 4.6
Alternative implementations for the XOR-split construct.

mechanism. The routing decision is made dynamically, allowing it to be deferred to the latest possible moment at runtime when the thread of control reaches the split construct.

Operation As illustrated in figure 4.6(a), depending on the results of the evaluation of the three arc conditions, the *Exclusive choice* pattern routes the thread of control to either the `book plane`, `book train`, or `book hire car` task.

Context There is one context condition associated with this pattern: the mechanism that evaluates the *Exclusive choice* is able to access any required data elements or other necessary resources when determining which of the outgoing branches the thread of control should be routed to.

Implementation Similar to the *Parallel split* pattern, the *Exclusive choice* pattern can be represented either explicitly via a specific construct or implicitly via disjoint conditions on the outgoing control-flow edges of a task. BPMN represents it explicitly using an Exclusive Decision (data-based) construct. BPMone represents the pattern implicitly via conditions on the outgoing control-flow edges from a plan. Oracle BPEL depicts it explicitly via conditions on the outgoing control-flow edges from an If activity (or a Switch activity for BPEL 1.1 processes), which must be specified in such a way that they are disjoint. Figure 4.7 illustrates the configuration of the pattern in the three BPM offerings.

Issues One of the difficulties associated with this pattern is ensuring that precisely one outgoing branch is triggered when the *Exclusive choice* is executed.

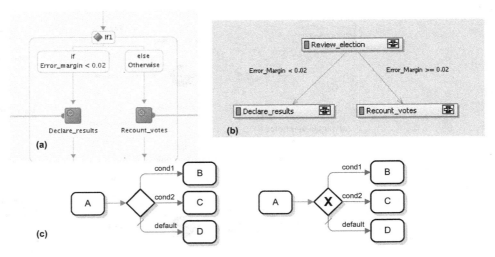

Figure 4.7
Exclusive choice configuration in (a) Oracle BPEL, (b) BPMone, and (c) BPMN.

Solutions The inclusion of default outgoing arcs on XOR-split constructs is an increasingly common means of ensuring that an outgoing branch is triggered (and hence the thread of control continues in the process instance) when the XOR-split is enabled and none of the conditions on outgoing branches evaluate to true. An associated issue is ensuring that no more than one branch is triggered. There are two possible approaches to dealing with this issue where more than one of the arc conditions will potentially evaluate to true. The first of these is to randomly select one of these arcs and allow it to proceed while ensuring that none of the other outgoing arcs is enabled. The second option, which is more practical in form, is to assign an evaluation sequence to the outgoing arcs that defines the order in which arc conditions will be evaluated. The means of determining which arc is triggered then becomes one of evaluating the arc conditions in sequential order until one evaluates to true. This arc is then triggered and the evaluation stops (i.e., no further arcs are triggered). In the event that none of the conditions evaluates to true, the default arc is triggered.

The *Exclusive choice* pattern is based on the premise that all of the information necessary to make the branching decision is available in the process instance at runtime. An alternative situation is also possible, which is described by the *Deferred choice* pattern, where the required decision information is not prescribed within the process definition and allowance is made for its availability being potentially delayed. As such, the time at which a branching decision can be made is *deferred* to the last possible moment at runtime. In such a scenario, there is in effect a race condition between the various outgoing branches from the choice construct. The actual decision as to which branch is taken is made when a user explicitly chooses one of the branches or conditions within the operating environment allow one of the branches to commence execution. The pattern that characterizes this scenario is described next.

Deferred choice

Description A point in a process where one of several branches is chosen based on interaction with the operating environment. Prior to the decision, all branches represent possible future courses of execution. The decision is made when an entity in the operating environment (typically a person) chooses to commence the first task in one of the branches (i.e., in effect there is a *race* between different branches, only one of which can ultimately be chosen). After the decision is made, the execution alternatives in branches other than the one selected are withdrawn.

Examples

- At the commencement of the *Resolve complaint* process, there is a choice between the *Initial customer contact* task and the *Escalate to manager* task. The *Initial customer contact* is initiated when it is started by a customer services team member. The *Escalate to manager* task commences 48 hours after the process instance commences. Once one of these tasks is initiated, the other is withdrawn.
- Once a customer requests an *airbag shipment*, it is either picked up by the *postman* or a *courier driver* depending on who can visit the customer site first. Once one of these pickups occurs, the other is informed that they are no longer required.

Motivation The *Deferred choice* pattern provides the ability to defer the *moment of choice* in a process (i.e., the moment as to which one of several possible courses of action should be chosen is delayed to the latest possible time and is based on factors external to the process instance) (e.g., incoming messages, environment data, resource availability, timeouts, etc.). Up until the point at which the decision is made, any of the alternatives presented as outgoing branches from the decision construct represent viable courses of future action.

Operation The operation of this pattern is illustrated in figure 4.6(b), in which the XOR split construct signifies a *moment of choice*. At this point, any of the subsequent tasks book plane, book train, or book hire car represent possible courses of action. Only when the user has selected one of them is the choice actually made, and at this point, the options that were not chosen are removed as possible future options, and the thread of control is directed to the selected branch.

Context There are no specific context conditions associated with this pattern.

Implementation This is a complex pattern. In order to successfully support it, an offering needs to provide the ability to define a moment of choice where a series of alternate actions are potentially made available as viable courses of action but only one can be selected. Typically this involves the use of a dedicated construct for this purpose, which can set up the required race condition among the various alternatives. Oracle BPEL provides support for it via the Pick activity and BPMN through the Exclusive Decision (event-based) construct. BPMone does not directly provide a notion of state, but it provides several ways of supporting this pattern through the use of user and system decisions on plan types and also by using arc guards that evaluate to NIL in conjunction with data elements to make the decision as to which branch is selected (this allows precisely one of the subsequent plans to be executed as determined by which one a user decides to commence first). Figure 4.8 illustrates the configuration of the *Deferred choice* in Oracle BPEL, BPMone, and BPMN.

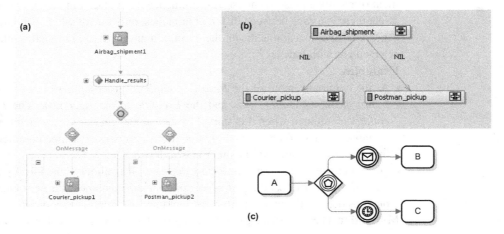

Figure 4.8
Deferred choice configuration in (a) Oracle BPEL, (b) BPMone, and (c) BPMN.

At first sight, the difference between the exclusive choice and the deferred choice may seem unimportant. However, both types of choices are relevant, and one type cannot be used to realize the other. This difference is well known in the context of concurrency theory and process semantics. Consider a process X with three activities A, B, and C. First, A is executed, then a choice is made between B and C. In another process Y, already at the start a choice is made as to whether A is followed by B or by C. In both processes (X and Y), two traces are possible: AB and AC. However, both processes behave differently. This difference is related to the difference between trace equivalence and bisimulation equivalence [83]. Process algebraic languages like CCS, CSP, ACP and so on denote this difference as $A(B+C) \neq AB + AC$ [27].

The deferred choice can be seen as $A(B+C)$ (i.e., after A executes, there is still a real choice between B and C). The explicit choice does not leave the choice open after executing A (i.e., it is better described by $AB + AC$).

4.2.3 OR-split

The OR-split construct where the thread of control is passed to one or several subsequent branches on a selective basis is directly characterized by the *Multi-choice* pattern described below.

Multi-choice

Description The divergence of a branch into two or more branches such that when the incoming branch is enabled, the thread of control is immediately passed to one or more of the outgoing branches based on a mechanism that selects one or more outgoing branches.

Synonyms Conditional routing, selection, OR-split, multiple choice.

Examples

- Depending on the nature of the emergency call, one or more of the *despatch-police*, *despatch-fire-engine*, and *despatch-ambulance* tasks is immediately initiated.
- After a network outage is detected, any or all of the *reboot-firewall*, *reset-router*, and *test-cable-connectivity* tasks may be initiated as required.

Motivation The *Multi-choice* pattern provides the ability for the thread of execution to be diverged into several concurrent threads in distinct branches on a selective basis. The decision as to whether to pass the thread of execution to a specific branch is made at runtime. It can be based on a variety of factors, including the outcome of a preceding task, the values of elements of specific data elements in the process, the results of evaluating an expression associated with the outgoing branch, or some other form of programmatic selection mechanism.

Operation The operation of the *Multi-choice* pattern is illustrated in figure 4.9 in the context of a car service scheduling process. After accepting a service booking, the thread of control can be passed to one or more of the following branches depending on the evaluation of the various arc conditions associated with each of them.

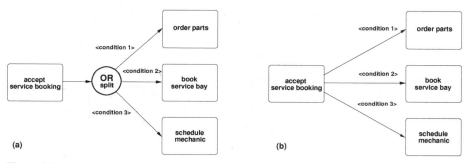

Figure 4.9
Multi-choice operation: (a) explicit depiction and (b) implicit depiction.

Context There is one context condition associated with this pattern: the mechanism that evaluates the *Multi-choice* is able to access any required data elements or necessary resources when determining which of the outgoing branches the thread of control should be routed to.

Implementation As with other branching and merging constructs, the *Multi-choice* pattern can be represented either implicitly or explicitly. BPMone provides support for the explicit form of the pattern implementing it via guards on arcs in static, dynamic, and sequential subplans. Oracle BPEL does so in a similar way by structuring the activities that are conditionally executed as parallel activities following a Flow activity branching construct and associating a skip condition with each of them based on an XPath expression whose evaluation indicates whether the activity is executed or skipped. BPMN provides three alternative representations, including the Inclusive Decision construct, the use of an implicit split with conditions on the arcs, and the Complex Condition construct. Figure 4.10 illustrates the configuration of the *Multi-choice* pattern in Oracle BPEL, BPMone, and BPMN.

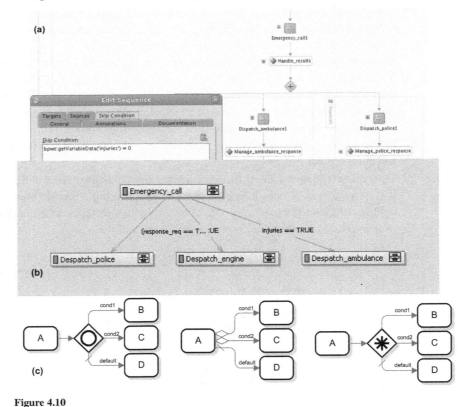

Figure 4.10

Multi-choice configuration in (a) Oracle BPEL (note the skip condition that can be specified for each branch), (b) BPMone, and (c) BPMN.

Issues Two issues have been identified with the use of this pattern. The first difficulty is ensuring that at least one outgoing branch is selected from the various options available. If this is not the case, then there is the potential for the process to stall. Second, where an offering does not support the *Multi-choice* construct directly, the question arises as to whether there are any indirect means of achieving the same behavior.

Solutions With respect to the first issue, the general solution to this issue is to enforce the use of a default outgoing arc from a *Multi-choice* construct, which is enabled if none of the conditions on the other outgoing arcs evaluates to true at runtime. The implementation approach for this is shown in figure 4.11(a).

For the second issue, a work-around that can be used to support the pattern in most offerings is based on the use of an AND-split immediately followed by an (binary) XOR-split in each subsequent branch. Another work-around is the use of an XOR-split with an outgoing branch for each possible task combination (e.g., a *Multi-choice* construct with outgoing branches to tasks B and C would be modeled using an XOR-split with three outgoing branches — one to each of the combinations of tasks B and C). These implementation approaches are depicted in figures 4.11(b) and (c).

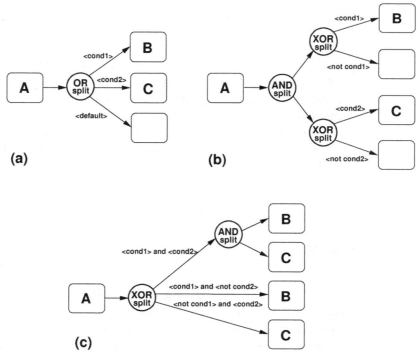

Figure 4.11

Alternative OR-split implementations.

4.2.4   Thread split

Unlike the branching constructs discussed up to this point, which direct the thread of control from one incoming branch into one or several subsequent branches, the *Thread split* does as its name infers and diverges the thread of control in a branch into two or more concurrent execution threads in the *same* branch. It is discussed below.

Thread split

Description At a given point in a process, a nominated number of execution threads can be initiated in a single branch of the same process instance.

Example

- At the completion of the *confirm paper receival* task, initiate three instances of the subsequent *independent peer review* task.

Motivation This pattern provides a means of triggering multiple execution threads along a branch within a given process instance. It is a counterpart to the *Thread merge* pattern (discussed in section 4.2), which merges multiple execution threads along the same branch. Unless used in conjunction with the *Thread merge* pattern, the execution threads will run independently to the end of the process.

The use of a *Thread split/Thread merge* combination provides a means of realizing task concurrency as it allows any task on a path between the *Thread split* and *Thread merge* constructs to execute multiple times and for these execution instances to occur concurrently. An alternative set of patterns related to concurrent task execution are provided by the multiple instance group of patterns presented in section 4.5.

Operation The operation of this pattern is illustrated in figure 4.12. One thread of control reaching the thread split construct results in 12 concurrent threads of control in the outcoming branch, each of which triggers a distinct instance of the `fill bottle` task (i.e., there are assumed to be 12 bottles in a carton).

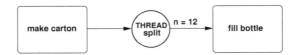

Figure 4.12
Thread split operation.

Context There is one context consideration for this pattern: the number of threads needing to be created (n) must be known at design time.

Implementation Implementation of this pattern implies that an offering is able to support the execution of processes in a non-safe context. The term *safe* originates from the safety property in a Petri net. A Petri net is *safe* if there can never be multiple tokens in the same place. In other languages, this means that the threads of control for a given process instance never reside at the same location. Many workflow offerings are unable to provide support for this property. BPMN provides direct support for the pattern by allowing the completionQuantity attribute to be specified for an activity indicating the number of tokens that will flow down the outgoing sequence flow at its conclusion. Oracle BPEL indirectly allows the same effect to be achieved via the Invoke activity in conjunction with suitably specified correlation sets. This pattern cannot be implemented in BPMone as it does not allow non-safe execution. However, this is compensated for by the strong support for its multiple instances patterns.

Issues One of the major considerations associated with the use of this pattern is what the implications are for any data elements associated with the thread of control that is being split. Are copies of these data elements similarly diverged for each of the concurrent execution threads or are all execution threads expected to share (and compete for) access to these data elements?

Solutions This issue is not explicitly addressed in BPMN, although the assumption appears to be that the data elements within a case are indeed shared by all diverging threads from a thread split. The workaround discussed above for Oracle BPEL results in a distinct set of data elements being passed to each invoked task.

The *Thread split* pattern is related to the multiple instances patterns (section 4.4). By separating the different threads into separate (sub-)instances, issues related to data can be solved more easily.

4.3 Synchronization patterns

Synchronization patterns describe situations where multiple threads of control on one or several branches need to be merged into a single outgoing branch. Such situations appear frequently in real-life processes where the contingent execution of a specific activity is halted until one or more preceding activities in the process have been completed. Typically these synchronization events are represented by specific constructs in a workflow context based on the number of incoming branches that need to be synchronized. There are four classes of variants that arise in practice:

- **AND-join**, where all incoming branches are active and a specified number of them need to be synchronized;
- **XOR-join**, where one of the incoming branches needs to be synchronized;
- **OR-join**, where some of the incoming branches are active and need to be synchronized; however, the specific number that require synchronizing is not known until runtime; and
- **Thread merge**, where there is only one incoming branch, but it has multiple threads of control flowing on it which need to be synchronized.

Each of these classes is discussed in more detail below.

4.3.1   AND-join variants

The AND-join is a widely supported construct in BPM offerings. It supports the synchronous merger of multiple incoming branches as illustrated in the example shown in figure 4.13, where it is not possible to start making tea until the water is boiled and the tea pot and tea leaves have been located. In general, the use of an AND-join implies that the thread of control is passed to the task that follows it once all preceding branches have completed execution. Despite the apparent simplicity of this notion, however, there are a variety of distinct ways in which this synchonization can occur depending on:

1. whether all incoming branches must have completed execution before the thread of control can be passed onto the subsequent branch;
2. what happens to any remaining incoming branches that have not (yet) completed execution when the thread of control is passed to the subsequent branch; and
3. what happens if there is more than one active thread of control in a given incoming branch.

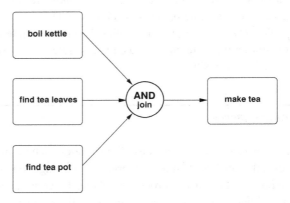

Figure 4.13

AND-join illustration.

Depending on the combination of these factors, there are a variety of distinct patterns that describe how each of these situations should be handled. In order to delineate the required pattern for a given situation, it is necessary to consider these factors in more detail.

Number of incoming branches requiring synchronization

In general, in order for the AND-join to fire, all of the incoming branches need to be activated for synchronization to occur. Once this has occurred, the thread of control can be passed on to the following task, and the join construct can reset allowing it to be triggered again. In this situation, the synchronization and reset actions occur simultaneously as all incoming execution threads are merged in one go; however, there may be scenarios where, although all incoming branches must be synchronized, the thread of control can be passed onto the subsequent branch when some threshold of the incoming branches have been activated (e.g., in figure 4.13 above, it might be acceptable in the interest of speeding up the overall time to make tea, to do so once two of the three preceding tasks have completed). It is important to note that when this approach to synchronization is taken, the synchronization action (i.e., the firing of the join) precedes the reset action, possibly by a significant amount of time. However, the two actions remain contingent, and once the join has fired, it cannot fire again until it has first reset. To relate this to the example above, it is not possible to start making a second pot of tea until all of the actions associated with making the first pot have been completed.

Having considered these points, it can now be seen that there are two essential variants to when the synchronization may occur based on the inputs to the incoming branches for the AND-join:

1. when all of the incoming branches to the join have been activated, and
2. when a subset n of the incoming branches ($1 \leq n < m$, where m is the total number of incoming branches) have been activated and the remaining $m - n$ branches are expected to complete at some future time.

These two variants correspond to the notions of a complete or full join and a partial join, respectively.[1] Both of these form the basis for individual patterns, which will be discussed subsequently.

Handling remaining branches

The second consideration for the AND-join is what happens to any remaining incoming branches when the threshold for firing is reached and the join is enabled. There are three possible options:

- do nothing with any other threads of control in unactivated branches and let them progress in their own time and space;
- block incoming branches, allowing any threads of control already in these branches to reach the join construct (and the join to reset when all incoming branches have been activated) but preventing new threads of control from entering any of the incoming branches until the join has reset; and
- cancel any threads of control in unactivated incoming branches.

---

1 Earlier patterns discussions have also presented the concept of a *Discriminator*, which corresponds to an AND-join that fires when one incoming branch has been activated. We do not consider this form of AND-join here as the partial join subsumes this concept.

Associated with all of these options is the overriding assumption that whatever happens to the tasks in the remaining incoming branches, once the join has fired, they cannot affect the outgoing thread of control from the join.

Handling multiple threads of control

The final consideration for the AND-join construct is whether incoming branches allow multiple threads of execution to flow through them for the same process instance. There are two possible options:

- only one thread of control can flow through each of the incoming branches to the join construct; and
- multiple threads of control are allowed in a branch.

There are various ways in which the threads of control in an incoming branch can be limited to a single thread. One of the most common ways of achieving this is by adopting a structured approach to workflow design as illustrated in figure 4.14, where the number of splits and join in a process are balanced. By doing so, the issue of dealing with multiple execution threads in a single branch is avoided.

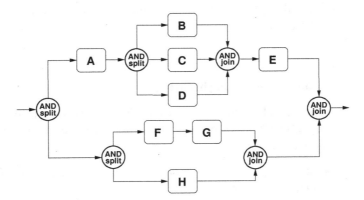

Figure 4.14
Example of structured workflow design.

In some systems, a conundrum arises in that, although they do not cater to multiple execution threads in a given branch, they do not explicitly prevent the situation from arising either. Where such situations arise, they tend to deal with it on a localized basis rather than enforcing a more general prevention policy. Two common means of dealing with this are:

- the *"Pac-man" approach*, where multiple execution threads arriving at a single task (when it is enabled) are consumed and coalesced into a single execution thread; and

- the *Blocking approach*, where a task or join cannot be enabled if its execution would result in the thread of control being passed to a point in the process at which another thread of control already resides.

AND-join pattern variants

As a consequence of the various pattern configurations described above, it is possible to arrive at five distinct variants for the AND-join pattern as illustrated by table 4.1. At first glance, it may seem that some of these pattern variants are actually more analogous to OR-join constructs, particularly those where it is possible to pass on the thread of control before all incoming branches have actually completed. However, there is an important distinction between the two types of joins that needs to be borne in mind: an AND-join always requires that all m incoming branches will ultimately be activated, although it allows for the actual synchronization to occur when n incoming branches have completed (where $n < m$). Both of these design criteria for an AND-join construct are known at design time. In contrast for an OR-join, although the number of incoming branches (m) is known at design time, the actual number that will be active (n) and require synchronization is not known until runtime.

Table 4.1

AND-join variants.

Pattern	Incoming branches to synchronize	Handling remaining branches	Multiple threads in same branch
Synchronization	all	N/A	not possible
Structured partial join	some	do nothing	not possible
Blocking partial join	some	block	allowed
Canceling partial join	some	cancel	not possible
Generalized AND-join	all	N/A	allowed

Each of these patterns is discussed in detail in the following sections. To start with, we examine the simplest case of all, the *Synchronization* pattern, which operates in a safe environment and triggers the following branch when precisely one execution thread has been received on each incoming branch.

Synchronization

Description The convergence of two or more branches into a single subsequent branch, such that the thread of control is passed to the subsequent branch when all input branches have been enabled.

Synonyms AND-join, full join, rendezvous.

Examples

- The *despatch-goods* task runs immediately after both the *check-invoice* and *produce-invoice* tasks are completed.
- Cash-drawer reconciliation can only occur when the store has been closed and the credit card summary has been printed.

Motivation *Synchronization* provides a means of reconverging the execution threads of two or more parallel branches. In general, these branches are created using one or more AND-split constructs earlier in the process model. The thread of control is passed to the task immediately following the synchronizer once all of the incoming branches have completed.

Operation The format of the *Synchronization* pattern is illustrated in figure 4.15. The synchronizer (i.e., the AND-join) requires all of its inputs to be enabled before the thread of control is passed to the output branch. In other words, tasks A, B, and C must complete before task D is triggered.

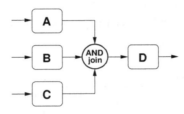

Figure 4.15
Synchronization pattern operation.

Context This pattern is based on the assumption that once the synchronizer has been activated and has not yet been reset, it is not possible for a thread of control to be received on any of the activated incoming branches. Similarly, it is not possible for multiple execution threads to be received on any incoming branch at any time.

Implementation The *Synchronization* pattern is widely supported. It can either be realized as an explicit construct within a process definition language — this is the approach taken in BPMN, which provides the Parallel Join construct for this purpose — or it can be represented implicitly via multiple input arcs to a task, as is the case in Oracle BPEL and BPMone.

Issues The use of the *Synchronization* pattern can potentially give rise to a deadlock in the situation where one of the incoming branches fails to deliver a thread of control to the join construct. This could be a consequence of a design error or that one of the tasks in the incoming branch failed to complete successfully (e.g., as a consequence of it experiencing some form of exception) or because the thread of control was passed outside of the branch.

Solutions None of the offerings examined provides support for resolving this issue, where the problem is caused by task failure in one of the incoming branches. Where this pattern is used in a structured context, the second possible cause of deadlock generally does not arise. The use of verification techniques can assist in ensuring that a design time process model is free from structures that may potentially lead to deadlock at runtime.

As we identified earlier in this section, a variation of the full join is to pass on the thread of control when some of the incoming branches have been enabled. This provides a means of expediting process execution by allowing a join to fire earlier than would normally be the case. This notion provides the basis for the *partial join*, where the join construct fires when a specified threshold of incoming branches have been activated. There are three possible forms of the partial join depending on whether (1) the process model in which it is utilized is structured in form, (2) it can be assumed that each incoming branch will be activated precisely once by blocking further threads from flowing through individual branches once the join has fired but not reset, and (3) remaining execution threads in branches are summarily canceled once the firing threshold for the join is reached. Each of these options is discussed subsequently.

Structured partial join

Description The convergence of two or more branches (say m) into a single subsequent branch following a corresponding divergence earlier in the process model, such that the thread of control is passed to the subsequent branch when n of the incoming branches have been enabled (where $1 \leq n < m$). Subsequent enablements of incoming branches do not result in the thread of control being passed on. The join construct resets when all active incoming branches have been enabled. The join assumes a structured context (i.e., there must be a single *Parallel split* construct earlier in the process model with which the join is associated, and it must merge all of the branches emanating from the *Parallel split*). These branches must all be structured in form.

Example
- Once two of the preceding three *Expenditure Approval* tasks have completed, start the *Issue Cheque* task. Wait until the remaining task has completed before allowing the *Issue Cheque* task to fire again.

Motivation The *Structured partial join* pattern provides a means of merging two or more distinct branches resulting from a specific AND-split construct earlier in a process into a single branch. The join construct does not require triggers on all incoming branches before it can fire. Instead a given threshold can be defined, which describes the circumstances under which the join should fire — typically this is presented as the ratio of incoming branches that need to be live for firing as against the total number of incoming branches to the join (e.g., a 2-out-of-3 join signifies that the join construct should fire when two of three incoming arcs are live). Subsequent completions of other remaining incoming branches have no effect on (and do not trigger) the subsequent branch. As such, the *Structured partial join* provides a mechanism for progressing the execution of a process once a specified number of concurrent tasks have completed rather than waiting for all of them to complete. **Operation** An indication of the process format in which a *Structured partial join* can be employed is illustrated in figure 4.16.

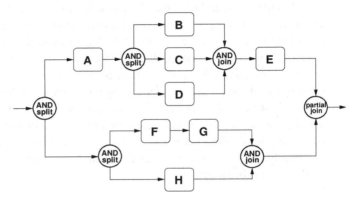

Figure 4.16
Structured partial join operation.

Context Two context conditions are associated with the use of this pattern: (1) once the *partial join* has been activated and has not yet been reset, it is not possible for another signal to be received on any already activated branch or for multiple signals to be received on any incoming branch. In other words, all input places to the *partial join* are safe. (2) Once the associated *parallel split* has been enabled, none of the tasks in the branches leading to the *partial join* can be canceled before the join has been triggered. The only exception to this is that it is possible for *all* of the tasks leading up to the *partial join* to be canceled.
Implementation One of the difficulties in implementing the *Structured partial join* is that it essentially requires a specific construct to represent the join if it is to be done in a tractable manner. BPMN provides support for the *Structured partial join* via the Complex Merge construct, where the activationExpression indicates the number of incoming gates that need to be enabled for the join to fire. There is no ability to represent the pattern in BPMone or Oracle BPEL.

There are two possible variants of this pattern that arise from relaxing some of the context conditions associated with it. Both of these improve on the efficiency of the join while retaining its overall behavior. The first alternative, the *Blocking partial join*, removes the requirement that each incoming branch can only be enabled once between join resets. It allows each incoming branch to be triggered multiple times, although the construct only resets when one triggering has been received on each input branch. Second, the *Canceling partial join* resolves the problem by canceling the other incoming branches to the join construct once a specified number (denoted n) of incoming branches have completed.

Blocking partial join

Description The convergence of two or more branches (say m) into a single subsequent branch following one or more corresponding divergences earlier in the process model. The thread of control is passed to the subsequent branch when n of the incoming branches have been enabled (where $1 \leq n < m$). The join construct resets when all active incoming branches have been enabled once for the same process instance. Subsequent enablements of designated branches are blocked until the join has reset.

Example

- Articles are selected for a journal by sending them to three domain experts for review. Once feedback about an article has been received from two of the three reviewers, an initial decision can be made as to whether to include it in the issue. It is important, however, that all three reviews are completed in order to ensure the final decision is based on feedback from all of the reviewers. Additional reviews may be requested for the article; however, they cannot be received or processed until the first three reviews have been received and processed.

Motivation The *Blocking partial join* is a variant of the *Structured partial join* that is able to operate in environments where there are concurrent process instances, particularly process instances that have multiple concurrent execution threads. Moreover, there is no necessity for the process to be structured in form. The major advantage of this pattern over the *Structured partial join* is that it demonstrates greater flexibility in that it is able to deal with the situation where a branch could potentially be triggered more than once (e.g., where the construct exists within a loop).

Operation Figure 4.17 illustrates the operation of this pattern. The *Blocking partial join* functions by keeping track of which incoming branches have been enabled and prevents them from being re-enabled until the join construct has reset as a consequence of receiving a trigger on each incoming branch. The traffic light symbols in each branch serve to illustrate the blocking effect. Not only are any further threads prevented from entering the branches once the blocking effect is in force, but the number of threads waiting to enter each of the blocked branches must be kept track of and retained for later execution. Once a thread of control has started to flow down a given input branch, no further execution threads can flow down that branch until the join has reset. In other words, for every designated branch, the blocking effect comes into force when a token enters it. Therefore, the specific entry points to the branches involved are an essential component of the pattern.

Context There are no specific context conditions associated with the pattern.

Implementation In order to effectively implement this pattern, an offering must be able to keep a record of which input branches have been triggered to the partial join construct

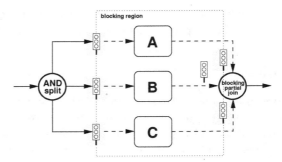

Figure 4.17
Blocking partial join operation.

for a given process instance in order to determine when it can fire. Additionally, it must provide a means of blocking individual incoming branches to the partial join once they have been enabled and the partial join has not yet been reset. These are complex requirements, and not surprisingly few offerings are able to offer direct support for this pattern. BPMN implements the pattern via the Complex Merge where the activationExpression indicates the number of incoming gates that need to be enabled for the join to fire. Once it has fired, the join remains blocked until a token is received on all other input gates that have not already received tokens. The pattern is not supported by BPMone or Oracle BPEL.

Canceling partial join

Description The convergence of two or more branches (say m) into a single subsequent branch following one or more corresponding divergences earlier in the process model. The thread of control is passed to the subsequent branch when n of the incoming branches have been enabled (where $1 \leq n < m$). Triggering the join also *cancels* the execution of all the other incoming branches and resets the construct.

Example

- Once the picture is received, it is sent to three art dealers for examination. Once two of the *prepare condition report* tasks have been completed, the remaining *prepare condition report* task is canceled (e.g., by notifying the dealer that it is no longer required), and the *plan restoration* task commences.

Motivation This pattern provides a means of expediting a process instance where a series of incoming branches to a join needs to be synchronized but only a subset of those tasks associated with each of the branches needs to be completed. The use of this pattern allows further resource usage to be minimized once a join decision has been made by canceling any incoming execution threads to the join that have not yet completed.

Operation The operation of this pattern is shown in figure 4.18. Once a sufficient number of the incoming branches to the join have been enabled in order for the join to fire, two

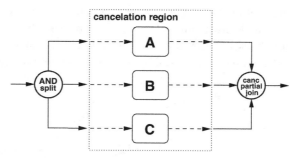

Figure 4.18
Canceling partial join operation.

actions occur simultaneously: the thread of control is passed to the following branch and any execution threads that remain within the cancelation region (for the same process instance) are removed. As a consequence of these two actions occurring at the same time, it is possible for the join to reset immediately, thus readying it for subsequent re-enablement.

Context There are no specific context conditions associated with the use of this pattern.

Implementation This pattern is not widely supported, and none of the offerings examined provides an implementation.

Issues The major difficulty with this pattern is in determining how much of the process model preceding the partial join is to be included in the cancelation region. Moreover, the cancelation of tasks is a challenge especially if things have side effects outside the scope of the system.

Solutions This first issue is easily addressed in structured processes as all of the branches back to the preceding split construct, which corresponds to the *Canceling partial join* should be subject to cancelation. In figure 4.19(a), it is easy to see that the area denoted by the dotted box should be the cancelation region. It is a more complex matter when the process is not structured (e.g., as in figure 4.19(b)) or other input arcs feed into the preceding branches to the *Canceling partial join* that are not related to the corresponding split as shown in figure 4.19(c). In both of these situations, the structure of the process preceding the *Canceling partial join* serves as a determinant of whether the pattern can be supported. In figure 4.19(b), a cancelation region can be conceived, which reaches back to the first AND-split and the pattern can be implemented based on this. In figure 4.19(c), the potential for other control-flows to be introduced that do not relate to the earlier AND-split means that the pattern probably cannot be supported in a process model of this form as it could lead to improper completion.

In highly concurrent environments, such as those where there are potentially multiple execution threads for a given process instance in the same branch, it may be desirable to allow a process to operate without blocking subsequent triggerings of any already enabled inputs to an AND-join that has not yet fired. In such a situation, it is conceivable that more than one control thread might arrive at an input to an AND-join prior to it being triggered. In order to deal with this situation, it may be desirable to preserve each of the distinct execution threads; hence, not all of them will be consumed when the join fires. The following pattern is intended to deal with process models requiring this capability.

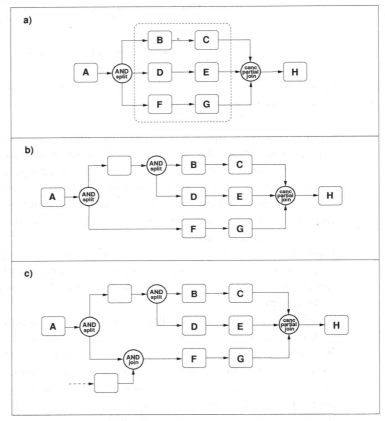

Figure 4.19
Determining the extent of the cancelation region for the canceling partial join.

Generalized AND-join

Description The convergence of two or more branches into a single subsequent branch such that the thread of control is passed to the subsequent branch when all input branches have been enabled. Additional triggers received on one or more branches between firings of the join persist and are retained for future firings. Over time, each of the incoming branches should deliver the same number of triggers to the AND-join construct (although obviously the timing of these triggers may vary).

Example

- Accumulate engine, chassis, and body components from the various production lines. When one or more of each of them has been received, use one of each component to assemble the basic car substructure.

Motivation The *Generalized AND-join* corresponds to one of the generally accepted notions of an AND-join implementation (the other situation is described by the *Synchronization* pattern) in which several paths of execution are synchronized and merged together. Unlike the *Synchronization* pattern, it supports the situation where one or more incoming branches may receive multiple triggers for the same process instance (i.e., a non-safe context) before the join resets.

Operation The form of the *Generalized AND-Join* is illustrated in figure 4.20. If any of tasks A, B, or C have executed more than once since the last firing of the AND-join, then one or more of the associated inputs to the AND-join may have more than one execution thread pending for them. Any excess execution threads are retained when the enablement conditions are met enabling the AND-join to fire. This approach to AND-join implementation relaxes the context condition associated with the *Synchronization* pattern that only allows it to receive one trigger on each incoming branch after activation but before firing. As a result, it is able to be used in concurrent execution environments such as process models, which involve loops as well as offerings that do not assume a safe execution environment. The classical Petri net (as discussed in section 2.4.1) uses semantics that are similar to this pattern. This shows that these semantics can be formulated easily, although their intended interpretation in practice tends to be unclear in situations involving non-safe behavior.

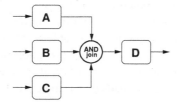

Figure 4.20
Generalized AND-join operation.

Context There are no specific context conditions associated with the pattern.

Implementation The need to provide persistence of triggerings (potentially between distinct firings of the join) means that this construct is not widely supported; where it is, its implementation tends to be problematic (e.g., in the Staffware workflow system, there is the potential for a race condition to arise when an enabled branch of an AND-join receives a second triggering and depending on the time at which it is received, the subsequent triggering may or may not be coalesced with the preceding thread of control in the branch).

Being a token-based process model, BPMN has an advantage in this regard and is able to support this pattern via the Parallel Join construct.

Issues As with the *Thread Split* and *Thread Merge* patterns, this pattern assumes that multiple threads of control may flow within a single process instance. This raises the question of whether each execution thread retains its own set of data elements or whether all execution threads are expected to share (and compete for) access to these data elements?

Solutions In BPMN, the assumption is that the data elements within a case are indeed shared by all execution threads in a process instance. As a consequence, there is not an issue with variations in data occurring between distinct firings of the join (where an additional triggering received on one incoming branch is retained for a subsequent firing). The pattern is not realizable in either Oracle BPEL or BPMone, which essentially support safe process execution.

The various patterns that correspond to the AND-join construct deal with situations where all of the incoming branches to a join are enabled. However, this is only one of the possible situations that might arise when it is necessary to merge several branches at any given point in a process. Another possibility that might arise is the merging of multiple incoming branches where precisely one of them may be active at any given time. The requirement is commonly supported by the XOR-join construct, which is discussed in detail in the following section.

4.3.2   XOR-join variants

There are two distinct variants of the XOR-join that may be utilized. Both of these options allow distinct executions threads flowing down differing branches to be merged into a single branch; however, they differ in their behavior in the face of concurrent execution threads. The *Simple merge* is able to merge two branches but is not able to deal with the situation where concurrent execution threads from two or more branches need to be merged simultaneously. The *Multi-merge*, however, is able to deal with this situation and merge concurrent threads into a single outgoing branch while still retaining their individual identities.

Simple merge

Description The convergence of two or more branches into a single subsequent branch such that each enablement of an incoming branch results in the thread of control being passed to the subsequent branch.

Synonyms XOR-join, exclusive OR-join, asynchronous join, merge.

Examples

- At the conclusion of either the *bobcat-excavation* or the *D9-excavation* tasks, an estimate of the amount of earth moved is made for billing purposes.
- After the *cash-payment* or *provide-credit* tasks, initiate the *produce-receipt* task.

Motivation The *Simple merge* pattern provides a means of merging two or more distinct branches without synchronizing them. As such, this presents the opportunity to simplify a process model by removing the need to explicitly replicate a sequence of tasks that is common to two or more branches. Instead, these branches can be joined with a simple merge construct and the common set of tasks need only be depicted once in the process model.

Operation Figure 4.21 illustrates the behavior of this pattern. Immediately after either task A, B, or C is completed, task D will be enabled. There is no consideration of synchronization, and there is the assumption that only one thread of execution will ever reach the merge construct at any time.

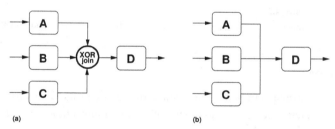

Figure 4.21
Simple merge operation: (a) explicit depiction, and (b) implicit depiction.

Context There is one context condition associated with the pattern: the merge construct will never receive another execution thread during the time that it is forwarding a previously received execution thread from an input branch to the outgoing branch.

Implementation Similar to patterns described earlier, this pattern can be represented either explicitly or implicitly. Oracle BPEL and BPMone represent this sort of join implicitly. BPMN can represent it both implicitly and also explicitly via the Exclusive Merge construct. Figure 4.22 illustrates the configuration of the pattern in the three BPM offerings.

Issues One issue that can arise with the use of this pattern occurs where it cannot be ensured that the merge will only ever receive a single execution thread at any time.

Solutions In this situation, the context conditions for the pattern are not met and it cannot be used; however, an alternative pattern — the *Multi-merge* (described subsequently) — is able to deal with the merging of branches in potentially concurrent situations.

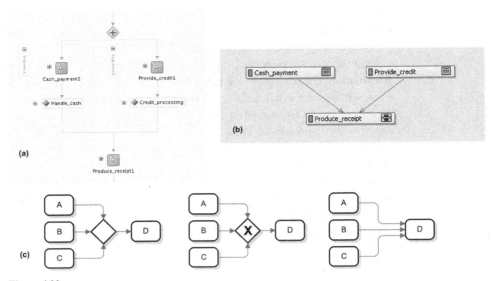

Figure 4.22
Simple merge configuration in (a) Oracle BPEL, (b) BPMone, and (c) BPMN.

Multi-merge

Description The convergence of two or more branches into a single subsequent branch such that each enablement of an incoming branch results in the thread of control being passed to the subsequent branch.

Synonyms XOR-join, exclusive OR-join, asynchronous join, merge.

Example

- The *lay-foundations*, *order-materials*, and *book-labourer* tasks occur in parallel. As each of them completes the *quality-review* task is run. By using a multi-merge construct, this task only needs to be specified once.

Motivation The *Multi-merge* pattern provides a means of merging distinct branches in a process into a single branch. Although several execution paths are merged, there is no synchronization of control-flow, and each thread of control that is currently active in any of the preceding branches will flow unimpeded into the merged branch.

Operation The operation of this pattern is illustrated in figure 4.23. Any threads of control on incoming branches from tasks A, B, or C will be passed on to the outgoing branch, hence enabling task D. Each execution thread is preserved. The distinction between this pattern and the *Simple merge* is that it is possible for more than one incoming branch to be active simultaneously and for the merge construct to still operate correctly.

Context There are no specific context conditions associated with this pattern (i.e., the context assumption for the simple merge pattern is dropped).

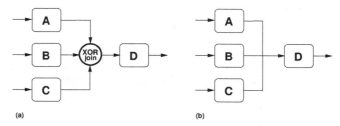

(a)   (b)

Figure 4.23

Multi-merge operation: (a) explicit depiction, and (b) implicit depiction.

Implementation BPMN directly implements this pattern via the Exclusive Merge construct. BPMone is able to support multiple concurrent threads through dynamic subplans; however, its highly structured nature does not enable it to provide general support for the *Multi-merge*. Similar considerations apply for Oracle BPEL. Although it supports concurrent execution within a Flow activity, it does not provide for just one thread (out of several active threads) to leave the Flow activity at a time. One workflow system that has particular difficulties with this pattern was Staffware (version 9), which attempted to maintain a safe process model by coalescing subsequent triggerings of a step while it is active into the same thread of control (cf. the Pac-man approach discussed on in section 4.2). This behavior was quite problematic as it created a race condition in which a variety of execution sequences were possible. For example, in the context of the process model in figure 4.23(b), depending on the time at which execution threads reached the XOR-join from tasks A, B, and C, 24 possible execution sequences (e.g., such as ABCD, ABDCD, ADBDCD, etc.) were possible, hence it was unable to support this pattern.

Another common synchronization scenario that can arise in processes is the merging of several branches where not all of them will necessarily be enabled. An illustration of such a situation is depicted in figure 4.24. When ordering a meal, it is first necessary to select options for each of the desired courses. At least one dish must be chosen if an order is to be placed, but there is no necessity to choose an option for each course (e.g., you might just want a main meal or two entrees).

The moment at which the place order task can commence is determined as follows: either all incoming branches have been activated or at least one incoming branch has been activated. Of those that have not been activated, it is not possible that they will be activated at some future time. Applying this definition to the restaurant example, when the place order activity commences, it is assumed that the desired courses have been selected when the order is placed.

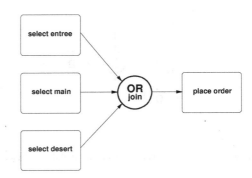

Figure 4.24
OR-join illustration.

4.3.3 OR-join variants

There are three distinct variants of the OR-join that may be utilized. Each of these variants operates in the same manner; however, they vary in the form that they take and the situations in which they can be utilized. Moreover, there is also a trade-off between generality and performance in each case.

- The *Structured synchronizing merge* is limited to supporting the notion of an OR-join in a structured process model. However, by virtue of the simplified context in which it operates, it is easier to implement in an efficient manner (i.e., the effort involved in determining whether the join can fire is limited).
- The *Local synchronizing merge* is able to be utilized in a more general context and is applicable to a wider range of process models (including unstructured ones and those involving loops). It uses locally available information (often termed *local semantics*) when making the decision as to whether it can fire; hence, it too is relatively efficient.
- The *General synchronizing merge* can be used in any form of process model and does not have any specific context restrictions associated with it; however, it requires a complete analyis of potential future states of the process instance in order to determine whether it can be enabled. Hence, it may suffer from poor runtime performance in order to achieve its universal applicability.

Each of these patterns is discussed in the following section.

Structured synchronizing merge

Description The convergence of two or more branches (which diverged earlier in the process at a uniquely identifiable point) into a single subsequent branch, such that the thread of control is passed to the subsequent branch when each active incoming branch has been enabled. The *Synchronizing merge* occurs in a structured context (i.e., there must be a single

Multi-choice construct earlier in the process model with which the *Synchronizing merge* is associated, and it must merge all of the branches emanating from the *Multi-choice*) . These branches must either flow from the *Multi-choice* to the *Synchronizing merge* without any splits or joins or they must be structured in form (i.e., balanced splits and joins).

Example

- Depending on the type of emergency, either or both of the *despatch-police* and *despatch-ambulance* tasks are initiated simultaneously. When all emergency vehicles arrive at the accident, the *transfer-patient* task commences.

Motivation The *Structured synchronizing merge* pattern provides a means of merging the branches resulting from a specific *Multi-choice* (or OR-split) construct earlier in a process into a single branch. Implicit in this merging is the synchronization of all the threads of execution resulting from the preceding *Multi-choice*.

Operation As already indicated, the *Structured synchronizing merge* pattern provides a means of merging the branches from a preceding *Multi-choice* construct and synchronizing the threads of control flowing along each of them. It is not necessary that all of the incoming branches to the *Synchronizing merge* are active in order for the construct to be enabled; however, all of the threads of control associated with the incoming branches must have reached the *Synchronizing merge* before it can fire.

There are two main approaches to implementing the *Structured synchronizing merge* pattern. The first of these implicitly restructures the process model following an OR-split such that the subsequent *Synchronizing merge* always receives precisely one trigger on each of its incoming branches, and no additional knowledge is required to make the decision as to when it should be enabled. It does this by notionally adding an alternate "bypass" path around each branch from the OR-split to the *Synchronizing merge*, which is enabled in the event that the normal path is not chosen. The "bypass" path is merged with the normal path for each branch prior to the *Synchronizing merge* ensuring that it always gets a trigger on all incoming branches and can hence be implemented using an AND-join construct. This approach is illustrated in figure 4.25(a). The dashed lines indicate the bypass path that is taken for each branch if it is not enabled by the OR-split.

The second solution shown in figure 4.25(b) does not require any modification to the process model but instead relies on communication from the OR-split to the *Synchronizing merge* of exactly how many incoming branches are active. Once the *Synchronizing merge* has received triggerings on each of these incoming branches, it can be enabled and pass on the thread of control.

Context There are two context conditions associated with the use of this pattern: (1) once the *Synchronizing merge* has been activated and has not yet been reset, it is not possible for another signal to be received on an activated branch or for multiple signals to be received on any incoming branch. In other words, all input places to the *Synchronizing merge* are safe. (2) Once the *OR-split* has been enabled, none of the tasks in the branches leading to the *Synchronizing merge* can be canceled before the merge has been triggered. The only

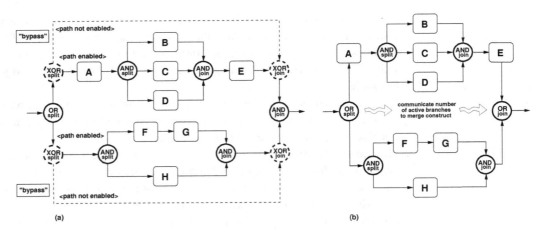

Figure 4.25
Structured synchronizing merge operation.

exception to this is that it is possible for *all* of the tasks leading up to the *Synchronizing merge* to be canceled.

Implementation In a structured context, merging of threads created by a preceding multi-choice is not possible through the use of AND/XOR-joins as one cannot guarantee that all active threads will be synchronized rather than a subset of them. Hence, there is the general requirement that a specific construct can provide the necessary merging and synchronization facilities in order to implement this pattern.

This pattern is directly supported in Oracle BPEL, BPMone, and BPMN. Oracle BPEL implements it using links within a Flow activity. The links indicate which branches within the Flow activity are activated, and only when all of these have completed can the Flow activity complete. BPMone supports the pattern within static, dynamic, and sequential subplans. Each plan model is a directed acyclic graph of nodes representing various plan elements and actions. Nodes with multiple incoming arcs wait for their predecessors to be completed or skipped. If all preceding nodes have been skipped or all incoming arcs have a guard evaluating to false, then a given node is skipped. Otherwise a node waits until preceding nodes (which have not been skipped) have completed before commencing execution. BPMN supports this pattern via the Inclusive Merge construct. Figure 4.26 illustrates the configuration of the pattern in the three offerings.

One consideration that arises with the implementation of the OR-join is providing a form that is able to be used in arbitrary loops and more complex process models that are not structured in form. The *Structured synchronizing merge* cannot be used in these contexts; however, both the *Local synchronizing merge* and the *General synchronizing merge* are able to be used in unstructured process models. The latter is also able to be used in arbitrary loops. The *Local synchronizing merge* only uses local information and tends to be more

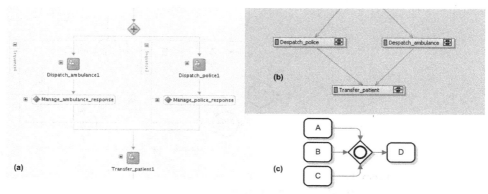

Figure 4.26
Structured synchronizing merge configuration in (a) Oracle BPEL, (b) BPMone, and (c) BPMN.

attractive from an implementation perspective as it is computationally less expensive than the *General synchronizing merge*.

Local synchronizing merge

Description The convergence of two or more branches that diverged earlier in the process into a single subsequent branch, such that the thread of control is passed to the subsequent branch when each active incoming branch has been enabled. Determination of how many branches require synchronization is made on the basis of information locally available to the merge construct.

Example

- Figure 4.27 provides an example of the *Local synchronizing merge* pattern. It shares a similar structure to the example presented in figure 4.25; however, the XOR-split between tasks B and C has the potential to route the thread of control outside of the path between the OR-split and the merge construct. Consequently, it is not possible to model the process fragment in a structured way. The local synchronizing merge construct must be able to determine when to fire on the basis of the current state and information that is locally available to it.

Motivation The *Local synchronizing merge* provides a deterministic semantics for the synchronizing merge, which does not rely on the process model being structured (as is required for the *Structured synchronizing merge*) but also does not require the use of non-local semantics in evaluating when the merge can fire. One significant advantage offered by the local synchronizing merge is that it is able to be used in a wider range of process structures, including ones that are nonstructured in form and also in processes that contain loops. However, there are some limitations. In particular, any loops within a process must either

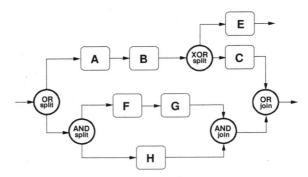

Figure 4.27
Example of a Local synchronizing merge.

wholly exist within a single branch between the merge construct and the preceding OR-split or the region from the preceding OR-split to the merge construct must be completely contained within the loop structure.

Operation Figure 4.28 illustrates one approach to implementing this pattern. It is based on the use of "true" and "false" tokens used to indicate whether a branch is enabled. When an OR-split is encountered, all outgoing branches have an execution thread passed to them. Encoded into each of these threads is a flag indicating whether the branch has been enabled. As the execution thread is passed down a branch, if it is a "true" token, then each task that receives the thread of control is executed; otherwise it is skipped (illustrated by the <path not enabled> route around each task). The *Local synchronizing merge* can be evaluated when every incoming branch has delivered an execution thread (indicating it is either active or to be skipped).

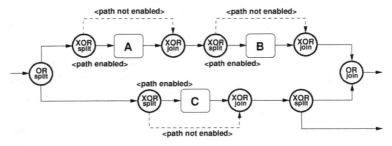

Figure 4.28
Local synchronizing merge operation.

Context There are two context conditions associated with the use of this pattern: (1) once the *Local synchronizing merge* has been activated and has not yet been reset, it is not possible for another signal to be received on an activated branch or for multiple signals to be received on any incoming branch (i.e., all input places to the *Local synchronizing merge* are safe), and (2) the *Local synchronizing merge* construct must be able to determine how many incoming branches require synchronization based on local knowledge available to it during execution.

Implementation As described for the *Structured synchronizing merge,* BPMone provides support for this pattern within static, dynamic, and sequential subplans by distinguishing skipped branches and active branches, thus allowing a given node in a plan to determine when it can fire on the basis of local information available to it. Oracle BPEL similarly distinguishes between active and skipped branches in a Flow activity and uses this information to determine when a Flow activity can complete. BPMN supports the pattern via the Inclusive Merge construct.

Issues The *Local synchronizing merge* cannot be part of a cycle in a process model unless the preceding OR-split (and all branches from the OR-split to the merge construct) are also part of the same cycle. If the merge construct is part of a cycle by itself, then its evaluation can be potentially problematic as there is the potential for execution threads from distinct loop iterations to arrive on the same input branch.

Solutions The *Local synchronizing merge* does not deal with this issue. However, the *General synchronizing merge* is able to offer a more powerful, general solution that operates in all forms of process model.

General synchronizing merge

Description The convergence of two or more branches that diverged earlier in the process into a single subsequent branch, such that the thread of control is passed to the subsequent branch when at least one incoming branch is enabled, and it is not possible to activate any branch that is not yet activated at some future stage without firing any of the OR-joins in the process model or disabling a currently activated incoming branch.

Examples

- Figure 4.29 provides an example of the *General synchronizing merge* pattern. It shares a similar fundamental structure to the example presented in figure 4.28. However, the loop involving task D and the path out of the loop to task E means that it is not possible to model it in a structured way or use local information to determine when the OR-join should be enabled.

- In parallel with the *Prepare Foreign Remittance* task, an optional *Check Payer Identity* task may run. This is mandatory for transfers greater than $10,000 but may be necessary in other circumstances as well. Depending on the verification bureau it accesses, it may return a confirmation of the payer's identity, a nonconfirmation, or an inconclusive result (in which case it needs to run again using a different verification bureau). Only positive confirmations are treated as successful completions of the *Check Payer Identity* task and trigger an outgoing execution thread. There is a synchronization point after the *Prepare*

The vicious circle paradox

One of the main considerations associated with join constructs is in determining when they are able to fire. For AND-joins, this is relatively simple – the outgoing branch can be enabled when all incoming branches have been triggered. In the illustration below, this corresponds to the time at which tasks A and B have completed. For XOR-joins, only one of the input branches needs to be triggered for the output branch to be enabled. In the example below, task C can be triggered when task A completes. Where the join construct is an OR-join however, the situation is more complex. Informally, an OR-join fires when "some" of its input branches have been enabled. The exact determination is generally taken to be that it can pass on the thread of control when all of the incoming branches that are going to be enabled have been enabled. Whilst conceptually simple, determining which branches might become enabled can be problematic. In the example below, it is questionable whether the OR-join should fire without knowledge of whether task B is likely to complete at some future time.

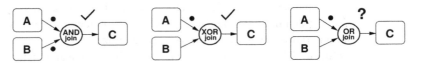

Indeed a broader view is required of the current state of the process when attempting to make the firing decision for an OR-join. This view is often termed "non-local semantics" and involves not only an examination of the current state of non-enabled input branches to the OR-join but also an assessment of whether they are ever likely to be triggered in the future. If it is possible that one of the inputs to the join that is not currently enabled might receive a thread of control, then the OR-join should wait until either it definitively knows that it will not receive any further triggerings on non-enabled branches or all expected triggerings have arrived. However, even the use of non-local semantics does not fully address the problem of determining OR-join enablement. The process model (called the "vicious circle") below illustrates the potential difficulties that can arise when evaluating these constructs.

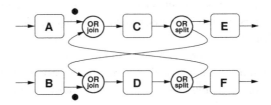

Tasks A and B have completed and the threads of control have advanced to the two OR-joins. Determining whether the join after task A needs to wait until the OR-split after D completes leads to the following conundrum. If the join after task A needs to wait until the OR-split after D completes, then, because of symmetry, the join after task B also needs to wait until the OR-split after C completes. If the join after task A does not wait, then the join after task B also does not need to wait. As a result, any of the joins may be triggered again indicating that the join should have waited. If the join after task A is forced to wait, then the join after task B also needs to wait. However, such behavior is also not possible because the process deadlocks and the joins should not have waited. Hence, whether the joins wait or not, there is a conundrum. This is the so-called vicious circle paradox Various attempts have been made to resolve this problem, however a general solution does not appear to exist. Detailed discussion of this issue can be found in [9] and [75].

Foreign Remittance task, and if the *Check Payer Identity* task has also been triggered, the process canot proceed until both tasks have completed.

Motivation This pattern provides a general approach to the evaluation of the *General synchronizing merge* (or OR-join) in processes. It is able to be used in nonstructured and highly concurrent processes, including process models that include arbitrary looping structures.

Operation This pattern provides general support for the OR-join construct that is widely utilized in modeling languages but is often only partially implemented or severely restricted in the form in which it can be used. The difficulty in implementing the *General synchronizing merge* stems from the fact that its evaluation relies on non-local semantics in order to determine when it can fire. The evaluation needs to consider all possible continuations and thus construct the state space for the current OR-join enablement.

The OR-join can only be enabled when the thread of control has been received from all incoming branches, and it is certain that the remaining incoming branches that have not been enabled will never be enabled at any future time. Determination of this fact requires a (computationally expensive) evaluation of possible future states for the current process instance.

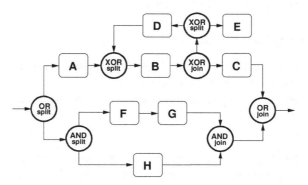

Figure 4.29
Example of a General synchronizing merge.

Context Unlike the previous synchronizing merge patterns, there are no specific context conditions associated with this pattern.

Implementation BPMN is the only one of the offerings examined to support this pattern. An algorithm describing an approach to implementing the *General synchronizing merge* has been developed and is described in [148]. However, this pattern is not widely supported by current commercial BPM tools.

Issues Three significant issues are associated with this pattern: (1) when determining whether an OR-join should be enabled in a given process instance, how should composite tasks which precede the OR-join be considered; (2) how should preceding OR-joins be handled; and (3) how can the performance implications of OR-join evaluation (which potentially involves a state space analysis for the case in which the OR-join appears) be addressed?

Solutions Solutions to all of these problems have been developed and are described in [148]. It provides a deterministic means of evaluating whether an OR-join should be enabled based on an evaluation of the current execution state of preceding tasks. It considers composite tasks to function in the same way as atomic tasks (i.e., they are either enabled or not), and there is no further consideration of the execution specifics of the underlying subprocess. Moreover, it is assumed that they will continue executing and pass the thread of control onto subsequent tasks when complete. In terms of the second issue, any preceding OR-joins are all considered to function either as XOR-joins or AND-joins when determining whether the task with which they are associated can be enabled. It also offers some potential solutions to the third issue involving the use of active and structural projection that limit the extent of the net that needs to be considered and hence the size of the state space evaluation required in order to establish whether the OR-join should be enabled. In addition, reduction rules can further reduce the size of the net that needs to be considered and hence may further reduce the associated state space. These two techniques are described in further detail in [147].

4.3.4   Synchronizing execution threads

In the same way that the *Thread split* pattern supports the creation of concurrent execution threads within a given branch, there is also a counterpart to this pattern — the *Thread merge* — that supports their coalesence into a single execution thread.

Thread merge

Description At a given point in a process, a nominated number of execution threads in a single branch of the same process instance should be merged together into a single thread of execution.

Example

- The *Plate Production* process collects requests for new or replacement licence plates. When ten requests have been received (as a result of either the *register-vehicle* or *process-replacement* tasks running), they are coalesced into a single execution of the *produce-plate* task, which produces ten sets of license plates.

Motivation This pattern provides a means of merging multiple threads flowing along the same branch within a given process instance. It is a counterpart to the *Thread split* pattern, which creates multiple execution threads along the same branch.

Operation The operation of this pattern is illustrated in figure 4.30, which is a counterpart to the example illustrated in figure 4.12 for the *Thread split*. In this example, the thread merge operator coalesces the twelve execution threads into a single one before commencing the `pack carton` task (i.e., a carton is packed with twelve filled bottles).

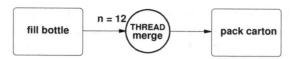

Figure 4.30
Thread merge operation.

Context There is one context consideration for this pattern: the number of threads needing to be merged (n) must be known at design time.

Implementation Implementation of this pattern implies that an offering is able to support the execution of processes in a non-safe context. This rules out many BPM offerings from providing any tractable forms of implementation. BPMN provides direct support for the pattern by specifying the startQuantity attribute for an Activity indicating the number of incoming execution threads that need to be received (and synchronized) before it can commence. Oracle BPEL provides an indirect means of implementation based on the correlation facility for feedback from the *Invoke* activity, although some programmatic housekeeping is required to determine when synchronization should occur. BPMone is unable to support the pattern as it requires process instances to execute in a safe context. However, it does provide extensive support for the multiple instances patterns, which provide a more controlled way of achieving a similar outcome to that of this pattern without the need for non-safe process execution. These are discussed in section 4.4.

Issues A significant issue associated with this pattern is how the data elements associated with the various coalesced execution threads are managed.

Solutions In BPMN, the assumption is that all thread instances share the same data elements. The correlation set facility in Oracle BPEL provides a means of accessing data elements in distinct execution threads that are being merged. However, the actual merging of data must be undertaken manually.

4.4   Repetition patterns

The controlled repetition of an individual task or a group of tasks is a fundamental requirement for business processes. In recognition of the importance of this need, there are a variety of ways in which it can be achieved depending on the manner in which the associated tasks need to be repeated. The most general form of repetition is characterized by the *Arbitrary cycles* pattern, which recognizes the existence of possible execution cycles within a process that result in one or more tasks being repeated. These cycles are unstructured in form and are represented by circular paths through a process rather than by a specific construct in the model. Moreover, it is possible that the cycle may have more than one entry or exit point and that not all tasks are executed the same number of times.

In contrast to this form of repetition, the *Structured loop* pattern describes a specific set of tasks that are repeated with a specific termination condition being evaluated either before or after each iteration. There is only one entry and exit point to the loop, and it is possible for the loop to be represented as a specific construct in the process model. In programming language terms, the *Structured loop* is analogous to implementing repetition using a *while...do* or *repeat...until* loop, whereas *Arbitrary cycles* are akin to achieving it using a *goto* statement, which shifts the point of control to another part of the process.

A third approach to repetition is described by the *Recursion* pattern, which characterizes situations where a specific task is repeated through self-invocation. These three patterns are discussed below.

Arbitrary cycles

Description The ability to represent cycles in a process model that have more than one entry or exit point. It must be possible for individual entry and exit points to be associated with distinct branches.

Synonyms Unstructured loop, iteration, cycle.

Example

- Figure 4.31 provides an illustration of the pattern with two entry points illustrated by arcs from the left-hand side of the figure.

Motivation The *Arbitrary cycles* pattern provides a means of supporting repetition in a process model in an unstructured way without the need for specific looping operators or restrictions on the overall format of the process model.

Operation The only consideration for facilitating this pattern is that the offering imposes no restrictions on cycles (i.e., does not enforce a block structure).

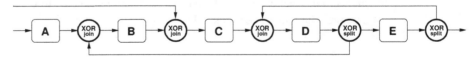

Figure 4.31

Arbitrary cycles example.

Context There are no specific context conditions associated with this pattern.

Implementation BPMN is capable of capturing the *Arbitrary cycles* pattern as it allows processes to be modeled that include cycles among the various nodes. Block structured offerings such as Oracle BPEL and BPMone are not able to represent arbitrary process structures.

Issues The unstructured occurrences of the *Arbitrary cycles* pattern are difficult to capture in some BPM offerings, particularly those that implement structured process models.

Solutions In some situations, it is possible to transform process models containing *Arbitrary cycles* into structured processes, thus allowing them to be captured in offerings based on structured process models. Further details on the types of process models that can be transformed and the approaches to doing so can be found in [72, 74].

Structured loop

Description The ability to execute a task or subprocess repeatedly. The loop has either a pretest or posttest condition associated with it that is either evaluated at the beginning or end of the loop to determine whether it should continue. The looping structure has a single entry and exit point.

Examples

- While the machine still has fuel remaining, continue with the production process.
- Only schedule flights if there is no *storm-identified* task.
- Continue processing photographs from the film until all of them have been printed.
- Repeat the *select player* task until the entire team has been selected.

Motivation There are three general forms of this pattern — the *while* loop, which equates to the classic `while...do` pretest loop construct used in programming languages; the *repeat* loop, which equates to the `repeat... until` posttest loop construct; and the *combination* loop, which amalgamates the two earlier forms and provides for both pre and posttesting during iteration.

The while loop allows for the repeated sequential execution of a specified task or a subprocess zero or more times providing a nominated condition evaluates to true. The pretest condition is evaluated before the first iteration of the loop and is reevaluated before each subsequent iteration. Once the pretest condition evaluates to false, the thread of control passes to the task immediately following the loop.

The repeat loop allows for the execution of a task or subprocess one or more times, continuing with execution until a nominated condition evaluates to true. The posttest condition is evaluated after the first iteration of the loop and is reevaluated after each subsequent iteration. Once the posttest condition evaluates to true, the thread of control passes to the task immediately following the loop.

The combination loop allows for the repeated sequential execution of a specified task or a subprocess zero or more times. It allows for pretest and posttest of continued iteration at different points in the overall loop structure, thus providing further flexibility in terms of the tasks at which the loop starts and ends (i.e., it doesn't need to start and end at the same point).

Operation As indicated above, there are three variants of this pattern: the while loop illustrated in figure 4.32(a), the repeat loop shown in figure 4.32(b), and the combination loop depicted in figure 4.32(c). Note that figure 4.32(c) allows for A, ABCD, ABCDE, ABCDEBCD, and so on.

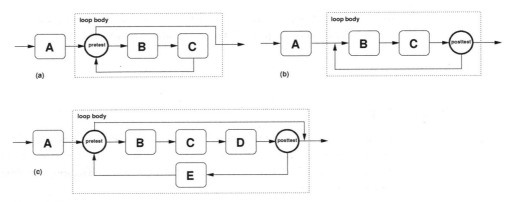

Figure 4.32
Structured loop examples.

Context There is one context condition associated with this pattern: only one instance of a loop can be active at any time (i.e., there can only be one thread of control in the loop body at any point).

Implementation The main consideration in supporting the *Structured loop* pattern is the availability of a construct within a modeling language to denote the repeated execution of a task or subprocess based on a specified condition. The evaluation of the condition to determine whether to continue (or cease) execution can occur either before or after the task (or subprocess) has been initiated. BPMone provides the sequential plan construct that allows a sequence of tasks to be repeated sequentially until a nominated condition is satisfied. Oracle BPEL directly supports pretested and posttested loops via the While and Repeat Until activities. BPMN allows both forms of repetition to be captured through the Loop Activity construct. Figure 4.33 illustrates the configuration of the pattern in Oracle BPEL, BPMone, and BPMN.

The last pattern in this group is the *Recursion* pattern where a part of the process can invoke itself.

Recursion

Description The ability of a task to invoke itself (or an ancestor in terms of the overall decomposition structure with which it is associated) during its execution.

Examples

- The *Validate Witness Statement* task ensures all testimony taken from witnesses during the investigation has been recorded correctly. It does this by checking the first witness statement that was received. If there are witness statements remaining to be processed, then it invokes another *Validate Witness Statement* task to deal with those statements; otherwise it completes and passes back control to the task that invoked it.

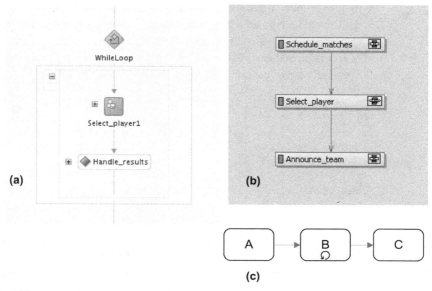

Figure 4.33
Structured loop configuration in (a) Oracle BPEL, (b) BPMone, and (c) BPMN.

- An instance of the *resolve-defect* task is initiated for each mechanical problem that is identified in the production plant. During the execution of the *resolve-defect* task, if a mechanical fault is identified during investigations that is not related to the current defect, then another instance of the *resolve-defect* is started. These subprocesses can also initiate further *resolve-defect* tasks should they be necessary. The parent *resolve-defect* task cannot complete until all child *resolve-defect* tasks that it initiated have been satisfactorily completed.

Motivation For some types of tasks, simpler and more succinct solutions can be provided through the use of recursion rather than iteration. In order to harness recursive forms of problem solving within the context of a process, a means of describing a task execution in terms of itself (i.e., the ability for a task to invoke another instance of itself while executing) is required.

Operation Figure 4.34 illustrates the format of the *Recursion* pattern. Task B can be realized as a process involving three tasks: A, B, and C. It is important to note that this implementation for task B also includes task B; hence, the task is described in terms of itself. A possible execution sequence is AB(AB(AC)C)C, where the brackets illustrate the recursion.

In order to implement this pattern, a process model requires the ability to denote the synchronous invocation of a task or subprocess within the same model. In order to ensure that use of recursion does not lead to infinite self-referencing decompositions, figure 4.34 contains one path (illustrated by task sequence AC) that is not self-referencing and will terminate normally. This corresponds to the *terminating condition* in mathematical descriptions of recursion and ensures that, where recursion is used in a process, the overall process will eventually complete normally when executed.

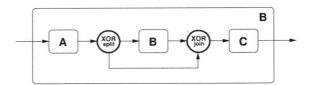

Figure 4.34
Recursion example.

Context There are no specific context conditions associated with this pattern.
Implementation In order to implement recursion within the context of a process, some means of invoking a distinct instance of a task is required from within a given task implementation. Of the offerings examined, only BPMN provides the ability for a task to directly invoke an instance of itself while executing. It achieves this via a Call Activity, which enables a Process or Global Task (which is defined outside the context of the calling Process) to be invoked. Recursion is possible where the Global Task/Process in turn contains a Call Activity that invokes the Global Task/Process.

4.5   Multiple instances patterns

The ability to specify that multiple instances of a task can execute concurrently is an important means of expediting work throughput and provides a mechanism for distributing a task across multiple resources. It is particularly suited to situations where the work outcome associated with the task can be similarly achieved by executing the task multiple times (e.g., in a criminal investigation, the *interview witnesses* task can be conceived as multiple instances of the [singular] *interview witness* task, each of which can be undertaken by a distinct investigator, hence speeding the completion of the overall work objective). Another example is the handling of a customer order that consists of multiple order lines: various activities (e.g., checking the availability of a particular item) need to be executed per order line.
There are a number of ways in which multiple task instances can be supported depending on three factors:

- the time at which the number of instances that will be executed is determined;

- the number of those instances that must be completed (i.e., synchronized) before any subsequent tasks can be triggered; and
- where only some of the instances are synchronized and the thread of control is passed on, what happens to the remaining instances (i.e., nothing or are they canceled).

Table 4.9 indicates how these factors correspond to specific multiple instances patterns. Each of these patterns is discussed subsequently in further detail.

Table 4.2

Multiple instance patterns key differentiating criteria (from [64]).

Pattern	Determination of execution instances	Instances to synchronize	Handling remaining tasks
Multiple instances without synchronization	runtime before task initiation	none	no action
Multiple instances with a priori design time knowledge	design time	all	no action
Multiple instances with a priori runtime knowledge	runtime before task initiation	all	no action
Multiple instances without a priori runtime knowledge	runtime before task completion	all	no action
Static partial join for multiple instances	runtime before task initiation	some	no action
Canceling partial join for multiple instances	runtime before task initiation	some	cancel
Dynamic partial join for multiple instances	runtime before task completion	some	no action

Multiple instances without synchronization

Description Within a given process instance, multiple instances of a task can be created. These instances are independent of each other and run concurrently. There is no requirement to synchronize them upon completion. Each of the instances of the multiple instance task that are created must execute within the context of the process instance from which they were started (i.e., they must share the same case identifier and have access to the same

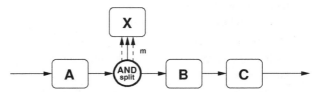

data elements), and each of them must execute independently from and without reference to the task that started them.

Synonyms Multi-threading without synchronization, spawn off facility.

Example

- A list of traffic infringements is received by the Transport Department. For each infringement on the list, an *Issue-Infringement-Notice* task is created. These tasks run to completion in parallel and do not trigger any subsequent tasks. They do not need to be synchronized at completion.

Motivation This pattern provides a means of creating multiple instances of a given task. It caters to situations where the number of individual tasks required is known before the spawning action commences, the tasks can execute independently of each other, and no subsequent synchronization is required.

Operation The operation of this pattern is illustrated in figure 4.35. There is a means of spawning off one or more instances of task X, which execute concurrently and are independent of the main thread of control. These instances may be created either simultaneously or sequentially (e.g., as part of a loop).

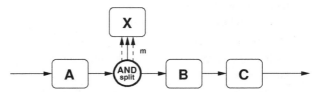

Figure 4.35
Multiple instances without synchronization operation.

Context There is one context condition associated with this pattern: the number of task instances to be created (m) is known at design time and is a fixed value.

Implementation Generally there are two approaches to implementing this pattern: either new task instances can be spawned off sequentially in a loop or additional (asynchronous) tasks instances can be created using a specific task initiation construct, which allows the new instances to execute concurrently with the main execution thread. Oracle BPEL supports the sequential variant of this pattern, creating instances using the Invoke activity within a loop based on a While or Repeat Until activity. BPMone supports the simultaneous variant via the dynamic subplan construct. BPMN supports both the sequential and concurrent variants of the pattern using the Multiple Instances Activity construct. The isSequential attribute indicates whether they are sequential or concurrent, the loopCardinality atttribute corresponds to an expression that determines the number of instances, and the behavior attribute is set to None, indicating that no synchronization or specific interaction is required when individual instances complete. Figure 4.36 illustrates the pattern configuration in each of the three BPM offerings.

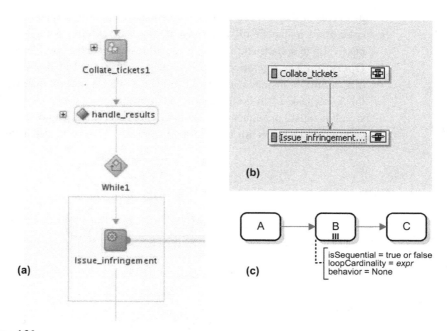

Figure 4.36
Multiple instances without synchronization configuration in (a) Oracle BPEL, (b) BPMone, and (c) BPMN.

Issues A major consideration with the use of this pattern is whether the newly created task instances operate in the same address space (i.e., share access to the same data elements) as the process instance from which they are created.

Solutions The data issues associated with multiple task instance are described at length in the *Multiple Instance Data* pattern discussed in chapter 5.

Multiple instances with a priori design time knowledge

Description Within a given process instance, multiple instances of a task can be created. The required number of instances is known at design time. These instances are independent of each other and run concurrently. It is necessary to synchronize the task instances at completion before any subsequent tasks can be triggered.

Example

• The annual report must be signed by all six directors before it can be issued.

Motivation This pattern provides the basis for concurrent execution of a nominated task a predefined number of times. It also ensures that all task instances are complete before subsequent tasks are initiated. One of the advantages offered by this pattern is that it saves the need to explicitly identify each instance of a task in the process model where multiple instances of the task run in parallel. Instead the pattern can be used to denote that multiple concurrent instances of a nominated task will execute with the thread of control being passed on to subsequent task(s) when all instances have completed.

Operation The operation of this pattern is illustrated in figure 4.37. Within the context of a "multiple instance" construct, it is possible for several distinct instances of a task (in this case, task B) to be triggered and subsequently synchronized. They can be triggered simultaneously or sequentially, but in either case, the thread of control is only passed on to subsequent tasks (in this case, task C) when all of the instances have completed execution.

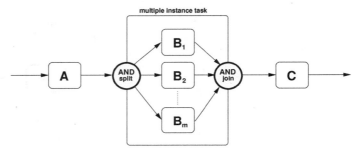

Figure 4.37
Multiple instances with a priori design time knowledge operation.

Context There is one context condition associated with this pattern: the number of task instances (m) is known at design time and is a fixed value.

Implementation In order to implement this pattern, an offering must provide a specific construct in the process model that is able to identify and initiate the actual number of concurrent task instances that are required. BPMone supports the concurrent variant of the pattern through the use of the dynamic subplan construct. BPMN support both options via the Multiple Instances Activity construct. The isSequential attribute indicates whether they are sequential or concurrent, the loopCardinality attribute corresponds to an expression that determines the number of instances, and the behavior attribute is set to All, indicating that an output token is produced when all instances complete. Oracle BPEL provides the For Each activity, which allows multiple instances of a task to be created either concurrently or sequentially. Figure 4.38 illustrates the configuration of the pattern in each offering.

Issues Many offerings provide a work-around for this pattern by embedding some form of task invocation within a loop. These implementation approaches have two significant problems associated with them: (1) the task invocations occur at discrete time intervals, and there is no requirement that they execute concurrently, with the potential consequence that all instances do not necessarily share the same process state during their execution; and (2) there is no consideration of the means by which the distinct task instances will be synchronized. These issues, together with the necessity for the designer to effectively craft the pattern themselves (rather than having it provided by the offering), rule out this form

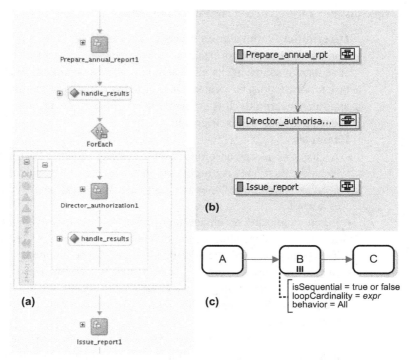

Figure 4.38
Multiple instances with a priori design time knowledge configuration in (a) Oracle BPEL, (b) BPMone, and (c) BPMN.

of implementation from being considered as satisfying the requirements for full support of this pattern.

Another issue associated with this and the following two multiple instances patterns is that of data handling in distinct task instances. In particular, how do individual task instances share access to data elements and what happens to instance-specific data elements when task instances complete execution.

Solutions One possibility that exists where this functionality is not provided by an offering but an analogous form of operation is required is to simply replicate the task in the process model between a split and join construct such that all instances of the task execute in parallel. Each instance of the task should be passed the same data elements at commencement (other than those data items that are specific to individual instances) to ensure that they execute in the same context.

Data handling for multiple instance tasks is a complex problem. The various ways in which data is utilized by multiple instance tasks are characterized by the data patterns described in chapter 5, in particular the *Multiple instance data*, *Task data*, and *Case data* patterns.

Multiple instances with a priori runtime knowledge

Description Within a given process instance, multiple instances of a task can be created. The required number of instances may depend on a number of runtime factors, including state data, resource availability, and interprocess communication, but is known before the task instances must be created. Once initiated, these instances are independent of each other and run concurrently. It is necessary to synchronize the instances at completion before any subsequent tasks can be triggered.

Examples

- A customer places an order for three books and two DVDs. Hence, within the order instance, there are five order line instances for which activities such as order picking need to be executed. Other activities such as process payment are executed for the order as a whole.
- When diagnosing an engine fault, multiple instances of the *check-sensor* task can run concurrently depending on the number of error messages received. When all messages have been processed, the *identify-fault* task can be initiated.
- In the review process for a paper submitted to a journal, the *review paper* task is executed several times depending on the content of the paper, the availability of referees, and the credentials of the authors. The review process can only continue when all reviews have been returned.
- When dispensing a prescription, the *weigh compound* task must be completed for each ingredient before the preparation can be compounded and dispensed.

Motivation The *Multiple instances with a priori runtime knowledge* pattern provides a means of executing multiple instances of a given task in a synchronized manner with the determination of exactly how many instances will be created being deferred to the latest possible time before the first of the tasks is started.

Operation The operation of the pattern is illustrated in figure 4.39. It is similar to that for the *Multiple instances with a priori design time knowledge* pattern with the main difference being that determination of the actual number of instances to start is deferred until runtime. Generally, this number is passed to or calculated by the multiple instance task construct when it is initiated. As with other multiple instances patterns, there are two variants of this pattern depending on whether the instances are created sequentially or simultaneously.

Context There is one context condition associated with this pattern: the number of task instances (m) is known at runtime prior to the creation of instances of the task. Once determined, the number of task instances is a fixed value.

Implementation BPMone supports the simultaneous variant of the pattern through the use of the dynamic subplan construct. BPMN supports both options via the Multiple Instances Activity construct. In the cases of BPMone and BPMN, the actual number of instances required is indicated through a variable passed to the construct at runtime. Oracle BPEL supports the pattern via the For Each activity, which allows multiple instances of a task to

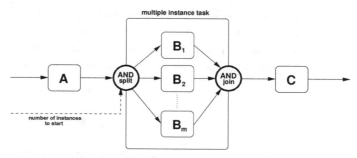

Figure 4.39
Multiple instances with a priori runtime knowledge operation.

run either concurrently or sequentially. The actual number of instances that are initiated can be passed to the construct at initiation (as an integer or an array) or alternatively calculated based on a specified expression when the construct is initiated.

Multiple instances without a priori runtime knowledge

Description Within a given process instance, multiple instances of a task can be created. The required number of instances may depend on a number of runtime factors, including state data, resource availability, and interprocess communications, and is not known until the final instance has completed. Once initiated, these instances are independent of each other and run concurrently. At any time while instances are running, it is possible for additional instances to be initiated. It is necessary to synchronize the instances at completion before any subsequent tasks can be triggered.

Example

- The despatch of an *oil rig* from factory to site involves numerous *transport shipment* tasks. These occur concurrently. Although sufficient tasks are started to cover initial estimates of the required transport volumes, it is always possible for additional tasks to be initiated if there is a shortfall in transportation requirements. Once the whole oil rig has been transported and all *transport shipment* tasks are complete, the next task (*assemble rig*) can commence.

Motivation This pattern is an extension to the *Multiple instances with a priori runtime knowledge* pattern, which defers the need to determine how many concurrent instances of the task are required until the last possible moment — either when the synchronization of the multiple instances occurs or the last of the executing instances completes. It offers more flexibility in that additional instances can be created "on the fly" without any necessary change to the process model or the completion conditions for the task.

Operation The operation of the pattern is illustrated in figure 4.40. It is similar to the *Multiple instances with a priori runtime knowledge* pattern, with the main difference being that there is a provision for the initiation of additional task instances once the task has commenced at runtime (and the initial group of instances have been started). Similar to other multiple instances patterns, there are two variants to this pattern depending on whether the initial round of instances are started sequentially or simultaneously.

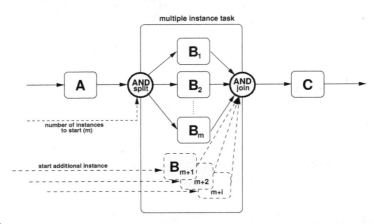

Figure 4.40
Multiple instances without a priori runtime knowledge operation.

Context There is one context condition associated with this pattern: the number of task instances is known at runtime prior to the completion of the multiple instance task (note that the final number of instances does not need to be known when initialising the MI task).
Implementation Only one of the offerings examined — BPMone — provides direct support for this pattern. It does this through the dynamic subplan construct. Neither BPMN nor Oracle BPEL provides a means of adding additional instances once the initial number of instances has been determined when the construct is first started.

The previous three multiple instances patterns assume that all task instances will complete before the thread of control is passed to subsequent tasks. However, this assumption has the potential to slow down overall process execution. The next three patterns seek to remedy this issue by providing a means of continuing on with subsequent tasks in the process once a subset of the concurrent task instances has completed execution. The various ways in which they operate are analogous to the *Blocking partial join* and *Canceling partial join* patterns discussed earlier.

Static partial join for multiple instances

Description Within a given process instance, multiple concurrent instances of a task (say m) can be created. The required number of instances is known when the first task instance commences. Once n of the task instances have completed (where n is less than m), the next task in the process is triggered. Subsequent completions of the remaining *m-n* instances are inconsequential. However, all instances must have completed in order for the join construct to reset and be subsequently re-enabled.

Example

- Examine ten samples from the production line for defects. Continue with the next task when seven of these examinations have been completed.

Motivation The *Static partial join for multiple instances* pattern is an extension to the *Multiple instances with a priori runtime knowledge* pattern, which allows the process instance to continue once a given number of the task instances have completed rather than requiring all of them to finish before the subsequent task can be triggered.

Operation The general format of the *Static partial join for multiple instances* pattern is illustrated in figure 4.41. The number of task instances to be started (m) and the number that must complete (n) for the partial join to be enabled and subsequent tasks to be enabled are known prior to task commencement and are generally specified in the design time process model. Once the partial join has been enabled, the remaining $m-n$ task instances can complete in their own time and have no effect on subsequent process execution.

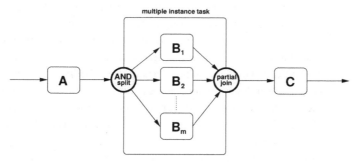

Figure 4.41
Static partial join for multiple instances pattern operation.

Context There are two context conditions associated with this pattern: (1) the number of concurrent task instances (denoted by variable m in figure 4.41) is known prior to task commencement, and (2) the number of tasks that need to be completed before subsequent tasks in the process model can be triggered is also known prior to task commencement.

Two variants of this pattern relax some of the restrictions described above. First, the *Canceling partial join for multiple instances* pattern removes the need to wait for all of the task instances to complete (to reset) by canceling any remaining task instances as soon as the join fires. These are explained later.

The second, the *Dynamic partial join for multiple instances* pattern, allows the value of m (i.e., the number of instances) to be determined during the execution of the task instances.

In particular, it allows additional task instances to be created "on the fly." This pattern is described later.

Implementation Although Oracle BPEL has a provision for specifying an early exit criterion that allows the construct to complete and pass on the thread of control before all task instances have completed, this results in any remaining task instances being canceled. Hence, this is not considered to constitute support for the pattern. BPMN also appears to offer support for this pattern via the Multiple Instances Activity construct; however, there is no means of triggering the partial join when n instances have completed without canceling the remaining m−n instances. BPMone does not support the pattern.

Canceling partial join for multiple instances

Description Within a given process instance, multiple concurrent instances of a task (say *m*) can be created. The required number of instances is known when the first task instance commences. Once *n* of the task instances have completed (where *n* is less than *m*), the next task in the process is triggered, and the remaining *m-n* instances are canceled.

Examples

- Run 500 instances of the *Protein Test* task with distinct samples. Once 400 have completed, cancel the remaining instances and initiate the next task.
- Ask five reviewers to examine a manuscript. Once three reviewers have completed their deliberations, withdraw the review request from the remaining reviewers.

Motivation This pattern is a variant of the *Multiple instances with a priori runtime knowledge* pattern that expedites process throughput by both allowing the process to continue to the next task once a specified number (*n*) of the multiple instance tasks have completed and also cancels any remaining task instances, negating the need to expend any further effort executing them.

Operation Figure 4.42 illustrates the operation of this pattern. It is similar in form to the *Static partial join for multiple instances* pattern but functions in a different way once the partial join has fired. At this point any remaining instances that have not already completed are withdrawn, allowing the associated AND-join to be re-enabled.

Context This pattern has the same context conditions as the *Static partial join for multiple instances* pattern: (1) the number of concurrent task instances (denoted by variable m in figure 4.42) is known prior to task commencement, and (2) the number of tasks that need to complete before subsequent tasks in the process model can be triggered is also known prior to task commencement.

Implementation This pattern relies on the availability of a *Cancel task* or *Cancel region* capability within an offering (see section 4.8 for further details on the operation of these patterns), and at least one of these patterns needs to be supported for this pattern to be facilitated. Oracle BPEL supports the pattern via the For Each activity, which allows multiple instances of a task to run either concurrently or sequentially. The actual number of

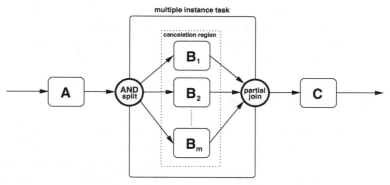

Figure 4.42
Canceling partial join for multiple instances operation.

instances that are to be executed is set at the time the construct is initiated. The For Each activity also has a provision for an early exit criterion based on a completion condition, which allows the construct to complete once a specified condition is satisfied or a certain number of instances has completed. When the early exit criterion has been satisfied, all remaining instances are canceled, and the thread of control is passed to subsequent tasks. Figure 4.43 illustrates the configuration of the completion condition for the pattern in Oracle BPEL. BPMN support both options via the Multiple Instances Activity construct. The

Figure 4.43
Canceling partial join for multiple instances configuration in Oracle BPEL.

isSequential attribute indicates whether they are sequential or concurrent, the loopCardinality atttribute corresponds to an expression that determines the number of instances, the behavior attribute is set to None, a null noneBehaviorEventRef is set to prevent individual activity completions triggering output events or tokens, and completionCondition is set to n to indicate that an output token should be produced when n activity instances have completed and the remainder should be canceled. BPMone does not support the pattern.

Dynamic partial join for multiple instances

Description Within a given process instance, multiple concurrent instances of a task can be created. The required number of instances may depend on a number of runtime factors, including state data, resource availability, and interprocess communications, and is not known until the final instance has completed. At any time while instances are running, it is possible for additional instances to be initiated, provided the ability to do so has not been disabled. A completion condition is specified, which is evaluated each time an instance of the task completes. Once the completion condition evaluates to true, the next task in the process is triggered. Subsequent completions of the remaining task instances are inconsequential, and no new instances can be created.

Example

- The dispatch of an *oil rig* from factory to site involves numerous *transport shipment* tasks. These occur concurrently, and although sufficient tasks are started to cover initial estimates of the required transport volumes, it is always possible for additional tasks to be initiated if there is a shortfall in transportation requirements. Once 90% of the *transport shipment* tasks are complete, the next task (*invoice transport costs*) can commence. The remaining *transport shipment* tasks continue until the whole rig has been transported.

Motivation This pattern is a variant of the *Multiple instances without a priori runtime knowledge* pattern that provides the ability to trigger the next task once a nominated completion condition is satisfied. The completion condition is usually based on state information relevant to the specific process instance (e.g., number of incoming branches that have completed execution). However, any deterministic condition that can be evaluated in the context of the process instance (even one that is not based on process-specific data) can be used as the completion condition. The pattern also provides the ability to disable the creation of additional task instances while still allowing already enabled instances to complete in their own time.

Operation Figure 4.44 illustrates the operation of this pattern. It is similar to the *Multiple instances without a priori design time knowledge* pattern, the main difference being that the thread of control is passed on when some (and not all) of the task instances have completed. The actual partial join condition is specified in the design time model and may be based on a number of task instances completing or may use an entirely different basis for assessing when the thread of control should be passed on. Additional task instances can be initiated at any time after the initial round of instances are started up until the time the partial join fires. Similar to other multiple instances patterns, there are two variants to this pattern depending on whether the initial round of instances is started sequentially or simultaneously. At any time after commencement of the multiple instance task (but before completion), it is possible for the ability to create further instances to be disabled.

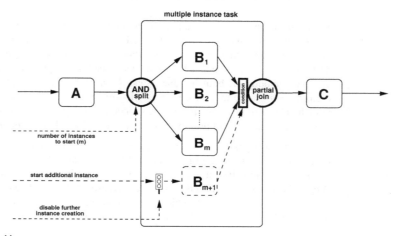

Figure 4.44
Dynamic partial join for multiple instances operation.

Context This pattern has two context conditions: (1) the number of concurrent task instances to be started initially (denoted by variable m in figure 4.44) is known prior to task commencement, and (2) it must be possible to access any data elements or other necessary resources required to evaluate the completion condition at the conclusion of each task instance.

Implementation Of the offerings identified, only BPMone allows the dynamic creation of multiple instance tasks (via dynamic subplans). However, it requires all of them to be completed before any completion conditions associated with a dynamic subplan (e.g., partial joins) can be evaluated and subsequent tasks can be triggered. This is not considered to constitute support for this pattern. Neither Oracle BPEL nor BPMN allows additional instances to be created dynamically as part of their multiple instance constructs. Hence, neither of these offerings supports the pattern.

4.6   Concurrency patterns

Concurrency patterns serve to provide a measure of control over concurrent execution within a given process instance. Five distinct patterns in this group allow various limitations to be imposed on parallel execution within a region of a process or within a set of tasks and also provide for contingent execution of a task when another branch is in a specified state. The specific concurrency patterns are as follows:

Deadlocks and livelocks

Just as in database systems and programming, where livelocks and deadlocks signal undesirable events, there are analogous concepts in BPM systems. A deadlock corresponds to a state in a process instance which is not the end state and from which no further execution is possible. The left-hand process model below shows a deadlocked process instance. The OR-split only enabled one outgoing branch – that to task A which has now completed. However, in order for the process instance to progress, the AND-join requires a thread of control on each incoming branch. This will never happen as the branch involving task B was never activated, hence the process instance will not progress any further even though it has not reached its end state.

A livelock corresponds to a state in a process instance that is not the end state and from which the process instance cannot ever reach the end state. Unlike a deadlock, where no further execution is possible, in a livelock it is possible for the process instance to progress, however the desired end state can never be reached. The right-hand process below shows a livelock where the thread of control has reached task C which will execute and pass it back to task B. In effect, there is an infinite loop involving tasks B and C and the process instance will never terminate.

Although there are mature analysis techniques that can detect deadlocks and livelocks in executing processes, few BPM offerings provide good support for verification. The most common approach to managing these issues is through the use of task deadlines which either cancel the process instance or escalate it to a suitable resource for manual intervention and resolution.

The notion of *soundness* [1] has been defined as one means of ensuring that a process will be free of deadlocks and livelocks. A process is sound if and only if:

1. there is always an option to complete: for each case it is always still possible to reach the designated end state;
2. proper completion is guaranteed: if the thread of control has reached the designated end state, then no other threads of control must exist within the process instance; and
3. there are no dead transitions: every task in the process model should be on an execution path from the start to the end node.

It is possible to analyse a process model statically to determine whether or not it is sound and a number of tools exist for doing do, such as the Woflan tool which can assess workflow models from the Staffware, MQSeries Workflow and COSA offerings as well as the generic Petri net format PNML. The Signavio BPMN editor also integrates with third-party facilities for assessing process model soundness.

- **Sequence**, where the execution of a set of tasks must occur in a specified order;
- **Interleaved routing**, where the execution of a set of tasks can occur in any order, provided that each task executes precisely once and that no two tasks in the set can execute simultaneously;
- **Interleaved parallel routing**, where a set of tasks, which have a partial ordering indicating the sequence in which they must be undertaken, are executed in any sequence that meets with the implied partial ordering, such that no two tasks in the set run simultaneously and each task executes precisely once;
- **Critical section**, where two or more regions of a process model are defined, such that only one thread of control can be active in all of the regions at any time; and
- **Milestone**, where the execution of a nominated task can only proceed when the thread of control in a distinct branch has reached a specific state.

Each of these patterns is discussed in more detail subsequently. The simplest structure within a process is the task sequence. It describes a strictly ordered set of tasks that execute one after the other and have no branching or merging behavior associated with them. This scenario is described by the *Sequence* pattern.

Sequence

Description A task in a process is enabled after the completion of a preceding task in the same process.

Synonyms Sequential routing, serial routing.

Examples

- The *verify-account* task executes after the credit card details have been captured.
- The *codacil-signature* task follows the *contract-signature* task.
- A receipt is printed after the train ticket is issued.

Motivation The *Sequence* pattern serves as the fundamental building block for processes. It is used to construct a series of consecutive tasks that execute in turn one after the other. Two tasks form part of a *Sequence* if there is a control-flow edge from one of them to the next, which has no guards or conditions associated with it.

Operation Figure 4.45 illustrates the *Sequence* pattern. It is simply a sequence of tasks that execute one after the other in a strict order.

Figure 4.45
Sequence operation.

Context There are no context conditions associated with this pattern.

Implementation The *Sequence* pattern is widely supported, and all of the offerings examined directly implement it as a linked series of tasks.

Issues One issue that arises with the use of this pattern occurs in situations where there is the possibility for concurrent execution threads to arrive at the same point in the process model where that point is not a join or synchronization operator.

Solutions This issue does not arise in BPMN, Oracle BPEL, or BPMone. However, there are systems where such a situation needs to be catered to. There are two main approaches to dealing with this: *coalescence* (also termed the "Pac-man" approach) and *prevention* (also termed the "blocking" approach). These approaches are exemplified by the Staffware v10 and COSA 5.1 workflow offerings. Where a second execution thread arrives at an already enabled task in Staffware, it is simply coalesced into the already active task. Thus, a race condition exists that may result in execution threads being lost in certain circumstances. COSA deals with this situation by preventing two execution threads reaching the same point simultaneously. Where a task has recently completed and a token resides in one or more of its output places, it is not possible for the task to be enabled again until the output tokens have exited from these output places (by progressing further in the process model).

Interleaved routing

Description Each member of a set of tasks must be executed once. They can be executed in any order, but no two tasks can be executed at the same time (i.e., no two tasks can be active for the same process instance at the same time). Once all of the tasks have completed, the next task in the process can be initiated.

Example

- The *check-oil*, *test-feeder*, *examine-main-unit*, and *review-warranty* tasks all need to be undertaken as part of the machine-service process. Only one of them can be undertaken at a time; however, they can be executed in any order.

Motivation The *Interleaved routing* pattern provides a means of specifying that a group of tasks must be executed without requiring that the actual execution sequence be nominated.

Operation Figure 4.46 illustrates the operation of this pattern. After A is completed, tasks X, Y, and Z can be completed in any order (but not concurrently). After all of them have been completed, task B can be undertaken.

Context There is one consideration associated with the use of this pattern: tasks must be initiated and completed on a sequential basis; in particular, it is not possible to suspend one task during its execution to work on another.

Implementation In order to effectively implement this pattern, an offering must have an integrated notion of state that is available during execution of the control-flow perspective. Oracle BPEL can achieve similar effects using isolated scopes within the context of a Pick activity. BPMone has a distinct foundation, making this pattern superfluous. The case

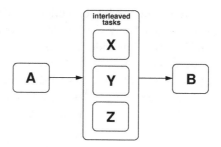

Figure 4.46
Interleaved routing operation.

handling paradigm allows multiple resources to view a case and its associated data. However, only at most one resource can actually work on the case at any point in time. Hence, interleaved routing is guaranteed. However, it is also possible for a resource to suspend a task during execution to work on another; hence, the context condition for this pattern is not fully satisfied. BPMN indirectly supports the pattern via an Ad-Hoc Sub-Process containing all of the Activities to be interleaved with ordering set to sequential. However, it is unclear what the required completionCondition should be to ensure each Activity is executed precisely once.

Interleaved parallel routing

Description A set of tasks has a partial ordering defining the requirements with respect to the order in which they must be executed. Each task in the set must be executed once, and they can be completed in any order that accords with the partial order. Moreover, any task in the set can be routed to resources for execution as soon as they are enabled. Thus, there is the provision within the partial ordering for *parallel routing* of tasks should more than one of them be enabled simultaneously, and there is no necessity that they be routed sequentially. However, there is an additional requirement — that no two tasks can be executed at the same time (i.e., no two tasks in the set can be active for the same process instance at the same time). Hence, the execution of tasks is also *interleaved*.

Examples

- When despatching an order, the *pick goods*, *pack goods*, and *prepare invoice* tasks must be completed. The *pick goods* task must be done before the *pack goods* task. The *prepare invoice* task can occur at any time. Only one of these tasks can be done at any time for a given order.

Motivation The *Interleaved parallel routing* pattern offers the possibility of relaxing the strict ordering that a process usually imposes over a set of tasks. A set of tasks may have a partial ordering, which implies that some tasks must be executed before others, but this ordering may not be as strict and complete as that implied by the *Sequence* pattern, and it allows for a variety of possible execution orderings. Should the need for ordering between tasks be relaxed completely, the *Interleaved routing* pattern applies instead.

Operation Figure 4.47 provides examples of *Interleaved parallel routing*. The set of tasks to be interleaved comprises A, B, C, X, and Y. There are two partial orderings implied in the set of tasks, such that A must execute before B, B before C, and X before Y. Three possible execution sequences are illustrated. Overall, there are ten permissible task orderings: ABCXY, ABXCY, AXBCY, XABCY, ABXYC, AXBYC, XABYC, AXYBC, XAYBC, and XYABC.

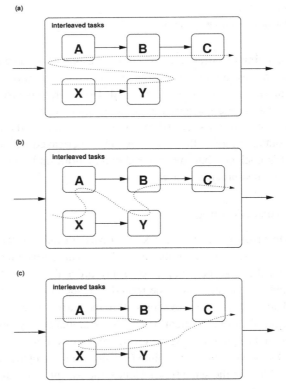

Figure 4.47
Examples of interleaved parallel routing.

Context One context condition is associated with this pattern: tasks must be initiated and completed on a sequential basis, and thus it is not possible to suspend one task during its execution to work on another.

Implementation In order to effectively implement this pattern, an offering must have an integrated notion of state that is available during execution of the control-flow perspective. Oracle BPEL can indirectly achieve similar effects using isolated scopes within the context of a Pick activity. It also has the shortcoming that every permissible execution sequence of interleaved tasks must be explicitly modeled. Figure 4.48 illustrates this configuration in Oracle BPEL.

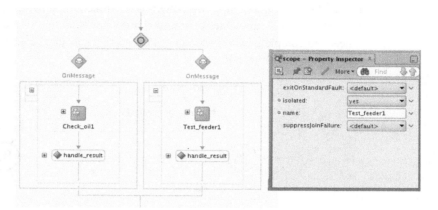

Figure 4.48
Interleaved routing configuration in Oracle BPEL.

As mentioned before, BPMone has a distinct foundation, making this pattern superfluous. At most one resource can actually work on the case at any point in time. Although interleaved routing is guaranteed, a resource can suspend a task during execution and resume work on it later. Therefore, the pattern is only partially supported. BPMN indirectly supports the pattern via an Ad-Hoc Sub-Process containing all of the Activities (and sequences of Activities) to be interleaved with ordering set to sequential. However, it is unclear what the required completionCondition should be to ensure each Activity is executed precisely once.

Critical section

Description Two or more connected subgraphs of a process model are identified as *critical sections*. At runtime for a given process instance, only tasks in one of these *critical sections* can be active at any given time. Once execution of the tasks in one *critical section* commences, it must complete before another *critical section* can commence.
Example
• Both the *take-deposit* and *insurance-payment* tasks in the holiday booking process require the exclusive use of the *credit-card-processing* machine. Consequently, only one of them can execute at any given time.
Motivation The *Critical section* pattern provides a means of preventing two or more sections of a process executing concurrently. Generally, this is necessary if tasks within a section require exclusive access to a common resource (either data or a physical resource)

necessary for a task to be completed. There are also regulatory situations (e.g., as part of due diligence or quality assurance processes) which necessitate that two tasks do not occur simultaneously.

Operation The operation of this pattern is illustrated in figure 4.49. Only one of the tasks A, B, C, F, and G can be active at any given time. Note that if one critical section starts, it needs to complete before another critical section can start (e.g., ABCFG and FGABC are allowed but AFBGC is not).

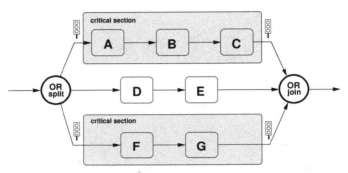

Figure 4.49
Critical section operation.

Context There are no specific considerations associated with the use of this pattern.

Implementation Although useful, this pattern is not widely supported among the offerings examined. Oracle BPEL allows it to be directly implemented through its isolated scope functionality. BPMone provides indirect support through the use of data elements as semaphores. In BPMN, there is no direct means of restricting concurrent access of two parts of a given process. A workaround is conceivable based on the use of a monitored condition (e.g., NoCriticalSectionExecuting, where each critical section is preceded by a Conditional Intermediate Event as part of the normal sequence flow, which is enabled when the critical section receives the thread of control and the monitored condition is true). Once the critical section commences, it sets the data condition to indicate a critical section is underway and resets it at its conclusion. A potential difficulty with this scheme is that checking and setting the data condition are not integrated as would be the case with traditional semaphore operations. Hence, it is conceivable that two critical sections could execute at the same time if they both received the thread of control and tested the monitored condition simultaneously.

Milestone

Description A task is only enabled when the process instance (of which it is part) is in a specific state (typically in a parallel branch). The state is assumed to be a specific execution point (also known as a *milestone*) in the process model. When this execution point is reached, the nominated task can be enabled. If the process instance has progressed beyond this state, then the task cannot be enabled (i.e., the deadline has expired) unless an execution thread returns to it at some future time as a consequence of iteration. Note that the execution does not influence the state itself (i.e., unlike normal control-flow dependencies, it is a test rather than a trigger).

Examples

- Most budget airlines allow the routing of a booking to be changed provided the ticket has not been issued.
- The *accept student enrollment* task can only execute while new enrollments are being accepted. This is after the *open enrollment* task has completed and before the *close off* enrollment task commences.

Motivation The *Milestone* pattern provides a mechanism for supporting the conditional execution of a task or subprocess (possibly on a repeated basis) where the process instance is in a given state. The notion of state is generally taken to mean that control-flow has reached a nominated point in the execution of the process instance (i.e., a *Milestone*). As such, it provides a means of synchronizing two distinct branches of a process instance, such that one branch cannot proceed unless the other branch has reached a specified state.

Operation The operation of the *Milestone* pattern is illustrated by figure 4.50. Task C cannot be enabled when it receives the thread of control unless the execution point in the top branch has reached (and not passed) the `milestone`.

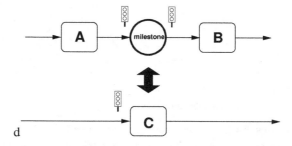

Figure 4.50
Milestone operation.

Context There are no specific context conditions for this pattern.

Implementation The necessity for an inherent notion of state within the process model means that the *Milestone* pattern is not widely supported. BPMone offers indirect support for the pattern through the introduction of a data element for each situation in which a *Milestone* is required. This data element can be updated with a value when the *Milestone* is reached, and the branch that must test for the *Milestone* achievement can do so using the BPMone milestone construct. Note that this is only possible in a data-driven system like BPMone. It is not possible to use variables this way in a classical control-flow driven system because a "busy wait" would be needed to constantly inspect the value of this variable. (Note that BPMone only reevaluates the state after each change with respect to data elements.) Figure 4.51 illustrates the configuration of the *Milestone* in BPMone. The pattern cannot be directly supported in Oracle BPEL. In BPMN, there is no direct support for conditional execution of activities based on the current state of a process. A workaround is possible based on the use of a Data Object to indicate that the process instance is in/not in a given state. The activity whose execution is conditional on the milestone is preceded by a Conditional Intermediate Event (similar to that specified for the *Critical section* pattern), which triggers the activity when it has been passed the thread of control, and the milestone Data Object is set indicating the process instance is in the required state. The various BPM systems based on Petri nets (e.g., COSA and YAWL) can easily support this pattern using a so-called self-loop (i.e., a task having the milestone place as input and output).

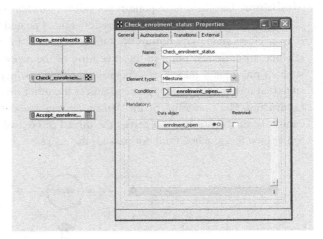

Figure 4.51
Milestone configuration in BPMone.

Issues As task C can only execute when the thread of control in the top branch is at a particular point, it is possible that a *Milestone* may cause a potential deadlock.
Solutions There are two potential solutions to this problem. One is to block task B from proceeding until task C has executed. The other is for task C to be preceded by a deferred choice construct, which provides an alternative path around the task (allowing it to be skipped) when the milestone is not enabled. The *Deferred choice* pattern is discussed in more detail in section 4.1.2.

4.7 Trigger patterns

Process execution typically does not occur in isolation from the broader operational environment in which it resides. There are a variety of situations where the execution of specific tasks within a process needs to be synchronized with or triggered by events outside of the environment in which the process operates. Therefore, two types of trigger patterns provide a way of achieving this objective. The *Transient trigger* provides a means of initiating a task on the basis of a signal from the environment once it has received the thread of control. The signal is ephemeral, and if it does not cause the immediate initiation of the task, it is lost. In other situations, the fact that the signal has occurred remains significant. This is recognized by the *Persistent trigger*, which allows triggers that have been sent to a task to be retained until the task receives the thread of control. Both patterns are discussed below.

Transient trigger

Description The ability for a task instance to be triggered by a signal from another part of the process or from the external environment. These triggers are transient in nature and are lost if not acted on immediately by the receiving task. A trigger can only be utilized if there is a task instance waiting for it at the time it is received.

Examples

- Start the *Handle Overflow* task immediately when the *dam capacity full* signal is received.
- If possible, initiate the *Check Sensor* task each time an *alarm trigger signal* is received.

Motivation Transient triggers are a common means of signaling that a pre-defined event has occurred and that an appropriate handling response should be undertaken — comprising either the initiation of a single task, a sequence of tasks, or a new thread of execution in a process. Transient triggers are events that must be dealt with as soon as they are received. In other words, they must result in the immediate initiation of a task. The process provides no form of memory for transient triggers. If they are not acted on immediately, then they are irrevocably lost.

Operation Figure 4.52 illustrates the operation of the pattern. Task A cannot proceed until it has received the required input trigger. If a trigger is sent to A and the thread of control has not yet reached the task, then the trigger is discarded.

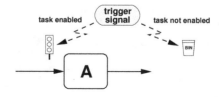

Figure 4.52
Transient trigger operation.

Context There are no specific context conditions associated with the pattern.

Implementation BPMN supports the pattern via a Message Event attached to an activity or inline within a Process. BPMone provides the ability for tasks to wait on specific data conditions that can be updated from outside the process. However, there is no direct means of testing for task enablement and immediately resetting the data condition where the task is not enabled. Oracle BPEL provides a mechanism for task triggering based on messages. However, all messages are assumed to be durable in form.

Issues One consideration that arises with the use of transient triggers is what happens when multiple triggers are received simultaneously or in a short time interval. Are the latter triggers inherently lost as a trigger instance is already pending or are all instances preserved (albeit for a potentially short timeframe)?

Solutions Although the offerings described above do not give any indication in this regard, for many other systems examined as part of the *Workflow Patterns Initiative* that do support transient triggers (cf. Staffware 10, COSA 5.1), it seems that in general transient triggers are lost if they are not immediately consumed. There is no provision for transient triggers to be duplicated.

Persistent trigger

Description The ability for a task instance to be triggered by a signal from another part of the process or from the external environment. These triggers are persistent in form and are retained by the process instance, for as long as it continues to execute, in the expectation they can be acted on by the receiving task at some future time.

Examples

- Initiate the *Staff Induction* task each time a *new staff member* event occurs.
- Start a new instance of the *Inspect Vehicle* task for each *service overdue* signal that is received.

Motivation Persistent triggers are inherently durable in nature, ensuring that they are not lost in transit and are buffered until they can be dealt with by the target task.

Operation Figure 4.53 illustrates the operation of a persistent trigger. In this case, all triggers are retained and consumed one by one when the thread of control reaches task A.

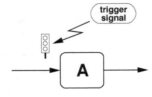

Figure 4.53
Persistent trigger operation.

Context There are no specific context conditions associated with the pattern.

Implementation BPMone provides the ability for tasks to wait on specific data conditions that can be updated from outside the process. Oracle BPEL provides a mechanism for this form of triggering via messages, and in all cases, the messages are assumed to be durable in nature, and can either trigger a stand-alone task or can enable a blocked task waiting on receipt of a message to continue. Figure 4.54 illustrates the configuration of the pattern in these offerings. In BPMN, message events are transient in nature, and no means is provided of buffering them for later consumption.

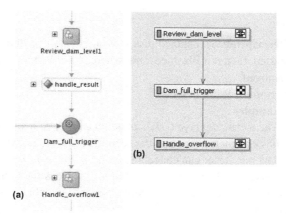

Figure 4.54
Persistent trigger configuration in (a) Oracle BPEL, and (b) BPMone.

4.8   Cancelation and completion patterns

A common requirement in the execution of business processes is to be able to cancel some (or all) of the tasks in a process instance on a selective basis. Generally, the cancelation action is linked to the process instance reaching a specified state (i.e., a certain task being executed), although in some situations (e.g., cancelation of an entire case), the triggering event can originate from outside of the process instance.

A variety of concepts fall under the notion of cancelation, depending on the extent of the cancelation action and the type of tasks that are being canceled. Consequently, there are five distinct patterns recognizing desirable capabilities in this area.

The five cancelation and completion patterns are:

- **Cancel task**, where a specific task instance is withdrawn when the process instance reaches a specified state;
- **Cancel multiple instance task**, where all instances of a multiple task instance are withdrawn when the process instance reaches a specified state;
- **Complete multiple instance task**, where the remaining instances of a multiple task instance are withdrawn when the process instance reaches a specified state (and, where relevant, subsequent tasks in the process are triggered);

- **Cancel region**, where all of the task instances in a specified part of the process are withdrawn when the process instance reaches a specified state; and
- **Cancel case**, where all of the task instances in a process are withdrawn.

Each of these patterns is discussed in further detail below.

Cancel task

Description An enabled task is withdrawn prior to or during its execution. If the task has started, then it is disabled, and, where possible, the currently running instance is halted and removed.

Synonym Withdraw task.

Examples

- The *assess damage* task is undertaken by two insurance assessors. Once the first assessor has completed the task, the second is canceled; and
- The purchaser can cancel the *building inspection* task at any time before it commences.

Motivation The *Cancel task* pattern provides the ability to withdraw a task that has been enabled or is already executing. This ensures that it will not commence or complete execution.

Operation The operation of the *Cancel task* pattern is illustrated by figure 4.55. When task A completes, any instances of task B that are currently executing (in the same process instance) are canceled. The cancelation of B involves removing any executing instances and also removing any references to it that may exist on users' task lists. Any tasks subsequent to B are not enabled as a result of the cancelation.

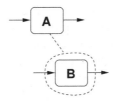

Figure 4.55
Cancel task operation.

Context There are no specific context conditions associated with the pattern.

Implementation The majority of the offerings examined provide support for this pattern within their process models. Oracle BPEL supports it using fault or compensation handlers attached to tasks, as does BPMN, which uses a Signal Event attached to the boundary of the activity to be canceled, which allows the cancelation to be initiated from anywhere within the process without it escalating beyond the intended activity instance. BPMone does not directly support the pattern, although tasks can be skipped and redone. Figure 4.56 illustrates the configuration of the pattern in Oracle BPEL, and BPMN.

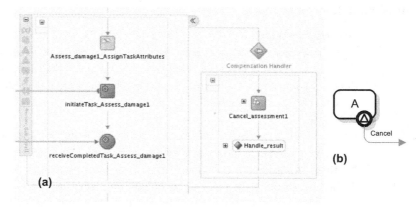

Figure 4.56
Cancel task pattern configuration in (a) Oracle BPEL, and (b) BPMN.

Issues It is important to note that cancelation is not guaranteed, and it is possible that the task will continue executing to completion. In effect, the cancelation versus continuation decision operates as a *Deferred choice*, with a race condition being set up between the cancelation event and the much slower alternative where the resource to whom the task is assigned completes it before the cancelation is processed.

Solutions In general, it is not possible to guarantee task cancelation. For all practical purposes however, it is much more likely that the cancelation will be effected than the user be able to complete it once the withdrawal has been initiated.

The *Cancel task* pattern handles the cancelation of atomic tasks. Where the task being canceled can potentially have multiple concurrent instances (i.e., it is a multiple instance task), two specific patterns deal with the early termination of associated task instances:

- *Cancel multiple instance task* acts as a *hard* cancelation of all task instances. It completely removes all task instances (enabled and executing) and does not pass on the thread of control to any subsequent tasks.
- *Complete multiple instance task* acts as a *soft* cancelation. It cancels any enabled or executing task instances but leaves any completed instances unaffected. The thread of control is passed on to subsequent tasks.

In effect, the first of these patterns operates as a cancelation operator for multiple instance tasks, removing any consequences of their execution, whereas the second only seeks to terminate their execution but leaves any work completed to that point intact. An additional difference between them is that MI task execution is reported as unsuccessful in the former situation but successful in the latter. The details of these two patterns are discussed subsequently.

Cancel multiple instance task

Description Within a given process instance, multiple instances of a task can be created. These instances are independent of each other and run concurrently. At any time, the multiple instance task can be canceled, and any instances that have not completed are withdrawn. Task instances that have already completed are unaffected. No tasks subsequent to the canceled task are enabled.

Example

- Run 500 instances of the *Protein Test* task with distinct samples. If any of these instances have not completed one hour after commencement, cancel them.

Motivation This pattern provides a means of canceling a multiple instance task at any time during its execution such that any remaining instances are canceled. No new instances may start; however, any instances that have already completed are unaffected by the cancelation.

Operation The operation of the *Cancel multiple instance task* pattern is illustrated by figure 4.57. When task A is enabled, any instances of task B that are currently executing (in the same process instance) are canceled. The cancelation of B involves removing any executing instances and also removing any references to them that may exist on users' task lists. Any tasks subsequent to B (i.e., task C) are not enabled as a result of the cancelation. The various instances of the canceled task (i.e., B_1, B_2, B_3) are not considered to have completed successfully (e.g., they are recorded as unsuccessful in the log).

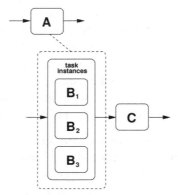

Figure 4.57
Cancel multiple instance task operation.

Context There is one context condition associated with this pattern: it is assumed that only one instance of each multiple instance task is executing for a given case at any time.

Implementation In order to implement this pattern, an offering also needs to support one of the Multiple instance patterns that provide synchronization of the task instances at completion (see section 4.5 for details). BPMN supports the pattern via a Multiple Instances Activity, which has a Signal Event attached to its boundary. When the Multiple Instances

Activity is to be canceled, a Signal Event is triggered to terminate any remaining instances. Oracle BPEL is able to support the pattern by associating a fault or compensation handler with a For Each activity. There is no ability to cancel multiple instance tasks in BPMone. Figure 4.58 illustrates the configuration of the pattern in Oracle BPEL and BPMN.

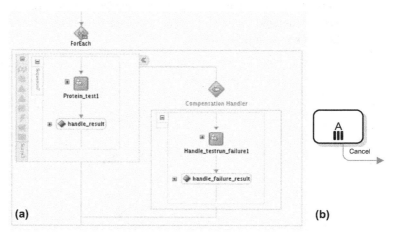

Figure 4.58
Cancel MI task pattern configuration in (a) Oracle BPEL, and (b) BPMN.

Complete multiple instance task

Description Within a given process instance, multiple instances of a task can be created. These instances are independent of each other and run concurrently. It is necessary to synchronize the instances at completion before any subsequent tasks can be triggered. During the course of execution, it is possible that the task needs to be forcibly completed such that any remaining instances are withdrawn and the thread of control is passed to subsequent tasks.

Examples

- Run 500 instances of the *Protein Test* task with distinct samples. One hour after commencement, withdraw all remaining instances and initiate the next task.

Motivation This pattern provides a means of finalizing a multiple instance task that has not yet completed at any time during its execution, such that any remaining instances are withdrawn and the thread of control is immediately passed to subsequent tasks. No new instances may start. Any instances that have already completed are unaffected by the cancelation.

Operation The operation of the *Complete multiple instance task* pattern is illustrated by figure 4.59. When task A completes, any instances of task B that are enabled (in the same process instance) are canceled. The completion of B involves removing any enabled and executing instances. Any instances that have already completed executing (in this example, task instance B_2) are unaffected. Any tasks subsequent to B (i.e., task C) are enabled once the completion is triggered. Any instances of the force completed task that had completed execution prior to the completion action are considered to have executed successfully (e.g., task instance B_2), and any canceled instances (e.g., B_1, B_3) are not considered to have completed successfully. These considerations are also reflected in associated entries in the execution log.

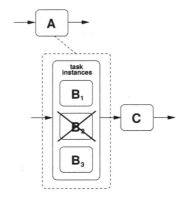

Figure 4.59
Complete multiple instance task operation.

Context There is one context condition associated with this pattern: only one instance of a multiple instance task can execute at any time.

Implementation In order to implement this pattern, an offering also needs to support one of the Multiple Instance patterns that provide synchronization of the task instances at completion. BPMN provides direct support for the pattern by specifying a completionCondition expression for a Multiple Instances Activity that can be set to true when required (e.g., by including an OR clause that tests whether a nominated Data Object is set). When the Data Object is set, the Activity is completed when the next instance completes successfully, any remaining activity instances are canceled, and subsequent Activites are triggered. BPMone provides indirect support for this pattern via the auto-complete condition on dynamic plans, which force-completes unfinished plans when the condition evaluates to true. However, this can only occur when all subplans have completed. Similarly, it also provides deadline support for dynamic plans, which ensures that all remaining instances are forced completed once the deadline is reached. However, this action also causes all subsequent tasks to be force completed as well. Oracle BPEL does not provide any means of force completing a multiple instance task (or indeed any other form of task).

The task cancelation patterns provide support for the withdrawal of individual task instances, but they do not scale well where a number of tasks in a process are subject to cancelation at the same time. For this reason, we introduce the *Cancel region* pattern.

Cancel region

Description The ability to disable a set of tasks in a process instance. If any of the tasks are already executing (or are currently enabled), then they are withdrawn. The tasks need not be a connected subset of the overall process model.

Examples

- Stop any tasks in the *Prosecution* process that access the *evidence* database from running.
- Withdraw all tasks in the *Waybill Booking* process after the *freight-lodgement* task.

Motivation The option of being able to cancel a series of (potentially unrelated) tasks is a useful capability, particularly when handling unexpected errors.

Operation The operation of the *Cancel region* pattern is illustrated by figure 4.60. When task A is enabled, any instances of tasks B, C, and G that are enabled or running (in the same process instance) are canceled. Once the cancelation action has been effected, no tasks subsequent to those canceled are enabled as a result of the cancelation action.

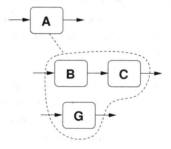

Figure 4.60
Cancel region operation.

Context There are no specific context conditions associated with the pattern.

Implementation The concept of cancelation regions is not widely supported. BPMone allows individual tasks to be skipped, but there is no means of canceling a group of tasks. BPMN offers partial support by enclosing the Activities that will potentially be canceled in a Sub-Process Activity and associating a Signal Event with the Sub-Process to trigger cancelation when it is required. The shortcoming of this approach is that the tasks in the subprocess must be a connected subgraph of the overall process model. Similarly, Oracle

BPEL only supports cancelation of tasks in the same scope. Hence, it only partially supports the ability to cancel an arbitrary group of tasks. YAWL is one of the few systems that fully supports this concept.

Issues One issue that can arise with the implementation of the *Cancel region* pattern occurs when the canceling task lies within the cancelation region. Although this task must run to completion and cause the cancelation of all of the tasks in the defined cancelation region, once this has been completed, it too must be canceled.

Solutions The most effective solution to this problem is to ensure that the canceling task is the last of those to be processed (i.e., the last to be terminated) of the tasks in the cancelation region. The actual cancelation should occur when the task to which the cancelation region is attached completes execution.

The flexibility of the *Cancel region* pattern makes it useful in a wide variety of situations when dealing with cancelation requirements. One scenario that merits further discussion is when an entire case is canceled. This involves not only the withdrawal of a series of individual task instances but also the bookkeeping associated with the removal of the case. Unlike the other cancelation/completion patterns, this event may need to be triggered either from within or outside of a process instance. Consequently, a distinct pattern is merited for this purpose — *Cancel case* — which we discuss next.

Cancel case

Description A complete process instance is removed. This includes currently executing tasks, those that may execute at some future time and all subprocesses. The process instance is recorded as having completed unsuccessfully.

Synonym Withdraw case.

Examples

- During an *insurance claim* process, it is discovered that the policy has expired. As a consequence, all tasks associated with the particular process instance are canceled.
- During a *mortgage application*, the purchaser decides not to continue with a house purchase and withdraws the application.

Motivation This pattern provides a means of halting a specified process instance and withdrawing any task instances associated with it.

Operation Cancelation of an entire case involves the withdrawal of all currently enabled task instances in a process instance. The cancelation may be initiated either from within the process instance or from the external environment.

Context There is an important context condition associated with this pattern: cancelation of an executing case must be viewed as unsuccessful completion of the case. This means that although the case was terminated in an orderly manner, this should not be interpreted in any way as a successful outcome. For example, where a log is kept of events occurring during process execution, the case should be recorded as incomplete or canceled.

Implementation There is reasonable support for this pattern among the offerings examined: Oracle BPEL provides the Exit activity for this purpose. BPMN provides support via the Terminate End Event that allows all executing Activities in a process instance to be terminated. BPMone provides partial support for the pattern through its ability to skip or redo entire cases.

The cancelation and completion patterns deal with exceptional situations that necessitate the removal of particular task or process instances. In contrast, the final group of control-flow patterns focus on the issue of case termination, an event that occurs for every process instance.

4.9   Termination patterns

A process instance can terminate in two distinct ways. One possibility is that it can be deemed to have finished when there is no more work to be done, either now or at any future time, for the process instance. The alternative option is that it can be considered to have completed when a specific state is reached in the process. These two scenarios provide the basis for the two termination patterns: *Explicit termination* and *Implicit termination*, discussed subsequently.

Explicit termination

Description A given process (or subprocess) instance should terminate when it reaches a nominated state. Typically this is denoted by one or more specific end nodes. When one of these end nodes is reached, any remaining work in the process instance is withdrawn, and the overall process instance is recorded as having completed successfully, regardless of whether there are any tasks in progress or remaining to be executed.

Example

- The example in figure 4.61 has two end nodes. Once the thread of control reaches one of these end nodes, the process instance is deemed complete, and all other work items associated with it are withdrawn.

Motivation The rationale for this pattern is that it represents a deterministic means of defining when a process instance can be designated as complete. This is when the thread of control reaches a defined state within the process model. Typically this is denoted by one or more designated termination nodes at the end of the model. Where there is a single end node in a process, its inclusion in other compositions is simplified.

Operation When a nominated state is reached in the process instance, typically this takes the form of one or more specified end nodes, the process instance is deemed complete, and all remaining task instances and execution threads are withdrawn.

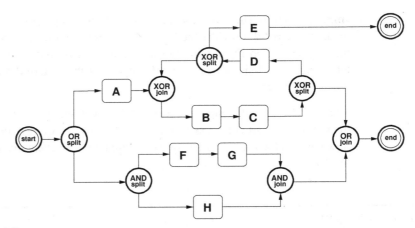

Figure 4.61
Explicit termination example.

Context There is one context condition associated with this pattern: every task in a process model must be on a path from a designated start node to a designated end node.

Implementation None of the offerings examined supports this pattern.

Issues One consideration that does arise where a process model has multiple end nodes is whether it can be transformed to one with a single end node.

Solutions For simple process models, it may be possible to simply replace all of the end nodes for a process model with links to an OR-join, which then links to a single final node. Another approach, not using the OR-join, is described in [73], where it is shown how a so-called "standard workflow" with multiple endpoints that is safe and always terminates can be transformed to an equivalent standard workflow with a unique endpoint. However, it is less clear for more complex process models involving multiple instance tasks whether they are always able to be converted to a model with a single terminating node.

Implicit termination

Description A given process (or subprocess) instance should terminate when there are no remaining work items that are able to be done either now or at any time in the future and the process instance is not in deadlock. There is an objective means of determining that the process instance has successfully completed.

Example

- In the example shown in figure 4.62, three distinct ending scenarios are possible: (1) complete after task F, (2) complete after task K, and (3) complete after task F and K. *Implicit termination* offers an effective way of determining when the process is complete as there is no single end task and there are several possible ending scenarios.

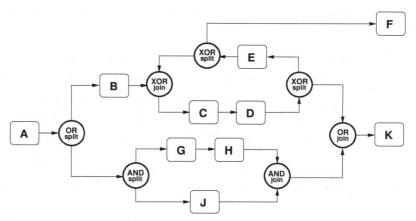

Figure 4.62
Implicit termination example.

Motivation The rationale for this pattern is that it represents the most realistic approach to determining when a process instance can be designated as complete. This is when there is no remaining work to be completed as part of it, and it is not possible that new work items will arise at some future time.

Operation The operation of this pattern is simple: once there are no remaining work items for a process instance and it is not possible that any new work items will arise at some future time, the case is deemed complete.

Context There are no specific context conditions associated with this pattern.

Implementation BPMone, Oracle BPEL, and BPMN all support this pattern.

Issues Where an offering does not directly support this pattern, the question arises as to whether it can implement a process model that has been developed based on the notion of *Explicit termination* (i.e., there needs to be an explicit task ending the case).

Solutions For simple process models, it may be possible to indirectly achieve the same effect by replacing all of the end nodes for a process with links to an OR-join, which then links to a single final node. However, it is less clear for more complex process models involving multiple instance tasks whether they are always able to be converted to a model with a single terminating node.

It is worthwhile noting that some languages do not offer this construct on purpose: the *Implicit termination* pattern makes it difficult (or even impossible) to distinguish proper termination from deadlock. Often it is only through examination of the process log that it is possible to determine whether a particular case has actually finished. Additionally, processes without explicit endpoints are more difficult to use in compositions.

4.10   Further reading

The following papers provide further background on some of the more complex issues raised in this chapter and are recommended as useful additional readings:

- [14] is the seminal Workflow Patterns paper that first motivated the use of the patterns as a means of delineating generic control-flow constructs. It identified twenty patterns relevant to the control-flow perspective of workflow systems and analyzed their implementation in fifteen commercial and research workflow systems. It triggered research efforts into the use of the patterns to evaluate the capabilities of a series of business process modeling languages and (proposed) web services standards. Subsequent efforts in this area used the twenty control-flow patterns to examine the control-flow capabilities of UML activity diagrams (both versions 1.4 and 2.0) [44, 114, 140], BPEL4WS [139], BML [141], and BPMN [97, 137, 142].
- The Vicious Circle paradox illustrating semantic problems related to looking ahead when determining the enabling of tasks is described in [9] and [75].
- [106], in which Rittgen proposes a means of OR-join implementation based on the direct communication of the number of active branches from a preceding divergence to the OR-join.
- [79], in which the notion of "dead path elimination" was introduced as an approach to OR-join evaluation in early IBM workflow offerings (e.g., FlowMark). This concept was subsequently subsumed in BPEL4WS.
- [74], in which Kiepuszewski et al. present a comprehensive discussion of the issues associated with structured workflows.
- [73], in which Kiepuszewski et al. examine a number of fundamental issues associated with the control-flow perspective in workflow systems, including consideration of issues such as termination semantics and the possibilities for semantically equivalent process model transformation.
- [148], in which Wynn et al. propose a general strategy for OR-join evaluation. The journal version of this article also investigates a series of optimization approaches for improving its operational performance. There are a multitude of articles about the OR-join (e.g., [43, 82, 130]).
- [1], in which van der Aalst discusses the application of Petri nets for describing the control-flow perspective of workflow and verifying their operational characteristics. See [11] for an overview of the state-of-the-art results in workflow verification.

5 Data Patterns

The control-flow forms the backbone of any process. However, it has long been recognized that the effective capture, management, and dissemination of data is a key part of any business process, and consequently the data perspective is identified as a first-class citizen (along with the control-flow perspective) in most contemporary BPM offerings. However, although the area of data modeling is well understood, there is less clarity associated with the features and capabilities necessary to support effective data utilization by business processes. Many process automation tools do not manage application data but leave this problem with the underlying application systems that they coordinate. Indeed one can divide data into two groups: data that is directly under the control of a BPM offering and data that is outside the BPM offering (but accessible from within it). The *data patterns* described in this chapter aim to describe the features and capabilities needed to support the handling of data in a process-oriented setting.

Section 5.1 provides an overview of the data patterns. As shown, they can be divided in four distinct groups. Section 5.2 describes the *data visibility patterns*. These describe the extent and manner in which data elements can be accessed and utilized. For example, a variable may only be visible within a particular scope of a single process instance, whereas another variable may be shared among different process instances. The *data interaction patterns*, described in section 5.3, focus on the manner in which data is communicated between active elements within a process. For example, there is a pattern describing the capability that allows the environment to push data into the process without a request from the process itself. The *data transfer patterns* are presented in section 5.4 and focus on the actual transfer of data (e.g., data transfer by value, data transfer by reference, locking, etc.). The *data-based routing patterns* described in section 5.5 connect the control-flow to the data-flow. For example, tasks may have preconditions or postconditions, and choices are often driven by data elements. Section 5.6 concludes the chapter by pointing out related work.

5.1 Overview of the data patterns

This chapter examines the range of concepts that apply to the representation and utilization of data within business processes. These concepts not only define the manner in which data in its various forms can be employed within a business process and the range of informational concepts that it is able to capture but also characterize the interaction of data elements with other process and environmental constructs. They are derived from a broad survey of contemporary process technology standards and tools, which suggests that the way in which data is structured and utilized within these offerings has a number of common characteristics. These can be divided into four distinct groups:

- **Data visibility** patterns, which relate to the extent and manner in which data elements can be accessed and utilized by various components in a process;
- **Data interaction** patterns, which focus on the manner in which data is communicated between active elements within a process;
- **Data transfer** patterns, which consider the means by which the actual transfer of data elements occurs between process elements and describe the various mechanisms by which data elements can be passed across the interface of a specific process element; and
- **Data-based routing** patterns, which characterize the manner in which data elements can influence the operation of other aspects of a process, particularly the control-flow perspective.

Each of these groups is discussed in detail in the following sections, starting with data visibility patterns.

5.2   Data visibility patterns

Within the context of a process, there are a variety of distinct ways in which data elements can be defined and utilized. Typically these variations relate to the process construct to which they are anchored (which in turn influences the scope in which they are accessible). More important, they directly influence the way in which the data element may be used (e.g., to capture *production* information, to manage *control* data, or for *communication* with the external environment). This section considers each of the potential contexts in which a data construct can be defined and utilized.

Task data

Description Data elements can be defined by tasks that are accessible only within the context of individual execution instances of that task.

Example

- The *working trajectory* variable is only used within the *Calculate Flight Path* task.

Motivation To provide data support for local operations at the task level. Typically these data elements are used to provide working storage during task execution for control data or intermediate results when manipulating production data.

Overview Figure 5.1 illustrates the declaration of a task data element (variable X in task B) and the scope in which it can be utilized (shown by the shaded region and the use() function). Note that it has a distinct existence (and potential value) for each instance of task B (e.g., in this example, it is instantiated once for each process instance because task B is executed at most once per instance).

Context There are no specific context conditions associated with this pattern.

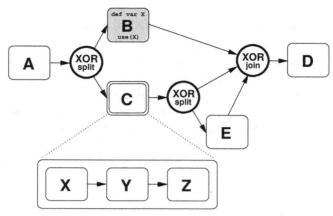

Figure 5.1
Task-level data visibility.

Implementation The implementation of task data takes one of two forms: either data elements are defined as parameters to the task, making them available for use within the task, or they are declared within the definition of the task itself. In either case, they are bound in scope to the task block and have a lifetime that corresponds to that of the execution of an instance of that task. BPMN directly supports the notion of task data via Activity Properties that serve as item-aware elements for storing data elements during the execution of an Activity. BPMone and Oracle BPEL provide indirect support by allowing data elements with greater scope to have their visibility restricted to a single task. BPMone supports the pattern using the restricted attribute for a data element that allows the places that it can be updated to be specified. Oracle BPEL associates a data element with a scope activity that limits its extent of usage to the defined block. For a task data element, this block must only contain one task.

Issues One difficulty that can arise is the potential for a task to declare a data element with the same name as another data element declared elsewhere at a different level within the process hierarchy (e.g., a surrounding scope, block, case, global) that can be accessed from within the task. This phenomenon is often referred to as "name clash."

A second issue that may require consideration can arise when a task is able to execute more than once (e.g., in the case of a multi-merge). When the second (or later) instance commences, should the data elements contain the values from the first instance or should they be re-initialized?

Solutions The first issue can be addressed through the use of a tight binding approach at the task level, restricting the use of data elements within the task to those explicitly declared by the task itself and those passed to the task as formal parameters. All of these data element names must be unique within the context of the task.

An alternative approach is employed in Oracle BPEL, which only allows access to the data element with the innermost scope in the event of name clashes. Indeed, this approach is proposed as a mechanism of "hiding" data elements from outer scopes by declaring another with the same name at the task level.

The second issue is not a major consideration for most offerings that initialize data elements at the commencement of each task instance. One exception to this is BPMone, which provides the option for a task instance that comprises part of a loop in a process to either refresh data elements on each iteration or retain their values from the previous instance (in the preceding or indeed any previous loop iteration).

Block data

Description Block tasks (i.e., tasks that can be described in terms of a corresponding subprocess) are able to define data elements that are accessible by each of the components of the corresponding subprocess.

Example

- All components of the subprocess that defines the *Assess Investment Risk* block task can utilize the *security details* data element.

Motivation The manner in which a block task is implemented is usually defined by its decomposition, which takes the form of a subprocess. It is desirable that data elements available in the context of the undecomposed block task are available to all of the components that make up the corresponding subprocess. Similarly, it is useful if there is the ability to define new data elements within the context of the subprocess that can be utilized by each of its components during execution.

Overview Figure 5.2 illustrates both of these scenarios. Data element M is declared at the level of the block task C and is accessible both within the block task instance and tasks X, Y, and Z in the corresponding subprocess. Similarly, data element N is declared within the context of the subprocess and is available to all task instances in the subprocess. Depending on the actual offering, it may also be accessible at the level of the corresponding block task.

Context There are no specific context conditions associated with this pattern.

Implementation The concept of block data is widely supported, and generally most offerings that support the notion of subprocesses implement it in some form. BPMone provides facilities for specifying data elements within the context of a subprocess. BPMN also does so via the Data Objects and Properties associated with a given Process or Sub-Process, which can be accessed throughout the Process or Sub-Process and within any associated Tasks or throughout any nested Sub-Processes. Oracle BPEL supports the incorporation of BPEL processes as components within a BPEL process via its Service Component Architecture (SCA), which supports a BPEL process being constructed in terms of other service-oriented technologies. These BPEL process elements are in effect subprocesses and have their own set of variables that serve as block variables within the subprocess.

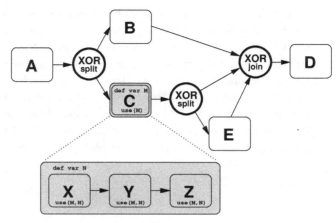

Figure 5.2
Block-level data visibility.

Issues A major issue associated with the use of block-level data is in managing concurrent access to it by distinct task instances in a case.

Another consideration in regard to block-structured tasks within a process is the handling of block data visibility, where cascading block decompositions are supported and data elements are implicitly inherited by subprocesses. As an example, in the preceding diagram, block data sharing would enable a data element declared within the context of task C to be utilized by task X, but if X were also a block task, would this data element also be accessible to task instances in the subprocess corresponding to X?

Solutions In order to ensure that usage of shared data elements by concurrent process elements does not lead to inconsistencies, Oracle BPEL provides the isolated flag, which when set enforces that access to any data elements associated with a scope or block is synchronized. BPMone and BPMN do not provide any facilities in this regard.

In terms of the second issue, the workflow tool Staffware deals with this by only allowing one level of block data inheritance by default (i.e., data elements declared in task instance C are implicitly available to X, Y, and Z but not to further subprocess decompositions). Where further cascading of data elements is required, this must be specifically catered to.

Scope data

Description Data elements can be defined that are accessible by a subset of the tasks in a case. The tasks do not necessarily need to reside within the same block within the process.

Example

- The *initial tax estimate* variable is only used within the *Gather Return Data*, *Examine Similar Claims*, and *Prepare Initial Return* tasks in the *Prepare Tax Return* process.

Motivation Where several tasks within a process coordinate their actions around a common data element or set of data elements, it is useful to be able to define data elements that are bound to that subset of tasks in the overall process.

Overview One of the major justifications for the use of scopes in processes is that they provide a means of binding data elements, error, and compensation handlers to sets of related tasks within a case. This allows for more localized forms of recovery action to be undertaken in the event that errors or concurrency issues are detected. Figure 5.3 illustrates the declaration of data element X, which is scoped to tasks A, B, and C. It can be freely accessed by these tasks but is not available to tasks D and E.

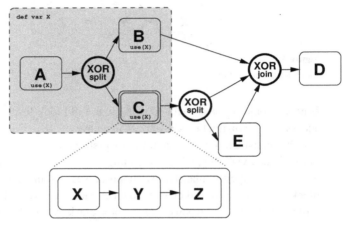

Figure 5.3
Scope-level data visibility.

Context There are no specific context conditions associated with this pattern.

Implementation The definition of scope data elements requires the ability to define the portion of the process to which the data elements are bound. This is potentially difficult in process descriptions that are based on a graphical process notation but less difficult for those that utilize a textual definition format such as XML particularly, where elements within a scope are not adjacent and lie in different parts of a process.

A significant distinction between scopes and blocks in a process context is that scopes provide a grouping mechanism within the same address space (or context) as the surrounding case elements. They do not define a new address space, and data passing to tasks within the scope does not rely on any specific data passing mechanisms other than normal task-to-task data transfer facilities.

Oracle BPEL is the only offering examined that fully supports the notion of scope data elements. It provides support for a scope construct, which allows related tasks, variables, and exception handlers to be logically grouped together. BPMone supports "restricted data elements," which can have their values set by nominated tasks, although they are more widely readable.

Issues The potential exists for variables named within a scope to have the same name as a variable in the surrounding block in which the scope is defined.

Solutions The default handling for this in Oracle BPEL is that the innermost context in which a variable is defined indicates which variable should be used in any given situation. Variables within a given scope must be unique.

Multiple instance data

Description Tasks that are able to execute multiple times within a single case can define data elements that are specific to an individual execution instance.

Example

- Each instance of the *Expert Assessment* task is provided with the *case history* and *test results* at commencement and manages its own *working notes* until it returns a *verdict* at completion.

Motivation Where a task executes multiple times, it is useful to be able to define a set of data elements that are specific to each individual execution instance. The values of these elements may be passed to the task instance at commencement, and at the conclusion of its execution, they can be made available (either on an individual basis or as part of an aggregated data element) to subsequent tasks. There are three distinct scenarios in which a task could be executed more than once:

1. Where a particular task is designated as a "multiple instance task" (i.e., the process modeling language provides a specific construct for denoting controlled task concurrency), and once it is enabled, multiple instances of it are initiated simultaneously (see also the multiple instance patterns in section 4.5).
2. Where distinct tasks in a process share the same implementation.
3. Where a task can receive multiple initiation triggers (i.e., several distinct instances can be started) during the operation of a case (see the multi-merge pattern in section 4.3.2).

Overview Each of these scenarios is illustrated in figure 5.4. In the top left-hand diagram, task E illustrates a multiple instance task. In the bottom left-hand diagram, task D is invoked twice (once after task B completes and also when task C or E completes). In the right-hand diagram, tasks C and E both share the same implementation that is defined by the subprocess containing tasks X and Y. In each of the cases shown, it is important that every execution has its private set of variables (so that things are not mixed up).

Context There are no specific context conditions associated with this pattern.

Implementation The ability to support distinct data elements in multiple task instances presumes the offering is also able to support data elements that can be bound specifically

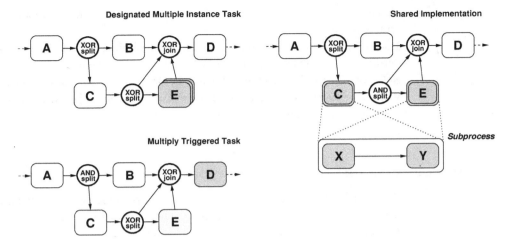

Figure 5.4
Alternative implementations of multiple instance tasks.

to individual tasks (i.e., *Task data*) in some form. Offerings lacking this capability are unable to facilitate the isolation of data elements between task instances for any of the scenarios identified above. In addition to this, there are also other prerequisites for individual scenarios as described below.

In order to support multiple instance data in the first of the scenarios identified above, the offering must also support designated multiple instance tasks, and it must provide facilities for composite data elements (e.g., arrays) to be split up and allocated to individual task instances for use during their execution and for these data elements to be subsequently recombined for use by later tasks.

The second scenario requires the offering to provide task-level data binding and support the capability for a given task to be able to receive multiple triggers, each of which results in a distinct execution instance (cf. the *Multi-merge* pattern). Each of the instances should have a mutually distinct set of data elements that can receive data passed from preceding tasks and pass them to subsequent tasks.

For the third scenario, it must be possible for two or more distinct block tasks to share the same implementation (i.e., the same underlying subprocess), and the offering must support block-level data. Additionally, these data elements must be able to be allocated values at commencement of the subprocess and for their values to be passed back to the calling (block) task once the subprocess has completed execution.

Of the various multiple instance scenarios identified, BPMone provides support for the first of them via its dynamic subplan construct. Oracle BPEL also supports the first scenario via the For Each activity, which allows multiple concurrent instances of a task to be initiated, each of which has its own set of distinct variables. Moreover, each instance can access a distinct value of a counter attribute, which can potentially serve as an index into a composite data element in the surrounding block, allowing each instance to utilize a distinct part of the data it contains. It also supports the third option, where a BPEL process component is included more than once as an element of a given BPEL process. BPMN can support all three scenarios. The individual properties associated with a task are unique to each task instance. Where multiple tasks share the same implementation via a Call Activity, the Properties or Data Objects are unique to each instance of the Call Activity. Multiple Instances Activities operate over a collection of data elements, with individual instances receiving a distinct element from the collection for processing.

Case data

Description Data elements are supported that are specific to a process instance or case. They can be accessed by all components of the process during the execution of the case.

Example

- The *employee assessment results* can be accessed by all of the tasks during this execution instance of the *Performance Assessment* workflow.

Motivation Data elements defined at the case level effectively provide global data storage during the execution of a specific case. Through their use, data can be made accessible to all process components without the need to explicitly denote the means by which it is passed between them.

Overview Figure 5.5 illustrates the use of the case-level data element X, which can be utilized by all of the tasks throughout a process (including those in subprocesses).

Context There are no specific context conditions associated with this pattern.

Implementation Most offerings support the notion of case data in some form. However, the approaches to its implementation vary widely. BPMN supports case data through Data Objects and Properties associated with a given Process, which can be accessed throughout the Process and within any associated Tasks or throughout any nested Sub-Processes. In BPMone, the default binding for data elements is at the case level, and they are visible to all of the components in a process. For Oracle BPEL, data elements defined at the level of the root BPEL process are accessible throughout the process instance.

Issues One consideration associated with case data is ensuring that case-level data elements are accessible, where required, to the components of a subprocess associated with a specific case (e.g., as part of the definition of a block task).

Solutions This issue can be addressed in one of two ways. In some offerings, subprocesses that are linked to a process model do not seem to be considered to be part of the same execution context as the main process. To remedy this issue, some tools (e.g., Staffware)

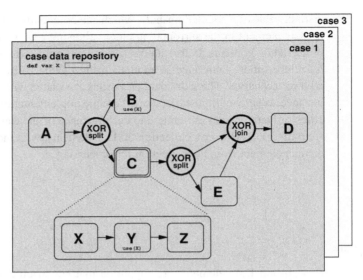

Figure 5.5
Case-level data visibility.

require that case-level data elements be explicitly passed to and from subprocesses as parameters in order to make them visible to the various components at this level. An alternative approach is to make these data elements visible to all subprocesses by default, as is the situation in BPMone.

Folder data

Description Data elements can be defined that are accessible by multiple cases on a selective basis. They are accessible to all components of the cases to which they are bound.
Example
- Selected instances of the *Approve Travel Request* task can access the *current cash reserves* data element regardless of the case in which they execute, provided they nominate the folder they require at case initiation.

Motivation Folder data provides a mechanism for sharing a data element between related task instances in different cases. This is particularly useful where tasks in multiple cases are working on a related problem and require access to common working data elements. Such data elements can also be used to dynamically configure the process for selected groups of cases (e.g., some checks are skipped when a folder variable is set to high).
Overview Figure 5.6 illustrates the notion of folder data. In essence, "folders" of related data elements are declared in the context of a process model prior to the execution of individual cases. Individual cases are able to nominate one or more of these "folders" that

their task instances should have access to during execution. Access may be read-only or read-write. In figure 5.6, two folders are declared (A and B) containing data elements X and Y, respectively. During the course of execution, case 1 and case 2 have access to folder A, whereas case 3 has access to both folders A and B. As there is only one copy of each folder maintained, should any of case 1, case 2, or case 3 execute concurrently, they will in effect share access to data element X. As a general rule, for folder data to be useful in an offering, the cardinality of the accessibility relationship between folders and cases needs to be m-n (i.e., data elements in a given folder need to be accessible to more than one case, and a given case needs to be able to access more than one data folder during execution). This implies that where two or more folders share the same naming convention for data elements, a given case can only access the variables in one of these folders at a time (otherwise it would not be possible to distinguish between the folders). In order to manage this situation, it is useful if cases can request access to additional folders during execution and relinquish access to folders they no longer need.

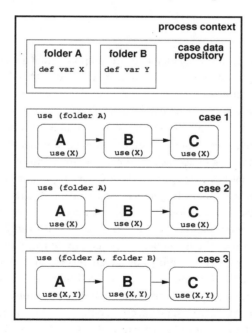

Figure 5.6
Folder data visibility.

Context There are no specific context conditions associated with this pattern.
Implementation None of the offerings examined implements this pattern. However, the COSA workflow system does offer the facility to share data elements between cases on a selective basis. It achieves this by allowing each case to be associated with a folder at

commencement. At any time during execution of the case, it is possible for the current folder to be changed. The type of access (read-only or read-write) and a range of access controls can be specified for each folder at design time. It is also possible to use folders as repositories for more complex data elements such as documents.

Issues As each folder defines its own context, one consideration that arises when a case (or a task instance within a case) has access to multiple folders is how naming clashes are resolved where two data elements in distinct folders share the same name. A second issue that arises is that of providing concurrency control for folder-level data.

Solutions The first issue is addressed in COSA by only allowing one case to access attributes from a given folder at a time. This is achieved using a specific Tool Agent library that governs access to data contained in folders. It is possible to change the folder to which a case refers at any time (again using a specific Tool Agent call). In terms of the second issue, similar considerations apply to those discussed for case data. In the case of COSA, there is no direct system support to address this problem.

Global data

Description Data elements are supported that are accessible to all components in each and every case of the process and are defined within the context of the process.

Example
- The *risk/premium matrix* can be utilized by all of the cases of the *Write Insurance Policy* workflow and all task instances within each case.

Motivation Some data elements have sufficiently broad applicability that it is desirable to make them accessible to every component in all cases of process execution. Data that falls into this category includes startup parameters to the operating environment, global application data frequently used, and production information that governs the potential course of execution that each case may take.

Overview Figure 5.7 illustrates the extent of global data visibility. Note that in contrast to case-level data elements, which are typically only visible to tasks in the case in which they are declared, global data elements are visible throughout all cases. Generally, they are defined in the context of the overall process environment and have a lifespan that is not linked to the execution of any individual or group of cases.

Context There are no specific context conditions associated with this pattern.

Implementation In order to make data elements broadly accessible to all cases, most offerings address this requirement by utilizing persistent storage, typically in the form of a database. This may be provided directly as an internal facility (e.g., a Data Store in the case of BPMN or entity variables based on Service Data Object [SDO] technology in the case of Oracle BPEL) or indirectly by linking in/accessing facilities in a suitable third-party product (e.g., Oracle BPEL and BPMone both provide a broad range of external data access facilities and adapters).

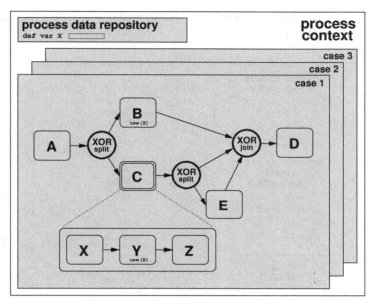

Figure 5.7
Global data visibility.

Issues The main issue associated with global data is in managing concurrent access to it by multiple processes.

Solutions As discussed for the *Folder data* pattern.

Environment data

Description Data elements that exist in the external operating environment are able to be accessed by components of processes during execution.

Example

- Where required, tasks in the *System Monitoring* workflow can access the *temperature sensor data* from the operating environment.

Motivation Direct access to environmentally managed data by tasks or cases during execution can significantly simplify processes and improve their ability to respond to changes and communicate with applications in the broader operational environment.

Overview External data may be sourced from a variety of distinct locations, including external databases, applications that are currently executing or can be initiated in the operating environment, and services that mediate access to various data repositories and distribution mechanisms (e.g., stock price feeds). These scenarios are illustrated in figure 5.8. Data elements in external data repositories, applications, and services (e.g., data elements

X, Y, and Z in this figure) are accessible throughout the various cases operating in the context of the process.

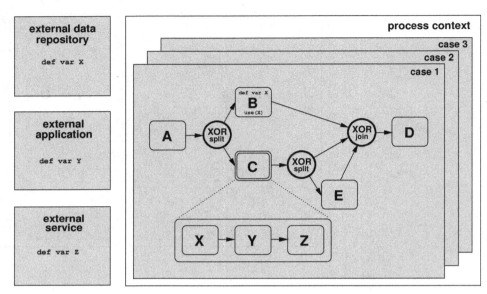

Figure 5.8
Environment data visibility.

Context There are no specific context conditions associated with this pattern.

Implementation The ability to access external data elements generally requires the ability to connect to an interface or interprocess communication (IPC) facility in the operating environment or to invoke an external service that will supply data elements. Facilities for achieving this may be either *explicitly* or *implicitly* supported by an offering.

Explicit support involves the direct provision by an offering of constructs for accessing external data sources. Typically these take the form of specific elements that can be included in the design-time process model. BPMone implements Mapping Objects, which allow data elements to be copied from external databases into the workflow engine, updated as required with case data, and copied back to the underlying database. It also allows text files to be utilized in workflow actions and has a series of interfaces for external database integration. Oracle BPEL provides a broad range of facilities for accessing data in external databases and invoking external web services in order to access and manipulate environment data elements.

Implicit support occurs in offerings that necessitate that access to external data occurs within individual task implementations. Typically this is facilitated by extending the program code corresponding to the task implementation to incorporate the required integration capabilities in order to access external data elements. This approach is also an option within Oracle BPEL.

5.3 Data interaction patterns

Data interaction relates to the manner in which data elements are trafficked between the various elements of a workflow process. In this section, we examine the various ways in which data elements can be passed between components in a process and how the characteristics of the individual components can influence the manner in which the actual transport of data elements occurs. Of particular interest is the distinction between the communication of data between components within a process as against the data-oriented interaction of a process element with the external environment.

5.3.1 Internal data interaction patterns

Data interaction between tasks

Description The ability to communicate data elements between one task instance and another within the same case. The communication of data elements between two tasks is specified in a form that is independent of the task definitions themselves.

Example
- The *Determine Fuel Consumption* task requires the coordinates determined by the *Identify Shortest Route* task before it can proceed.

Motivation The passing of data elements between tasks is a fundamental aspect of BPM offerings. In many situations, individual tasks execute in their own distinct address space and do not share significant amounts of data on a global basis. This necessitates the ability to move commonly used data elements between distinct tasks.

Overview All BPM offerings support the notion of passing parameters from one task to another. However, this may occur in a number of distinct ways depending on the relationship between the data perspective and control-flow perspective within the offering. There are three main approaches as illustrated in figure 5.9.

- *Integrated control-flow and data channels* — where both control-flow and data are passed simultaneously between tasks utilizing the same channel. In the example, task B receives the data elements X and Y at exactly the same time that control-flow is passed to it from A. While conceptually simple, one of the disadvantages of this approach to data passing is that it requires all data elements that may be used some time later in the process to be passed with the thread of control regardless of whether the next task will use them. For example, task B does not use data element Y, but it is passed to it because task C will subsequently require access to it.

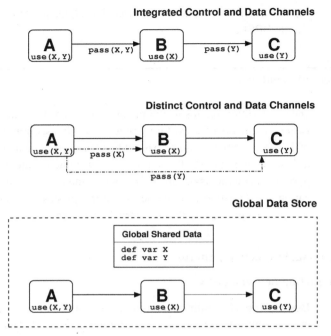

Figure 5.9

Approaches to data interaction between tasks (from [116]).

- *Distinct data channels* — where data is passed between tasks via explicit data channels that are distinct from the process control-flow links within the process design. Under this approach, the coordination of the passing of data and control-flow is usually not specifically identified. It is generally assumed that when control-flow is passed to a task that has incoming data channels, the data elements specified on these channels will be available at the time of task commencement.
- *Global data store* — where tasks share the same data elements (typically via access to globally shared data) and no explicit data passing is required (cf. the *Case data* and *Folder data* patterns). This approach to data sharing is based on tasks having shared a priori knowledge of the naming and location of common data elements. It also assumes that the implementation is able to deal with potential concurrency issues that may arise where several task instances seek to access the same data element.

Context There are no specific context conditions associated with this pattern.

Implementation Surprisingly, the third strategy described above is the most common approach to data passing adopted in workflow offerings. BPMone facilitates the passing of data through case-level data repositories accessible by all tasks. Oracle BPEL utilizes a combination of the first and third approaches. Variables can be bound to scopes within a process definition that may encompass a number of tasks, but there is also the ability for messages to be passed between tasks when control-flow passes from one task to another. BPMN also supports the first and third approaches. In general, data passing is explicitly defined using Data Associations. However, Data Objects or Properties associated with a given Process can be implicitly accessed throughout the Process and any nested Sub-Processes and within any associated Tasks.

Issues There are several potential issues associated with the use of this pattern. First, where there is no data passing between tasks and a common data store is utilized by several tasks for communicating data elements, there is the potential for concurrency problems to arise, particularly if the process involves parallel execution paths. This may lead to inconsistent results depending on the task execution sequence taken.

A second consideration arises when data and control-flow are passed along the same channel. In this situation, there is the potential for two (potentially differing) copies of the same data element to flow to the same task,[1] necessitating that the task decide which is the correct version of the data element to use in its processing activities. (Note that the use of dedicated data channels for data passing usually implies that data elements are indivisible. Hence, this problem does not arise in this situation.)

A third consideration where data and control-flow occur via distinct channels is that of managing the situation where control-flow reaches a task before the required data elements have been passed to it.

Solutions The first issue — concurrency control — can be handled in a variety of different ways. BPMone avoids the problem by only allowing one active user or process that can update data elements in a case at any time (although other processes and users can access data elements for reading). Oracle BPEL supports isolated scopes that allow compensation handlers to be defined for groups of tasks that access the same data elements, which ensure that access to a given data element can be restricted to a single task instance at any given time.

In terms of the second issue, no general solutions to this problem have been identified. Of the offerings observed, only Oracle BPEL supports the simultaneous passing of control-flow and data along the same channel, and it does not provide a solution to the issue.

Although not observed in any of the offerings examined, the third issue can generally be addressed by ensuring that a task instance receiving data waits for all of the required data elements to arrive before commencing execution. An alternative solution involves the use of default values for missing data elements.

---

1 For example, access to a given data element may be required in three branches within a process, requiring the original data element to be replicated and passed to one or more tasks in each branch. The difficulty arises where the data element is altered in one branch and the branches subsequently converge at a join operator.

Data interaction between block task and subprocess decomposition

Description The ability to pass data elements between a block task and the corresponding subprocess that defines its implementation. Any data elements that are available to the block task are able to be utilized in the associated subprocess either directly or by passing them to the subprocess at its commencement and back at its completion.

Examples

- *Customer claims* data is passed to the *Calculate Likely Tax Return* block task, whose implementation is defined by a series of tasks in the form of a subprocess. The *customer claims* data is passed to the subprocess and is visible to each of the tasks in the subprocess.
- The *Determine Optimal Trajectory* subprocess passes the coordinates of the *launch* and *target locations* and the *flight plan* back to the block task.

Motivation In order for subprocesses to be used in an effective manner within a process model, a mechanism is required that allows relevant data elements to be passed to and from them during their execution.

Overview Block or composite tasks are analogous to the programmatic notion of procedure calls and indicate a task whose implementation is described in further detail at another level of abstraction (typically elsewhere in the process model) using the same range of process constructs. The question that arises when data is passed to a block element is whether it is immediately accessible by all of the tasks that define its actual implementation or if some form of explicit data passing must occur between the block task and the subprocess. Typically one of three approaches is taken to handling the communication of parameters from a block task to the underlying implementation and back again at its completion. Each of these is illustrated in figure 5.10.

- *Implicit data passing* — data passed to the block task is immediately accessible by all sub-tasks, which make up the underlying implementation. In effect the main block task and the corresponding subprocess share the same address space, and no explicit data passing is necessary. As a consequence, any changes made to these data elements made by tasks in the subprocess are immediately recognized in the block task.
- *Explicit data passing via parameters* — data elements supplied to the block task must be specifically passed as parameters to the underlying subprocess implementation at its commencement and back at its completion. The second example in figure 5.10 illustrates how parameters can be used to map data elements at block task level to data elements at subprocess level with distinct names. This capability provides a degree of independence in the naming of data elements between the block task and subprocess implementation and is particularly important in the situation where several block tasks share the same subprocess implementation.
- *Explicit data passing via data channels* — data elements supplied to the block task are specifically passed via data channels to all tasks in the subprocess that require access to

them. At the completion of the subprocess, any required data elements are returned to the block task via data channels.

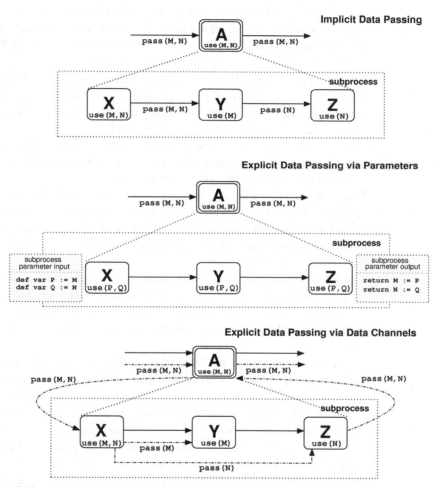

Figure 5.10
Approaches to data interaction between block tasks and corresponding subprocesses.

Context There are no specific context conditions associated with this pattern.

Implementation All of these approaches are utilized in various combinations in the offerings examined. The first approach does not involve any actual data passing between block activity and implementation. Rather the block-level data elements are made accessible to the subprocess. This strategy is utilized by BPMone and BPMN for data passing to subprocesses. In all cases, the subprocess is presented with the entire range of data elements utilized by the block task, and there is no opportunity to limit the scope of items passed. Oracle BPEL achieves the same effect through the use of entity variables managed by an SDO facility provided by one of the services making up the process implementation.

The second approach necessitates the creation of new data elements at the subprocess level to accept the incoming data values from the block activity. Oracle BPEL utilizes the second approach to interact with external services and (sub-)processes via partner links. Similarly, BPMN supports an explicit data passing strategy based on Call Activity parameters for passing data to and from a Process or Global Task. DataInputs (and DataOutputs, where the data passing is from subprocess to parent task) are specified to indicate data input and output requirements for the relevant sub-process.

The third approach relies on the passing of data elements between tasks to communicate between block task and subprocess. Workflow systems such as Staffware utilize this mechanism for passing data elements to subprocesses.

Issues One consideration that may arise where the explicit parameter passing approach is adopted is whether the data elements in the block task and the subprocess are independent of each other (i.e., whether they exist in independent address spaces). If they do not, then there is the potential for concurrency issues to arise where tasks executing in parallel update the same data element.

Another difficulty that can arise occurs when there is not a strict correspondence between the data elements returned from the subprocess and the receiving data elements at block task level. For example, the subprocess returns more data elements than the block task is expecting, possibly as a result of additional data elements being created during its execution.

Solutions The first issue can arise where subprocess data elements are passed as fields rather than parameters (as is done in Staffware). The resolution to this issue is to map the input fields to fields with distinct names not used elsewhere during execution of the case. In BPMN, where data is passed via parameters from a Call Activity to a Global Task or Process, the assumption is that the data elements exist in distinct address spaces.

The second situation does not arise in BPMN, Oracle BPEL, or BPMone. However, for other offerings, it can be solved in one of two ways. Some systems such as Staffware support the ability for block tasks to create data elements at block task level for those data items at subprocess level, which it has not previously encountered. Other products (such as the WebSphere MQ Workflow system) require a strict mapping to be defined between subprocess and block task data elements to prevent this situation from arising.

Data interaction with multiple instance tasks

Description The ability to pass data elements from a preceding task to a subsequent task that is able to support multiple execution instances. This may involve passing the data elements to all instances of the multiple instance task or distributing them on a selective basis. The data passing occurs when the multiple instance task is enabled. At the conclusion of the various task instances, the distributed data elements are coalesced so they can be passed to subsequent tasks.

Motivation Where a task is capable of being invoked multiple times, a means is required of controlling which data elements are passed to each of the execution instances. This may involve ensuring that each task instance receives all of the data elements passed to it (possibly on a shared basis) or distributing the data elements across each of the execution instances on some predefined basis. For practical applications, it is obvious that not all instances should do exactly the same thing. As each execution instance of a multiple instance task effectively operates independently from other instances, there is also the requirement to pass on these data elements at the conclusion to subsequent tasks.

Examples

- The *Identify Witnesses* task passes the *witness list* to the *Interview Witnesses* task. This data is available to each instance of the *Interview Witnesses* task at commencement.
- The *New Albums List* is passed to the *Review Album* task, and one task instance is started for each entry on the list. At commencement, each of the *Review Album* task instances is allocated a distinct entry from the *New Album List* to review.
- At the conclusion of the various instances of the *Record Lap Time* task, the *list of lap times* is passed to the *Prepare Grid* task.

Overview There are four potential approaches to passing data elements to multiple instance tasks as illustrated in figure 5.11. As a general rule, it is possible to either pass a data element to all task instances or distribute one item from it (assuming it is a composite data element such as an array or a set) to each task instance. Indeed the number of task instances that are initiated may be based on the number of individual items in the composite data element. Data passing may be by value or by reference. The specifics of each of these approaches are discussed below.

- *Instance-specific data passed by value* — this involves the distribution of a data element passed by value to task instances on the basis of one item of the data element per task instance (in the example shown, task instance B_1 receives M[1], B_2 receives M[2], etc.). As the data element is passed by value, each task instance receives a copy of the item passed to it in its own address space. At the conclusion of each of the task instances, the data element is reassembled from the distributed items and passed to the subsequent task instance.
- *Instance-specific data passed by reference* — this scenario is similar to that described above except that the task instances are passed a reference to a specific item in the data element rather than the value of the item. This approach avoids the need to reassemble the data element at the conclusion of the task instances.
- *Shared data passed by value* — where a distinct copy of a specific data element is passed to each task instance. This is useful where the data element is not intended to be updated by the task. Where such a data element is updated, a potential problem arises at the time

at which each of the distinct copies of the data element need to reconciled and a single value passed on to subsequent tasks.

- *Shared data passed by reference* — in this situation, all task instances are passed a reference to the same data element. While this allows all task instances to access the same data element, it does not address the issue of concurrency control should one of the task instances amend the value of the data element (or indeed if it is altered by some other component of the process).

In general, data is passed from a multiple instance task to subsequent tasks when a certain number of the task instances have concluded. The various scenarios in which this may occur are illustrated in figure 5.11. These usually coincide with the passing of control from the multiple instance task, although data and control-flow do not necessarily need to be fully integrated. In the case where data elements are passed by reference, the location rather than the values are passed on at task completion (obviously this implies that the data values may be accessed by other components of the process prior to completion of the multiple instance task as they reside in shared storage).

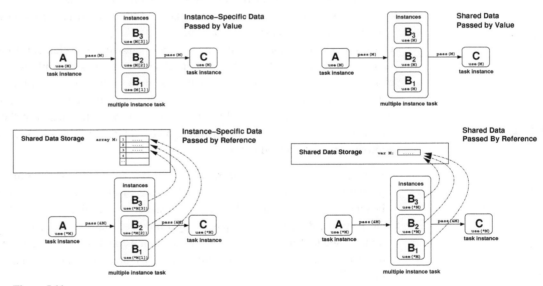

Figure 5.11
Data interaction approaches for multiple instance task (based on [116]).

Context There are no specific context conditions associated with this pattern.
Implementation BPMone provides facilities for instance-specific data to be passed by reference, whereby an array can be passed to a designated multiple instance task, and specific subcomponents of it can be mapped to individual task instances. At the conclusion of these task instances, it provides the ability to aggregate instance-specific data from each of them

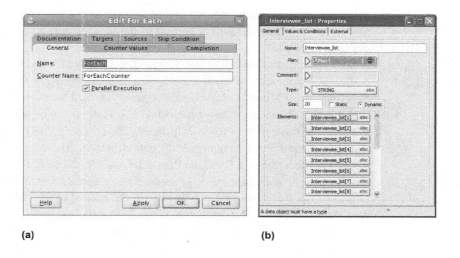

(a)   (b)

Figure 5.12
MI data in (a) Oracle BPEL, and (b) BPMone.

and passed it a subsequent task. BPMone also allows for shared data elements to be passed by reference to all task instances. In this situation, there is no requirement to aggregate these elements at the conclusion of the task instances. Oracle BPEL facilitates multiple instance tasks via the For Each construct. There are several distinct ways in which data elements can be provided to the individual task instances. Instance-specific data can be passed to each task instance by reference through the use of an index variable, which enables each instance to access distinct parts of an array variable residing in the same scope as the For Each activity. Alternatively, shared data elements can either be passed by reference (each task instance can directly access any variables in the surrounding scope) or by value (using the Assign activity). In BPMN, instance-specific data passed by value is supported. Each instance receives an element from the data collection passed to the Multiple Instances Activity at commencement. These elements are coalesced at the conclusion of each instance, and the data collection is updated accordingly. The entire data collection is passed from the Multiple Instances Activity at its conclusion. Figure 5.12 illustrates the configuration of the composite variables passed to the various instances of a MI task in Oracle BPEL and BPMone.

Issues Where a task is able to execute multiple times but not all instances are created at the same time, one issue that arises is whether the values of data elements are set for all execution instances at the time at which the multiple instance task is first initiated or whether they can be set after this occurs for the invocation of a specific task instance.

Another issue for BPM offerings that support designated multiple instance tasks involves the partitioning of composite data elements (such as an array) in a way that ensures each task instance receives a distinct portion of the data element that is passed to each of the multiple task instances.

A third issue that arises with multiple instance tasks is identifying the point at which the output data elements from them are available (in some aggregate form) to subsequent tasks.

Solutions In BPMone, multiple instance tasks are facilitated via the Dynamic Plan construct, which allows the data for individual task instances to be specified at any time prior to the actual invocation of the task instance. The passing of data elements to specific task instances is handled, via Mapping Array data structures. These can be extended at any time during the execution of a Dynamic Plan, allowing for new task instances to be created "on the fly" and the data corresponding to them to be specified at the latest possible time. In Oracle BPEL, this situation can only arise in the context of the For Each activity, in which case each task instance receives the values of the data elements when it is initiated. The situation is the same in BPMN, and the data values passed to individual instances are based on those in the data collection passed to the Multiple Instances Activity at commencement. The number of activity instances is also known at this time, and additional instances cannot be added during execution.

BPMone addresses the second problem through mapping objects that allow sections of a composite data element in the form of an array (e.g., $X[1]$, $X[2]$, etc.) to be allocated to individual instances of a multiple instance task (known as a dynamic plan). Each multiple task instance only sees the element it has been allocated, and each task instance has the same naming for each of these elements (i.e., X). At the conclusion of all the multiple instances, the data elements are coalesced back into the composite form together with any changes that have been made. BPMN partitions the input data collection passed to a Multiple Instances Activity into discrete segments for individual activity instances in a similar way and recombines these at the conclusion of each instance. Oracle BPEL achieves this effect through the use of an index variable in the context of a For Each activity in order to provide distinct execution instances with the ability to access distinct parts of an array variable in the same scope as the For Each activity. However, there is no means of enforcing access restrictions on portions of the array data to individual task instances.

In the case of BPMone, the third issue is dependent on where the data elements are accessed. The BPMone engine allows parallel task instances to access output data elements from other instances even if these instances have not yet completed (i.e., the values obtained, if any, may not be final). However, subsequent task instances (i.e., those after the multiple instance task) can only rely on the complete composite data element being available. In Oracle BPEL, the output values are made available as soon as each instance completes. In BPMN, the output data collection is only available when all instances of a Multiple Instances Activity have completed.

Data interaction between cases

>   **Description** The passing of data elements from one case of a process during its execution
>   to another case that is executing concurrently.
>
>   **Example**
>   - During execution of a case of the *Re-balance Portfolio* workflow, the *best price* identified
>   for each security is passed to other cases currently executing.
>
>   **Motivation** Where the results obtained during the course of one process instance are likely
>   to be of use to other cases, a means of communicating them to both currently executing
>   and subsequent cases is required.
>
>   **Overview** Direct support for this pattern requires the availability of a function within the
>   BPM offering that enables a given case to initiate the communication (and possibly up-
>   dating) of data elements with a distinct process instance (illustrated via ❶ in figure 5.13).
>   Alternatively, it is possible to achieve the same outcome indirectly by writing them back
>   to a shared store of persistent data[2] known to both the initiating and receiving cases. This
>   may be either an internally maintained facility at process level ❷ or an external data repos-
>   itory ❸.
>
>   Each of these approaches requires the communicating cases to have a priori knowledge of
>   the location of the data element that is to be used for data passing. They also require the
>   availability of a solution to address the potential concurrency issues that may arise when
>   multiple cases wish to communicate.
>
>   **Context** There are no specific context conditions associated with this pattern.
>
>   **Implementation** BPMN provides Data Stores as a means of passing data elements between
>   distinct process instances. Similarly, Oracle BPEL can utilize entity variables based on
>   SDO technology to pass data elements between different cases. In the case of BPMone, it
>   is possible to achieve the same result indirectly using the methods described above.
>
>   **Issues** The main consideration associated with this pattern is in establishing an effective
>   means of linking related cases and their associated data elements together in order to ensure
>   that the data passing between them occurs in a predictable way.
>
>   **Solutions** None of the offerings examined addresses this need. However, there are BPM
>   offerings that do provide solutions to the issue. In Vectus, it is possible to relate cases.
>   There are four types of relationships: "parent," "child," "sibling," and "master." These re-
>   lationships can be used to navigate through cases at runtime. For example, one case can
>   schedule tasks in another flow, terminate a task in another flow, create new cases, and so
>   on. It is also possible to share data using a dot notation similar to that used in the Object
>   Constraint Language used in UML. The "master" relation can be used to create a proxy

---

2 Although this does not constitute "true" case to case data passing, it indirectly achieves the same outcome.

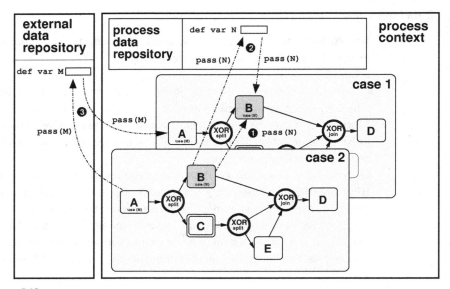

Figure 5.13
Data interaction between cases.

shared by related cases to show all tasks related to these cases. A similar construct is also present in the Bizagi[3] product.

5.3.2   External data interaction patterns

External data interaction involves the communication of data between a component of a process and some form of information resource or service that operates outside of the context of the process environment. The notion of being external to the context of the process environment applies not only in technology terms but also implies that the operation of the external service or resource is independent of that of the process. The various types of interactions between elements of a process and the broader operational environment are considered in this section.

Data interaction — process to environment — push-oriented

Description The ability to initiate the passing of data elements from a process to a resource or service in the operating environment.

3 http://www.visionsoftware.biz

Examples

- The *Calculate Mileage* task passes the *mileage data* to the *Corporate Logbook* database for permanent recording.
- At its conclusion, each case of the *Perform Reconciliation* workflow passes its results to the *Corporate Audit* database for permanent storage.
- At any time the *Process Tax Return* process may save its working data to an external data warehouse facility.

Motivation The passing of data from a process to an external resource is most likely to be initiated by a task during its execution, although other schemes are possible, such as automated data synchronization or backup to an external repository on a periodic basis. Depending on the specific requirements of the data passing interaction, it may be necessary to connect to an existing API or service interface in the operating environment or to actually invoke an application or service to which to forward the data.

Overview Figure 5.14 illustrates two approaches to data passing between a process and the operating environment. In the first of them (indicated by ❶), the data passing is initiated by a task during process execution and involves a case data element being passed to an external process. In the second (indicated by ❷), the data passing is initiated by some form of case-based event (e.g., receipt of a signal) and occurs independently of process execution. There is a wide range of ways in which this pattern can be facilitated. However, these tend to divide into two categories:

- *Explicit integration mechanisms* — where the process environment provides specific constructs for passing data to the external environment such as adapters.
- *Implicit integration mechanisms* — where the data passing occurs implicitly within the programmatic implementations that make up tasks and related constructs in the process and is not directly supported by the process environment.

In both cases, the data passing activity is described in the process definition and usually occurs during process execution. Any data items that are accessible in the context of the process (e.g., parameters, task, scope, block, case, folder and global data) may be transferred.

Context There are no specific context conditions associated with this pattern.

Implementation BPMone enables data to be passed to external applications using the Operation Action construct and to external databases using Mapping Objects. BPMN supports the pattern via a Message Flow from an Activity to the boundary of a Pool representing the environment. Oracle BPEL provides a range of facilities for passing data elements to external services, applications, and repositories, ranging from external service invocations through to the use of a dedicated Notification Service. Figure 5.15 illustrates the facilities available in Oracle BPEL, BPMone, and BPMN for passing data elements from a process instance to the operational environment.

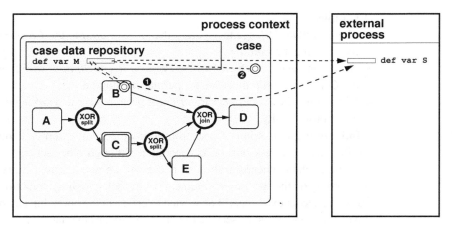

Figure 5.14
Push-oriented data interaction from a process to the operating environment.

Issues One difficulty that can arise when sending data to an external application is knowing whether it was successfully delivered. This is particularly a problem when the external application does not provide immediate feedback on delivery status (e.g., the interaction is not synchronous).

Solutions The most general solution to this problem is for a subsequent task in the case to request an update on the status of the delivery using a construct, which conforms to the *Data interaction — environment to process — pull-oriented* pattern and requires an answer to be provided by the external application. Alternatively, the external application can lodge a notification of the delivery using some form of *Event-based task trigger* or by passing data back to the process (e.g., using the *Data interaction —environment to process — push-oriented* pattern). This is analogous to the messaging notion of asynchronous callback.

Data interaction — environment to process — pull-oriented

Description The ability in a process to request data elements from resources or services in the operational environment.

Examples

- The *Determine Cost* task must request *cattle price* data from the *Cattle Market System* before it can proceed.
- At any time, cases of the *Process Suspect* process may request additional data from the *Police Records System*.
- The *Monitor Portfolios* process is able to request *new market position* download from the *Stock Exchange* at any time.

Motivation Processes require the means to proactively seek the latest information from known data sources in the operating environment during their execution. This may involve accessing the data from a known repository or invoking an external service in order to gain access to the required data elements.

Overview Figure 5.16 illustrates two approaches to data passing between the operating environment and a process where the data interaction is initiated by the process. In the first of them (indicated by ❶), a task instance in the executing process requests a data element from the operating environment. In the second (indicated by ❷), the data passing occurs independently of specific events related to process execution, and a data element in the process environment is updated with data received from the operating environment. Similar to the *Data interaction — process to environment — push-oriented* pattern, the facilitation of this pattern can be based on either explicit or implicit integration mechanisms. Any data element in the context of the overall process (i.e., task, case, global data, etc.) can be updated as a consequence of the use of this pattern.

Context There are no specific context conditions associated with this pattern.

Implementation BPMone utilizes Mapping Objects to extract data elements from external databases. Oracle BPEL provides a range of adapters and services for accessing data elements in external applications and repositories. BPMN does not directly support this pattern as Message Flows are assumed to be push-oriented interactions.

Issues One difficulty with this style of interaction is that it can block progress of the requesting case if the external application has a long delivery time for the required information or is temporarily unavailable.

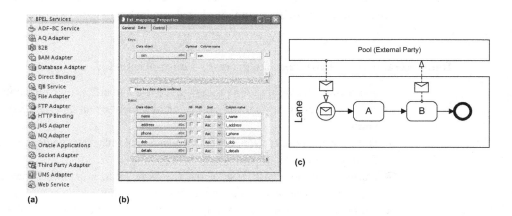

Figure 5.15

Facilities for data passing facilities from a process instance to the operating environment in (a) Oracle BPEL, (b) BPMone, and (c) BPMN.

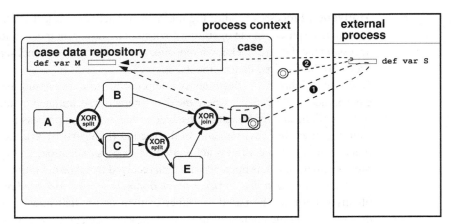

Figure 5.16
Pull-oriented data interaction between a process and the operating environment.

Solutions One potential solution to this problem is for the requesting entity not to wait for the requested data (i.e., continue execution either immediately or after a nominated time-out) and to implement some form of asynchronous notification of the required information (possibly along the lines of the *Data interaction — environment to process — push-oriented* pattern). The disadvantage of this approach is that it complicates the overall interaction by requiring the external application to return the required information via an alternate path and necessitating the process environment to provide notification facilities. Another possible solution is to nominate default values for the required data elements if they are not immediately available from the external application.

Data interaction — environment to process — push-oriented

Description The ability for a process to receive and utilize data elements passed to it from services and resources in the operating environment on an unscheduled basis.

Examples

- During execution, the *Review Performance* task may receive new *engine telemetry* data from the *Wireless Car Sensors*.
- During execution, each case of the *Evaluate Fitness* workflow may receive additional *fitness measurements* data from the *Biometry system*.
- All *mining permits* data currently available is passed to the *Develop Mining Leases* process.

Motivation An ongoing difficulty for processes is establishing mechanisms that enable them to be provided with new items of data as they become available from sources outside of their execution environment. This is particularly important in areas of volatile information, where updates to existing data elements may occur frequently but not on a scheduled basis (e.g., price updates for equities on the stock market). This pattern relates to the ability of processes to receive new items of data as they become available without needing to proactively request them from external sources or suspend execution until updates arrive.

Overview Figure 5.17 illustrates two approaches to data passing between the operating environment and a process where the data interaction is initiated by an entity in the operating environment. In the first (indicated by ❶), the action of updating the value of a data element in the process context is undertaken by a specific task instance based on the receival of a request to do so. In the second (indicated by ❷), the data passing occurs independently of specific events related to process execution, and a data element in the process environment is directly updated with data received from the operating environment.

As for the previous two patterns, approaches to this pattern can be divided into *explicit* and *implicit* mechanisms. The main difficulty that arises in its implementation is in providing external processes with the addressing information that enables the routing of data elements to the relevant target (i.e., the specific process instance, task instance, and variable location). Potential solutions to this include the provision of externally accessible execution monitors by offerings that indicate the identity of currently executing process and task instances recording their identity with a shared registry service in the operating environment.

An additional consideration is the ability of processes to be able to asynchronously wait for and respond to data passing activities without impacting their actual progress. This necessitates the availability of asynchronous communication facilities — typically at the task level — either provided as some form of (*explicit*) task construct by the BPM system or able to be (*implicitly*) included in the programmatic implementations of tasks.

Context There are no specific context conditions associated with this pattern.

Implementation All of the offerings examined support this pattern in some form. BPMone allows the value of case data and also data elements associated with task forms to be updated via the chp_dat_setval and chp_frm_setfield API calls. BPMN supports the pattern using a Message Flow from the Pool representing the environment to the relevant Activity. Oracle BPEL provides support via the Receive activity and message event handlers, which allow a task to receive a message and update a specified variable with its value.

Issues The major difficulty associated with this pattern is in providing a means for external applications to identify the specific task instance in which they wish to update a data element.

Solutions In general, the solution to this problem requires the external application to have knowledge of both the case and the specific task in which the data element resides. Details of currently executing cases can only be determined with reference to the process environment, and most offerings provide a facility or API call to support this requirement. The

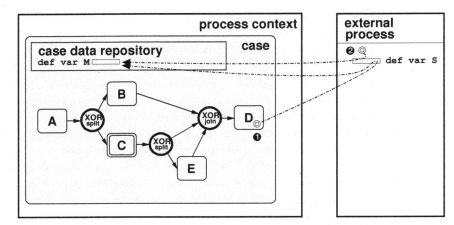

Figure 5.17
Push-oriented data interaction between the operating environment and a process.

external application will most likely require a priori knowledge of the identity of the task in which the data element resides.

Data interaction — process to environment — pull-oriented

Description The ability of a process to receive and respond to requests for data elements from services and resources in the operational environment.

Examples

- During execution, the *Assess Quality* task may receive requests for current data from the *Quality Audit* web service handler. It must provide this service with details of all current data elements.
- Each case of the *Handle Visa* process must respond to data requests from the *Immigration Department*.
- At any time, the *Monitor Portfolios* process may be required to respond to requests to provide data on any portfolios being reviewed to the *Securities Commissioner*.

Motivation In some cases, the requests for access to various forms of process data are initiated by external entities. These requests need to be handled as soon as they are received but should be processed in a manner that minimizes any potential impact on the process from which they are sourcing data.

Overview The ability to access data from a process can be handled in one of two ways as illustrated in figure 5.18. Either the request from the operating environment for a specific data element can be forwarded to a task instance, which can locate and return the required value (as indicated by ❶), or a specific facility can be provided for accessing the value of a data element (as indicated by ❷). In both cases, the request from the operating environment is typically directed to some form of API provided by an offering in order for it to be serviced.

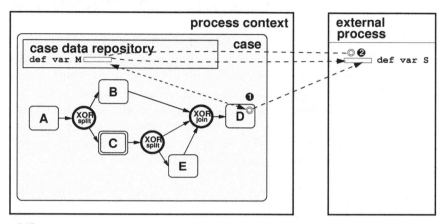

Figure 5.18
Push-oriented data interaction between the operating environment and a process.

Context There are no specific context conditions associated with this pattern.

Implementation BPMone supports the pattern via the chp_dat_getval API call, which provides the ability for external processes to interactively query case-level data elements. Oracle BPEL provides support for the pattern via the Reply activity, which returns the value of a specified variable in response to an earlier Receive request. BPMN does not directly support this pattern as Message flows are assumed to be push-oriented interactions.

Issues Similar difficulties exist with the utilization of this pattern to those identified above for the *Data interaction — environment to process — push-oriented* pattern.

Solutions As detailed above for the *Data interaction — environment to process — push-oriented* pattern.

5.4   Data transfer patterns

Data transfer patterns are essentially an adjunct to the data interaction patterns presented earlier. They aim to augment the earlier group of patterns by considering the manner in which the actual transfer of data elements occurs between one process component and another, with a particular focus on the various mechanisms by which data elements can be passed across the interface of a process component. The specific style of data passing that is used in a given scenario depends on a number of factors, including whether the two components share a common address space for data elements, whether it is intended that a distinct copy of an element is passed as against a reference to it, and whether the component

Data consistency

Although much of the focus of workflow technology has been on ensuring the consistency and correctness of control-flow, an equally important aspect of workflow execution is managing data consistency. One of the main motivations for utilizing workflow technology is providing a better means of routing work to the right resources. The availability of any necessary data is a prerequisite to delivering against this objective. One of the major difficulties faced when data is shared between and potentially manipulated by a number of concurrent task instances within a process is in ensuring that a consistent view is maintained of it by the various task instances that may be utilizing it.

The figure below illustrates a fragment of a medical review process where patient cases are examined and any necessary escalations are triggered. The solid lines between tasks indicate control-flow and the dashed lines indicate data flow. Illustrated in the figure are the three main types of data that may be utilized within a process. For each of these, different mechanisms are adopted in order to ensure that their recorded values remain consistent.

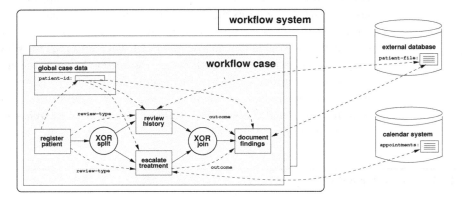

First of all, *task-specific* data elements (e.g., `review-type`, `outcome`) are utilized to pass working data between limited numbers of tasks. Typically these data elements are passed from one task instance to another within a given case and their existence is defined in the context of the tasks between which they are passed typically as task variables. As the "ownership" of each data element resides with a specific task instance at any given point in time, responsibility for maintaining the consistency of the data element also resides with this task. This is relatively straightforward as the limited scope of the data element ensures that it is not accessible to any other task instances.

The second type of data element is *shared* data (as illustrated by the `patient-id` global variable) which is accessible either by a subset of or by all task instances within a case. This type of data corresponds to data elements which are used simultaneously by a number of potentially concurrent task instances.

In order to ensure that all task instances utilize a given shared data element on a consistent basis, there is the need to serialize its usage such that any updates to its value by a given task instance result in any other task instances being informed of its updated value. This can be achieved in one of two ways: either *locks* can be used to prevent concurrent access to individual shared data elements in much the same way as is traditionally done in database systems or *isolated scopes* can be utilized to prevent concurrent execution of a given section of a process to which shared data elements are attached.

Finally *external* data corresponds to data elements which exist outside of the context of the workflow process (e.g., `patient-file`, `appointments`) but which are utilized and possibly updated during its execution. This class of data presents a particular problem from a consistency perspective as the ownership of the data element does not reside with the workflow system. Furthermore, the information content of these data elements is often quite complex in form. External data may correspond to documents, database tables, image files, etc. rather than simple data values like integer and string. In general the most common means of managing the consistency of these data elements from the workflow standpoint is to communicate the key to the data element rather than the full content when passing it between task instances during execution. This limits the potential for inconsistencies to be introduced by the workflow itself during data passing (e.g., as a result of data type and representational differences between the workflow and database). Secondly, the retrieval and usage of the data element should occur as close as possible to its actual point of usage in the process in order to ensure that the most current value is utilized and to minimize any potential waiting time for the data element. Some workflow offerings provide specific facilities for interacting with third party applications and databases using specialized adapters that allow data access to occur directly from individual task instances. One of the most interesting options in this area is the "copy-in copy-out" functionality provided by BPMone which allows a record from an external database to be retrieved at the beginning of a task instance and locked during the duration of its execution with the updated results written back to the database at completion.

receiving the data element can expect to have exclusive access to it. These variations give rise to a number of distinct patterns as described below.

Data transfer by value

Description The ability of a process component to receive incoming data elements by value, avoiding the need to have shared names or common address space with the component(s) from which it receives them.

Examples

- At commencement, the *Identify Successful Applicant* task receives values for the *required role* and *salary* data elements.
- Upon completion, the *Identify Successful Applicant* task passes the value of *successful applicant name* to the next task.

Motivation Under this scenario, data elements are passed as values between communicating process components. There is no necessity for each process component to utilize a common naming strategy for the data elements or for components to share access to a common data store in which the data elements reside. This enables individual components to be written in isolation without specific knowledge of the manner in which data elements will be passed to them or the context in which they will be utilized.

Overview Figure 5.19 illustrates the passing of the value of data element R in task instance A to task instance B where it is assigned to data element S. In this example, a transient variable G (depending on the specific implementation, this could be a data container, a case, or a global variable) is used to mediate the transfer of the data value from task instance A to task instance B, which do not share a common address space.

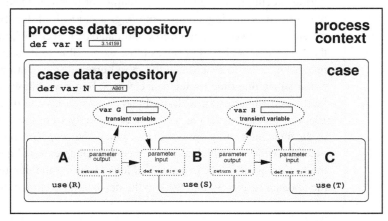

Figure 5.19

Data transfer by value.

Context There are no specific context conditions associated with this pattern.

Implementation This approach to data passing is commonly used for communicating data elements between tasks that do not share a common data store or wish to share task-level (or block-level) data items. The transfer of data between process components is typically based on the specification of mappings between them identifying source and target data locations. In this situation, there is no necessity for common naming or data type equivalance of data elements as only the data values are actually transported between interacting components. BPMN supports this style of data passing using Data Associations, which copy the value of a data element from one Data Object/Property to another. Oracle BPEL provides the option to pass data elements between activities using the Assign activity or using messages — both approaches rely on the transfer of data between process components by value.

Data transfer — copy in/copy out

Description The ability of a process component to copy the values of a set of data elements from an external source (either within or outside the process environment) into its address space at the commencement of execution and to copy their final values back at completion.

Example

- When the *Review Witness Statements* task commences, copy in the *witness statement* records and copy back any changes to this data at task completion.

Motivation This facility provides components with the ability to make a local copy of data elements that can be referenced elsewhere in the process instance. This copy can then be utilized during execution, and any changes that are made can be copied back at completion. It enables components to function independently of data changes and concurrency constraints that may occur in the broader process environment.

Overview The manner in which this style of data passing operates is shown in figure 5.20.

Context There are no specific context conditions associated with this pattern.

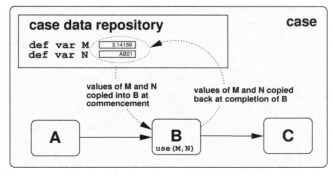

Figure 5.20

Data transfer — copy in/copy out.

Implementation While not a widely supported data passing strategy, BPMone and BPMN do offer limited support for it. In some cases, its use necessitates the adoption of the same naming strategy and structure for data elements within the component as used in the environment from which their values are copied. BPMone utilizes this strategy for accessing data from external databases via the InOut construct. BPMN supports this approach to data passing for global Processes or Global Tasks, which receive the DataInputs of the associated Call Activity at commencement and map back their output to the DataOutputs of the Call Activity at conclusion. This occurs implicitly; no specific DataAssociation is required. Oracle BPEL is able to utilize a range of adapters for accessing databases as part of an SOA-based composite application.

Issues Difficulties can arise with this data transfer strategy, where data elements are passed to a subprocess that executes independently (asynchronously) of the calling process. In this situation, the calling process continues to execute once the subprocess call has been made, and this can lead to problems when the subprocess completes and the data elements are copied back to the calling process as the point at which this copy back will occur is indeterminate.

Solutions There are two potential solutions to this problem:

- Do not allow asynchronous subprocess calls.
- In the event of asynchronous subprocess calls occurring, do not copy back data elements at task completion.

Data transfer by reference — unlocked

Description The ability to communicate data elements between process components by utilizing a reference to the location of the data element in some mutually accessible location. No concurrency restrictions apply to the shared data element.

Example

- The *Finalize Interviewees* task passes the location of the *interviewee shortlist* to all subsequent tasks in the *Hire* process.

Motivation This pattern is commonly utilized as a means of communicating data elements between process components that share a common data store. It involves the use of a named data location (which is generally agreed at design time) that is accessible to both the origin and target components and, in effect, is an implicit means of passing data as no actual transport of information occurs between the two components.

Overview Figure 5.21 illustrates the passing of two data elements M and N (global and case level, respectively) by reference from task instance A to B. Note that task instance B accepts these elements as parameters to internal data elements R and S, respectively.

Context There are no specific context conditions associated with this pattern.

Implementation Reference-based data passing requires the ability for communicating process components to have access to a common data store and to utilize the same reference

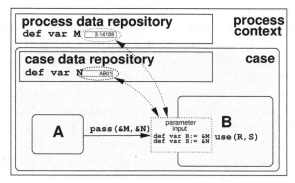

Figure 5.21
Data transfer by reference — unlocked.

notation for elements that they intend to use co-jointly. There may or may not be communication of the location of shared data elements via the control-flow channel or data channel (where supported) at the time that control-flow passes from one component to the next. BPMone and Oracle BPEL both support data passing strategies based on access to a common data store by the various activities in a process instance. BPMN does not provide support for this pattern.

Issues The major issue associated with this form of data utilization is that it can lead to problems where two (or more) concurrent task instances access the same data element simultaneously. In the event that two or more of the task instances update the shared data element in a short interval, there is the potential for the "lost update problem" to arise where one of the task instances unwittingly overwrites the update made by another.

Solutions The solution to this issue is to provide a means of limiting concurrent access to shared data elements where updates to its value are required. There are a variety of possible solutions to this, but the use of read and write locks is the most widely utilized scheme. The *Data transfer by reference — with lock* pattern embodies this solution.

Data transfer by reference — with lock

Description The ability to communicate data elements between process components by passing a reference to the location of the data element in some mutually accessible location. Concurrency restrictions are implied with the receiving component receiving the privilege of read-only or dedicated access to the data element. The required lock is declaratively specified as part of the data passing request.

Example

- At conclusion, the *Allocate Client Number* task passes the locations of the *new client number* and *new client details* data elements to the *Prepare Insurance Document* task, which receives dedicated access to these data items.

Motivation As for the previous pattern, this pattern communicates data elements between process components via a common data store based on common knowledge of the name of the data location. It provides the additional ability to lock the data element ensuring that only one task can access and/or update it at any given time, thus preventing any potential update conflicts between concurrent tasks that may otherwise attempt to update it simultaneously or continue to use an old value of the data element without knowledge that it has been updated.

Overview This approach is an extension of the *Data Transfer by Reference — Unlocked* pattern identified above, in which there is also the expectation that the originating process component has acquired either read-only or exclusive (write) access to the specific data elements being passed (i.e., a read or write lock). The process component that receives these data elements can choose to relinquish this access level (thus making them available to other process components), or it may choose to retain it and pass it on to later components. There is also the potential for the access level to be promoted (i.e., from a read to a write lock) or demoted (i.e., from a write to a read lock).

Context There are no specific context conditions associated with this pattern.

Implementation Oracle BPEL provides an approach to concurrency control based on the use of isolated scopes that allow fault and compensation handlers to be defined for groups of process activities and allow access to a given data element to be restricted to a single task instance at any given time. BPMone provides limited support for a style of write lock that allows the primary case to modify data while still enabling it to be accessible for reading by other processes. BPMN does not provide support for this pattern.

Data transformation — input

Description The ability to apply a transformation function to a data element prior to it being passed to a process component. The transformation function has access to the same data elements as the receiving process component.

Example

- Prior to passing the *transform voltage* data element to the task *Project_demand*, convert it to standard ISO measures.

Motivation The use of transformation functions provides a direct means of specifying that, at runtime, the values of data elements should be transformed before being passed to the designated parameters of a process component. This eliminates the need to add (artificial) tasks to perform these transformations. These functions can be internal to the process or could be externally facilitated.

Overview In the example shown in figure 5.22, the `prepare()` function intermediates the passing of the data element G between task instances A and B. At the point at which control-flow is passed to B, the results of performing the `prepare()` transformation function on data element G are made available to the input parameter S.

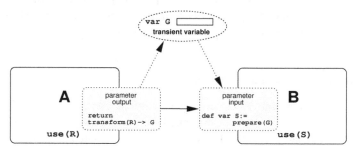

Figure 5.22
Data transformation — input and output.

Context There are no specific context conditions associated with this pattern.
Implementation BPMone provides limited facilities for the transformation of input data elements through the use of mappings and derived elements. Similarly, BPMN provides support for the pattern via the transformation Expression, which forms part of a Data Association. Oracle BPEL has a number of facilities for transforming input data elements, including the use of XPath functions and bpelx extensions as part of an Assign activity.

Data transformation — output

Description The ability to apply a transformation function to a data element immediately prior to it being passed out of a process component. The transformation function has access to the same data elements as the process component that initiates it.
Example
- Summarize the *spatial telemetry data* returned by the *Satellite Download* task before passing it to subsequent activities.

Motivation As for the *Data transformation — input* pattern.
Overview This pattern operates in a similar manner to the *Data transformation — input* pattern. However, in this case, the transformation occurs at the conclusion of the task (e.g., in figure 5.22, the `transform()` function is executed at the conclusion of task A immediately before the output data element is passed to data element G).
Context There are no specific context conditions associated with this pattern.
Implementation As described for the *Data transformation — input* pattern, except that the facilities identified are used for transforming the data elements passed from a task instance rather than for those passed to it.

5.5   Data-based routing patterns

Whereas the preceding patterns have described characteristics of data elements and their usage in isolation from other process perspectives (i.e., control-flow, resource, etc.), the data-routing patterns focus on the various ways in which data elements can interact with other perspectives and influence the overall operation of a process instance.

Task precondition — data existence

Description Data-based preconditions can be specified for tasks based on the presence of data elements at the time of execution. A precondition can utilize any data elements available to the task with which it is associated. A task can only proceed if the associated precondition evaluates to true.

Example
- Only execute the *Run Backup* task when *tape_loaded_flag* exists.

Motivation The ability to deal with missing data elements at the time of task invocation is desirable. This allows corrective action to be taken during process execution rather than necessitating the raising of an error condition and halting any further action.

Overview The operation of this pattern is illustrated in figure 5.23. Typically data existence preconditions are specified on task input parameters[4] in the process model as illustrated in figure 5.23. In this context, data existence refers to the ability to determine whether a required parameter has been defined and provided to the task at the time of task invocation and whether it has been assigned a value. One of five actions is possible where missing parameters are identified:

- Defer task commencement until they are available.
- Specify default values for parameters to take when they are not available.
- Request values for them interactively from BPMS users.
- Skip this task and trigger the following task(s).
- Kill this thread of execution in the case.

Context There are no specific context conditions associated with this pattern.

Implementation This pattern is implemented in a variety of different ways among the offerings examined. BPMone provides the milestone construct, which, among other capabilities, provides data synchronization support allowing the commencement of a subsequent task to be deferred until nominated data elements have a value specified. BPMN supports

---

4 For the purposes of this discussion, the term *parameters* is used in a general manner to refer both to data elements that are formally passed to a task and also to those that are shared between a task and its predecessor and passed *implicitly*.

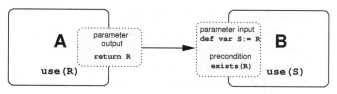

Figure 5.23

Task precondition — data existence.

the pattern via by delaying commencement of an Activity until required input data elements are available. Oracle BPEL provides exception handling facilities where an attempt to utilize an uninitialized variable is detected. These can be indirectly used to provide data existence precondition support at the task level but require each task to be defined as having its own scope with a dedicated fault handler to manage the uninitialized parameters accordingly.

Issues A significant consideration in managing preconditions that relate to data existence is being able to differentiate between data elements that have an undefined value and those that are defined to be empty or null.

Solutions BPMone provides facilities to test whether data elements have been assigned a value. Oracle BPEL provides a standard fault type for detecting and managing uninitialized data elements. BPMN does not distinguish between the two scenarios.

Task precondition – data value

Description Data-based preconditions can be specified for tasks based on the value of specific parameters at the time of execution. The preconditions can utilize any data elements available to the task with which they are associated. A task can only proceed if the associated precondition evaluates positively.

Example

- Execute the *Rocket Initiation* task when *countdown* is 2.

Motivation The ability to specify value-based preconditions on parameters to tasks provides the ability to delay execution of the task (possibly indefinitely) where a precondition is not satisfied.

Overview The operation of this pattern is similar to that in figure 5.23 except that the precondition is value-based rather than a test for data existence. There are three possible alternatives where a value-based precondition is not met:

- The task can be skipped and the subsequent task(s) initiated.
- Commencement of the task can be delayed until the required precondition is achieved.
- This thread of execution in the case can be terminated.

Context There are no specific context conditions associated with this pattern.

Implementation This pattern is directly implemented by BPMone through the milestone construct, which enables the triggering of a task to be delayed until a parameter has a specified value. Oracle BPEL provides the ability to execute tasks on a conditional basis through the use of link conditions. By specifying a link condition to a task, call it A, which corresponds to the required data values and creating a parallel *empty* task in the business process that has a link condition that is the negation of this, task A will be skipped if the required data values are not detected. BPMN supports the pattern by preceding an Activity by a Conditional Intermediate Event, which tests for the required data value.

Task postcondition — data existence

Description Data-based postconditions can be specified for tasks based on the existence of specific parameters at the time of task completion. The postconditions can utilize any data elements available to the task with which they are associated. A task can only complete if the associated postcondition evaluates positively.

Example

- Do not complete the *Rocket Initiation* task until *ignition data* is available.

Motivation Implementation of this pattern ensures that a task cannot complete until specified output parameters exist and have been allocated a value.

Overview Figure 5.24 illustrates this pattern. The specification of a data-based postcondition on a task effectively creates an implicit decision at the end of the task. If the postcondition is met, then the thread of control is passed to one or more of the outgoing branches from the task (e.g., task B is enabled if the postcondition exists(R) is met). There are two possible scenarios where the postcondition is not met:

1. the thread of control can be routed back to the beginning of the task (which may or may not result in the task being executed again), or
2. it can be routed to the end of the task (which is analogous to suspending the task).

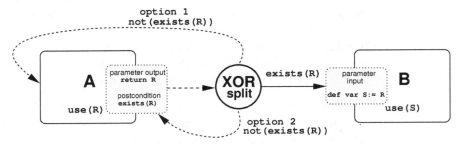

Figure 5.24

Task postcondition — data existence.

The implication of both scenarios, however, is that the task does not pass on control-flow until the required parameters exist and have defined values.

Context There are no specific context conditions associated with this pattern.

Implementation Two alternatives exist for the implementation of this pattern. Where tasks that have effectively finished all of their processing but have a nominated data existence postcondition that has not been satisfied, either the task could be suspended until the required postcondition is met or the task could be implicitly repeated until the specified postcondition is met.

BPMone provides direct support for this pattern by allowing data element fields in task constructs, called plan elements, to be specified as mandatory, thus ensuring they have a value specified before the plan element can complete execution. BPMN does not allow the thread of control to pass from an Activity until all output data elements are available. Oracle BPEL provides a standard fault type for detecting and managing uninitialized data elements.

Issues As for the *Task precondition — data existence* pattern.

Solutions As for the *Task precondition — data existence* pattern.

Task postcondition — data value

Description Data-based postconditions can be specified for tasks based on the value of specific parameters at the time of execution. The postconditions can utilize any data elements available to the task with which they are associated. A task can only complete if the associated postcondition evaluates positively.

Example

- Execute the *Fill Rocket* task until *rocket-volume* is 100%.

Motivation Implementation of this pattern would ensure that a task could not complete until nominated output parameters had a particular data value, are in a specified range, or have a certain relationship to each other (e.g., $x < y$).

Overview Similar to the *Task Postcondition — Data Existence* pattern, two options exist for handling the achievement of specified values for data elements at task completion:

- Delay execution until the required values are achieved.
- Implicitly re-run the task.

Again, the task does not pass on control-flow until the postcondition is met.

Context There are no specific context conditions associated with this pattern.

Implementation BPMone provides direct support for this pattern by requiring data element fields in task constructs to have a specified value before the plan element can complete execution. Oracle BPEL provides a standard fault type for detecting and managing data elements not meeting a specified condition. BPMN supports the pattern by following an Activity with a Conditional Intermediate Event, which tests for the required data value.

Event-based task trigger

Description The ability for an external event to initiate or resume a task and to pass data elements to it.

Example

- Initiate the *Emergency Shutdown* task immediately after the *Power Alarm* event occurs and pass the *alarm code* data element.

Motivation

The *Event-based task trigger* pattern provides the ability for one or more data elements to be passed to the initiated/resumed task instance when the trigger executes. As such it provides an effective mechanism for process synchronization and interprocess communication. The *Transient trigger* and *Persistent trigger* control-flow patterns described earlier are similar. However, they are purely event-based, and no data content is passed when they are triggered. They are able to be extended through the use of this pattern should these facilities be required.

Overview Three distinct scenarios may arise in the context of this pattern as illustrated in figure 5.25. In all situations, the capability is available to pass data elements at the same time that the trigger is sent to the relevant task. The first alternative (illustrated by the *start_A*() function) is that the task instance to be initiated is the first task in the process. This is equivalent in control-flow terms to starting a new case in which A is the first task instance.

The second alternative (illustrated by the *start_B*() function) is that the external event is triggering the resumption of a task instance that is in the middle of a process. The task instance has already had control-flow passed to it, but its execution is suspended pending occurrence of the external event trigger. This situation is shown in figure 5.25, with task instance B already triggered as a result of task instance A completing but halted from further progress until the event from *start_B*() occurs.

The third alternative is that the task instance is isolated from the main control-flow in the process, and the only way in which it can be initiated is by receiving an external event stimulus. Figure 5.25 shows task instance C, which can only be triggered when the event stimulus from *start_C*() is received.

Context There are no specific context conditions associated with this pattern.

Implementation This facility generally takes the form of an external interface to the process environment that provides a means for applications to trigger the execution of a specific task instance. All three variants of this pattern are directly supported by BPMone, BPMN, and Oracle BPEL, and in all cases, the passing of data elements as well as process triggering are supported. In each case, the underlying trigger support is persistent in nature.

Data-based task trigger

Description Data-based task triggers provide the ability to trigger a specific task when an expression based on data elements in the process instance evaluates to true. Any data element accessible within a process instance can be used as part of a data-based trigger expression.

Example

- Trigger the *Re-balance Portfolio* task when the *loan margin is less than 85%*.

Motivation This pattern provides a means of triggering the initiation or resumption of a task instance when a condition based on data elements in the process instance is satisfied.

Overview This pattern is analogous to the notion of active rules or event-condition-action (ECA) rules as found in active databases. A specific data-based trigger expression is associated with a task that is to be enabled in this way.

Context There are no specific context conditions associated with this pattern.

Implementation The pattern is directly supported in BPMone through the specification of a condition corresponding to the required data expression on a milestone construct immediately preceding the to-be-triggered task. When the data condition is met, the task is then triggered. BPMN supports this pattern via the Conditional Event construct. Oracle BPEL can provide support by using its Business Rule service component within a BPEL process. Many BPM offerings do not directly support this pattern. However, in some cases, it can be constructed for offerings that support the *Event-based trigger* pattern by simulating event-based triggering within the context of the process instance. This is achieved by nominating an event that the triggered task should be initiated/resumed on and then establishing a data monitoring task that runs (continuously) in parallel with all other tasks and monitors data values for the occurrence of the required triggers. When one of them is detected, the task

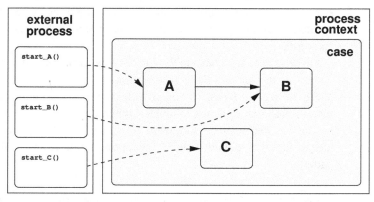

Figure 5.25
Event-based task trigger.

that requires triggering is initiated by raising the event that it is waiting on. The only caveat to this approach is that additional care is required where the process environment supports the *Implicit termination* control-flow pattern. In this situation, there is the potential for problems to arise in determining when a process instance is complete, as, by default, the monitoring task could potentially run indefinitely even after all other tasks in the process instance have completed. Hence, the determination of case completion needs careful management. This scenario is illustrated in figure 5.26. Task instance A is to be triggered when *trigger condition* evaluates to true. A task instance is set up to monitor the status of *trigger condition* and to complete and pass control-flow to A when it occurs. By adopting the strategy illustrated in figure 5.26, the pattern can be indirectly implemented in Oracle BPEL.

Figure 5.26
Data-based task trigger.

Data-based routing

Description Data-based routing provides the ability to alter the control-flow within a case based on the evaluation of data-based expressions. A data-based routing expression is associated with each outgoing arc of an OR-split or XOR-split. It can be composed of any data-values, expressions, and functions available in the process environment, provided it can be evaluated at the time the split construct with which it is associated completes. Depending on whether the construct is an XOR-split or OR-split, a mechanism is available to select one or several outgoing arcs to which the thread of control should be passed based on the evaluation of the expressions associated with the arcs.

Example
- If *alert* is *red*, then execute the *Inform Fire Crew* task after the *Handle Alert* task; otherwise run the *Identify False Trigger* task.

Motivation *Data-based routing* provides the ability to define data-based conditions on arcs between tasks in a process to indicate when these arcs can be enabled. This pattern is used by the *Exclusive choice* and *Multi-choice* control-flow patterns to indicate the selection mechanism that should be used for routing control-flow in the context of each of these patterns.[5]

---

5 Note that for the *Data-based routing* pattern, it is a hard requirement that the routing decision is based on the evaluation of data-based expressions, whereas for the *Exclusive choice* and *Multi-choice* patterns, the routing decisions can be based on a variety of possible mechanisms that may or may not be data-related

Overview Figure 5.27 illustrates data-based routing expressions as conditions associated with the control-flow branches from one task to another. These expressions can utilize task-level data passed from the completing task as well as any other data elements that are accessible to the task. In the example shown, task C will be triggered once A completes (as the value of data element M is greater than 3.0), task D will not, and task B may be triggered depending on the value of data element R that is passed from A.

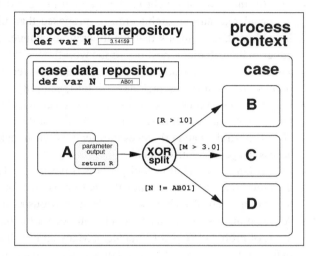

Figure 5.27
Data-based routing.

Context There is one context condition associated with this pattern: the mechanism that evaluates the *Data-based routing* is able to access any required data elements when determining which of the outgoing branches the thread of control should be passed to.

Implementation Both the *Exclusive choice* and *Multi-choice* usages of this construct are supported by Oracle BPEL and BPMN. BPMone only supports the *Exclusive choice* variant.

5.6   Further reading

Although the data perspective is deemed to be an essential part of a business process model and data handling is an integral part of most workflow systems, there is surprisingly little literature in this area that merits further reading. Worthwhile publications include the following:

- The data patterns discussed in this chapter were introduced in [116].

- A general classification of runtime data usage in workflow systems is provided by the WfMC in [144].
- Three general approaches to dataflow within workflow systems (explicit, implicit, and shared data store) are proposed in [117]. It also discusses the issue of data validation, and seven distinct data problems are identified that can prevent a process from functioning correctly.
- In [46], the issue of synchronizing internal process data with external data repositories is considered, and an architecture is proposed that allows policies to be specified for individual data elements that identifies how changes in the value of the data element either in the external repository or the workflow will be propagated.
- The issue of warehousing workflow audit data has received significant focus. Worthwhile publications in this area include [30], [86], and [48].
- In [146], a comprehensive access control scheme is described for data in workflow systems, which takes factors such as the identity of the requesting user, role, task, and associated constraints and privileges into account when making decisions to whether to allow access to specific data elements.
- In [126], a set of dataflow anti-patterns is described. These patterns capture undesirable dataflows (e.g., reading a data value before its creation, etc). These patterns can be used to develop analysis techniques that detect obvious mistakes with respect to data.
- As mentioned several times, concurrent access to shared data elements may cause all kinds of problems (e.g., lost updates). Many authors have worked on transaction support in the context of WFM systems. For example, the techniques presented in [135] originate from databases but can be applied to concurrency control in process management.

6 Resource Patterns

After discussing patterns related to the control-flow perspective and the data perspective, we now focus on the third perspective: *resources*. Existing languages and tools focus on control-flow and combine this focus with mature support for data in the form of XML and database technology (often provided by third-party tools). As a result, control-flow and data management are well addressed by existing languages and systems (either directly or indirectly by incorporating external capabilities). Unfortunately, *less attention has been devoted to the resource perspective*. This continues to be the case even with relatively recent advances such as BPEL, which does not mandate any degree of direct support for resources in business processes based on web services. In the case of BPEL (as with many other BPM offerings), it is left to individual vendors to decide how resources will be integrated with a BPEL-enabled process. Similarly, languages like XPDL, the "Lingua Franca" proposed by the Workflow Management Coalition (WfMC), has a simplistic view of the resource perspective and provides minimal support for modeling workers, organizations, work distribution mechanisms, and so on. John Seely Brown (a former chief scientist at Xerox) succinctly captures the current predicament: "Processes don't do work, people do!" [32]. In other words, it is not sufficient to simply focus on control-flow and data issues when capturing business processes, the resources that enable them need to be considered as well.

Section 6.1 starts by providing an overview of the resource patterns. These include: *creation patterns* (section 6.2), *push patterns* (section 6.3), *pull patterns* (section 6.4), *detour patterns* (section 6.5), *auto-start patterns* (section 6.6), *visibility patterns* (section 6.7), and *multiple resource patterns* (section 6.8). Pointers for further reading are provided in section 6.9.

6.1 Overview of the resource patterns

This chapter focuses on the resource perspective. The resource perspective centers on the modeling of resources and their interaction with a BPM offering. Resources can be both human (e.g., a worker) or nonhuman (e.g., plant and equipment). Nevertheless, our focus will only be on human resources. Although BPM offerings typically identify human resources, they know little about them. For example, in a workflow system like Staffware, a human resource is completely specified by the work queues they can see. This does not do justice to the capabilities of the people using such systems. Staffware also does not leave a lot of "elbow room" for its users since the only thing users can do is to execute the work items in their work queues (i.e., people are treated as automatons and have little influence over the way work is distributed). The limitations of existing offerings motivated the patterns collection presented in this chapter. The following sections discuss the range of *Resource Patterns* that have been identified in business process modeling languages and systems. These are grouped into a series of specific categories depending on the specific focus of individual patterns as follows:

- **Creation** patterns, which describe design time work distribution directives that are nominated for tasks in a process model;
- **Push** patterns, which describe situations where the system proactively distributes work items to resources;
- **Pull** patterns, which relate to situations where individual resources take the initiative in identifying and committing to undertake work items;
- **Detour** patterns, which describe various ways in which the distribution and lifecycle of work items can deviate from the directives specified for them at design time;
- **Auto-start** patterns, which identify alternate ways in which work items can be automatically started;
- **Visibility** patterns, which indicate the extent to which resources can observe pending and executing work items; and
- **Multiple-resource** patterns, which identify situations where the correspondence between work items and resources is not one-one.

The approach to integrating people with business processes varies widely between BPM offerings. Indeed even among the offerings examined in this book, there is little commonality in the way in which human resources are represented or work is distributed to them.

- BPMone supports an organizational model that is exclusively role-based and is defined in terms of a role hierarchy. Correspondences are established between individual users or groups of users and roles. Users involved in a business process are characterized in terms of the roles that they possess. All work allocations are role-based and are triggered at the request of individual users based on their ability to take on new work items.
- Oracle BPEL provides support for a sophisticated organizational model both in terms of the definition of individual resources and their various attributes, and also in terms of the relationships between them. Moreover, it provides a wealth of options for handling the distribution of work items to both individual resources and groups of resources and for managing its conduct through to completion. It also caters to the realities of work performance in an operational environment and includes facilities such as escalations and reassignments, where specified distribution practices in a business process go awry and provides a framework for binding a wealth of organizational and extra-organizational capabilities and services into processes by virtue of its service-oriented architecture.
- BPMN provides a different perspective on the distribution of work by virtue of its status as both a modeling language and an execution language for business processes. At a conceptual level, Pools and Swimlanes can be used to denote the responsibility for undertaking specific activities. When used at an executable level, it supports User Tasks based on the WS-HumanTask specification to more rigorously define the way in which

tasks should be assigned to resources and their associated lifecycle at runtime. It also incorporates a basic organizational model that identifies distinct resources and provides various grouping concepts.

In subsequent sections, we will examine the various resource patterns that have been delineated in business processes. We start with creation patterns, which characterize frequently occurring design time directives for the distribution of work in a business process.

6.2   Creation patterns

Creation patterns correspond to limitations on the manner in which a work item may be executed. They are specified at design time, usually in relation to a task, and serve to restrict the range of resources that can undertake work items that correspond to the task. They also influence the manner in which a work item can be matched with a resource that is capable of undertaking it.

The essential rationale for creation patterns is that they provide a degree of clarity about how a work item should be handled after creation during the offering and allocation stages prior to it being executed. This ensures that the operation of a process conforms with its intended design principles and operates as efficiently and deterministically as possible.

In terms of the work item lifecycle, creation patterns come into effect when a work item is created. This state transition occurs at the beginning of the work item lifetime and is illustrated by the bold arrow in figure 6.1. This arc is labeled `S:create`, indicating that the transition is initiated by the system (hence, the `S:` prefix as against an `R:` prefix that would indicate the transition being initiated by a resource) and that it corresponds to a `create` action (i.e., the creation of a new task instance or work item).

For all of these patterns, it is assumed that there is an associated organizational model that allows resources to be uniquely identified and that there is a mechanism to distribute work items to specific resources identified in the organizational model. As creation patterns are specified at design time, they usually form part of the process model that describes a business process.

Direct distribution

Description The ability to specify at design time the identity of the resource(s) to which instances of a task will be distributed at runtime.

Example

- The *Fix Bentley* task must only be undertaken by *Fred*.

Motivation *Direct distribution* offers the ability for a process designer to precisely specify the identity of the resource to which instances of a task will be distributed at runtime. This is particularly useful where it is known that a task can only be effectively undertaken

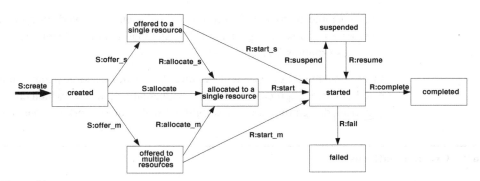

Figure 6.1
Creation patterns (from [113]).

by a specific resource as it prevents the problem of unexpected or nonsuitable resource distributions arising at runtime by ensuring work items are routed to specific resources, a feature that is particularly desirable for critical tasks.

Overview The *Direct distribution* pattern is specified as a relationship between a task and a (nonempty) group of resources. At runtime, work items associated with the task are distributed to one or more of these resources.

Context There are no specific context conditions associated with this pattern.

Implementation The use of *Direct distribution* necessitates the inclusion of the identity of specific resources in a process definition. Consequently, any changes in the staffing arrangement for specific tasks in a process also require changes to the process model. For this reason, many BPM offerings do not offer support for this pattern, preferring instead to use the indirection mechanism provided by the next pattern — *Role-based distribution* — which isolates the process model from specific staffing considerations. Oracle BPEL allows a Human Task to be directly allocated to a specific user. At an abstract level, BPMN utilizes the notion of Pools for identifying how Tasks will be assigned at runtime.

As a Pool can correspond to an individual or a role, it directly supports this pattern. Additionally, Tasks can be assigned to a specific resource on the basis of associated expressions or parameterized queries. BPMone does not provide the ability to directly specify the identity of a resource to whom a task should be distributed; however, the same effect can be achieved where a role is used to specify the task distribution, and there is a 1-1 correspondence between resources and roles. Figure 6.2 illustrates the configuration of the *Direct distribution* pattern in Oracle BPEL and BPMN.

Issues One of the main drawbacks of this approach to work distribution is that it effectively defines a static binding of all work items associated with a task to a single resource. This removes much of the advantage associated with the use of process technology for managing work distribution as the BPM offering is offered little latitude for optimizing the distribution of work items in this situation.

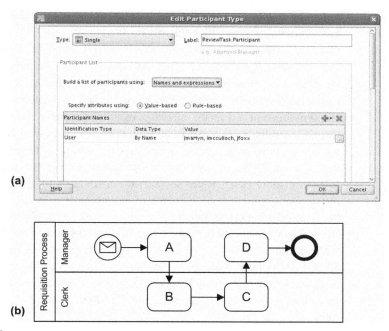

Figure 6.2
Direct distribution pattern in (a) Oracle BPEL, and (b) BPMN.

Solutions There is no real solution to this problem other than using role-based distribution.

Role-based distribution

Description The ability to specify at design time one or more roles to which instances of a task will be distributed at runtime. Roles serve as a means of grouping resources with similar characteristics. Where an instance of a task is distributed in this way, it is distributed to all resources that are members of the role(s) associated with the task.

Example

- Instances of the *Approve Travel Permit* task must be executed by a *Manager*.

Motivation Perhaps the most common approach to work item distribution within BPM offerings, *Role-based distribution* offers the means to route work items to suitably qualified resources at runtime. The decision as to which resource actually receives a given work item is deferred until the moment at which it becomes "runnable" and needs to be distributed to a resource in order for it to proceed. One advantage offered by *Role-based distribution* is that roles can be defined for a given process that identify the various classes of available resources to undertake work items. Task definitions within the process model can nominate the specific role to which they should be routed; however, the actual population of individual roles occurs at runtime. Moreover, the population of a role can change over time, reflecting changes in staffing with an organization, but this does not necessitate changes to process definitions in which the role is utilized.

Overview The *Role-based distribution* pattern is specified as a relationship between a task and a (nonempty) group of roles. At runtime, work items associated with the task are distributed to one or more of the resources participating in these roles.

Context There are no specific context conditions associated with this pattern.

Implementation All of the offerings examined support *Role-based distribution* in some form. Generally, roles serve as groupings of resources with similar characteristics or authority and provide a means of decoupling the routing of a work item from that of resource management. BPMone supports multiple users per role and allows a user to play different roles in distinct cases. Roles serve as the main basis of work item distribution, although resources have a reasonable degree of autonomy in selecting the work items (and cases) that they will undertake rather than having work items directly assigned to them. Oracle BPEL allows one or more application roles to be used for identifying potential resources to whom a Human Task may be assigned. At an abstract level, BPMN supports roles through the use of Pool and Swimlane constructs. At an executable level, BPMN allows Tasks to be assigned to a role on the basis of expressions or parameterized queries. Figure 6.3 illustrates the configuration of the pattern in BPMone, which bases its distribution strategy on roles.

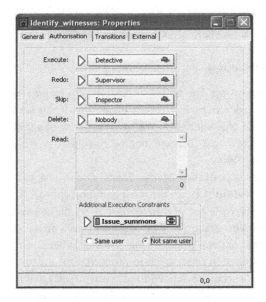

Figure 6.3
Role-based distribution pattern in BPMone: instances of task identify_witnesses should be executed by a resource having role Detective.

Issues In most BPM offerings, the concepts of roles and groups are relatively synonymous. Roles serve as an abstract grouping mechanism (i.e., not just for resources with similar characteristics or authority, but also for identification of organizational units; e.g., teams, departments, etc.) and provide a means of distributing work across a number of resources simultaneously. One difficulty that can arise with this use of roles occurs where the intention is to offer a work item to several resources with the expectation that they will all work on it.

Solutions Oracle BPEL provides support for group-based work distribution. It provides a multitude of configuration options for defining how such tasks should be routed to group members, how they should be undertaken (e.g., by a single participant, multiple group members in parallel, multiple members in sequence, rule-based selection mechanisms for choosing amongst group members), and how task completion should be assessed where multiple resources undertake it (e.g., specified number of group member completions, expression-based completion conditions, voting, etc). BPMN allows Tasks to be assigned to group-based roles on the basis of expressions or parameterized queries. BPMone does not provide support for this approach to work distribution as part of its role-based distribution mechanism.

Deferred distribution

Description The ability to specify at design time that the identification of the resource(s) to which instances of a task will be distributed will be deferred until runtime.

Example

- Identification of who will execute the *Assess Damage* task is deferred until runtime. During execution of a case, the *next_resource* field will hold the identity of the resource to whom instances of the task should be allocated.

Motivation *Deferred distribution* takes the notion of indirect work distribution one step further and allows the process designer to defer the need to identify the resource for a specific task (or work items corresponding to the task) until runtime. By doing so, the flexibility of the work distribution within a process is maximized and actual work assignments can be deferred until the last possible moment at runtime, allowing current workloads and resource commitments in the operating environment to be taken into account when making task allocations.

Overview The *Deferred distribution* pattern is specified as a relationship between a task and some form of indirection mechanism. This may be a (nonempty) group of data elements, a dynamic routing expression, or a business rule. At runtime, when an instance of the task is triggered, the value of the data element(s) is determined or the routing expression or business rule is evaluated to give a set of resources to which work items associated with the task may be distributed. The result of this evaluation may be the identity of one or more specific resources or it may be a role to which the relevant work item can be assigned.

Context There is one context condition associated with this pattern: the offering supports direct or role-based distribution.

Implementation Oracle BPEL provides a number of alternatives for supporting this pattern. Task assignments can be specified dynamically based on task assignment patterns, XPath expressions, or business rules. There is also the provision for an external routing service to be utilized to determine task assignment at runtime. When these assignment features are utilized, they identify a specific user, group, or role to whom a work item should be assigned. BPMN allows the actual identification of the identity of the resource or role to which a task is distributed to be delayed to runtime.

Issues The main issue associated with the use of this pattern is handling the situation where the distribution function or rule does not identify a specific user or group to assign the work item to.

Solutions Oracle BPEL supports the notion of an Error Assignee for individual tasks, which identifies a specific resource who can deal with a failed task assignment. In the event of a failed assignment of a work item (or other error conditions related to work item routing), the Error Assignee resource is advised of the error condition and can resolve the situation by assigning the work item to a specific resource on an ad-hoc basis, reassigning it to the user or group previously identified in the assignment criteria for the task, or an assignment error can be raised indicating that the assignment problem is terminal and nonrecoverable. Although not precisely specified by BPMN, the assumption is that a compensation event can be specified to handle the occurrence of this situation for a Task.

Authorization

Description The ability to specify the range of privileges that a resource possesses in regard to the execution of a process. These privileges are independent from the actual work distribution and define the range of actions that a resource can initiate when undertaking work items associated with tasks in a process.

Examples

- In a call center, only users with the manager role can reorder work items in the queue.
- Only *Senior Managers* can suspend instances of the *conduct audit* task.

Motivation Through the specification of authorizations on task definitions, it is possible to define a security framework over a process that is independent of the way in which work items are actually routed at runtime. This can be used to restrict the range of resources that can access details of a work item or request, execute, or redistribute it. This ensures that unexpected events that may arise during execution (e.g., work item delegation by a resource or reallocation to another resource outside of the usual process definition) do not lead to unexpected resources being able to undertake work items.

Overview The *Authorization* pattern takes the form of a set of relationships between resources and the privileges that they possess in regard to a given process. These privileges define the range of actions that the resource can initiate. They are intended to be orthogonal to the work distribution directives specified for individual tasks in a process and can include operations such as:

- the ability to select the next work item that they will execute;
- the ability to execute more than one work item simultaneously;
- the ability to reorder work items in their worklist;
- the ability to suspend and resume instances of a task during execution;
- the ability to reallocate instances of a task that have been commenced to another user;
- the ability to deallocate instances of a task that have not been commenced and allow them to be re-allocated to another user;
- the ability to delegate instances of a task that have not been commenced to another user;
- the ability to skip instances of a task; and
- the ability to access data elements associated with a task.

Context There are no specific context conditions associated with this pattern.

Implementation Oracle BPEL provides a number of access rules that prescribe the specific actions that a resource can undertake with respect to a given work item. These include actions such as acquiring, delegating, escalating, withdrawing, and completing the work item. BPMone uses roles as the main basis for case and work item distribution. Roles are organized as hierarchies, and only resources that directly (or indirectly) possess a required role are able to view and execute a specific work item. BPMone provides facilities for limiting access to data items associated with a work item; however, it does not provide any further ability to limit user actions with respect to individual work items. For a BPMN Task based on a WS-HumanTask implementation, a range of operation authorizations can be specified. Figure 6.4 illustrates the authorization capabilities available in Oracle BPEL.

Issues The range of resources that are authorized to undertake a task may not correspond with those to which it could be assigned based on the current resource pool within the BPM offering.

Solutions As described for the *Deferred distribution* pattern, Oracle BPEL provides the Error Assignee facility to deal with situations where a task assignment fails or where no authorized user exists that can start or undertake the task. This ensures that there is always a user that can progress a work item in this situation.

Separation of duties

Description The ability to specify that two tasks must be executed by different resources in any given case. This is also known as the "four-eyes principle" (i.e., at least two persons should have worked on selected cases).

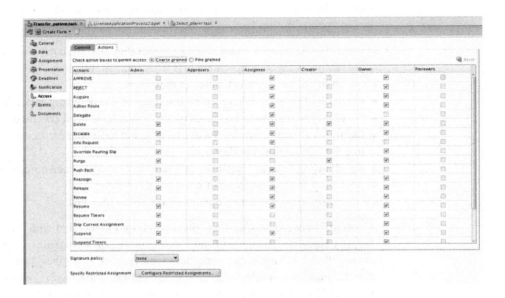

Figure 6.4
Authorization facilities available in Oracle BPEL.

Example

- Instances of the *Countersign cheque* task must be allocated to a different resource to that which executed the *Prepare cheque* task in a given case.

Motivation *Separation of duties* allows for the enforcement of audit controls within the execution of a given case. The *Separation of duties* constraint exists between two tasks in a process model. It ensures that within a given case, work items corresponding to the latter task cannot be executed by resources that completed work items corresponding to the former task. Another use of this pattern arises with BPM offerings that support multiple task instances. In this situation, the degree of parallelism that can be achieved when a multiple instance task is executed can be maximized by specifying that as far as possible, no two task instances can be executed by the same resource (assuming that there are a multitude of suitable resources able to undertake distinct task instances).

Overview The *Separation of duties* pattern relates a task t to a number of other tasks that precede it in the process. Within a given case, work items corresponding to task t cannot be distributed to any resource that previously completed work items corresponding to tasks with which t has a *Separation of duties* constraint. As it is possible that preceding tasks may have executed more than once within a given case (e.g., they may be contained within a loop or have multiple instances), a number of resources may be excluded from undertaking instances of task t.

Context There are no specific context conditions associated with this pattern.

Implementation BPMone provides the ability to specify at task level a link with another (preceding) task. At runtime, the work item corresponding to the task cannot be allocated to the same resource as that which undertook the last instance of the work item corresponding to the linked task. Oracle BPEL can achieve a similar effect through the use of an XPath expression or a custom assignment directive in the Assignment section for a Human Task that specifies that the resource(s) to whom it can be assigned cannot include the resource to which a preceding task in the same case has been allocated. For a BPMN Task based on a WS-HumanTask implementation, peopleAssignments can be defined based on XPath functions, including the except operation, which allows separation of duties constraints to be enforced for task distributions.

Issues The use of this pattern can lead to situations where no resources remain that are able to execute a given work item due to the resource exclusions that have been imposed.

Solutions As described for the *Deferred distribution* pattern.

Case handling

Description The ability to allocate all work items within a given case to the same resource that started the case.

Example

- All tasks in a given case of the *Prepare defence* process are allocated to the same *Legal Advisor*.

Motivation *Case handling* is a specific approach to work distribution that is based on the premise that all work items in a given case are so closely related that they should all be undertaken by the same resource. The identification of the specific resource occurs when a case (or the first work item in a case) requires allocation.

Case handling may occur on either a "hard" or "soft" basis. In the former situation, work items within a given case are allocated exclusively to the same resource that must complete them all. In the latter, work items within a given case are routed to an initial resource that is identified as having initial responsibility for them and subsequently delegates them to other resources or allows them to nominate work items they would like to complete.

Overview The *Case handling* pattern takes the form of a relationship between a process and one or more resources or roles. When an instance of the process is initiated, a resource is selected from the associated set of resources and roles and the process instance is allocated to this resource. It is expected that this resource will execute work items corresponding to tasks in this process instance.

Context There are no specific context conditions associated with this pattern.

Implementation This approach to work distribution is not generally supported by BPM offerings such as those examined. Only BPMone (which describes itself as a case handling system) provides direct support.

Retain familiar

Description The ability to allocate a work item to the same resource that undertook a preceding work item for the same case.

Example

- If there are several suitable resources available to undertake the *Prepare Match Report* work item, it should be allocated to the same resource that undertook the *Umpire Match* task in a given workflow case.

Motivation Distributing a work item to the same resource that undertook a previous work item is a common means of expediting a case. As the resource is already aware of the details of the case, it saves familiarization time at the commencement of the work item. Where the two work items are sequential, it also offers the opportunity for minimizing switching time as the resource can commence the latter work item immediately on completion of the former.

This pattern is a more flexible version of the *Case handling* pattern discussed earlier. It only comes into effect when there are multiple resources available to undertake a given work item, and where this occurs, it favors the allocation of the work item to the resource that undertook a previous work item in the case. Unlike the *Case handling* pattern (which operates at the case level), this pattern applies at the work item level and comes into play when a work item is being distributed to a resource.

The *Chained execution* pattern is related to this pattern and is designed to expedite the completion of a case by automatically starting subsequent work items once the preceding work item is complete.

Overview The *Retain familiar* pattern takes the form of a one-one relationship between a task and a preceding task in the same process. Where it holds for a task, when an instance of the task is created in a given case, it is distributed to the same resource that completed the nominated preceding task in the same case. If the preceding task has been executed more than once, then it is distributed to one of the resources that completed it previously.

Context There are no specific context conditions associated with this pattern.

Implementation Not surprisingly, this pattern enjoys wider support than the *Case handling* pattern. BPMone provides a facility in the design time workflow model to enforce that a task must be executed by the same resource as another specified task in the case. Oracle BPEL achieves it through the use of an XPath expression or a custom assignment directive in the Assignment section for a Human Task that specifies that the resource to whom it is assigned should be the same as the resource that undertook a nominated preceding task in the same case. For a BPMN Task based on a WS-HumanTask implementation, this pattern is supported by setting the actual owner to the same value as the actual owner of another task.

Capability-based distribution

Description The ability to distribute work items to resources based on specific capabilities that they possess. Capabilities (and their associated values) are recorded for individual resources as part of the organizational model.

Example

- Instances of the *Airframe Examination* task should be allocated to an *Engineer* with an aeronautics degree, an Airbus in-service accreditation, and more than 10 years experience in Airbus servicing.

Motivation The *Capability-based distribution* pattern provides a mechanism for offering or allocating work items to resources through the matching of specific requirements of work items with the capabilities of the potential range of resources that are available to undertake them. This allows for a much more fine-grained approach to selecting the resources suited to completing a given task.

Overview Within a given organizational model, each resource is assumed to be able to have *capabilities* recorded for them that specify their individual characteristics (e.g., qualifications, previous jobs) and their ability to undertake certain tasks (e.g., licenses held, trade certifications). Similarly, it is assumed that *capability functions* can be specified that take a set of resources and their associated capabilities and return the subset of those resources that conform to a required range of capability values. Each task in a process model can have a capability function associated with it. Figure 6.5 illustrates the manner in which the *Capability-based distribution* pattern operates with a capability function, matching a work item to a resource on the basis of both resource capabilities and work item attributes.

Capability-based distribution can be either push- or pull-based (i.e., the actual distribution process can be initiated by the system or the resource). In the former situation, the system determines the most appropriate resource(s) to which a work item should be routed. In the latter, a resource initiates a search for an unallocated work item(s) that it is capable of undertaking.

Context There are no specific context conditions associated with this pattern.

Implementation *Capability-based distribution* is based on the specification of capabilities for individual resources. Capabilities generally take the form of attribute-value pairs (e.g., "signing authority," "$10M"). A dictionary of capabilities can be defined in which individual capabilities have a distinct name and the type and potential range of values that each capability may take can also be specified. Similarly, tasks can also have capabilities recorded for them. In the case of resources, details of their individual capabilities are often recorded in repositories or directories external to the BPM offering. Such repositories provide a reference of organizational resources and their characteristics that can be used

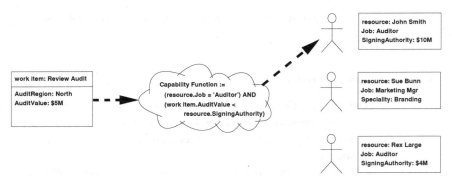

Figure 6.5
Capability-based distribution.

by individuals and systems throughout the organization. They are often based on organizational directory standards such as X.500 or LDAP.

The actual capability-based distribution process is generally based on capability functions (in some form of procedural or declarative language) that are evaluated at runtime and determine how individual work items can be matched with suitable resources. These may be arbitrarily complex in nature depending on the range of capabilities that require matching between resources and work items and the approach that is taken to ranking the matches that are achieved to select the most appropriate resource to undertake a given work item. Oracle BPEL provides support for arbitrarily complex XPath expressions that can use a range of internal and external data elements related to resources to determine how a given work items should be assigned. BPMone uses case queries to determine which cases can be allocated to a specific resource. These can include data elements relating to both the case and the individual resource. In BPMN, there is no support for routing tasks to resources based on additional capability attributes that the resources may possess.

Issues One issue associated with push-oriented *Capability-based distribution* is that it is possible for capability functions to identify more than one possible resource to which a work item may be assigned. Where this occurs, the work item may either be offered to multiple resources or assigned to one of the identified resources on a specific basis. It is also possible for the capability function to return an empty set of possible resources.

A second issue relates to pull-oriented *Capability-based distribution*, in that it is possible for a resource to identify more than one work item that it is capable of undertaking.

Solutions The first of these issues is not necessarily a problem, although it may result in suboptimal resource allocations. It can be avoided through more precise definition of capability functions. As an example, if the intention of the competence function in figure 6.5 was to allocate the task to a single auditor, then a ranking function (e.g., `minimum`) should be included in the competence function to ensure only a single resource is returned. The problems associated with an empty return value can be avoided by testing whether the capability function returns an empty set and, if so, assigning a default value for the resource. Oracle provides facilities to address both of these issues through the use of dynamic assignment functions (e.g., LEAST_BUSY, MOST_PRODUCTIVE) to limit assignment to a single resource and the Error Assignee facility to ensure assignment succeeds even in the event of problems with capability-based assignment functions.

The second issue should not generally result in difficulties. Under a pull-based distribution strategy (such as that employed in BPMone), resources should anticipate the possible return of multiple work items.

History-based distribution

Description The ability to distribute work items to resources on the basis of their previous execution history.

Examples

- Allocate the *Finalize heart bypass* task to the *Surgeon* who has successfully completed the most of these tasks.
- Allocate the *Core extraction* task to the *drill operator* that has the lowest utilization over the past 3 months.

Motivation *History-based distribution* involves the use of information on the previous execution history of resources when determining which of them a work item should be distributed to. This is an analogue to common human experience when determining who to distribute a specific work item to which considers factors, such as who has the most experience with this type of work item or who has had the least numbers of failures when tackling similar tasks.

Overview *History-based distribution* assumes the existence of *historical distribution functions*, which take a set of resources and the previous execution history for the process and return the subset of those resources that satisfy the nominated historical criteria. These may include factors such as the resource that least recently executed a task, has executed it successfully the most times, has the shortest turnaround time for the task, or any other combination of requirements that can be determined from the execution history. Each task in a process model can have a historical distribution function associated with it.

Context There are no specific context conditions associated with this pattern.

Implementation For a BPMN Task based on a WS-HumanTask implementation, peopleAssignments can be defined based on XPath functions, including historical execution data provided by the getTaskHistory function. Oracle BPEL can provide indirect support for the pattern through the use of custom or external assignment services that retain details of historical execution in a form that allows it to be utilized when distributing task instances at runtime.

Issues The main difficulty with facilitating this distribution strategy is that it requires a range of historical execution information be retained in a readily accessible form and introduces additional complexity in the distribution of work items.

Solutions There is no immediate solution to this issue. Supporting this pattern does introduce additional complexity into BPM offerings. Where a history-based distribution strategy is not directly supported by an offering, modifications are required to the process in order to achieve this. The only recommendation that can be made in this situation is to gather and manage the least amount of execution history for each resource that is required to facilitate the chosen work distribution strategy.

Organizational distribution

Description The ability to distribute work items to resources based on their position within the organization and their relationships with other resources.

Examples

- The *Review Audit* work item must be allocated to a resource that is employed in a *Partner* position.
- The *Authorize Expenditure* work item must be allocated to the *Manager* of the resource that undertook the *Claim Expenditure* work item in a given case.

Motivation Most offerings provide some degree of support for modeling the organizational context in which a given process operates. This is an important aspect of business process modeling and implementation as many work distribution decisions are made in the context of the organizational structure and the relative position of individual resources both in the overall hierarchy and also in terms of their relationships with other resources. The ability to capture and emulate these types of work distribution strategies is an important requirement if BPM offerings are to provide a flexible and realistic basis for managing work in an organizational setting.

Overview *Organizational distribution* assumes the existence of *organizational distribution functions*, which take a set of resources and the organizational model associated with a process and return the subset of those resources that satisfy the nominated organizational criteria. These may include factors such as members of a specified department, resources holding a certain position, resources that report to a nominated individual, or any other combination of requirements that can be determined from the organizational model. Each task in a process model can have an organizational distribution function associated with it.

Context There are no specific context conditions associated with this pattern.

Implementation The degree of support for this pattern varies widely. Oracle BPEL supports a comprehensive organizational model for resources associated with BPEL processes. Any of the information captured by this model together with organizational data captured in external repositories can be used for work distribution purposes. For a BPMN Task based on WS-HumanTask, organizational distribution can only be specified based on group membership and role participation for individual resources. BPMone extends the notion of *Role-based distribution* and provides limited support for organizational structures in the form of role hierarchies, which can be used when distributing work items to users.

Automatic execution

Description The ability for an instance of a task to execute without needing to utilize the services of a resource.

Example

- The *End of Day* work item executes without needing to be allocated to a resource.

Motivation Not all tasks within a process need to be executed under the auspices of a human resource; some are able to execute independently once the specified enabling criteria are met.

Overview Where a task is nominated as *automatic*, it is initiated immediately when enabled. Similarly, upon its completion, subsequent tasks are triggered immediately.

Context There are no specific context conditions associated with this pattern.

Implementation BPMone, Oracle BPEL, and BPMN all provide facilities for defining tasks that can run automatically within the context of the process environment without requiring distribution to a resource.

6.3   Push patterns

Push patterns characterize situations where newly created work items are proactively offered or allocated to resources by the system. These may occur indirectly by advertising work items to selected resources via a shared worklist or directly with work items being allocated to specific resources. In both situations, however, the system takes the initiative and causes the distribution process to occur. Figure 6.6 illustrates (as bold arcs) the potential state transitions associated with push-based distribution:

- `S:offer_s` corresponds to a work item being offered to a single resource.
- `S:offer_m` corresponds to a work item being offered to multiple resources (one of which will ultimately execute it).
- `S:allocate` corresponds to a work item being directly allocated to a resource immediately after it has been created.

Nine push patterns have been identified. These divide into three distinct groups. The first three patterns identify the actual manner of work distribution — whether the system offers

User empowerment

There are a variety of different ways in which work distribution can occur within BPM systems. In many cases the actual approach selected will be governed by the nature of the process that is being automated and the enabling technology. In general most BPM systems only support a limited range of ways of distributing individual work items. Moreover, they often tend to leave the distribution of work items largely under the auspices of the system rather than providing individual users with some degree of ambit in terms of how and when work is distributed. This is unfortunate, particularly in light of prevailing views in the area of human resource management which suggest that individuals are both more motivated and more productive when they have some degree of control over the work that they are responsible for completing. The short-comings of many offerings are further compounded by the fact that the same approach to work distribution is not necessarily suitable for every task in a process. High volume, repetitive, short duration tasks are suited to a centralized distribution approach to workers whereas long duration, knowledge intensive activities are best assigned to resources based on consultation with them. The diagram below outlines common approaches to work distribution based on the manner in which individual resources procure the work items that they will undertake and the degree of flexibility they have in selecting when they will commence them.

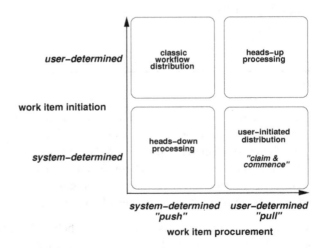

Heads up processing is perhaps the optimal approach to work distribution in business processes. It allows the user to nominate the time at which they are ready to receive new work allocations and also to select the moment at which they will start a given work item, hence providing them with a degree of autonomy in planning their commitments. The system distributes the work to the user at their request and also responds to signals from a user when they have commenced and completed specific work items.

User empowerment

Case handling is a specific type of heads up processing that provides users with maximal flexibility by allowing them to not only choose the timing of work item procurement and commencement but also allowing them to undertake work items in a given process instance in an order of their own choosing. Whilst it empowers users to undertake work items in their own particular way, it is not a general solution as it is best suited to processes in which individual tasks are tightly interrelated and need to be undertaken by the same resource or a group of tightly coupled resources.

Classic workflow distribution is a widely implemented approach based on a system-oriented allocation of work items to users. It involves the system distributing available work in process instances as it becomes executable. Typically the user has little freedom in selecting what type of work they want to do, however they are able to nominate the approach that they will take to undertaking work.

Heads down processing is the converse of the heads up processing approach discussed earlier. It offers individual workers almost no autonomy and allocates work items to them on a pre-emptive basis at a time of the system's choosing. The user has no choice in the timing of work item commencement and is typically expected to commence working on an assigned task immediately.

User-initiated distribution offers the individual worker a little more autonomy allowing them to choose the timing at which work items are distributed but they must still commence an assigned work item immediately or at a time of the system's choosing. Often with these distribution strategies, the underlying technology does not differentiate between work items being allocated to a specific resource and the time at which they are commenced and these two states are considered to be the same.

Existing BPM offerings typically support one of these approaches to work distribution. Hopefully it is clear from this discussion that there are a range of possible approaches to work distribution that may need to be catered for in a given process and that there are significant opportunities for enhancements in this area.

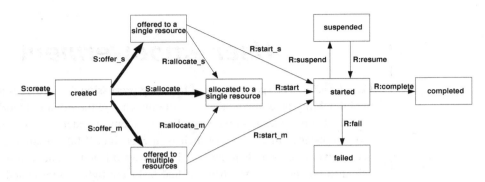

Figure 6.6
Push patterns (from [113]).

the work item to a single resource, to multiple resources, or whether it allocates it directly to a single resource.[1] These patterns correspond directly to the bold arcs in figure 6.6.

The second group of patterns relates to the means by which a resource is selected to undertake a work item where there are multiple possible resources identified. Three possible strategies are described — random allocation, round robin allocation, and shortest queue. These patterns correspond to alternate ways in which the S:offer_s and S:allocate transitions may occur.

The final three patterns identify the timing of the distribution process, and in particular the relationship between the availability of a work item for offer/allocation to resources and the time at which it commences execution. Three variants are possible — work items are offered/allocated before they have commenced (early distribution), after they have commenced (late distribution), or the two events are simultaneous (distribution on enablement). These patterns do not have a direct analogue in figure 6.6 but relate to the time at which the S:offer_s, S:offer_m and S:allocate transitions may occur with respect to the work item's readiness to be executed (i.e., already started, immediate start, or subsequent start).

Distribution by offer — single resource

Description The ability to distribute a work item to a selected individual resource on a nonbinding basis.
Example
• The *Prepare defense* work item is offered to a selected *Barrister*.

---

1 These patterns assume a one-to-one correspondence between resources working on a work item and work items being processed. In other words, resources cannot work on different work items simultaneously and it is not possible that multiple resources work on the same work item. In section 6.8, this requirement is discussed further and relaxed slightly.

Motivation This pattern provides a means of distributing a work item to a single resource on a nonbinding basis. The resource is informed of the work item being offered but is not committed to executing it and can either ignore the work item or redistribute it to other resources should it choose not to undertake it.

Overview Offering a work item to a single resource is the process analogy to the act of "asking for consideration" in real life. If the resource decides not to undertake it, then the onus is still with the system to find another suitable resource to complete it. Once a task has been enabled that is distributed on this basis, a means of actually informing the selected resource of the pending work item is required. The mechanism chosen should notify the resource that a work item exists that it may wish to undertake; however, it should not commit the resource to its execution, and it should not advise any other resources of the potential work item. Typically this is achieved by adding the work item to the worklist of the selected user with an offered status, although other notification mechanisms are possible. This pattern directly corresponds to the state transition denoted by arc `S:offer_s` in figure 6.6.

Context There are no specific context conditions associated with this pattern.

Implementation Oracle BPEL offers the ability to distribute work items on this basis where they are distributed to a group that only contains one member. In this situation, the user must claim the item before it is deemed to be assigned to them. BPMone operates on a "pull-oriented" basis, where individual users trigger the distribution of suitable work items to them at a time of their own choosing rather than having the system distribute work items to them. For BPMN Tasks based on WS-HumanTask, the pattern is supported by assigning a work item associated with the Task to a work queue that only has one group member. The resource must claim the work item before it is allocated to them.

Distribution by offer — multiple resources

Description The ability to distribute a work item to a group of selected resources on a nonbinding basis.

Example

- The *Sell portfolio* work item is offered to multiple *Stockbrokers*.

Motivation This pattern provides a means of distributing a work item to multiple resources on a nonbinding basis. The resources are informed of the work item being offered, but are not committed to executing it, and can either ignore the work item or redistribute it to other resources should they choose not to undertake it.

Overview Offering a work item to multiple resources is the process analogy to the act of "calling for a volunteer" in real life. It provides a means of advising a suitably qualified group of resources that a work item exists, with the expectation that one of them will actually commit to undertaking the activity, although the onus is still with the system to find a suitable resource should none of them agree to undertake it. Once a task has been enabled that is distributed on this basis, a means of actually informing the selected resources of the pending work item is required. The mechanism chosen should notify the resources that a work item exists that they may wish to undertake; however, it should not commit any of the resources to its execution. Typically this is achieved by adding the work item to the worklists of the selected resources with an offered status, although other notification mechanisms are possible. This pattern directly corresponds to the state transition denoted by arc `S:offer_m` in figure 6.6.

Context There are no specific context conditions associated with this pattern.

Implementation There are a variety of ways in which this pattern might be supported. Work items offered to multiple resources can be included on dedicated work queues for each of the individual resources, each resource may have a distinct work queue for group items as against that for work items individually allocated to them, or resources may have the ability to view a shared group work queue in addition to their own dedicated work queue. When a resource elects to undertake (or even starts) a work item that has been offered to several resources, it may either be removed from the work queues of the other resources or it may be left there, but they may no longer be able to select it. BPMone supports this pattern. By default, a work item is offered to all of the participants of the role(s) that correspond to the work item. Similarly, Oracle BPEL supports it for group- and role-based task allocations. For BPMN Tasks based on WS-HumanTask, the pattern is supported by setting multiple potential owners for a task instance in the Created or Ready state.

Distribution by allocation — single resource

Description The ability to distribute a work item to a specific resource for execution on a binding basis.

Example

- The *Cover Comalco AGM* work item should be allocated to the *Finance Sub-editor*.

Motivation This pattern provides a means of distributing a work item to a single resource on a binding basis. The resource is informed of the work item being distributed to them and is committed to executing it.

Overview Allocating a work item to a single resource is the process analogy to the act of "appointing an owner" in real life. It involves the system directly assigning a work item to a resource without first offering it to other resources or querying whether the resource will undertake it. In doing so, it passes the onus of ensuring the work item is completed to the selected resource.

This approach to work distribution shares some similarities with the work distribution strategy known as "heads down" processing, as it offers the resource little or no input into the work that they are allocated. In many implementations, resources are simply allocated a new work item once the previous one is completed, and they are not offered any insight into what work items might lay ahead for them.

Once a task has been enabled that is distributed on this basis, a means of actually informing the selected resource of the pending work item is required. The mechanism chosen should notify the resource that a work item exists that they must undertake. Typically this is achieved by adding the work item to the worklist of the selected resource with an allocated status, although other notification mechanisms are possible. This pattern directly corresponds to the state transition denoted by arc S:allocate in figure 6.6.

Context There are no specific context conditions associated with this pattern.

Implementation Where a specific resource has been identified during the course of work item distribution, this is the standard means of allocating a work item to a resource. It is done pre-emptively by the system and necessitates that the resource actually execute the work item unless it has recourse to a means of rejecting it. All of the offerings examined support *direct allocation* of work items to individual resources. In the case of BPMone, the allocation is initiated by the resource, whereas for Oracle BPEL, it occurs at the instigation of the system. For BPMN Tasks based on WS-HumanTask, the pattern is supported by setting a single potential owner for a task instance in the Created or Ready state.

Random allocation

Description The ability to allocate a work item to a selected resource chosen from a group of eligible resources on a random basis.

Example

- The *Judge case* work item is allocated to a *Magistrate* on a random basis.

Motivation *Random allocation* provides a nondeterministic mechanism for allocating work items to resources.

Overview This pattern provides a means of restricting the distribution of a work item to a single resource. Once the possible range of resources that a work item can be distributed to has been identified at runtime, one of these is selected at random to execute the work item.

Context There are no specific context conditions associated with this pattern.

Implementation Oracle BPEL supports the pattern through the use of an XPath-based dynamic assignment function that randomly selects a user from a list of users or groups. There is no support for this approach to work allocation in BPMN or BPMone.

Round robin allocation

Description The ability to allocate a work item to a selected resource chosen from a group of eligible resources on a cyclic basis.

Example

- Work items corresponding to the *Umpire Match* task are allocated to each available *Referee* on a cyclic basis.

Motivation *Round robin allocation* provides a means of allocating work items to resources on an equitable basis.

Overview This pattern provides a fair means of restricting the distribution of a work item to a single resource. Once the possible range of resources that a work item can be distributed to has been identified at runtime, one of these is selected on a cyclic basis to execute the work item. The intention being that, over time, each resource receives the same number of work items. One means of choosing the appropriate resource is to select the resource that undertook the task least recently. An alternative to this is for the system to keep track of the number of times each resource has completed each task, allowing the one who has undertaken it the least number of times to be identified.

Context There are no specific context conditions associated with this pattern.

Implementation Oracle BPEL directly supports the pattern through the use of the ROUND_ROBIN dynamic assignment function. There is no support for this approach to work allocation in BPMN or BPMone.

Issues By its nature, *Round robin allocation* requires details of individual resource allocations to be maintained so that a decision can be made as to which resource should be used when the next allocation decision is made.

Solutions Where a BPM offering does not directly support *Round robin allocation*, it is left to the auspices of the process developer to implement a strategy for this form of allocation.

Shortest queue

Description The ability to allocate a work item to a selected resource chosen from a group of eligible resources on the basis of having the shortest work queue.

Example

- The *Heart Bypass Procedure* is allocated to the *Surgeon* who has the least number of operations allocated to them.

Motivation *Shortest queue* provides a means of allocating work items to resources such that the chosen resource should be able to undertake the work item as soon as possible.

Overview *Shortest queue* distribution provides a means of allocating work items to resources with the intention of expediting the throughput of a process instance by ensuring that work items are allocated to the resource that is able to undertake them in the shortest possible timeframe. Typically the shortest timeframe means the resource with the shortest work queue, although other interpretations are possible.

Context There are no specific context conditions associated with this pattern.

Implementation Oracle BPEL directly supports the pattern through the use of the LEAST_BUSY dynamic assignment function. There is no support for this approach to work allocation in BPMN or BPMone.

Early distribution

Description The ability to advertise and potentially distribute a work item to resources ahead of the moment at which it is actually enabled.

Example

- The *Captain BA12 London — Bangkok flight* work item is offered to potential *Chief Pilots* at least two weeks ahead of the time that it can commence.

Motivation *Early distribution* provides a means of notifying resources of upcoming work items ahead of the time at which they need to be (or can be) executed. This is useful where resources are able to provide some form of forward commitment (or booking), indicating they they will execute and complete a work item at some future time. It also provides a means of optimizing the throughput of a case by ensuring that minimal time is spent waiting for resource distribution during case execution.

Overview Where a process contains a task that is identified as being subject to *Early distribution*, the existence of any work items corresponding to the task can be advertised to resources as soon as an instance of a process is initiated. Depending on the nature of the specific BPM offering, these advertisements may simply be an advance notification or (as in some case handling systems) they may constitute an actual offer or allocation of a work item. However, in both cases, such notifications do not imply that the work item is ready for execution, and it is only when the process advances to the task to which the work item corresponds that the work item can actually be commenced.

Context There are no specific context conditions associated with this pattern.

Implementation None of the offerings examined directly supports this pattern, suggesting that the focus of production BPM offerings tends to be on the management and completion of current work rather than on planning the optimal execution strategy for future work items. BPMone provides the ability for a resource to view future work items and potentially commence work on them even though they are not the next items in the process sequence. The case handling paradigm offers a different approach to work allocation, and the Further Reading section at the end of the chapter gives some links to material on the subject.

Distribution on enablement

Description The ability to advertise and distribute a work item to resources at the moment that the task to which it corresponds is enabled for execution.

Example

- The *Delivery Round* work item is allocated to a *Paper boy* at the time it is required to commence.

Motivation The simultaneous advertisement and distribution of a work item when the task to which it corresponds is enabled constitutes the simplest approach to work distribution from a resource perspective as it ensures that any work item that a resource receives in its work list can be immediately acted upon.

Overview Distribution of a work item at the time that the task to which it corresponds is enabled for execution is effectively the standard mechanism for work distribution in a BPM offering. The enablement of a task serves as the trigger for the system to create an associated work item and make it available to resources for execution. This may occur indirectly by placing it on the work lists for individual resources or on the global worklist or directly by allocating it to a specific resource for immediate execution.

Context There are no specific context conditions associated with this pattern.

Implementation The approach to work item enablement is most commonly supported by BPM offerings. BPMN, Oracle BPEL, and BPMone directly support it.

Late distribution

Description The ability to advertise and distribute a work item to resources after the task to which the work item corresponds has been enabled for execution.

Example

- The *Service Car* work item is only allocated to a *Mechanic* after the car has been delivered for repair and the mechanic has less than five items in his or her worklist.

Motivation *Late distribution* of work items effectively provides a means of "demand driving" a process by only advertising or allocating work items to resources after the tasks to which they correspond have already been enabled for execution. This could potentially be much later than the time the tasks were enabled. By adopting this approach, it is possible to reduce the current volume of work in progress within a process instance. Often this strategy is undertaken with the aim of preventing resources from becoming overwhelmed by the apparent workload even though they may not be required to undertake all of it themselves.

Overview Where a task is identified as being subject to *Late distribution*, the enablement of the task does not necessarily result in the associated work items being distributed to resources for execution. Generally other factors are taken into consideration (e.g., number of active work items, available resources, etc.) before the decision is made to advise resources of its existence. This approach to work distribution provides the system with flexibility in determining when work items are made available for execution and offers the potential to reduce context switching when resources have multiple work items that they are attempting to deal with. This approach to work distribution is often used in conjunction with "heads down" processing, where the focus is on maximizing work throughput and the distribution of work is largely under the auspices of the system. At the other end of the spectrum to this approach is *Case handling*, where the distribution and management of work are largely at the discretion of individual resources.

Context There are no specific context conditions associated with this pattern.

Implementation BPMN and BPMone do not support the notion of *Late distribution* for newly created work items. However, a similar notion is supported by Oracle BPEL through the notion of the ad-hoc routing strategy tasks, where the actual assignment of a human task occurs in two stages. When it is first enabled, it is allocated to an administrator. Then based on the contextual knowledge of the administrator about the state of the current process instance and available resources, a suitable resource is identified to actually undertake the task, and it is allocated to them on an ad-hoc basis.

6.4   Pull patterns

Pull patterns correspond to the situation where individual resources are made aware of specific work items that require execution, either via a direct offer from the system or indirectly through a shared worklist. The commitment to undertake a specific task is initiated by the resource rather than by the system. Generally, this results in the work item being placed on the specific worklist for the individual resource for later execution, although in some cases the resource may elect to commence execution on the work item immediately. The various state transitions associated with pull patterns are illustrated in figure 6.7.

- `R:allocate_s` corresponds to the situation where a work item has been offered to a single resource and the resource has indicated it will commit to executing the work item at some future time.
- `R:allocate_m` corresponds to the situation where a work item has been offered to multiple resources and one of the resources has indicated it will commit to executing the work item at some future time. The work item is deemed to be allocated to that resource and is no longer available to the other resources to which it was offered.
- `R:start_s` corresponds to the situation where a work item that has been offered to a single resource is started by that resource.
- `R:start_m` corresponds to the situation where a work item that has been offered to multiple resources is started by one of those resources.
- `R:start` corresponds to the situation where a work item that has been allocated to a single resource is started by that resource.

Six pull patterns have been identified. These can be divided into two distinct groups. The first three patterns identify the specifics of the actual "pull" action initiated by the resource, with a particular focus on the work item state before and after the interaction. These patterns correspond to the bold arcs in figure 6.7. The second group of patterns focus on the sequence in which the work items are presented to the resource and the ability of the system and the individual resource to influence the sequence and manner in which they are displayed. The final group of patterns illustrates the degree of freedom that the resource has in selecting the next work item to execute. The patterns in the second group are orthogonal to the ones in the first group. They do not have a direct analogue in figure 6.7 but apply to all of the "pull" transitions illustrated as bold arcs.

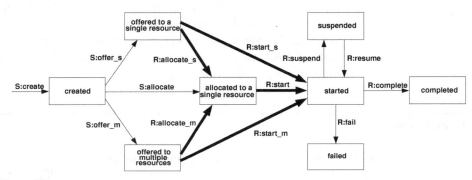

Figure 6.7
Pull patterns (from [113]).

Note that the distinction between push and pull patterns is identified by the initiator of the various transitions. For the push patterns in figure 6.6, the state transitions for work items are all triggered by the system, whereas in figure 6.7, which denotes pull patterns, the transitions are initiated by individual resources. Other characteristics of interest that ultimately lead to additional pull patterns relate to whether the resource has the ability to reorder their own work sequence or it is determined by the system, and whether a resource can select which work item they wish to commence next from those on its work queue.

Resource-initiated allocation

Description The ability for a resource to commit to undertake a work item without needing to commence working on it immediately. After allocation, the resource is responsible for the execution of the work item.

Example

- The *Clerk* selects the *Town Planning* work items that she will undertake today, although she only commences working on one of these at this point.

Motivation This pattern provides a means for a resource to signal its intention to execute a given work item at some point, although it may not commence working on it immediately.

Overview There are two variants of this pattern as illustrated by the bold arcs in figure 6.7, depending on whether the work item has been offered to a single resource (R:allocate_s) or to multiple resources (R:allocate_m). In both cases, the work item has its status changed from *offered* to *allocated*. It remains in the worklist of the resource that initiated the allocation. If the work item has been offered to multiple resources, then it is necessary to remove it from all other worklists in which it may have appeared as an offer. This ensures that only the resource to which it is now allocated can actually commence working on it.

Context There are no specific context conditions associated with this pattern.

Implementation The implementation of this pattern generally involves the removal of the work item from a globally accessible or shared worklist and its placement on a work queue specific to the resource to which it is allocated. It is supported by both BPMone and Oracle BPEL in much the same way, although in BPMone, the allocation occurs at the case level, whereas in Oracle BPEL, it occurs at the work item level. In BPMone, cases are retrieved for a given resource via a case query that specifies the distribution criteria for cases that can be allocated to the resource. Where a resource executes a case query and a matching case is identified, all of the work items in the case are effectively allocated to the resource. Each of these work items is listed in the resource's work tray but is not commenced until specifically requested by the resource. In Oracle BPEL, work items corresponding to tasks that are specified with a single participant type appear in the worklist of all users associated with the user lists, groups, or application role to whom they are routed until one of them claims the work item. Once this occurs, they are removed from the worklist of all users other than the one that has claimed them. For BPMN Tasks based on WS-HumanTask, the pattern is supported via the claim function provided the task instance is offered to more than one user. It is automatically started if only offered to one user.

Resource-initiated execution — allocated work item

Description The ability for a resource to commence work on a work item that is allocated to it.

Example

- The *Courier Driver* selects the next *Delivery* work item that is allocated to it and commences work on it.

Motivation Where a resource has work items that it has committed to execute but has not yet commenced, a means of signaling their commencement is required. This pattern fulfills that requirement.

Overview This pattern corresponds to the R:start transition illustrated in figure 6.7. It results in the status of the selected work item being changed from *allocated* to *started*. It remains in the same worklist.

Context There are no specific context conditions associated with this pattern.

Implementation The general means of handling that a work item has been allocated to a resource is to place it on a resource-specific work queue. This ensures that the work item is not undertaken by another resource and that the commitment made by the resource to which it is allocated is maintained. BPMone supports the concept of resource-specific work queues and provides mechanisms in the worklist handlers for resources to indicate that an allocated work item has been commenced. In Oracle BPEL, no differentiation is made between the time that a work item is allocated to a resource and the time that it is started. For BPMN Tasks based on WS-HumanTask, the pattern is supported via the start function.

Resource-initiated execution — offered work item

Description The ability for a resource to select a work item offered to it and commence work on it immediately.

Example

- The *Courier Driver* selects the next *Delivery* work item from those offered and commences work on it.

Motivation In some cases, it is preferable to view a resource as being committed to undertaking a work item only when the resource has actually indicated that it is working on it. This approach to work distribution effectively speeds throughput by eliminating the notion of work item allocation. Work items remain on offer to the widest range of appropriate resources until one of them actually indicates they can commence work on it. Only at this time is the work item removed from being on offer and allocated to a specific resource.

Overview There are two variants of this pattern as illustrated by the bold arcs in figure 6.7, depending on whether the work item has been offered to a single resource (R:start_s) or multiple resources (R:start_m). In both cases, the work item has its status changed from *offered* to *started*. It remains in the worklist of the resource that initiated the work item. In the latter case, the work item has been offered to multiple resources, and it is therefore necessary to remove it from all other worklists in which it may have appeared as an offer. This ensures that only one resource can actually work on it.

Context There are no specific context conditions associated with this pattern.

Implementation For BPMN Tasks based on WS-HumanTask, the pattern is supported via the start function. Oracle BPEL does not differentiate between allocated and started work items; hence, the act of claiming a work item by a user effectively starts it as well. This pattern is not supported by BPMone. The approach is commonly adopted by workflow systems such as Staffware and COSA for distributing work items to shared work queues (e.g., group queues). For these systems, a work item remains on the queue until a resource indicates that it has commenced it. At this point, its status changes, and no other resource can execute it, although it remains on the shared queue until it is completed.

System-determined work queue content

Description The ability of the system to control the content and sequence in which work items are presented to a resource for execution.

Example

- Depending on the configuration specified in the process model, the workflow engine presents work items to resources either in order of work item priority or date created.

Motivation This pattern provides the system with the ability to specify the ordering and content of work items in a resource's worklist. In doing so, the intention is that the system can influence the sequence in which concurrent work items are executed by resources by managing the information presented for each work item.

Overview Where an offering provides facilities for specifying the default ordering in which work items are presented to resources, the opportunity exists to enforce a work ordering policy for all resources or on a group-by-group or individual resource basis. Such ordering may be time-based (e.g., FIFO, LIFO, EDD) or relate to data values associated with individual work items (e.g., cost, required effort, completion time). The ordering and content of work lists can be specified individually for each user or on a whole-of-process basis.

Context There are no specific context conditions associated with this pattern.

Implementation Where this concept is supported by individual BPM offerings, it is generally done so in terms of a single ordering sequence for all resources. BPMone, Oracle BPEL, and BPMN do not provide the ability to enforce default orderings of work items. However, the Staffware workflow system does, and it supports the ordering of work items on a priority basis for each resource's worklist. It also supports the dynamic reordering of worklists as the priorities of individual work items change.

Resource-determined work queue content

Description The ability for resources to specify the format and content of work items listed in the work queue for execution.

Example

- The *Coordinator* resource has a worklist ordered by time of receipt.

Motivation Enabling resources to specify the format, content, and ordering of their work queue provides them with a greater degree of flexibility in both the selection of individual work items from those offered to them for execution and also in the sequence in which they tackle work items that they have committed to execute or have been allocated to them.

Overview Typically this pattern manifests itself as the availability of a range of sorting and filtering options that resources can access to tailor the format of their worklist. These options may be either transient views that they can request or alternately can take the form of permanent configuration options for their work lists.

Context There are no specific context conditions associated with this pattern.

Implementation For those offerings that provide some form of worklist handler for resources to interact with the BPM offering, the ability to be able to sort and filter work items is relatively commonplace. BPMone allows the user to specify "case queries" that define the type of cases that are retrieved into their work tray. Oracle BPEL allows resources to order the sequence of the work items in their worklist and also to vary the information that is displayed about individual work items. For BPMN Tasks based on WS-HumanTask, the simple and advanced query functions provide the ability for users to restrict and format the content of their worklists.

Selection autonomy

Description The ability for resources to select a work item for execution based on its characteristics and their own preferences.

Example

- Of the outstanding *Pruning* work items, the *Head Gardener* chooses the one for execution they feel they are best suited to.

Motivation The ability for a resource to select the work item that they will commence next is a key aspect of the "heads up" approach to process execution. It aims to empower resources and let them have the flexibility to prioritize and organize their own individual work sequence. As such it is a logical corollary to the *Resource-determined work queue content* pattern, enabling users to not only select how they are advised of work but also the sequence in which they will undertake it.

Overview This pattern is a common feature provided by worklist handlers in most BPM offerings. It typically manifests itself in one of two forms: either a resource is able to execute multiple work items simultaneously, and thus can initiate additional work items of their choice at any time, or they are limited to executing one work item at a time, in which case they can only commence a new work item when the previous one is complete, although they can choose which work item they will commence next. Where a system implements "heads down" processing, it is common for the *Selection autonomy* pattern to be disabled and for the system to determine which work item a resource will execute next.

Context There are no specific context conditions associated with this pattern.

Implementation BPMone, Oracle BPEL, and BPMN all support this pattern, allowing individual resources to execute multiple work items simultaneously.

Issues One consideration associated with this pattern is whether resources are still offered complete flexibility to choose which work item they will undertake next when there are urgent work items allocated to them or whether the system can guide their choice or dictate that a specific work item will be undertaken next.

Solutions Where autonomy is offered to resources in terms of the work items that they choose to execute, it is typically not revoked even in the face of pressing work items. Oracle BPEL provides the notion of notifications in relation to work items that, among other things, can be used to advise users of urgent work items. BPMone and BPMN do not provide any facilities in this regard.

6.5   Detour patterns

Detour patterns refer to situations where work item distributions that have been made to resources are interrupted by either the system or at the instigation of the resource. As a consequence of such events, the normal sequence of state transitions for a work item is varied. The range of possible scenarios for detour patterns are illustrated in figure 6.8.

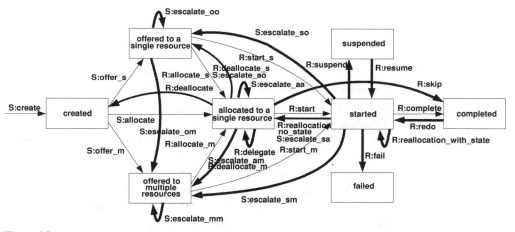

Figure 6.8
Detour patterns (from [113]).

There are a number of possible impacts on a work item depending on its current state of progression and whether the detour was initiated by the resource with which the work item was associated or by the system. These include:

- *delegation* — where a resource allocates a work item previous allocated to it to another resource;
- *escalation* — where the system attempts to progress a work item that has stalled by offering or allocating it to another resource;
- *deallocation* — where a resource makes a previously allocated or started work item available for offer and subsequent allocation;
- *stateful reallocation* — where a resource allocates a work item that it has started to another resource and the current state of the work item is retained;
- *stateless reallocation* — where a resource allocates a work item that it has started to another resource but the current state is not retained (i.e., the work item is restarted);
- *suspension/resumption* — where a resource temporarily suspends execution of a work item or recommences execution of a previously suspended work item;
- *skipping* — where a resource elects to skip the execution of a work item allocated to it;

- *redo* — where a resource repeats execution of a work item completed earlier; and
- *pre-do* — where a resource executes a work item that is ahead of the current execution point in a case.

Each of these actions relates to one or more transitions in figure 6.8 and corresponds to a specific pattern described below.

Delegation

Description The ability for a resource to allocate an unstarted work item previously allocated to it (but not yet commenced) to another resource.

Example

- Before going on leave, the *Chief Accountant* passed all of their outstanding work items on to the *Assistant Accountant*.

Motivation *Delegation* provides a resource with a means of re-routing work items that it is unable to execute. This may be because the resource is going to be unavailable (e.g., on vacation) or because they do not wish to take on any more work.

Overview *Delegation* is usually initiated by a resource via their worklist handler. It removes a work item that is allocated to them (but not yet commenced) and inserts it into the worklist of another nominated resource. It is illustrated by the R:delegate transition in figure 6.8.

Context There are no specific context conditions associated with this pattern.

Implementation Generally, the ability to delegate work items is included in the worklist handler for a BPM offering. Oracle BPEL provides users with the ability to transfer work items allocated to them to another nominated user or group. This can be done via the Delegate function, which gives the delegatee the delegator's privileges or via the Reassign function, where the work item is reassigned to users or groups managed by the delegator but without any elevated privileges (i.e., the delegatee does not receive the privileges of the delegator when executing the work item). For BPMN Tasks based on WS-HumanTask, the pattern is supported via the delegate function for tasks in the Reserved state. There is no support for this in BPMone.

Issues One consideration associated with the *Delegation* pattern is what happens where a work item is delegated to a user who is not authorized to execute it.

Solutions In Oracle BPEL, the approach taken to delegation/reassignment generally ensures that this situation does not arise. Should subsequent (and possibly unrelated) issues occur with task assignment, the Error Assignee provides a fallback to enable the situation to be resolved. Executable BPMN does not provide support in this area.

Escalation

Description The ability of a system to distribute a work item to a resource or group of resources other than those it has previously been distributed to in an attempt to expedite the completion of the work item.

Example

- The *review earnings* work item was reallocated to the *CFO*. It had previously been allocated to the *Financial Accountant*, but the deadline for completion had been exceeded.

Motivation *Escalation* provides the ability for a system to intervene in the conduct of a work item and assign it to alternative resources. Generally this occurs as a result of a specified deadline being exceeded, but it may also be a consequence of pre-emptive load balancing of work allocations undertaken automatically by the system or manually by the process administrator in an attempt to optimize process throughput.

Overview There are various ways in which a work item may be escalated depending on its current state of progression and the approach that is taken to identifying a suitable party to which it should be reassigned. The possible range of alternatives are illustrated by the S:escalate_oo, S:escalate_om, S:escalate_ao, S:escalate_sm, S:escalate_am, S:escalate_mm, S:escalate_so, S:escalate_sa, and S:escalate_aa transitions in figure 6.8. An escalation action is triggered by the system or process administrator and results in the work item being removed from the worklists of all resources to which it was previously offered or allocated and added to the worklists of the users to which it is being reassigned in either an offered or allocated state.

Context There are no specific context conditions associated with this pattern.

Implementation Oracle BPEL allows escalations to be specified for a task enabling associated work items that have exceeded a specified deadline to be reallocated to another (typically more senior) resource for resolution. It also supports the manual escalation of work items from the worklist handler. For BPMN Tasks based on WS-HumanTask, escalations can be specified, and both commencement and completion deadlines are supported together with logical conditions that restrict their application. There is no support for escalations in BPMone.

Deallocation

Description The ability of a resource (or group of resources) to relinquish a work item that is allocated to it (but not yet commenced) and make it available for distribution to another resource or group of resources.

Example

- As progress on the *Conduct initial investigation* work item is not sufficient, the *Level 1 support officer* resource has made it available for reallocation to another *Support Agent*.

Motivation *Deallocation* provides resources with a means of relinquishing work items allocated to them and making them available for redistribution to other resources. This may occur for a variety of reasons, including insufficient progress, availability of a better resource, or a general need to unload work from a resource.

Overview There are three possible variations to *Deallocation*: the work item can be offered to a single resource or multiple resources, or the work item can be placed back in the newly created state and the allocation process can recommence from the beginning. These transitions are illustrated by the R:deallocate_s, R:deallocate_m, and R:deallocate arcs in figure 6.8.

Context There are no specific context conditions associated with this pattern.

Implementation Oracle BPEL provides the Release action for work items assigned to groups or multiple users, which allows the user who claims the work item to release it for completion by other users. Additionally, it provides the Withdraw action, which allows the owner of a task or a task administrator to cancel execution of the task and enables the business process to determine what happens with it next. For BPMN Tasks based on WS-HumanTask, the pattern is supported via the release or forward functions for Tasks in the Reserved state. There is no support for deallocation in BPMone.

Issues One problem that can arise when deallocating a work item is that it could ultimately be reallocated to the same resource from which it was previously retrieved.

Solutions As the act of deallocating a work item is generally disjoint from that of reallocating it, the potential always exists for reallocation to the same resource unless active measures are taken to ensure that this does not occur. Generally, there are three approaches for doing this:

- Make the resource unavailable for the period in which the reallocation will occur so that it is not considered in the work item redistribution.
- Stop the resource from accepting new allocations or offers.
- Ensure that the distribution algorithm does not attempt to allocate a work item to a resource to which it has previously been allocated.

In Oracle BPEL, the distribution of work items is triggered by resources electing to claim new work items; hence, the expectation is that the resource releasing the work item does not attempt to claim any subsequent work items immediately afterward. If they do, there is the potential for the deallocated work item to be allocated to them once again. In executable BPMN, the solution to this issue relies on the third approach identified above.

Stateful reallocation

Description The ability of a resource to allocate a work item that they are currently executing to another resource without loss of state data.

Example

- The *Senior Partner* has suspended work on the *Building Society Audit Plan* work item and passed it to the *Junior Project Manager* for further work.

Motivation *Stateful reallocation* provides a resource with the ability to offload currently executing work items to other resources while maintaining the current state of the work item and the results of work undertaken on it to date. In the main, this centers on the ability to retain the current values of all data elements associated with the work item. It is motivated by the need for a resource to pass on a work item to another resource without losing the benefit of any work that has already been undertaken in regard to it.

Overview This pattern corresponds to the `R:reallocation_with_state` arc in figure 6.8. It is interesting to note the similarities between this pattern and the *Delegation* pattern. Both patterns result in a work item being reassigned to another resource. The main difference between them is that *Delegation* can only occur for a work item that has not yet commenced execution, whereas this pattern applies to work items currently being executed.

Context There are no specific context conditions associated with this pattern.

Implementation Oracle BPEL supports the transfer of work items to another resource. As it does not differentiate between allocated and started work items, any associated state data is also transferred intact. For BPMN Tasks based on WS-HumanTask, the pattern is supported via the forward function for Tasks in the InProgress state. There is no support for reallocation in BPMone.

Issues There are two potential issues associated with the reallocation of a work item to another resource while still preserving state information: (1) managing the transfer of state data without introducing issues related to the concurrent use of the same data elements, and (2) ensuring the resource to which the work item is reallocated is entitled to execute it and access the associated state information.

Solutions There are a number of potential solutions to the first of these issues. One solution is to limit access to relevant state data elements to the resource executing the work item. This is the approach adopted in Oracle BPEL, which uses scopes and associated event handlers to prevent concurrent access to shared variables by multiple resources.

Oracle BPEL enforces a series of rules to ensure that work items can only be reallocated to resources that are authorized to execute them. It does not impose any specific access restrictions on variables associated with work items or global variables; hence, any data that was accessible to the relinquishing resource will also be accessible to the resource acquiring the work item.

Executable BPMN does not provide solutions to either of these issues.

Stateless reallocation

Description The ability for a resource to reallocate a work item that it is currently executing to another resource without retention of state.

Example

- As progress on the *Recondition Engine* work item is not sufficient, it has been reallocated to another *Mechanic* who will restart it.

Motivation *Stateless reallocation* provides a lightweight means of reallocating a work item to another resource without needing to consider the complexities of state preservation. In effect, when this type of reallocation occurs, all state information associated with the work item (and hence any record of effective progress) is lost, and the work item is basically restarted by the resource to which it is reassigned.

Overview This pattern is illustrated by the R:reallocation_no_state arc in figure 6.8. It has similarities in terms of outcome with the *Delegation* and *Escalation* patterns, in that the work item is restarted except that in this scenario, the work item has already been partially executed prior to the restart. This pattern can only be implemented for work items that are capable of being redone without any consequences relating to the previous execution instance(s).

Context There are no specific context conditions associated with this pattern.

Implementation None of the offerings examined — BPMN, BPMone, or Oracle BPEL — directly implements this approach to reallocation. It is included in this taxonomy as it constitutes a useful simplification of the *Stateful reallocation* pattern.

Issue While partially executing a work item, there may be all kinds of side effects outside the direct control of the BPM system (e.g., a phone call or bank transfer may have happened before a stateless reallocation). As a result, a customer may be contacted multiple times, a payment made twice, or a room booked twice.

Solution The only way to address side effects outside of the system is to add compensation measures. If a work item is reallocated, then all side effects need to be compensated. This may imply additional actions.

Suspension/resumption

Description The ability for a resource to suspend and resume execution of a work item.

Example

- The *Secretary* has suspended all *Board Meeting* work items while the *Board* is being reconstituted.

Motivation In some situations, during the course of executing a work item, a resource reaches a point where they are not possible to progress the work item any further (e.g., lack of time to finish the work item due to an upcoming meeting). *Suspension* provides the ability for a resource to signal a temporary halt to the system of any work on the particular work item they are undertaking and switch their attention to another.

Overview *Suspension* and *Resumption* actions are generally initiated by a resource from their worklist handler. A suspended work item remains in the resource's worklist, but its state is generally notated as *suspended*. It is able to be restarted at some future time. This pattern is illustrated by the R:suspend and R:resume arcs in figure 6.8.

Context There are no specific context conditions associated with this pattern.

Implementation Oracle BPEL provides facilities for suspending and resuming claimed work items. For BPMN Tasks based on WS-HumanTask, the pattern is supported via the suspend and resume functions. These actions are not supported in BPMone.

Skip

Description The ability for a resource to skip a work item allocated to it and mark the work item as complete.

Example

- The *Ground Curator* elected to skip the *Roll Pitch* work item previously allocated to it.

Motivation The ability to skip a work item reflects the common approach to expediting process instances by simply ignoring noncritical activities and assuming them to be complete, such that work items associated with subsequent tasks can be commenced.

Overview The *Skip* pattern is generally implemented by providing a means for a resource to advance the state of a work item from *allocated* to *completed* without explicitly starting work on the work item. This pattern is illustrated by the R:skip arc in figure 6.8.

Context There are no specific context conditions associated with this pattern.

Implementation BPMone provides the ability for a resource to skip work items allocated to them. For BPMN Tasks based on WS-HumanTask, the pattern is supported via the skip function. It is not possible in Oracle BPEL as there is no differentiation between allocated and started tasks (once a work item is committed to a single user, it is effectively in the *claimed* state).

Issues The main consideration that arises where work items could potentially be skipped is how to deal with data gathering requirements (e.g., forms that need to be completed by the resource) that are embodied within the work item. In the situation where a work item is skipped, it is generally just marked as complete, and no further execution is attempted. Subsequent work items that may be expecting data elements or other side effects resulting from the skipped work item could potentially be compromised.

A second issue relates to authorization, in particular whether any user to whom a work item is allocated can skip it or only a specific range of denoted users.

Solutions Where an offering supports the ability for work items to be skipped, it is important that subsequent work items do not necessarily rely on the output of previous work items unless absolutely necessary. The use of static data elements such as default parameter values can avoid many of the consequences of data not being received. More generally, however, in order to avoid these problems, the ability is required within a BPM offering to specify work items that must be completed in full (i.e., cannot be skipped) and to specifically identify any resources that are allowed to initiate a skip action.

Typically the second issue is addressed by identifying which actions an assigned user may undertake when dealing with a task. The skip action in particular is one that must be specifically allowed for the task. Sometimes an additional restriction is also imposed on the range of users that may undertake the skip action. This is the approach that BPMone takes, and the skip action is an authorization setting for individual plans that can be specified for nominated roles.

Executable BPMN does not provide solutions to either of these issues.

Redo

Description The ability for a resource to redo a work item that has previously been completed in a case. Any subsequent work items (i.e., work items that correspond to subsequent tasks in the process) must also be repeated.

Example
- The *Inspector* has decided to redo the *Interview Key Witness* work item.

Motivation The *Redo* pattern allows a resource to repeat a work item that has previously been completed. This may be based on a decision that the work item was not undertaken properly or because more information has become available that alters the potential outcome of the work item.

Overview The *Redo* pattern effectively provides a means of "winding back" the progress of a case to an earlier task. The difficulties associated with doing this where a process instance involves multiple users means the pattern is not a common feature of BPM offerings. However, for situations where all of the work items in a case are allocated to the same user (e.g., in a case handling system), the problem is more tractable. One consideration in utilizing this pattern is that although it is possible to regress the execution state in a case, it is generally not possible to wind back the state of data elements. Hence, any necessary reversion of data values needs to be managed at the level of specific applications and is not a general feature. This pattern is illustrated by the R: redo arc in figure 6.8.

Context There is one context condition associated with this pattern: any shared data elements (i.e., block, scope, case data, etc.) cannot be destroyed during the execution of a case.

Implementation BPMone provides the ability to redo a previously completed work item. It is not possible in BPMN or Oracle BPEL.

Issues Redoing a previously completed work item can have significant consequences on the execution of a case. In particular, the validity of any subsequent work items is questionable as redoing a preceding work item may impact data elements utilized by these work items during their execution. Similar to stateless reallocation, there can also be problems related to side effects outside of the control of the BPM system (e.g., redoing a task should not result in double payments or bookings).

Solutions BPMone addresses this issue by requiring any work items that depend on a "redone" work item to also be repeated before the case can be marked as complete. Work items that have side effects need to be compensated in order to roll back safely.

Pre-do

Description The ability for a resource to execute a work item ahead of the time that it has been offered or allocated to resources working on a given case. Only work items that do not depend on data elements from preceding work items can be "pre-done."

Example

- The *Inspector* has completed the *Charge Suspect* work item even though the preceding *Interview Witness* work items have not yet been completed.

Motivation The *Pre-do* pattern provides resources with the ability to complete work items in a case ahead of the time that they are required to be executed (i.e., prior to them being offered or allocated to resources working on the case). The motivation for this is that overall throughput of the case may be expedited by completing work items as soon as possible regardless of the order in which they appear in the actual process specification.

Overview The *Pre-do* pattern effectively provides a means of completing the work items in a case in a user-selected sequence. There are difficulties associated with doing this, where later work items rely on data elements from earlier work items. Hence, the pattern is not a common feature. However, for situations where all of the work items in a case are allocated to the same user and there is less data coupling or the implications of shared data can be managed by resources (e.g., in a case handling system), the problem is more tractable. This pattern is not illustrated in figure 6.8.

Context There is one context condition associated with this pattern: any shared data elements (i.e., block, scope, case data, etc.) must exist at the beginning of the case.

Implementation BPMone provides the ability to pre-do a work item. It is not possible in BPMN or Oracle BPEL.

Issues One consideration associated with pre-doing work items is the fact that outcomes of preceding work items that are executed after the time at which the "pre-done" work item is completed may result in the "pre-done" work item being repeatedly re-executed.

Solutions There is no immediate solution to this problem other than careful selection of work items that are to be done in advance. As a general rule, work items that are to be "pre-done" should not be dependent on data elements that are shared with preceding work items or the outcome of these work items.

6.6 Auto-start patterns

Auto-start patterns relate to situations where execution of work items is triggered by specific events in the lifecycle of the work item or the related process definition. Such events may include the creation or allocation of the work item, completion of another instance of the same work item, or a work item that immediately precedes the one in question. The state transitions associated with these patterns are illustrated by the bold arcs in figure 6.9.

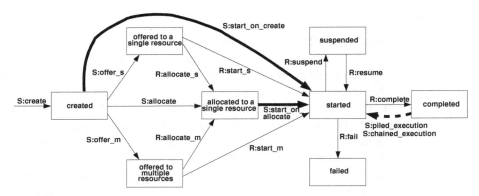

Figure 6.9
Auto-start patterns (from [113]).

Commencement on creation

Description The ability for a resource to commence execution on a work item as soon as it is created.

Example

- The *End of Month* work item is allocated to the *Chief Accountant* who must commence working on it as soon as it is allocated to his work queue.

Motivation The ability to commence execution on a work item as soon as it is created offers a means of expediting the overall throughput of a case as it removes the delays associated with allocating the work item to a suitable resource and also the time that the work item remains in the resource's work queue prior to it being started.

Overview Where a task is specified as being subject to *Commencement on Creation*, when the task is initiated in a process instance, the associated work item is created, allocated, and commenced simultaneously. This pattern is illustrated by the transition S:start_on_create in figure 6.9. The pattern can be viewed as combining S:allocate and S:start_on_allocate in one atomic action.

Context There are no specific context conditions associated with this pattern.

Implementation All offerings that support *Automatic* work items (i.e., work items that can execute without requiring allocation to a resource) provide limited support for the notion of *Commencement on creation*. More complex, however, is the situation where a work item must be allocated to a human resource as this implies that creation, allocation, and commencement must occur simultaneously. This approach to work distribution is possible in Oracle BPEL, which does not differentiate between allocated and commenced work items, by specifying an automatic allocation for the task to a single user. This will ensure it is assigned to a specific user as soon as it is enabled. The pattern is not supported in executable BPMN as tasks must be explicitly started by an owner.

Commencement on allocation

Description The ability to commence execution on a work item as soon as it is allocated to a resource.

Example

- Work on the *Practice Tower Block Fire Drill* work item commences as soon as it is allocated to a *Fire Team* resource.

Motivation Although combined creation, allocation, and commencement of work items promotes more efficient process throughput, it is restrictive and necessitates the identification of the assigned resource at the time of work item creation. This obviates much of the advantage of the flexible resource assignment strategies offered by BPM offerings. Commencing work items at the point of allocation does not require resource identity to be determined as early in the work item lifecycle while still retaining some of the benefit of expediting work throughput.

Overview Where a task is specified as being subject to *Commencement on allocation*, the act of allocating an associated work item in a process instance also results in it being commenced. In effect, it is put into the worklist of the resource to which it is allocated with a *started* status rather than an *allocated* status. This pattern is illustrated by the transition S:start_on_allocate in figure 6.9. Upon allocation, the commencement action for the work item is immediately triggered by the system. This contrasts with the situation where, of their own volition, a user immediately commences a work item that has been offered to them without explicitly requesting that it be allocated to them as illustrated by the R:start_S and R:start_m transitions. In this situation, the allocation action is implied.

Context There are no specific context conditions associated with this pattern.

Implementation The potential exists to implement this pattern in one of two ways: (1) *Commencement on allocation* can be specified within the process model, and (2) individual resources can indicate that items in their worklist are to be initiated as soon as they are received. As Oracle BPEL does not differentiate between allocated and commenced work items, it is able to support the former approach through the use of automatic allocation. The pattern is not supported in executable BPMN as tasks must be explicitly started by an owner.

Piled execution

Description The ability to initiate the next instance of a task (perhaps in a different case) once the previous one has completed with all associated work items being allocated to the same resource. The transition to *Piled execution* mode is at the instigation of an individual resource.

Example

- The next *Clean Hotel Room* work item can commence immediately after the previous one has finished, and it can be allocated to the same *Cleaner*.

Motivation *Piled execution* provides a means of optimizing task execution by pipelining instances of the same task and allocating them to the same resource.

Overview *Piled execution* involves a resource undertaking work items corresponding to the same task sequentially. These work items may be in different cases. Once a work item is completed, if another work item corresponding to the same task is present in the work queue, then it is immediately started. In effect, the resource attempts to work on *piles* of the same types of work items. The aim with this approach to work distribution is to allocate similar work items to the same resource, which aims to undertake them one after the other, thus gaining from the benefit of exposure to the same task. This pattern is illustrated by the transition R:piled_execution in figure 6.9. It is important to note that this transition is represented by a dashed line because it jumps from one work item to another (i.e., it links the life-cycles of two different work items, typically in distinct cases).

Context There are no specific context conditions associated with this pattern.

Implementation To implement this pattern requires like work items to be allocated to the same resource and the ability for the resource to undertake related work items on a sequential basis, immediately commencing the next one when the previous one is complete. Moreover, it is possible for multiple resources to be in piled execution mode for a given task at the same time. This is a relatively sophisticated requirement, and none of the offerings examined supports it. It is included in this taxonomy as it constitutes a logical extension of the concept that underpins the *Commencement on creation* pattern, enabling instances of the same task across multiple cases to be allocated to a single resource.

Chained execution

Description The ability to automatically start the next work item in a case once the previous one has completed. The transition to *Chained execution* mode is at the instigation of the resource.

Example

- Immediately commence the next work item in the *Emergency Rescue Coordination* process when the preceding one has completed.

Motivation The rationale for this pattern is that case throughput is expedited when a resource is allocated sequential work items within a case, and when a work item is completed, its successor is immediately initiated. This has the effect of keeping the resource constantly progressing a given case.

Overview *Chained execution* involves a resource undertaking work items in the same case in "chained mode," such that the completion of one work item immediately triggers its successor, which is immediately placed in the resource's worklist with a *started* status.

This pattern is illustrated by the transition R:chained_execution in figure 6.9. It is important to note that this transition is represented by a dashed line because it jumps from one work item to another (i.e., it links the lifecycles of two different work items within the same case).

Context There are no specific context conditions associated with this pattern.

Implementation In order to implement this pattern effectively, the majority (if not all) of the work items for a given case need to be allocated to the same resource, and it must execute them in a strict sequential order. This approach to work distribution is best addressed by a case handling system, and not surprisingly BPMone offers direct support for it. Oracle BPEL is able to support it for processes where individual tasks are all allocated to a single participant type. This implies that subsequent tasks are initiated and assigned to the same user as the preceding task completes execution. The pattern is not supported in executable BPMN.

Issues *Chained execution* offers a means of achieving rapid throughput for a given case. However, in order to ensure that this does not result in an arbitrary delay of other cases, it is important that cases are distributed across the widest possible range of resources and that the distribution only occurs when a resource is ready to undertake a new case.

Solutions This issue is managed in BPMone by defining Work Profiles that distribute cases appropriately and ensuring that resources only request new case allocation when they are ready to commence the associated work items.

The relationship between the *Piled execution* and *Chained execution* patterns is immediately evident when the operation of the two patterns is illustrated visually in terms of the sequence in which work items are executed. In figure 6.10(a), in a piled execution situation, a resource sequentially undertakes instances of the same task across multiple cases, whereas in figure 6.10(b), in a chained execution scenario, a resource sequentially undertakes work items corresponding to subsequent tasks in the same case.

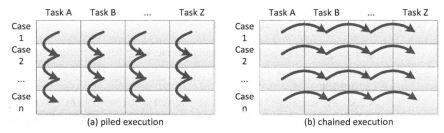

Figure 6.10
Work item execution: Piled execution vs Chained execution.

6.7   Visibility patterns

Visibility patterns classify the various scopes in which work item availability and commitment are able to be viewed by resources. They give an indication of how open to scrutiny the operation of a BPM offering is.

Configurable unallocated work item visibility

Description The ability to configure the visibility of unallocated work items by process participants.

Example

- The *Process Worker* can only see the unallocated work items that may be subsequently allocated to them or they can volunteer to undertake.

Motivation The pattern denotes the ability of a BPM offering to limit the visibility of unallocated work items — either to potential resources to which they may subsequently be offered or allocated or to completely shield knowledge of created but not yet allocated work items from all resources.

Overview The ability to view unallocated work items is usually implemented as a configurable option on a per-user basis. Of most interest is the ability to view work items in an *offered* state.

Context There are no specific context conditions associated with this pattern.

Implementation Oracle BPEL provides the ability to monitor the status of unallocated (i.e., ready) work items via the Process Workspace facility. The content that is displayed to a given resource can be configured in a variety of ways. This pattern is indirectly supported for BPMN Tasks based on WS-HumanTask, via the advanced query function which allows the results returned to be restricted according to the authorization of the invoking user. However, this feature is not a mandatory part of WS-HumanTask. There are no such facilities in BPMone.

Configurable allocated work item visibility

Description The ability to configure the visibility of allocated work items by process participants.

Example

- All *site workers* can view the allocated work items list for the day.

Motivation The pattern indicates the ability of a BPM offering to limit the visibility of allocated and started work items.

Overview The ability to view allocated work items is usually implemented as a configurable option on a per-user basis. It provides resources with the ability to view work items in an *allocated* or a *started* state. These work items may belong to other users.

Role-Based Access Control

BPMS technology attempts to optimize the routing of work items to the right person in an organization. Consequently there has been a significant degree of focus on the manner in which work routing directives can be specified in a process model. Less attention has been paid however to the authorization framework in which a process operates. This is particularly important in an organizational context as all resources do not operate with the same range of privileges and the technological support for process execution needs to accord with the degree of organizational authority that individual resources actually possess.

Of particular importance is the ability to precisely define the operations that a resource can perform with respect to an individual task and the extent of their ability to re-route instances of a task to resources other than those for whom it was originally intended. Specifying privileges in a workflow context is most effectively done at an individual task level for individual users or groups of users. The use of roles is an ideal grouping mechanism for this purpose as roles in a workflow system are typically used to group users having similar responsibilities and levels of authority.

Conceived as a generalized approach to access control in software systems, the Role-Based Access Control model (commonly referred to as RBAC) is one potential option for specifying access privileges within a workflow system. Having undergone a lengthy formulation and standardization process, RBAC represents the current state of thinking in supporting large-scale authorization management based on the needs of both industrial users and the research community. The UML class diagram below indicates the main elements of the RBAC Model.

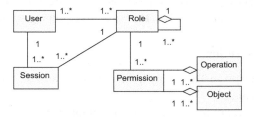

Permissions in a system are oriented around a hierarchy of roles. A permission defines a set of operations that are allowed to be performed on a designated set of objects. Users play one or several roles which provide them with particular privileges during the various execution Sessions in which they participate. In BPMS terms, an object can correspond to any resource used during BPMS execution such as a data item, a work item etc., and an operation describes allowable actions in the context of that object e.g. forward a work item, write a specific data variable.

Whilst there are several research prototypes which demonstrate the integration of RBAC in a BPMS context, the general set of notions embodied in the RBAC standard have not yet made their way into mainstream workflow offerings.

Context There are no specific context conditions associated with this pattern.

Implementation Oracle BPEL provides the ability to monitor the status of allocated (i.e., claimed) work items via the Process Workspace facility. The content that is displayed to a given resource can be configured in a variety of ways. BPMone provides support for this pattern by limiting the visibility of allocated work items to those resources that have the same role as the resource to which a work item is allocated. This pattern is indirectly supported for BPMN Tasks based on WS-HumanTask, via the advanced query function which allows the results returned to be restricted according to the authorization of the invoking user. However, this feature is not a mandatory part of WS-HumanTask.

6.8   Multiple resource patterns

Up to this point, the focus of this catalogue of patterns has been on situations where there is a one-to-one correspondence between the resources and work items in a given allocation or execution. In other words, resources cannot work on different work items simultaneously, and it is not possible that multiple resources work on the same work item. In situations where people are not restricted by IT, there is often a many-to-many correspondence between the resources and work items in a given allocation or execution (e.g., a team of people working on a single work item or a manager who is multitasking). Therefore, it may be desirable to support this using process technology. This section discusses patterns relaxing the one-to-one correspondence between resources and work items that has been assumed previously.

Let us first consider the one-to-many situation (i.e., resources *can* work on different work items simultaneously). This is a fairly simple requirement supported by most systems.

Simultaneous execution

Description The ability for a resource to execute more than one work item simultaneously.

Example

- The *Bank Teller* can conduct multiple *foreign exchange* work items at the same time.

Motivation In many situations, a resource does not undertake work items allocated to it on a sequential basis, but rather it commences work on a series of work items and multitasks between them.

Overview The *Simultaneous execution* pattern recognizes more flexible approaches to work item management, where the decision as to which combination of work items will be executed and the sequence in which they will be interleaved is at the discretion of the resource rather than the system.

Context There are no specific context conditions associated with this pattern.

Implementation All of the offerings examined allow a resource to execute multiple work items simultaneously. In most tools, the resource can undertake any combination of work items, although BPMone (being a case handling tool) limits the group of simultaneous work items to those that comprise the activities in a dynamic plan.

Simultaneous execution is easy to support, and most contemporary systems support this one-to-many correspondence between the resources and work items in a given allocation or execution. Unfortunately, it is more difficult to support a many-to-one correspondence (i.e., multiple resources working on the same work item). This is a pity since for more complicated activities, people tend to work in teams and collaborate to jointly execute work items. Moreover, there is also a lack of consideration for work items that require access to multiple nonhuman resources (e.g., plant and equipment, fuel, consumables, etc.) in order to proceed. Given the limited support of today's BPM offerings, only one pattern is proposed, which implies a many-to-one correspondence.

Additional resources

Description The ability for a given resource to request additional resources to assist in the execution of a work item that it is currently undertaking.

Example

- The *Blast Furnace Operator* has requested additional *Propane Gas Supplies* before continuing with the *Alloy Preparation* work item.

Motivation In more complex scenarios, a given work item may require the services of multiple resources in order for it to be completed (e.g., a machine operator, machine and fuel, additional staff). These resources may be durable in nature and capable of continual reuse, or they may be consumable. By providing the ability to model scenarios such as these, a BPM offering provides a more accurate depiction of the way in which work is actually undertaken in a production environment.

Overview This pattern recognizes more complex work distribution and resource management scenarios, where simple unitary resource allocation is not sufficient to deal with the constraints that tasks may experience during execution.

Context There are no specific context conditions associated with this pattern.

Implementation Oracle BPEL supports the notion of *Ad Hoc* routing, which allows a user to whom a work item is assigned to invite other users to participate in the task. It also supports the concept of group tasks allowing multiple users to work on a single work item. BPMN allows multiple resources to work on a given Task. BPMone only allows a single resource to work on any given task instance.

6.9 Further reading

Worthwhile further reading on the resource aspects of business process modeling and process-aware information systems more generally includes the following:

- The resource patterns discussed in this chapter were introduced in [113].
- [68] gives an overview of MOBILE — one of the first and perhaps most influential attempts to model the various perspectives of workflow systems in an integrated manner with detailed consideration of organizational and resource issues.
- The area of business or enterprise modeling [51, 57, 80, 128] presents an interesting alternative approach to capturing the details of the resource perspective. Rather than focusing on process-related issues, it aims to describe an organization in detail from a number of different standpoints in order to better understand its purpose and the way in which it can better deliver against corporate objectives.
- One line of research into resource modeling and enactment in a workflow context has focused on the design of resource managers that can manage organizational resources and enforce resource policies. [41], [78], and [67] are interesting readings in this area.
- The RBAC (Role-Based Access Control) model [52] is a widely used mechanism for access control in software systems that is equally applicable in a workflow context. It provides a means of ensuring that only suitable and authorized users are selected to execute a given work item.
- A number of meta-models [15, 87] have been proposed, which aim to document the various attributes of resources that are important in a BPM context and to describe the relationships between these attributes.
- In [98], a conceptual data model is presented reflecting the requirements for broader support for the resource perspective than present in contemporary workflow management systems (e.g., the involvement of more than one resource in the execution of a task or the inclusion of nonhuman resources). In [99], this work is elaborated upon, and a requirements analysis is conducted in order to determine what it means for a workflow management system to be "schedule-aware" and thus be able to interact with a scheduling system. This analysis has a range of implications for workflow management support for the resource perspective as this would need to be enhanced and expanded in a number of ways.

IV CONCLUSION

The workflow patterns that we have presented in the previous three chapters provide the basis for describing the main characteristics of a business process. However, there are also other aspects of a business process that have a generic form that can effectively be captured using patterns. In this chapter, we examine seven additional pattern collections that deal with other related business process perspectives.

- *Exception handling patterns* describe strategies for dealing with unusual or unexpected situations that might arise during the operation of a business process;
- *Service interaction patterns* characterize the various ways in which two (or more) independent processes might communicate with each other during their execution;
- *Flexibility patterns* identify a range of ways that the control-flow perspective of a process can be altered in order to enhance its ability to deal with changes that might arise during its execution;
- *Change patterns and change support features* delineate the specific ways in which the control-flow perspective of a process model can be amended to cater for permanent changes that have arisen in the operational environment;
- *Scientific workflow patterns* identify control-flow and data design considerations that are specifically relevant to scientific workflows;
- *Workflow time patterns* provide a basis for describing the time-related aspects of a business process; and
- *Workflow activity patterns* describe recurrent business functions that arise when modeling business processes.

We will provide an introduction to each of these collections in the following sections.

7.1 Exception handling patterns

In common with other areas of software engineering, the notion of the exception is also utilized in the context of business processes to describe deviations from normal behavior that might arise during process execution. Exceptions can be classified as either *expected* or *unexpected* [47] depending on whether their occurrence might reasonably be foreseen. For expected exceptions, it is possible to define exception handling strategies that can be invoked should a nominated set of exceptional circumstances be detected during process execution. In this section, we overview the exception handling patterns proposed by Russell et al. [112], a group of patterns that aim to describe the various approaches that can be adopted within a process to deal with an exception that has been detected.[1]

The exception handling patterns are premised on the notion that an exception is a distinct, identifiable event that occurs during the execution of a business process. Exceptions are assumed to arise in the context of a specific work item, and their occurrence is expected to be immediately detectable. A variety of different approaches may be taken to handling an exception. However, in general, the actual strategy that is selected is based on four main considerations:

- The type of exception that has been detected;
- How to manage the work item that detected the exception;
- How to manage other work items in the case in which the exception was detected, as well as in related cases; and
- What recovery strategy should be pursued to deal with the exception.

By precisely describing these factors for a given exception, a specific handling strategy can be delineated for it that deals with the affected work item and more generally mitigates the overall effects of the exception on the execution of related processes. Each of these factors will be discussed in more detail in sections 7.1.1 – 7.1.4. This then provides the basis for the definition of exception handling patterns, which are subsequently discussed in section 7.1.5, and their use in describing the exception handling capabilities of the BPMN, Oracle BPEL, and BPMone offerings, which are presented in section 7.1.6. The exception handling patterns have been operationalized in the YAWLeX graphical exception handling language, which is briefly introduced in section 7.1.7.

7.1.1   Exception types

Five distinct causes of exceptions are recognized in the exception pattern framework, each of which may serve as the basis for the definition of an exception handling pattern. These are as follows.

Work item failure (WIF) occurs when a currently executing work item is unable to continue executing or progress any further in its current execution state. This type of exception may be triggered in a variety of ways, including user-initiated termination of a work item, system-initiated intervention to address a stalled work item, or failure of a hardware, software, or network resource associated with a work item.

Deadline expiry (DEX) occurs when a work item has exceeded commencement or completion deadlines that are associated with its execution.

---

1 Note that the exception handling patterns focus on dealing with expected exceptions where the required handling strategy can be defined ahead of process execution. Unexpected exceptions cannot be anticipated prior to their actual occurrence and hence need to be dealt with by other mechanisms.

Resource unavailability (RUN) arises when a work item is unable to gain access (either on a shared or an exclusive basis) to one or more resources that it requires during its execution. These may be data resources that contain information required for the work item to execute or physical resources (human or nonhuman) that are necessary to actually perform the work item.

External trigger (EXT) relates to the receival by a work item of some form of signal initiated from a source external to the work item (and possibly outside the context of the executing process) indicating that an event has occurred that affects the work item and requires some form of handling. There are a variety of possible forms the signal can take, including interprocess communication events, software events, or hardware interrupts.

Constraint violation (CVI) occurs where a constraint that is specified as part of the process model is violated. Constraints typically take the form of operational invariants or pre/postconditions over control-flow, data, or resource elements in a process that need to be maintained to ensure its integrity and operational consistency is preserved.

7.1.2   Dealing with exceptions at work item level

The exception handling patterns are based on the notion that an exception occurs primarily in the context of a specific work item. This applies even where the exception does not specifically impact a single work item (e.g., where a constraint violation related to case data is detected). However, the notion is retained for all forms of exception handling pattern on the basis that the detection and reaction to the occurrence of an exception is generally initiated by a single work item that is currently executing.

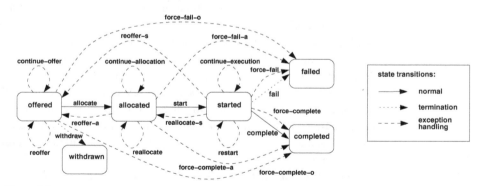

Figure 7.1
Lifecycle of a work item (based on [112]).

The way in which the detecting work item handles an exception largely depends on the state that it is currently in and its state after the exception has been dealt with. To determine the range of possible options, we first need to consider the various states through which a work item passes during execution. These are illustrated in figure 7.1. The solid arrows show the way a work item progresses during normal execution. There are two possible variations to this course of events shown in the figure as dotted arcs where: (1) a work item is withdrawn because it has been allocated to another resource (arc connecting state offered to state withdrawn), and (2) a work item fails (arc from state started to state failed). Figure 7.1 also illustrates as dashed arcs the fifteen possible state transitions that may occur for a work item when it is subject to exception handling. Each of these arcs constitutes an alternate approach to dealing with the work item that detected the exception. There are subtle differences between each of these transitions, and in order to distinguish among them, we briefly describe each in turn:

1. **continue-offer (OCO)** — the work item has been offered to one or more resources, and there is no change in its state as a consequence of the exception;

2. **reoffer (ORO)** — the work item has been offered to one or more resources, and as a consequence of the exception, these offers are withdrawn, and the work item is once again offered to one or more resources (these resources may not necessarily be the same as those to which it was offered previously);

3. **force-fail-o (OFF)** — the work item has been offered to one or more resources, these offers are withdrawn, and the state of the work item is changed to failed. No subsequent work items on this path are triggered;

4. **force-complete-o (OFC)** — the work item has been offered to one or more resources, these offers are withdrawn, and the state of the work item is changed to completed. All subsequent work items are triggered;

5. **continue-allocation** (ACA) — the work item has been allocated to a specific resource that will execute it at some future time, and there is no change in its state as a consequence of the exception;

6. **reallocate (ARA)** — the work item has been allocated to a resource, this allocation is withdrawn, and the work item is allocated to a different resource;

7. **reoffer-a (ARO)** — the work item has been allocated to a resource, this allocation is withdrawn, and the work item is offered to one or more re- sources (this group may not necessarily include the resource to which it was previously allocated);

8. **force-fail-a (AFF)** — the work item has been allocated to a resource, this allocation is withdrawn, and the state of the work item is changed to failed. No subsequent work items are triggered;

9. **force-complete-a (AFC)** — the work item has been allocated to a resource, this alloca-tion is withdrawn, and the state of the work item is changed to completed. All subsequent work items are triggered;

10. **continue-execution (SCE)** — the work item has been started, and there is no change in its state as a consequence of the exception;

11. **restart (SRS)** — the work item has been started, progress on the current execution instance is halted, and the work item is restarted from the beginning by the same resource that was executing it previously;

12. **reallocate-s (SRA)** — the work item has been started, progress on the current execution instance is halted, and the work item is reallocated to a different resource for later execution;

13. **reoffer-s (SRO)** — the work item has been started, progress on the current execution instance is halted, and it is offered to one or more resources (this group may not necessarily include the resource that was executing it);

14. **force-fail (SFF)** — the work item is being executed, any further progress on it is halted, and its state is changed to failed, and no subsequent work items are triggered; and

15. **force-complete (SFC)** — the work item is being executed, further progress on it is halted, and its state is changed to completed, and all subsequent work items are triggered.

7.1.3 Dealing with exceptions at the case level

The third consideration in describing an exception handling strategy is how to handle the exception at the level of the case, in particular deciding how other work items that may currently be executing or may execute in the future in the current case and other related cases should be dealt with. There are three possible options in this regard:

- **Continue with current case (CWC)** — the current case should be continued, and there should be no intervention in the execution of any other work items in the case;
- **Remove current case (RCC)** — selected or all remaining work items in the current case should be removed or canceled; or
- **Remove all cases (RAC)** — selected or all remaining work items in both the current case and all other executing cases that correspond to the same process model are removed.

7.1.4 Recovery action

The final consideration in regard to exception handling is what action should be taken to mitigate the effects of the exception that has been detected. There are three alternate courses of action in this regard:

- **No action (NIL)** — do nothing;
- **Rollback (RBK)** — rollback the effects of the exception by undoing the results of executing preceding work item(s) based on the state changes recorded in an execution log; or
- **Compensate (COM)** — compensate for the effects of the exception by executing an alternative task or subprocess.

7.1.5   Taxonomy of exception handling patterns

An exception handling pattern provides a succinct and precise means of describing an exception handling strategy and the context in which it applies. Exception handling patterns take the form of four-tuples comprising the following elements as described in the preceding sections:

- The type of exception detected;
- How the current work item should be handled;
- How the case and other related cases in the process model in which the exception occurs should be handled; and
- What recovery action (if any) is to be undertaken.

As an example, the pattern WIF-SFF-CWC-COM specified for a work item failure exception for the *check ledger totals* task indicates that if a failure of an associated work item is detected, then the work item should be terminated, have its state changed to failed, and the nominated compensation task or process should be invoked. No action should be taken with other work items in the same case. It is important to note that this pattern only applies to instances of the work item that fail once started; it does not apply to instances in the offered or allocated states (which if required should have distinct patterns nominated for them).

7.1.6   Support for exception handling patterns

The exception handling patterns provide an effective means of assessing and comparing the exception handling capabilities of various BPM offerings. In total, 135 distinct exception handling patterns can be conceived. Further details on the range of these patterns can be found in [112]. Figure 7.1 provides an indication of the extent of support for these patterns in the three BPM offerings — BPMN, BPMone, and Oracle BPEL — that we have looked at earlier. It is notable how sparse the range of exception handling support is and the extent to which it differs between offerings. Note that for space reasons, some exception handling pattern fragments are shown using a form of regular expression, e.g., SRS-CWC-(NIL|COM) corresponds to the pattern fragments SRS-CWC-NIL and SRS-CWC-COM.

7.1.7   YAWLeX: an exception handling language

The exception handling patterns provide an effective means of describing strategies for dealing with expected exceptions within a BPM offering, but in themselves they do not offer any direct guidance into how these strategies might be operationalized. Mindful of this conceptual gap, the graphical exception handling language YAWLeX was developed. It had the aim of providing a simple graphical means of specifying exception handling strategies based on the exception handling patterns. Figure 7.2 illustrates the various constructs of which YAWLeX is comprised.

Table 7.1

Exception handling pattern support in BPMN, BPMone, and Oracle BPEL.

	BPMN	BPMone	Oracle BPEL
Work item failure (**WIF-**)	SRS-CWC-(NIL|COM) SFF-(CWC|RCC)-(NIL|COM|RBK)		SRS-CWC-(NIL|COM|RBK) SFF-(CWC|RCC)-(NIL|COM|RBK)
Deadline expiry (**DEX-**)	OCO-CWC-(NIL|COM) OFF-CWC-(NIL|COM) OFF-RCC-(NIL|COM|RBK) ACA-CWC-(NIL|COM) AFF-CWC-(NIL|COM) AFF-RCC-(NIL|COM|RBK) SCE-CWC-(NIL|COM) SRS-CWC-(NIL|COM) SFF-CWC-(NIL|COM) SFF-RCC-(NIL|COM|RBK)	AFC-CWC-NIL SFC-CWC-NIL	ORO-CWC-(NIL|COM) ORA-CWC-(NIL|COM) OFF-(CWC|RCC)-(NIL|COM|RBK) ARO-CWC-(NIL|COM) ARA-CWC-(NIL|COM) AFF-(CWC|RCC)-(NIL|COM|RBK) SRO-CWC-(NIL|COM) SRA-CWC-(NIL|COM) SCE-CWC-(NIL|COM) SRS-CWC-(NIL|COM|RBK) SFF-(CWC|RCC)-(NIL|COM|RBK)
Resource unavailability (**RUN-**)	OFF-CWC-(NIL|COM) OFF-RCC-(NIL|COM|RBK) AFF-CWC-(NIL|COM) AFF-RCC-(NIL|COM|RBK) SRS-RCC-(NIL|COM|RBK) SFF-CWC-(NIL|COM) SFF-RCC-(NIL|COM|RBK)		ORA-CWC-(NIL|COM) OFF-(CWC|RCC)-(NIL|COM|RBK) ARA-CWC-(NIL|COM) AFF-(CWC|RCC)-(NIL|COM|RBK) SRA-CWC-(NIL|COM) SRS-CWC-(NIL|COM|RBK) SFF-(CWC|RCC)-(NIL|COM|RBK)
External trigger (**EXT-**)	ORO-CWC-(NIL|COM) OFF-CWC-(NIL|COM) OFF-RCC-(NIL|COM|RBK) ARA-CWC-(NIL|COM) AFF-CWC-(NIL|COM) AFF-RCC-(NIL|COM|RBK) SCE-CWC-(NIL|COM|RBK) SRS-CWC-(NIL|COM|RBK) SFF-CWC-(NIL|COM) SFF-RCC-(NIL|COM|RBK)		ORO-CWC-(NIL|COM) OFF-(CWC|RCC)-(NIL|COM|RBK) ARA-CWC-(NIL|COM) AFF-(CWC|RCC)-(NIL|COM|RBK) SCE-CWC-(NIL|COM) SRS-CWC-(NIL|COM|RBK) SFF-(CWC|RCC)-(NIL|COM|RBK)
Constraint violation (**CVI-**)	ORO-CWC-(NIL|COM) OFF-CWC-(NIL|COM) OFF-RCC-(NIL|COM|RBK) ARA-CWC-(NIL|COM) AFF-CWC-(NIL|COM) AFF-RCC-(NIL|COM|RBK) SCE-CWC-(NIL|COM) SRS-CWC-(NIL|COM|RBK) SFF-CWC-(NIL|COM) SFF-RCC-(NIL|COM|RBK)	AFC-CWC-NIL SFC-CWC-NIL AFC-CWC-COM SFC-CWC-COM	ORO-CWC-(NIL|COM) OFF-(CWC|RCC)-(NIL|COM|RBK) ARA-CWC-(NIL|COM) AFF-(CWC|RCC)-(NIL|COM|RBK) SCE-CWC-(NIL|COM) SRS-CWC-(NIL|COM|RBK) SFF-(CWC|RCC)-(NIL|COM|RBK)

Figure 7.3 provides an example of the use of YAWLeX. It defines the exception handling strategy for the *complete audit* task when a deadline expiry exception is detected. When this occurs, the associated work item is paused and allocated to a different resource than the one currently responsible for it. A compensation task is run to deal with any potential issues that may have arisen as a consequence of its late completion. The task is then rewound to the beginning and restarted. YAWLeX has been implemented in the YAWL open-source workflow offering. Further details are available at www.yawlfoundation.org.

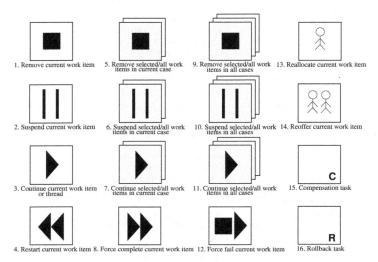

Figure 7.2

YAWLeX: exception handling language primitives (from [112]).

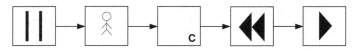

Figure 7.3

Example of YAWLeX exception handling strategy for deadline expiry exception handling of *complete audit* task (from [112]).

7.2   Service interaction and correlation patterns

Business processes do not operate in isolation. They execute in the context of an organization and interact with various participants and data sources within the organization during their operation. They may also interact with other business processes. In the case of interorganizational business processes, it is common that the overarching business process involves several organizational participants and is realized by a series of distinct organization-centric processes, which interact with each other on a service-oriented basis as each organization fulfills its part of the broader business initiative.

There are a number of recurrent characteristics of these interprocess interactions. In an effort to precisely delineate them, Barros et al. [28] proposed a collection of thirteen *Service Interaction Patterns* relevant when describing service compositions involving the *choreography* and *orchestration* of multiple service providers, as well as when dealing with associated lower level issues such as addressing and message typing. An overview of these patterns is presented in section 7.2.1.

Interactions between business processes are typically based on the exchange of messages between activities within those processes. Where a business process engages in multiple interactions with other business processes, the need arises to match incoming messages that it may receive with messages that it (or more specifically constituent activities within the process) sent or received earlier. This matching process is termed *correlation* and becomes a significant issue once the number of interacting process instances begins to scale up. In an effort to define the recurrent scenarios arising during message correlation, in 2007, Barros et al. [29] proposed a series of *Correlation Patterns*. We briefly introduce these in section 7.2.2.

The sheer diversity of ways in which business processes might possibly interact and the range of associated issues led to efforts by Mulyar et al. [89, 90] to establish an overarching framework for describing service-oriented interactions between processes. This framework considers the various styles of interaction as pattern families and provides detailed guidance on the various ranges of configuration options that apply to each family. We discuss this framework in section 7.2.3.

7.2.1   Original service interaction patterns

The original set of thirteen service interaction patterns aimed to provide a collection of generic benchmarks against which the capabilities of emerging web service functionality, particularly in the areas of choreography and orchestration, could be assessed. The scope of the patterns was intended to encompass a wide range of interactions, including bilateral, multilateral, competing, atomic, and causally related scenarios.

The patterns are categorized on the basis of three orthogonal dimensions:

- *Number of participants involved in the interaction*: either two (i.e., bilateral interactions, which may be one-way [simplex] or two-way [duplex]) or unbounded (i.e., multilateral);
- *Number of messages exchanged between two parties in a given interaction*: either one or two (single-transmission interaction) or unbounded (multitransmission interaction); and
- For two-way interactions: *whether the party receiving a response is the same as the sender that initiated the response (round-trip interaction) or not (routed interaction).*

This results in four distinct groups of patterns that contain a total of thirteen patterns. These are illustrated in tables 7.2 and 7.3, together with indicative examples of their usage. In [16], twenty-three service interaction patterns are described in terms of Petri nets (including various anti-patterns).

Oracle BPEL provides the ability for process instances to interact through the use of Invoke, Receive, and Reply activities. Partner links are used to denote particular interactions between two processes. Further details on these constructs can be found in chapter 3. BPMN supports Message-based interactions beween process instances. BPMone does not explicitly cater to interactions between distinct process instances.

Table 7.2

Service interaction patterns (from [28]).

Pattern	Definition
	Single-transmission bilateral interaction patterns
1. Send	A message is sent by one party to another party. *Example:* A party sends an email message.
2. Receive	A message is received by one party from another party. *Example:* A party receives an email message.
3. Send/receive	A party sends a message to another party and then receives a response to the original message from them. *Example:* A party sends a purchase order to a supplier who responds with either a confirmation or out of stock message.
	Single-transmission multilateral interaction patterns
4. Racing incoming messages	A party anticipates receiving one of several possible messages. These messages may differ in content and originate from different sources. These variations affect the manner in which they are ultimately processed. *Example:* A power station load management system receives current load measurement readings, fuel level readings and regular weather report messages. Depending on their content, receipt of any of these messages may trigger a change in power generation levels.
5. One-to-many send	A party sends a number of identical or logically related messages to various other parties. *Example:* A weather monitoring station sends periodic notifications to interested parties.
6. One-from-many receive	A party receives a number of logically related messages emanating from a series of independent events at various parties. These messages are expected to arrive in a nominated timeframe such that they can be correlated as a single event. *Example:* A grain processor receives notifications from various growers of grain that they have available in local siloes. Depending on the level of grain available at a given time, the grain processor may choose to accept/commence work on an order for processed grain.
7. One-to-many send/receive	A party sends a number of identical or logically related messages to various other parties. Responses to these messages are expected to arrive in a nominated timeframe however there is the potential both for messages not to be delivered or sent in the first place. The requested interaction may or not be successful depending on the specific responses received. *Example:* A portfolio manager needs to acquire a specified set of stocks to rebalance their current holdings. They send requests to various brokers for quotes on the complete transaction. The brokers may or may not respond to these requests depending on their current stock holdings and their view of the potential profitability of the transaction.

Table 7.3

Service interaction patterns (cont.) (from [28]).

Pattern	Definition
Multitransmission interaction patterns	
8. Multiresponses	A party sends a request to another party who sends one or more replies in response. The first party receives these until no further responses are required. Thereafter they are not accepted. The determination of no further responses can be initiated by either party on the basis of a temporal condition or message content. No further responses are expected after one or more of the following events: (1) the first party sends a request to stop, (2) a deadline set by the first party expires, (3) the first party does not receive any replies for a nominated timeframe or (4) the second party sends a message to the first party indicating there will be no further replies. *Example:* An entertainment venue sends a request to a cab company to start sending cabs once a show has finished. Each time a new cab is despatched, the cab company advises the venue of the number of the cab number that was sent. When no more cabs are required, the venue advises the cab company. If no further cabs are available, the cab company advises the venue accordingly.
9. Contingent requests	A party sends a request to another party. If they do not receive a response in a specified timeframe, they send a request to a third party. *Example:* A construction company sends a request for a materials quote to a supplier required within a given timeframe. If no response is received by the deadline, the quote is sent to another supplier.
10. Atomic multicast notification	A party sends notifications to a number of other parties that a certain number of them are required to accept within a given period. Depending on the responses received, the interaction may or may not be successful. *Example:* A travel agent sends notifications to various suppliers that their quotes have been accepted and they should now confirm their supply. If all suppliers cannot confirm availability within a specified timeframe, the itinerary to which they relate is cancelled.
Routing patterns	
11. Request with referral	A party sends a request to another party stating that any follow-up responses should instead be directed to several other parties (P1 ... Pn) depending on the outcome of a number of specific conditions. Fault responses are sent by default to these other parties, however they could instead be sent to yet another nominated party (which may be the original initiating party). *Example:* After a profitability review, a wholesaler decides to stop supplying certain unprofitable items. It sends notifications to all clients who have current orders for these products that they should send future orders to other nominated wholesalers (identified on a product-by-product basis).
12. Relayed request	A party makes a request to another party who subsequently delegates it to other third parties (P1 ... Pn). These third parties then continue interactions with the first party and the second (referring) party is allowed to observe these interactions including any associated faults. All interacting parties are aware of (and agree to) the observation by the second party of their interactions. *Example:* A government trade agency introduces overseas commodities buyers to local mining companies. Future interactions occur directly between the overseas buyers and mining companies although the trade agency receives a copy of the various interactions.
13. Dynamic routing	A routing request determines how a request is routed among a number of parties. The routing order is not fixed and a request may be received by more than one party. When the receiving parties have completed, another group of parties is determined and sent the request. Routing is dynamically determined on the basis of request data and additional data gathered along the way. *Example:* A medical review board reviews the outcomes of problematic surgical procedures. A request for review can be triggered by any member of the board and is routed to relevant specialists who are members of the board for their opinion. If they need further advice or have questions about matters outside of their expertise, the specialist in turn may route the request to other members of the board for further investigation.

7.2.2   Correlation patterns

Where a business process interacts with several other business processes, the correlation of incoming and outgoing messages is a major consideration and can take a number of forms. The *Correlation Patterns* proposed by Barros et al. [29] attempt to lay out a framework for describing the various scenarios in which correlation might occur.

The correlation patterns are based on three main concepts: *events*, *conversations*, and *process instances*. Events correspond to records of communication events and are akin to the messages exchanged between communicating business processes. Conversations are groups of communication events between different business processes, which are related to a specific business goal. Process instances are specific execution instances of a business process. Eighteen distinct correlation patterns have been identified and are detailed in tables 7.4 and 7.5, together with indicative examples of their usage.

Eight of the twenty-three service interaction patterns in [16] focus on correlation. Also [84] lists various correlation mechanisms in the context of services.

Oracle BPEL provides support for correlation via the *correlation set*. This is a set of data elements that is associated with an individual message sent between two process instances. The definition of the correlation set is shared by both communicating parties. When a message is sent from one party to another, the values of the various data elements making up the correlation set are fixed, thus allowing the message to be matched with other preceding messages by the receiving party. BPMN caters for both key-based correlation of Messages based on specific payload items and also for context-based correlation, where the Process context (i.e., its Data Objects and Properties) can dynamically influence the matching criterion. BPMone does not provide any form of message correlation facilities.

7.2.3   Service interaction pattern framework

The patterns discussed in the previous two sections identify a broad range of issues associated with the interaction of two or more business processes. However, they do not give any guidance as to the actual configuration of a specific interaction scenario. As a remedy to this shortcoming, Mulyar et al. [89, 90] have proposed an overarching framework for describing the various approaches to service interaction and the range of configuration options for each of them. In this framework, the alternative approaches to service interaction are divided in terms of five pattern families as illustrated in figure 7.4. For each pattern family, a series of configurable attributes are defined that allow a series of different service interaction scenarios to be catered to depending on their specific settings. The five distinct pattern families in the service interaction pattern framework are as follows:

- The *Multiparty Multimessage Request-Reply Conversation* pattern family describes the ways in which a given party can interact with several other parties in a conversation involving the exchange of multiple messages to achieve some common business objective.

Table 7.4

Correlation patterns (from [29]).

Pattern	Definition
Function-based correlation patterns	
C1. Key-based correlation	Events are grouped together based on their sharing of at least one identifier. *Example:* All messages include an attribute identifying the process instance from which they originated.
C2. Property-based correlation	Events are grouped based on the evaluation of a function applied to the values of a given set of attributes. *Example:* All events originating from customers with a postcode in the range 4000 - 4999 are grouped together (label= "intrastate") as against all others (label = "interstate").
C3. Time-interval-based correlation	Events are grouped on the basis of their timestamps. *Example:* All events from 30 days prior to today until the present time are grouped together (label = "recent") as against all others (label = "older").
Chained correlation patterns	
C4. Reference-based correlation	Given an anchor event and a function for a specific attribute of this event, a subsequent event is considered to be correlated to this anchor event if the function applied to the given attribute in the subsequent event yields the value of the anchor event. *Example:* All incoming credit note requests contain a reference to the original order to which they apply. On the basis of this reference, the original order is identified along with the responsible sales representative and the credit note request is grouped together with the original order as part of the sales representative's responsibilities.
C5. Moving time-window correlation	Events are not only correlated based on a shared property, but also on having the same resource involved and having both occurred within a specified timeframe. *Example:* Incoming orders for a given customer received in the same calendar month are grouped together and fulfilled in a single delivery at the end of that month.
Conversation patterns	
C6. Conversation overlap	Two independent conversations which have one or more message events in common. *Example:* During a conversation about scheduling a delivery time, a change of address message is exchanged. This message triggers a conversation to advise internal departments of the new address.
C7. Hierarchical conversation	A conversation involves several sub-conversations which can be spawned off and merged into distinct conversations. *Example:* During the course of a quote preparation process, several quotes are sought from subcontractors who supply individual services that form part of the overall master quote. The number of these that are required is not known until runtime and the conversations regarding subcontractor quotes must be complete before the overall quote preparation process can complete.
C8. Fork	A conversation is fragmented into several conversations which are not merged at any future time. *Example:* Large orders received by a component supplier are split into several production runs, each of which is fulfilled in parallel by a separate manufacturing facility.
C9. Join	Conversations with different origins are merged into a single conversation. *Example:* Several distinct deliveries that are required for a customer in a given timeframe are merged into a single delivery.
C10. Refactor	Based on a common characteristic, a number of conversations is identified to be refactored. *Example:* Goods received from different suppliers by a wholesaler are repackaged into consignments for specific retailers based on orders received from them.

Table 7.5

Correlation patterns (cont.) (from [29]).

Pattern	Definition
Process instance to conversation relationships	
C11. One process instance – one conversation	The ability to specify that a conversation does not involve multiple process instances undertaken by the same resource. *Example:* Fulfillment of an order is handled by a single instance of a process.
C12. Many process instances – one conversation	The ability to specify that a conversation can involve several process instances undertaken by the same resource. *Example:* A sales order is passed from the warehouse once they have completed and despatched it to the accounts section for invoicing. Each section has individual process instances which handle the order.
C13. One process instance – many conversations	The ability to specify that the instances of a given process instance can be involved in several conversations. *Example:* A wholesaler seeks tenders from various manufacturers for the production of a component. Only one is selected to actually produce the component.
C14. Initiate conversation	The ability to specify that for any conversations started in the context of a given instance of a process that that specific process instance is to be identified as the initiator of the conversation. *Example:* A customer requests a return authority for a faulty product they purchased thus triggering a conversation about the specific issue and the way in which the item should be returned to the supplier.
C15. Follow conversation	The ability to specify that a process instance can be identified as having the role of a follower (or responder) in a conversation it participates in where the conversation was created within a distinct process instance. *Example:* A manufacturer organizes the despatch of an order, and creates a process instance in order to do this, in response to an order received from a wholesaler.
C16. Leave conversation	The ability to specify that a process instance can decide to cease participation in a conversation. *Example:* A manufacturer indicates to a customer that they no longer produce the item requested and cancels the associated order.
C17. Multiple consumption	The ability to specify that a communication event can be consumed multiple times by distinct process instances. *Example:* The receipt of an order from a customer triggers the order handling process. As it contains a request for an item classified as a dangerous good, it also results in an instance of the dangerous goods tracking process being initiated.
C18. Atomic consumption	The ability to specify that a series of communication actions can trigger an action event. *Example:* A manufacturer organizes a despatch to a wholesaler once enough goods to fill a container have been ordered by them.

- The *Renewable Subscription* pattern family delineates the possible scenarios associated with long-running conversations (termed subscriptions) between two parties, which involve the request and delivery of goods or services over a specified period or under a defined set of terms. Either party can take the initiative to initiate, renew, or terminate the subscription.
- The *Message Correlation* pattern family describes the range of possible ways in which a party receiving a stream of incoming messages can correlate related messages with the conversation to which they pertain.

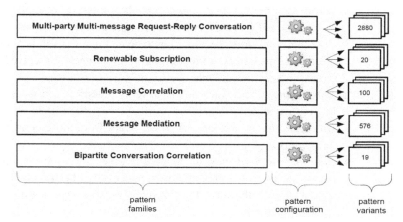

Figure 7.4
Pattern families in the service interaction pattern framework (from [90]).

- The *Message Mediation* pattern family delineates the range of situations where a conversation between two parties is enabled using the services of a third intermediary party known as a "mediator." The mediator may act in a number of different capacities depending on the specific scenario and may provide services ranging from simple introduction and message routing between the parties through to providing identity shielding of the communicating parties.
- The *Bipartite Conversation Correlation* pattern family describes possible approaches to message correlation in the context of a long-running conversation between two parties, where there is an ongoing accumulation of knowledge relevant to both the conversation and the way in which messages may be correlated.

We outline the capabilities of each of these pattern families in the following sections.

Multiparty Multimessage Request-Reply Conversation
This pattern family provides a range of possible options describing how a party can interact with multiple other parties in the context of a multimessage conversation. It delineates the following configurable parameters:

- *N:* list of subrequests sent in a single message.
- *M:* list of responding parties in the conversation.
- *Possibility of nonresponding parties:* whether some of the responding parties will ignore a request issued to them.
- *Possibility of missing replies:* whether the responding party will fail to reply to some of the subrequests.

- *Sorting of the queued messages:* the ordering discipline for response messages (i.e., FIFO, LIFO) based on some message attribute or none.
- *Enabling condition:* the condition to be met in order for the requestor to consume a reply message. This can be a timeout, minimal number of received messages, or a condition based on message content.
- *Consumption index:* the number of reply messages consumed by the requestor from the incoming queue.
- *Utilization index:* the number of messages from those consumed used by the requestor during processing.
- *Consumption frequency:* the number of times the requestor consumes messages from the incoming queue. Possible options are once only (then remaining messages are destroyed), a fixed number of times (after this remaining messages are destroyed), and as long as they continue to arrive.

The various combinations of these attributes allow 1,072 possible situations to be described using the pattern family. The permissible configurations are described in [89]. As describing individual pattern configurations is a potentially onerous task, an intuitive graphical notation has been developed for the pattern family that allows specific pattern configurations to be succinctly defined. An example of the use of this notation is shown in figure 7.5. It shows the default configuration for the pattern family.

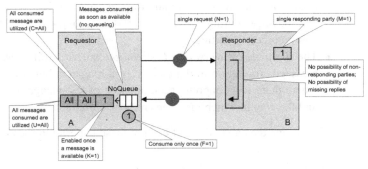

Figure 7.5
Default pattern configuration for Multiparty Multimessage Request-Reply pattern family (from [89]).

Interestingly, this pattern variant can be directly implemented by Oracle BPEL along with a number of other variants, including:

- There is the potential for multiple subrequests in a message (i.e., $N > 1$) if the message sent takes the form of a complex variable whose type is known to both the requestor and responder;
- A requestor can deal with the possibility of a nonresponding party using fault handling functionality;

- Depending on the reply logic implemented in the responder, there is the possibility for missing replies;
- If queuing support is required by the requestor (FIFO, LIFO, etc.), the receiving activity needs to be included in a loop to enable sufficient reply messages to be aggregated. Sorting functionality is not directly supported and would need to be explicitly implemented; and
- Alternate enablement conditions can be realized (e.g., timeouts can be achieved via a Wait activity, message content tests and minimal message thresholds can be implemented where the receiving activity is contained in a loop, and these conditions are explicitly tested for as part of the loop termination condition).

Renewable Subscription

This pattern family provides a range of possible options for configuring subscription-based interactions associated with the ordering and delivery of goods or services, typically on a periodic basis, between two parties. The two interacting parties are termed the *customer* and the *provider* depending on who supplies the goods and services and who consumes them. As a subscription is often intended to be an ongoing supply arrangement, there are two important events that arise during its lifetime. The first of these is its *initiation* (i.e., the time at which the request for the subscription is first raised). The second event is its *renewal* (i.e., the time at which a decision is made as to whether to continue the supply for a new term or terminate it). Six distinct types of subscriptions are possible depending on who initiates a subscription, who renews it, and whether it is renewed manually or automatically. These are listed in table 7.6.

Table 7.6
Renewable subscription types (from [89]).

Subscription Type	Initiator	Renewer
Customer-initiated Automatically-renewed	Customer	n/a
Provider-initiated Automatically-renewed	Provider	n/a
Customer-initiated Customer-renewed	Customer	Customer
Provider-initiated Customer-renewed	Provider	Customer
Customer-initiated Provider-renewed	Customer	Provider
Provider-initiated Provider-renewed	Provider	Provider

The following parameters apply to this pattern family and can be configured to yield distinct pattern alternatives:

- *Subscription type:* intended variant of the subscription from those listed in table 7.6.
- *Expected initiation confirmation (Qi):* whether the provider expects confirmation from the customer to a subscription initiation offer that has been sent to them. This parameter

only applies to provider-initiated subscriptions and provides the basis for manual or automated subscription initiation, where customer interaction (i.e., acceptance, rejection) is either mandatory or optional.

- *Expected renewal confirmation (Qr):* whether the provider expects confirmation from the customer to a subscription renewal offer that has been sent to them. This parameter only applies to provider-initiated subscriptions and provides the basis for manual or automated subscription renewal where customer interaction (i.e., acceptance, rejection) is either mandatory or optional.

The various combinations of these attributes allow for 20 distinct types of renewable subscription to be configured. Similar to the Multiparty Multimessage Request-Reply pattern family, a graphical notation allows specific pattern configurations to be succinctly defined. In addition to the overall pattern configuration, it has additional dynamic attributes that describe the specific characteristics of an individual subscription, including the product or service being delivered (*Prod)*, the subscription period (*SP*), the number of instalments being delivered (*Nr*), the response period in which a subscription offer must be accepted (*RP*), the customer response to the subscription initiation or renewal request (*Ri* and *Rr*), and the provider response to the subscription initiation and renewal request (*PRi* and *PBr*).

An example of the use of this notation is shown in figure 7.6. The top interaction sequence shows a subscription offer from the provider for "service," which involves the delivery of eleven installments (*Nr*) over a twelve-month period (*SP*), where the subscription offer must be taken up within ten days (*RP*), and the customer must explicitly accept a subscription offer (*Qi*) with a "yes" response. The response from the customer indicates whether the customer accepts the request (*Ri*). The bottom interaction sequence shows a renewal request from the customer. The provider confirms these details of the request in their reply and acknowledges their acceptance of this (*PRr*). Request and reply messages are denoted by *REQ* and *RPL*, respectively, with the suffix *c* or *p* indicating whether the message was sent by the customer or provider.

Each of the six subscription types associated with the pattern family can be implemented using Oracle BPEL. Similarly, all possible values associated with the Expected initiation confirmation (*Qi*) and Expected renewal confirmation (*Qr*) parameters can be handled, thus allowing all twenty variants of the pattern family to be implemented. The notion of subscriptions is not supported in BPMone and only in a limited way in BPMN.

Message Correlation

The third pattern family identifies the range of ways in which a party can correlate messages it receives with preceding and current conversations in which it is involved. The act of correlation involves either establishing the correspondence of the message to a pre-existing conversation or identifying that it is indeed a new conversation. The act of correlation is based on the use of *credentials*, which establish the identity of a participant and the conversation in which they are involved.

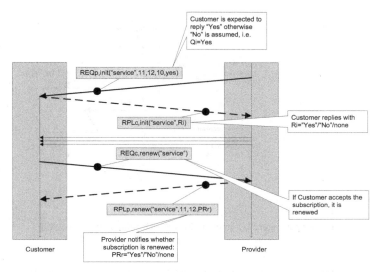

Figure 7.6
Provider-initiated customer-renewed subscription example (based on [89]).

This pattern family has the following configuration parameters:

- *Message sender details (From):* the information revealed by the message sender about their identity. This may include one or (ideally) both the sender identity and the conversation identifier.
- *Message receiver details (To):* the information included by the message sender about the receiver's identity. This may include one or (ideally) both the receiver identity and the conversation identifier.
- *Message sender credentials before correlation (You):* the extent of the receiver's knowledge about the sender's identity and the conversation identifier before message correlation has occurred.
- *Message sender credentials after correlation (You'):* the extent of the receiver's knowledge about the sender's identity and the conversation identifier after message correlation has been completed.

Through various settings of these parameters, 100 distinct configurations of the pattern family are possible. Similar to previous pattern families, there is also a graphical notation for message correlation as illustrated in figure 7.7.

Oracle BPEL is able to cater to the majority of the pattern variants in the Message Correlation pattern family except for those where the identity of the message receiver is underspecified by the sender. These are problematic as BPEL does not allow the intended

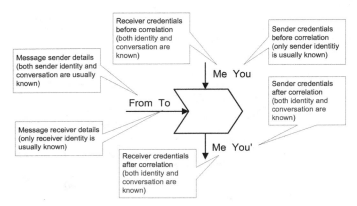

Figure 7.7

Default pattern configuration for Message Correlation (based on [89]).

target for a message to be omitted or for a message to be sent to an arbitrary party. Correlation can be based on native BPEL correlation facilities or it can use these facilities in conjunction with WS-Addressing. The latter combination offers the most flexibility when implementing pattern variants.

Message Mediation

The *Message Mediation* pattern family delineates a range of possible interaction scenarios involving two loosely coupled parties (the *customer* and the *provider*) who are brought into contact by a third party (the *mediator*). Initially, communication between the two parties occurs via the mediator. This may be because the parties are unaware of each other's identity or because they do not wish to interact directly. There are two distinct types of message mediation: *Mediated Interaction*, where the mediator handles all interaction between the two parties; and *Message Introduction*, where the mediator introduces the two parties and they interact directly with each other thereafter.

For the mediated interaction variant, there are the following configuration parameters:

- *Customer request for specific provider (Them1):* this may include either or (ideally) both the provider's identity and the conversation identifier, which are forwarded by the mediator at the customer's request.
- *Customer's permission to expose their credentials (Expose1):* whether the customer grants permission for their identity to be revealed to the provider.
- *Visibility of the provider's credentials (Expose3):* whether the provider grants permission for the mediator to reveal their identity to the customer.
- *Provider's knowledge of the credentials of the customer (Them3):* information revealed by the provider in the response to the mediator about the customer's credentials.

- *Information about the message sender in the response from provider to mediator (From3):* information revealed by the provider about their credentials in the response to the mediator.
- *Information about the message sender in the response from mediator to customer (From4):* information revealed by the mediator about their credentials in the response to the customer.

There are 320 potential configurations of this pattern family variant depending on the specific parameter settings used. Figure 7.8 illustrates the graphical notation used for representing specific pattern configurations. Requests from one participant to another are illustrated by the arrows between the relevant participants, and the items on the arcs indicate the significant information exchanged in the request (in addition to the message content). These items may be settings for specific configuration parameters (illustrated in italics), static attributes set for a specific pattern instantiation, or dynamic attributes set during pattern operation. All interactions between the customer and the provider are routed via the mediator.

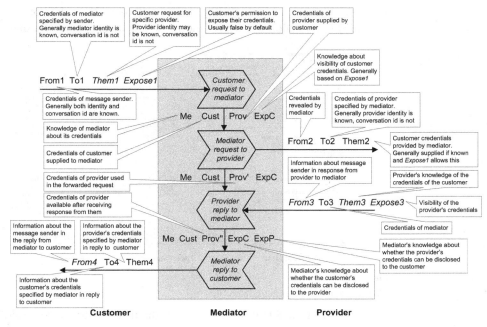

Figure 7.8

Mediated Interaction example (based on [89]).

For the mediated introduction variant, there are the following parameters:

- *Customer request for specific provider (Them1):* this may include either or (ideally) both the provider's identity and the conversation identifier, which are forwarded by the mediator at the customer's request.
- *Information about the message sender in the request from mediator to provider (From2):* information revealed by the mediator about their credentials in the request to the provider.
- *Information about the message sender in the response from provider to customer (From5):* information revealed by the provider about their credentials in the response to the customer.
- *Information about the mediator exposed by provider to customer (Them5):* information revealed by the provider about the mediator's credentials in the response to the customer.

There are 320 potential configurations of this pattern family variant depending on the specific parameter settings used (see [90] for details). In none of the 320 configurations are the customer and provider directly interacting. There is another set of patterns modeling the situation where the mediator establishes contact after which the provider directly contacts the customer without passing messages through the mediator. This is referred to as Mediated Introduction. Figure 7.9 shows the graphical notation for these patterns.

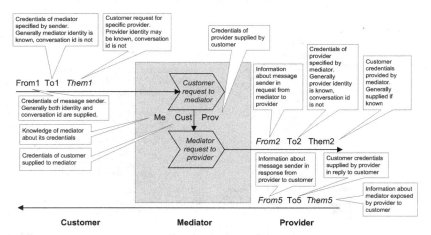

Figure 7.9
Mediated Introduction example (based on [89]).

Oracle BPEL is able to realize most of the pattern variants in the Message Mediation pattern family through the use of shared BPEL correlation sets and WS-Addressing. Only those where the identity of the message receiver is underspecified by the sender cannot be implemented. As discussed previously, these are problematic as BPEL does not allow the intended target for a message to be omitted or for a message to be sent to an arbitrary party.

Bipartite Conversation Correlation

The final pattern family in the service interaction pattern framework — *Bipartite Conversation Correlation* — deals with the issue of varying correlation information in the context of a long-running conversation between two parties. This may arise for a variety of different reasons ranging from a lossy communication channel through to the accidental or deliberate omission of necessary correlation information by the party sending a message intended as part of an ongoing conversation. At any stage in the conversation between two parties — hereafter termed *requestor* and *responder* — there is the potential that information necessary for message correlation is unavailable. Each message between requestor and responder is expected to include credentials for both parties, in addition to the message content in order to support message correlation, although there is the potential for incompleteness of certain credentials.

There are eighteen distinct *Bipartite Conversation Correlation* pattern configurations, all of which can be depicted via the graphical notation illustrated in figure 7.10. This includes denotation of configurable parameters along with static and dynamic attributes and succinctly illustrates the interactions between requestor and responder.

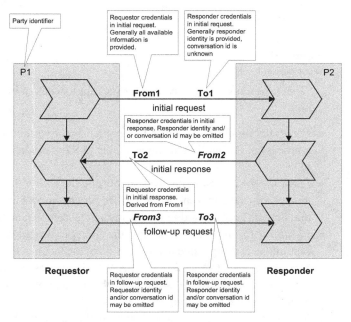

Figure 7.10

Bipartite Conversation Correlation pattern notation (based on [89]).

Oracle BPEL is able to realize all of the pattern variants in the Bipartite Conversation Correlation pattern family through the use of shared BPEL correlation sets and WS-Addressing.

7.3   Flexibility patterns

Flexibility patterns were proposed by Mulyar et al. [89, 91] as a catalogue of approaches for enhancing process flexibility. Flexibility is considered to be the ability of a business process to deal with changes in the operational environment through the pursuit of alternate execution paths, which may not have been foreseen or are not explictly catered to by the process model. The taxonomy of flexibility types previously introduced in section 3.5 is shown again in figure 7.11 [121].

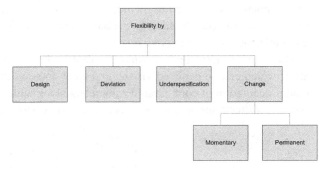

Figure 7.11
Taxonomy of flexibility types.

This taxonomy recognizes five distinct approaches to incorporating flexibility in a process:

- *Flexibility by design* involves the explicit incorporation of flexibility mechanisms into a process at design time using available process modeling constructs such as splits and joins;
- *Flexibility by deviation* involves supporting the ability for individual process instances to temporarily deviate from the prescribed process model in order to accommodate changes that may be encountered in the operating environment at runtime;
- *Flexibility by underspecification* is the ability to deliberately underspecify parts of a process model at design time in anticipation of the fact that the required execution details will become known at some future time. When a process instance encounters an underspecified portion of a process at runtime, the missing part can be instantiated in accordance with the required operational outcomes and then executed; and
- *Flexibility by change* caters to changes in the operational environment by actually amending the process model. There are two approaches to this:

  — *Flexibility by momentary change* involves change to the process model corresponding to a specific process instance. Any other process instances are unaffected by the change; and

— *Flexibility by permanent change* involves changing the process model for all process instances. This may involve migrating any other currently executing instances from the old to the new process model.

On the basis of these approaches, thirty-four flexibility patterns have been proposed that identify strategies for increasing the flexibility of a business process in various ways. These are divided into eight distinct groups depending on the pattern intent and are summarized in tables 7.7 and 7.8.

Each of the three offerings that we have examined throughout the course of this book provides some degree of flexibility support. Table 7.9 provides an assessment of flexibility pattern support in BPMN, BPMone, and Oracle BPEL using the same evaluation scale as utilized in earlier chapters. It is notable that design time flexibility is relatively well supported by all offerings. Similarly, BPMone demonstrates relatively strong support for the flexibility by deviation patterns as a consequence of its case handling foundations. Oracle BPEL also has reasonable support in this area. The other types of process flexibility enjoy almost no support. These results mirror the extent of flexibility support found in BPM offerings on a more general basis. Although there is relatively general support for design time flexibility, other aspects of process flexibility are not catered to to the same degree.

7.4   Change patterns and change support features

In an effort to provide a better basis for describing the capabilities of business process offerings when dealing with process change, Weber et al. [103, 133, 134] have proposed a series of eighteen change patterns and seven change support features. These consider changes effected at both the level of the process instance and the overall process model (i.e., type level). There are similarities between these patterns and the flexibility by momentary and permanent change patterns discussed in section 7.3. However, the change patterns include design alternatives as part of their formulation and are augmented with the change support features, which allow for a more fine-grained description of the manner in which a change feature is effected by an offering. The change patterns are divided into two groups:

- *Adaptation patterns*, which describe structural modifications to a process at the type or instance level. These changes do not need to be anticipated ahead of the time and can be made to any part of the process; and
- *Patterns for changes in defined regions*, which do not facilitate structural changes to the process but enable underspecified parts of the process to be completed. Unlike the adaptation patterns, they *do* need to be anticipated as part of the design time process model, and the extent of the application is limited to those parts of the design time model that are deliberately underspecified.

Table 7.7

Flexibility patterns.

FLEXIBILITY PATTERNS				
Design	*Deviation*	*Underspecification*	*Momentary Change*	*Permanent Change*
Flexible initiation: *Flexibility in the way process instances are initiated*				
FP-1: Alternative entry points	**FP-2: Entrance skip**	**FP-3: Undefined entry**	**FP-4: Momentary entry change**	**FP-5: Permanent entry change**
Include alternative start tasks in the design time process definition	At process initiation, there is the option of starting execution from any task subsequent to the nominated start task	A process definition has an underspecified beginning. At initiation, there is the option of completing the process definition by including an appropriate start task	At process initiation, there is the option of changing the process model for the current instance such that it has an alternative start task	At process initiation, there is the option of changing the process model such that it has an alternative start task. Any existing process instances are migrated to the new process definition
Flexible termination: *Flexibility in the way process instances terminate*				
FP-6: Alt. exit points	**FP-7: Term. skip**	**FP-8: Undefined exit**	**FP-9: Moment. exit-point chg**	**FP-10: Perm. exit-point chg**
Include alternative end tasks in the design time process definition	During process execution, there is the option of completing execution by skipping all future tasks to the nominated end task	A process definition has an underspecified ending. During execution, there is the option of completing the process definition by including an appropriate end task	During process execution, there is the option of changing the process model for the current instance such that it has an alternative end task	At process execution, there is the option of changing the process model such that it has an alternative exit task. Any existing process instances are migrated to the new process def'n
Flexible selection: *Flexibility in selecting an execution path*				
FP-11: Choice	**FP-12: Task substitution**	**FP-13: Late selection**	**FP-14: Momentary choice insertion**	**FP-15: Permanent choice insertion**
Include alternative execution paths in the design time process definition such that the desired path can selected at runtime	Allow the currently enabled task to be substituted with another (later) task in the process	A process definition has an underspecified region which may be completed at runtime to allow a path other than the default execution path to be taken	During process execution, there is the option of changing the process model for the current instance to include a choice between a task in the current model and an alternative task not previously foreseen	At process execution, there is the option of changing the process model to include a choice between a task in the current model and an alternative task not previously foreseen. Any existing process instances are migrated to the new process definition
Flexible reordering: *Flexibility in the execution ordering of tasks*				
FP-16: Interleaving	**FP-17: Swap**		**FP-18: Moment. reordering**	**FP-19: Perm. reordering**
Include alternative execution paths in the design time process definition such that alternative execution sequences exist for two tasks allowing them to be executed in either order but not concurrently	Allow the execution order of the current process instance to be changed such that the currently enabled task is swapped with its successor		During process execution, there is the option of changing the process model for the current instance such that a given task is moved to another place in the model	During process execution, there is the option of changing the process model such that a given task is moved to another place in the model. Any existing process instances are migrated to the new process definition

Table 7.8

Flexibility patterns (cont.).

Design	Deviation	Underspecification	Momentary Change	Permanent Change
Flexible elimination: *Flexibility in eliminating task execution*				
FP-20: Foreseen bypass path	**FP-21: Task skip**		**FP-22: Momentary task eliminat'n**	**FP-23: Permanent task elimination**
Include alternative execution paths in the design time process definition such that a nominated task can be bypassed	Allow the execution of the currently enabled task in a process to be skipped		During process execution, there is the option of changing the process model for the current instance such that a given task is removed from the process model	During process execution, there is the option of changing the process model such that a given task is removed from the process model. Any existing process instances are migrated to the new process def'n
Flexible extension: *Flexibility in enabling an alternative execution path*				
	FP-24: Task invocation	**FP-25: Late creation**	**FP-26: Momentary task insertion**	**FP-27: Permanent task insertion**
	Allow a task which has not yet been invoked to be executed before the currently enabled task in a process instance	A process definition has an underspecified region which may be completed at runtime to allow previously unanticipated tasks to be included in the process	During process execution, there is the option of changing the process model for the current instance such that a given task is added to the process model	During process execution, there is the option of changing the process model such that a task is added to the process model. Any existing process instances are migrated to the new process definition
Flexible concurrency: *Flexibility in enabling concurrent task execution*				
FP-28: Parallelism			**FP-29: Moment'y task parallelization**	**FP-30: Permanent task parallelization**
Include parallel execution paths in the design time process definition such that two independent tasks can execute concurrently or in any order			During process execution, there is the option of changing the process model for the current instance such that two independent tasks can execute concurrently or in any order	During process execution, there is the option of changing the process model such that two independent tasks can execute concurrently or in any order. Any existing process instances are migrated to the new process definition
Flexible repetition: *Flexibility in enabling repetitious task execution*				
FP-31: Iteration	**FP-32: Redo**		**FP-33: Momentary loop insertion**	**FP-34: Permanent loop insertion**
Include loops in the design time process definition such that a nominated task can be repeatedly executed on a conditional basis	Allow a previously completed task in a process instance to be repeated		During process execution, there is the option of changing the process model for the current instance such that a task can be inserted in a loop allowing it to be repeatedly executed on a conditional basis	During process execution, there is the option of changing the process model such that a task can be inserted in a loop allowing it to be repeatedly executed on a conditional basis. Any existing process instances are migrated to the new process definition

Table 7.9

Flexibility pattern support in BPMN, BPMone, and Oracle BPEL (based on [89, 91]).

Nr	Pattern	BPMN	BPMone	Oracle BPEL
Flexibility by Design				
FP-1	Alternative entry points	+	−	+
FP-6	Alternative exit points	+	−	+
FP-11	Choice	+	+	+
FP-16	Interleaving	+	+	+
FP-20	Foreseen bypass path	+	+	+
FP-28	Parallelism	+	+	+
FP-31	Iteration	+	+	+
Flexibility by Deviation				
FP-2	Entrance skip	+/−	+/−	+/−
FP-7	Termination skip	+	+	+
FP-12	Task substitution	+	+/−	+
FP-17	Swap	−	+	−
FP-21	Task skip	+	+	+
FP-24	Task invocation	+	+	+
FP-32	Redo	+	+	+
Flexibility by Underspecification				
FP-3	Undefined entry	−	−	−
FP-8	Undefined exit	−	−	−
FP-13	Late selection	−	−	−
FP-25	Late creation	+	−	+
Flexibility by Momentary Change				
FP-4	Momentary entry change	−	−	−
FP-9	Momentary exit change	−	−	−
FP-14	Momentary choice insertion	−	−	−
FP-18	Momentary reordering	−	−	−
FP-22	Momentary task elimination	−	−	−
FP-26	Momentary task insertion	−	−	−
FP-29	Momentary task parallelization	−	−	−
FP-33	Momentary loop insertion	−	−	−
Flexibility by Permanent Change				
FP-5	Permanent entry change	−	−	−
FP-10	Permanent exit change	−	−	−
FP-15	Permanent choice insertion	−	−	−
FP-19	Permanent reordering	−	−	−
FP-23	Permanent task elimination	−	−	−
FP-27	Permanent task insertion	−	−	−
FP-30	Permanent task parallelization	−	−	−
FP-34	Permanent loop insertion	−	−	−

Change patterns define strategies for the immediate structural adaptation of processes or the denotation of required adaptation in the process model and its deferral to runtime. Change support features operate at a more detailed level and provide additional information on how well an offering supports process change and the particular capabilities it has in this area. Further details of the adaptation patterns, patterns for changes in defined regions, and change support features are included in the following sections.

Adaptation patterns

There are fourteen adaptation patterns that describe the various ways in which a process can be structurally transformed. These operate at a sufficiently high level of abstraction, thus ensuring that process soundness is preserved when they are utilized. Two general design choices apply to the use of all patterns (the scope of the pattern and the object the pattern operates on) and additional choices that apply to specific patterns. All design choices are able to be used for the further specialization of pattern application based on the use of relevant parameters when specific patterns are applied. Tables 7.10 and 7.11 list the adaptation patterns, associated design choices, and examples of their use.

Patterns for changes in defined regions

Four patterns for changes in defined regions allow specific change decisions to be deferred to runtime by deliberately underspecifying parts of the design time process model. Although these notions are captured at the level of the process type (i.e., in the process model), they are effected at runtime at the level of the individual process instance. Table 7.11 lists these patterns, relevant design choices, and examples of their use.

Change support features

Seven change support features provide additional facilities that an offering should provide to enable the change patterns to be successfully utilized in practice. They provide further details in areas such as (F1) specific runtime features provided by an offering to assist in process change, (F2) extent of support for instance specific changes, (F3) ability to only allow correct changes, (F4) extent of facilities for tracing process changes, (F5) extent of access control facilities for process changes, (F6) availability of support for reusing previously defined change operations, and (F7) facilities for dealing with concurrent changes. The range of options for each of the change support features and their applicability to the process type (T), process instance (I), or both levels (T+I) are listed in table 7.12.

As an indication of the use of the change patterns, in table 7.13, an assessment of the capabilities of BPMone are presented. Although it does not provide any direct support for process change at the type level and minimal support at the level of individual process instances, the change support features provide a succinct characterization of underlying features that it provides, which may provide a foundation for future enhancements to the offering to support dynamic process change.

Table 7.10

Adaptation patterns (from [38, 107]).

General Design Choices for Adaptation Patterns (Apply to All Patterns) *A: Scope of pattern:* (1) process instance level, (2) process type level *B: Pattern operates on:* (1) atomic activity, (2) subprocess, (3) region (hammock) *Note that some patterns also have an additional design choice C*	
Pattern	**Definition**
AP1: Insert process fragment	A process fragment is included in a process definition *Example:* For a specific customer, a new quality check task is added to the dangerous goods shipping process *Design choices:* *C: new fragment is added:* (1) between an activity and its successor, (2a/2b) between activity sets with or without additional condition
AP2: Delete process fragment	A process fragment is removed from a process definition *Example:* For a particular customer, the prepare paper manifest is no longer required as part of the warehouse order fulfilment process (as it is now sent by EDI when the order is despatched).
AP3: Move process fragment	A process fragment is relocated from its current place to another part of a process definition *Example:* For any orders deemed to be suspicious, the credit check process is moved from its usual position prior to order despatch to the beginning of the take order process *Design choices:* *C: how to re-insert the migrated fragment:* (1) between an activity and its successor, (2a) between activity sets unconditionally, (2b) between activity sets with additional condition
AP4: Replace process fragment	A process fragment is substituted with a different process fragment in a process definition *Example:* For new repairs, the compression test activity is replaced by the engine operation test activity in the warranty service process
AP5: Swap process fragments	Two process fragments that form part of a process definition are interchanged *Example:* In the despatch freight process, the order of the book delivery and prepare manifest activities are interchanged with each other
AP6: Extract sub-process	A process fragment in a process definition is removed and turned into a subprocess that is referenced from where the fragment was originally located *Example:* To reduce the complexity of the conduct audit process, the tax-related activities are encapsulated in a separate subprocess which is to be carried out by members of the tax consulting group
AP7: Inline sub-process	A subprocess to which one or more process definitions refer is dispensed with and its constituent activities are directly included in these process definitions *Example:* The credit check subprocess which was previously outsourced to the credit department is now to be conducted by sales staff as part of the order fulfilment process and the activities involved are now subsumed into the order fulfilment process.
AP8: Embed process fragment in a loop	A process fragment in a process definition is selected to become part of a newly introduced loop *Example:* In the composition analysis process for a particular compound, the spectrograph activity may need to be run multiple times
AP9: Parallelize process fragments	A number of process fragments in sequential order are transformed into branches of a parallel construct *Example:* There is no longer any requirement to execute the check credit and prepare activities for the order fulfilment process sequentially and they can now run concurrently
AP10: Embed proces fragment in a conditional branch	A process definition is changed such that a process fragment is included in a conditional construct *Example:* The credit check activity in the order fulfilment process is now only run for medium and high value orders
AP11: Add control dependency	A control-flow arc is inserted in a process definition *Example:* The order fulfilment process is amended so that the despatch order activity can only execute when the produce invoice task has completed. This was not previously a requirement and is achieved by adding a control-flow arc from the despatch order to the produce invoice activity
AP12: Remove control dependency	An existing control-flow arc is extracted from a process definition *Example:* The execution of the fund loan activity is no longer contingent on the audit sign-off activity and the control-flow arc between these two activities can be removed
AP13: Update condition	A transition condition associated with a control-flow arc in a process definition is changed *Example:* The credit check activity now only needs to be undertaken for high value orders and not medium value orders as was the case previously

Table 7.11

Adaptation patterns (cont.) and Late selection of process-fragment patterns (from [38, 107]).

Pattern	Definition
AP14: Copy process fragment	A process fragment in a process definition is replicated in another part of the process definition *Example:* The criminal record check activity is to be performed at the end of the staff procurement process prior to the hire activity as well as at the commencement of the process as was previously the case *Design choices:* *C: how to reinsert the migrated fragment:* (1) between an activity and its successor, (2a) between activity sets without additional condition, (2b) between activity sets with additional condition
PP1: Late selection of process fragments	For specific activities (denoted with a placeholder in the process model) the corresponding implementation can be chosen at runtime *Example:* The actual implementation chosen for the service MRI equipment activity depends on the results of the earlier diagnosis and ship parts activities *Design Choices:* *A Selection of implementation:* (1) automatic (based on rules), (2) manual by user, (3) semi-automatic (combination of (1) and (2)) *B Realization of activity:* (1) activity, (2) subprocess *C Timing of late selection:* (1) before placeholder activity is enabled, (2) at enablement
PP2: Late modeling of process fragments	For particular parts of a process model (denoted with a placeholder in the process model) the corresponding implementation can be chosen at runtime for each process instance *Example:* Determination of how the remainder of the fault rectification will be undertaken depends on the results obtained from the earlier diagnostic activities in the process *Design Choices:* *A Building blocks for modeling:* (1) any of the process fragments in modeling repository, (2) a subset of the process fragments in the repository (based on some constraint), (3) new activities/process fragments can be modeled *B Extent of modeling freedom:* (1) all modeling constructs and change patterns available at process type level, (2) a restricted set of modeling constructs and change patterns *C Timing of late modeling:* (1) at process commencement, (2) before instantiation of placeholder activity, (3) on reaching a nominated process state *D Starting point for modeling:* (1) start from scratch, (2) work from a predefined template
PP3: Late composition of process fragments	At design time, a respository of process fragments is defined. At runtime, the actual process definition adopted for a given process instance is instantiated based on fragments from the repository *Example:* The actual process adopted for the ad-hoc fault resolution process is determined on a case-by-case basis based on the issue at hand by following one or more documented resolution strategies *Design Choices:* *A Building blocks for modeling:* (1) any of the process fragments in modeling repository, (2) a subset of the process fragments in the repository (based on some constraint), (3) new activities/process fragments can be modeled
PP4: Multi instance activity	The ability to execute a nominated activity a number of times. The exact determination of the number of times is made at runtime *Example:* The label production activity is run multiple times during the despatch process depending on the number of parcels in the delivery. The number of times it will run is not known until the complete order has been packed for shipment.

7.5   Scientific workflow patterns

There is increasing use of workflow technology in the scientific domain as a means of automating the conduct of scientific experiments, leading to greater efficiencies in their conduct and improved accuracy. In contrast to business-oriented workflow systems, which tend to focus on issues of control-flow, in scientific workflow, data management is one of the key considerations. As a consequence, data flow and data management considerations

Table 7.12

Change support features (from [38, 107]).

Feature	Scope	Options
F1: Schema evolution, version control and instance migration	T	No version control - existing schema is overwritten F1[1]: executing instances are cancelled F1[2]: executing instances remain
		Version control F1[3]: no migration, old and new instances co-exist F1[4]: all instances migrated F1[5]: controlled instance migration
F2: Support for instance-specific changes	I	Unplanned changes F2[1a]: temporary F2[1b]: permanent
		Preplanned changes F2[2a]: temporary F2[2b]: permanent
F3: Correctness of changes	I + T	N/A
F4: Traceability and analysis of changes	I + T	F4[1]: traceability of changes F4[2]: semantic annotation of changes F4[3]: change mining
F5: Access control for changes	I + T	F5[1]: changes can be restricted to specific users F5[2]: application of change patterns can be restricted F5[3]: authorization can be based on element being changed
F6: Change reuse	I	N/A
F7: Change concurrency control	I + T	F7[1]: uncontrolled concurrent access F7[2]: concurrent changes prohibited F7[3]: concurrent changes of structure/state controlled by offering F7[4]: concurrent changes at type/instance level

Table 7.13

Change patterns and change support features supported in BPMone.

Change pattern support at type level	
N/A	
Change pattern support at instance level	
AP2 - Delete fragment	A[2], B[1]
Change support features	
[F1] Schema evolution, version control and instance migration	F1[3]
[F2] Instance specific changes	F2[1b,2b]
[F4] Traceability and analysis	F4[1]
[F5] Access control for changes	F5[1,2,3]
[F7] Change concurrency support	F7[3]

(e.g., data provenance, fault tolerance of data sets in the face of partial execution re-runs) receive significantly greater prominence than is the case in workflow in other domains.

In scientific workflows, both data and control-flow dependencies are equally significant in the design and execution of processes. This duality leads to a greater range of potential process models as both data and control-flow dependencies need to be combined in the same model. Consequently, a range of additional design choices than may ordinarily arise in business-oriented workflows. A significant distinction is the existence and flow of both control and data tokens within a scientific workflow. In [149], Yildiz et al. nominate six scientific workflow patterns to aid in the design of such processes. These patterns are divided into three groups.

Single-activity patterns

These patterns focus on characterizing modeling situations pertaining to a single-individual activity in a scientific workflow, where the activity may have a single or multiple input and output dependencies with preceding and subsequent activities.

Pattern 1: *Single activity with one input and one output dependency*

Over time, an activity receives a number of tokens on its single input port and emits a (possibly different) number of tokens on its single output port. The number of tokens required for activation of the activity or produced on the output port at completion can be specified at design time or runtime. Design considerations can include: (1) the number of input and output tokens and whether these are fixed or variable, (2) the types of tokens received/produced (these can be the same or different [i.e., control and data]), and (3) the order of input tokens (these can be received in different orders if they are produced by different sources).

This pattern corresponds to the commonly occurring scenario of an activity in a process that has a single input and a single output link. Two significant implementation considerations arise in its use: (1) providing support for deterministic means of specifying the activation condition where the activity may potentially receive multiple input tokens, and (2) in the event that the number of input tokens received is greater than those required for activation, determining what to do with the excess tokens.

Pattern 2: *Single activity with multiple input and/or multiple output dependencies*

Over time, an activity receives a number of tokens on its range of input ports and emits a (possibly different) number of tokens on its range of output ports. As for Pattern 1, tokens can be either control or data tokens and can be fixed or variable. By default, all incoming ports must contain tokens for the activity to fire, although a subset of ports can be specified as sufficient for activation. A similar design choice is possible for output ports, which by default must produce tokens on each output after completion unless otherwise specified.

This pattern corresponds to the situation where an activity in a process has several input and/or output links. The major implementation consideration lies in dealing with scenarios where there may not be tokens on all input ports (particularly in the case of data tokens) but activation is required. Potential solutions center on the specification of the activation condition. A similar issue arises with activations that do not result in a token on each output port. Options in this case include the replication of a token from a productive output port or the creation of "dummy" tokens.

Control and data flow patterns

This group of patterns delineate situations where multiple activities (which may execute sequentially or concurrently) depend on data elements from a single preceding activity.

Pattern 3: *Sequential control and sequential data*

At least two sequential activities are interdependent both in terms of control and data flow. The activation of such activities requires both control and data tokens on their input ports. The number of data tokens can be fixed or variable, with activation occurring when both the control token is received and the required number of data tokens.

This pattern is a composition of Patterns 1 and 2 and consequently shares the same implementation issues — most significantly where the tokens received differ from those required for activation (either excess or paucity).

Pattern 4: *Sequential control and concurrent data*

At least three activities are sequentially connected by control-flow arcs and share a common data dependency on the same activity. The activation of such activities requires both control and data tokens on their input ports. In effect, the data tokens are shared by the three activities.

The major implementation consideration with this pattern lies in managing the shared access to a single token or a set of tokens by several discrete activities. Changes to the shared token(s) by any of the activities, or consumption of the token, can have significant consequences and therefore need to be managed with care.

Token quantity patterns

These patterns deal with situations where the number of data tokens flowing needs to be synchronized in order to enable subsequent activities to be activated.

Pattern 5: *Synchronization of sequential data tokens*

A number of data tokens pass through a series of sequential activities where, upon receipt of a data token, an activity consumes it and produces another data token. At some subsequent point in the workflow, the processing of data tokens is synchronized before subsequent activities are executed. The synchronization may need to deal with different numbers of tokens from each preceding activity (e.g., due to multiple executions).

This pattern shares similar implementation considerations with preceding patterns in terms of dealing with potential mismatches between token availability and requirements for synchronization. It can be implemented in two ways: (1) tokens passing through the sequential activities are counted and compared with a globally available value of tokens to be synchronized, or (2) the synchronization point has two inputs (akin to an AND-join) — one that receives a token indicating the number of data tokens processed by the sequential activities and a second from the final of the sequential activities indicating the number of data tokens processed.

Pattern 6: *Data token duplication*

An activity requires a token from each of two activities that it is connected to. As these preceding activities do not produce tokens at the same rate, tokens are duplicated for the activity producing at the slower rate so they are "balanced."

The main implementation consideration associated with this pattern is determining how many tokens need to be duplicated. Typically, additional token counting infrastructure will need to be incorporated in a given workflow in order to support the pattern.

The patterns discussed above are particularly relevant to scientific workflow tools, and for this reason, their occurrence in business-focused tools such as those as illustrative examples for other pattern catalogues is not considered here.

7.6   Workflow time patterns

Workflow time patterns aim to provide a systematic basis for identifying, assessing, and comparing the time-related capabilities across a variety of distinct process-aware information systems.

Lanz et al. [76, 77] propose a set of ten time patterns based on an evaluation of process models and case studies from four distinct domains and a detailed literature review. In line with the patterns philosophy, they require a candidate pattern to be observed at least three times before including it in their final list of time patterns. Each of the resultant patterns is documented in the problem-solution format traditionally used when describing patterns, along with potential design choices that allow for pattern variants in distinct implementation technologies, context details that define or restrict their usage, examples of their use in practice and references to related patterns, and known uses in the literature and mainstream technologies. The operational semantics of the time patterns are formalized on the basis of temporal execution traces. There is also a comprehensive survey of the occurrence of the patterns across a range of process-related technologies and modeling formalisms. Four distinct categories of time patterns are described.

Category I: Durations and time lags

This group of patterns focuses on characterizing time durations of process elements and time lags between them.

Pattern TP1: Times lags between two activities A specified time lag between two (potentially arbitrary) activities needs to be enacted. It may need to comply with pre-existing roles and requirements and may or may not be binding.

Pattern TP2: Durations A specific process element has a restriction on its overall duration. This may include waiting and/or processing times. It may be determined by factors external to the element and may or may not be binding.

Pattern TP3: Time lags between arbitrary events A specified time lag between two distinct events occurring during the execution of a process instance needs to be enacted. It may need to comply with pre-existing roles and requirements and may or may not be binding.

Category II: Restrictions of process execution points

This group of patterns identifies various types of time-related restrictions on process execution.

Pattern TP4: Fixed date element A particular process element needs to be executed at a specific date/time. Such a process element may also determine the earliest/latest start or completion of preceding/subsequent process element(s). Failing to meet the deadline may result in the process element or even the entire process instance becoming obsolete.

Pattern TP5: Schedule restricted elements There is a schedule that may impose a restriction on the execution of a specific process element.

Pattern TP6: Time-based restrictions Specific process elements may have restrictions on the number of times they can execute in a given time frame. These restrictions may be necessary to deal with underlying resource restrictions during process execution.

Pattern TP7: Validity period There is a validity period that restricts the timeframe during that a particular process element can execute. This may be necessary to deal with distinct versions of a process element (e.g., during rollout and decommissioning activities) and provides a means of ensuring that only one valid version of the process element is available at any given point in time.

Category III: (Time-dependent) variability

This pattern group comprises a single pattern that focuses on situations where control flow varies depending on the execution time of specific activities or events or there are time lags between these activities and events.

Pattern TP8: Time-dependent variability Time-related aspects may influence control-flow during process execution (e.g., different execution paths are chosen or different sub-process fragments are selected).

Category IV: Recurrent process elements

This pattern group comprises patterns related to cyclic elements and periodicity in business processes. The number of repetitions may be specified explicitly, calculated based on time lags or end dates, or may depend on a specific exit condition.

Pattern TP9: Cyclic elements A specific process element is executed repeatedly with time lags between individual iterations.

Pattern TP10: Periodicity A specific process element is executed on a periodic basis, with subsequent executions occurring with some form of regularity with respect to a particular reference scheme (e.g., a calendar). There is potential for exceptions to the regular execution schedule.

An alternative scheme for time patterns is proposed by Niculae [92], based on a comprehensive review of the workflow literature. In this pattern catalogue, discovery is based on concepts derived from the literature rather than actual observation in practice. Niculae identifies eleven patterns and for each of them nominates design decisions, the motivation for the pattern, implementation suggestions, and an evaluation with respect to the broader workflow literature. A notation is also provided for the patterns. In essence, the first ten of these overlap with the time patterns identified by Lanz et al. However, the final pattern T-RD (Required Delay) is novel. The specifics of each of the Niculae patterns are listed below.

Pattern T-TD: Task duration The capability to prescribe at design time the maximum duration of the execution of an activity.

Pattern T-D: Deadline The capability to prescribe at design time the time at which an activity must be executed.

Pattern T-RTCS: Repetitive time constraint with calendar support The capability to prescribe at design time that a given activity must be executed on a periodic basis as defined by some form of rule.

Pattern T-NTC: Negative time constraint The capability to prescribe at design time that a specific activity cannot be performed at a nominated time.

Pattern T-SR: Schedule restricted The capability to prescribe at design time that an activity can only be performed in accordance with a particular schedule.

Pattern T-TBR: Time-based restriction The capability to prescribe at design time that an activity can only be performed a limited number of times in a specified period.

Pattern T-VP: Validity period The capability to prescribe at design time that the lifespan of all work items of a given activity must fall within a particular period of validity.

Pattern T-TDV: Time-dependent variability The capability to prescribe at design time that time-related factors may influence control-flow during execution of a process.

Pattern T-TC2A: Time constraint between two activities The capability to prescribe at design time that a specified time lag needs to be observed between two given activities.

Pattern T-TC2E: Time constraint between two events The capability to prescribe at design time a time lag between two events which must be observed during process execution.

Pattern T-RD: Required delay The capability to prescribe at design time that two sequential activities must have a nominated delay between the completion of the first and the commencement of the second.

Table 7.14 identifies the correspondences between the two catalogues of time patterns and identifies the extent of support for each of them in BPMN, BPMone, and Oracle BPEL using the same evaluation scale as used elsewhere in earlier chapters. In this evaluation a "+" rating indicates support for stated intention of the pattern, although not all design options may necessarily be supported. Nonetheless, it is interesting to observe the extent of time pattern support underscoring the significance of the time dimension in business processes.

Table 7.14

Time pattern support in BPMN, BPMone, and Oracle BPEL.

Lanz et al Pattern	Niculae Pattern	BPMN	BPM one	Oracle BPEL
TP1: Time lags between two activities	T-TC2A: Time constraints between two activities	+	+	+
TP2: Durations	T-TD: Task duration	+	+	+
TP3: Time lags between arbitrary events	T-TC2E: Time constraints between two events	+/−	−	+/−
TP4: Fixed date element	T-D: Deadline	+	+	+
TP5: Schedule restricted element	T-SR: Schedule restricted T-NTC: Negative time constraint	−	−	−
TP6: Time based restriction	T-TBR: Time based restriction	−	−	−
TP7: Validity period	T-VP: Validity period	−	−	−
TP8: Time dependent variability	T-TDV: Time dependent variability	+	+	+
TP9: Cyclic element	T-RTCS Repetitive time constraint with calendar support	+/−	+	+/−
TP10: Periodicity	T-RTCS Repetitive time constraint with calendar support T-NTC: Negative time constraint	+/−	+/−	+/−
N/A	T-RD: Required delay	+	+	+

7.7 Workflow activity patterns

Workflow activity patterns [125] focus on the recurrent business functions in processes that have generic semantics. Seven such patterns have been identified through examination of a wide range of candidate process models. A summary of these patterns is provided below.

Pattern WAP1: Approval An artifact requires the approval of one or more organizational roles. The required evaluation may be undertaken once by a single resource or multiple times (sequentially or concurrently) by multiple resources, with a final decision made at the conclusion of the evaluations.

Pattern WAP2: Question-answer A question arises during process execution that requires answering. Execution of the process does not continue until an appropriate answer is obtained.

Pattern WAP3: Unidirectional performative A request for execution of a specified activity is routed to one or several process participants. Execution of the process continues without waiting for a response.

Pattern WAP4: Bidirectional performative A request for execution of a specified activity is routed to one or several process participants. Execution of the process only continues when responses have been received for all requests that have been issued.

Pattern WAP5: Notification One or several process participants are advised of the status or outcome of an activity.

Pattern WAP6: Informative An information request is sent to one or several process participants. Execution of the process only continues when responses have been received for all requests that have been issued.

Pattern WAP7: Decision Answers to one or more requests sent to process participants determine which subsequent branches will be taken.

The generic format of these patterns eases their capture in a wide range of business process formalisms and technologies, and they are all able to be represented in BPMN, BPMone, and Oracle BPEL.

7.8 Endword

This chapter has presented an introduction to seven patterns collections in the BPM domain. Unlike the patterns presented in chapters 4, 5, and 6, which deal with fundamental process considerations, these collections focus on higher order issues relevant to process definition, operation, and maintenance and provide solutions to problems that arise in areas such as exception handling, flexibility, service interaction, and dynamic process change. In doing so, they provide a valuable source of ideas and guidance for professionals involved in the design and deployment of new business processes and also for those involved in the creation of new enabling technology in the BPM domain.

8 Epilogue

This book informs the reader about a number of patterns collections in the BPM domain. A thorough understanding of the patterns in these collections provides a timeless understanding of the essential ingredients of business process modeling and automation. The BPM field continues to evolve; new support environments and standards come and go. However, the fundamentals of BPM remain largely unchanged, and focusing on these rather than current commercial offerings makes it easier for both students and professionals to weather the onslaught of new approaches, buzzwords, and marketing speak.

The workflow patterns for the control-flow, data, and resource perspectives are the result of a thorough analysis over a period of more than a decade and have been used widely, by both us and other practitioners, for the assessment of languages, tools (both commercial and open source), and (proposed) standards. They have become an accepted way of determining the comparative suitability of a particular approach to business process specification. As such, they have been used in a variety of tool selection processes. It is important to note at this point that the patterns are about *suitability* and not *expressive power*. Although any programming language is Turing complete, you would not use one to build a BPM solution from scratch. Therefore, statements that patterns can be programmed in a particular BPM environment miss the essence of what the patterns are about. Any pattern can be programmed in any programming language; suitability of a process specification language is about the *effort* required to realize patterns in that language.

Organizations looking for a BPM solution should not simply count the number of patterns supported by each system and then select the one that supports the most. Instead one should identify the patterns that are most important and see how well they are supported. Some of the BPM systems support many patterns but are also complex and require enormous configuration efforts. Compare selecting a BPM system to buying a means of transport: sometimes a truck is more convenient than a car, sometimes the car is preferable. The patterns give a means to make a well-informed decision.

The patterns have also been used in the development of the YAWL workflow language, the BPMN standard, and they have influenced language adaptations in BPM environments. There is no other independent and comprehensive approach to assessing a language's ability to capture business scenarios. This is not to say, however, that the patterns collections are complete (how could this even be determined?) and cannot be extended or improved in the future.

The workflow patterns collections presented in this book can be extended with pattern collections for perspectives that have not yet been delineated or are insufficiently documented. Some examples of such collections can be found in the previous chapter. The introduction of these collections raises the question as to what constitutes a "good" collection of patterns? A patterns collection needs to satisfy a few essential requirements:

- *Patterns should derive from a need, not a particular solution.* The description of a pattern should make the need it aims to address clear without being tied to particular ways of realizing this need.
- *The need a pattern aims to address should be real.* There are different ways of determining this. For example, one may have observed the pattern in a number of scenarios in different application domains or recognized that the pattern is directly supported by one (or more) tool(s). The latter justification is based on the assumption that if a vendor is willing to provide direct support for a particular pattern, then it must have been observed a number of times; otherwise it would not have been worth the investment necessary to support it.
- *It is important to determine the right level of granularity for a pattern.* Patterns become meaningless if they are too general or too specific. A pattern that is too general cannot be applied for a real purpose, whereas a pattern that is too specific is either better ignored or generalized to a pattern that covers a number of relevant dimensions. Ultimately, the "proof is in the pudding," and if a collection of patterns does not provide any new insight into the state of the art, it is not of any value. As such, a pattern collection should have been thoroughly validated (e.g., by using it to analyze the relevant problem domain and seeing whether it yields any innovative insights or learnings).
- *A pattern definition should cover a range of issues* and, for instance, not just consist of a brief description and an example. The pattern should be properly motivated, one or more examples should be given, and its manifestation in the state of the art should be discussed, as well as the various trade-offs and issues that may exist in its realization. It is also beneficial to include an explicit description of criteria that help determine to what extent a pattern is supported by a certain offering.

Although the above represent requirements that a pattern collection should fulfill, sometimes requirements arise that we feel are not necessary or impossible to satisfy. For example, a pattern does not need to be formally (i.e., mathematically) defined. For some perspectives (e.g., control-flow), this offers some real benefits, whereas this approach would not suit other perspectives and may limit desirable interpretations of the patterns and diminish their accessibility. Formalizing a pattern using a particular language helps to clarify the pattern, but it may also introduce a bias, excluding other solution approaches. For example, in [115], we provide colored Petri nets for all control-flow patterns. However, these should be seen as examples illustrating the desired behavior and not as a formal specification of the patterns. Obviously, there is a trade-off between generality and precision [13, 31]. In this book, we kept things as informal as possible to ensure accessibility and to avoid a bias toward particular notations. Completeness of a patterns collection constitutes an example of a requirement that often cannot be achieved. The reason is that this requires an accepted yardstick that in many cases simply does not exist; if it did, there would not have been a need for a patterns collection in the first place. For example, how can one determine completeness of the control-flow patterns? What would one use as a benchmark? While completeness can often not be achieved, *comprehensiveness* is a desirable quality of a patterns collection.

Language development

As mentioned earlier, the workflow patterns have been used as the basis for YAWL (Yet Another Workflow Language).[1] YAWL provides comprehensive support for the control-flow, the resource, and the exception handling patterns. The language has a formal foundation, which makes the development of sophisticated verification solutions possible, and there is support for dynamic as well as declarative workflows. YAWL is supported by an open source environment that has a Service-Oriented Architecture (SOA), and complex functionality has been realized through the provision of new services communicating through well-defined interfaces with existing components in this environment. The YAWL environment started out as a reference implementation, demonstrating that comprehensive patterns support is feasible and illustrating how this may be achieved. Over time, the environment matured to the point where it is now able to be used in a production environment. The YAWL experience demonstrates the power of using patterns as a starting point for language development.

The development of YAWL was (partially) intended to counter early vendor claims that comprehensive patterns support would not be feasible. This belief may not have been restricted to the vendor community. In fact, an anonymous reviewer of the original workflow patterns paper wrote, "I do not think that such complex patterns can be used in real life workflow systems." The perception may also exist that it may not be desirable to provide comprehensive patterns support as this leads to languages/systems that are too complex for practitioners. The development of YAWL and broader trends in the field of BPM in recent years contradict this perception. Recent languages tend to offer increased patterns support (consider e.g., XPDL 1.0 vs. BPEL), and in some cases, the patterns have provided input during their development (notably BPMN). Having said this, comprehensive support for the resource perspective, flexibility, and process integration is still evolving in current standards and commercial offerings.

A promising trend in recent years is the emergence of open source BPM offerings. These can leverage the traditional benefits of open source software, including cost and adaptability considerations. Although generally speaking (and apart from YAWL) their patterns-based support is not as strong as the mainstream commercial offerings, they have become a worthwhile alternative. One of the reasons for this is that comprehensive patterns support is not necessarily required in all cases. If a detailed analysis of the pattern requirements in

1 www.yawlfoundation.org

a problem domain reveals that support for only a certain subset of the patterns is needed, tools supporting this subset may be perfectly adequate. Some open source offerings claim to be based on the workflow patterns, and it is hoped that workflow patterns support increases in this space in the coming years.

Need for empirical validation

The patterns are based on a detailed analysis of various WFM/BPM systems. Moreover, practical experiences obtained through a multitude of evaluations resulted in reformulations and further refinements of the patterns. Systems such as Staffware, WebSphere MQ Workflow, FLOWer, COSA, iPlanet, SAP Workflow, Filenet, jBPM, OpenWFE, Enhydra Shark, WebSphere Integration Developer, and Oracle BPEL, and languages/standards such as BPMN, XPDL, BPEL, UML, and EPCs have been analyzed using the patterns. Moreover, we have been interacting with workflow vendors, consultants, end-users, and analysts regarding the patterns. Nevertheless, there is an ongoing need for empirically validating the patterns. For example, in [131, 132], five workflow projects conducted by ATOS/Origin were to get quantitative data about the frequency of patterns. The results of this analysis showed that in many of ATOS/Origin's projects, workflow designers were forced to adapt the process or resort to spaghetti-like diagrams or coding because particular patterns were not supported by the WFM system. The project also showed a positive correlation between the patterns being used and the patterns that were well supported (e.g., the processes developed using Staffware had much more parallelism than the processes developed using Eastman Enterprise Workflow). This example shows that patterns tend to be used frequently if they are supported well. This indicates that process design is influenced by patterns support. A more elaborate empirical validation of the workflow patterns is welcome.

Workflow patterns can be validated by collecting large collections of process models. However, with the increasing availability of event data, it is also possible to apply process mining techniques [3] to discover frequent process patterns. Experience obtained by applying process mining in more than 100 organizations shows that processes are often much more involved than what people would like to think. Typically, 80% of the process instances can be described by a rather simple process model. However, to model the remaining 20%, more advanced patterns are needed. Such observations indicate the need for more empirical studies into the importance of the various workflow patterns. Such analysis should not be limited to what organizations are using but also what is needed.

Conclusion

The notion of patterns has become established in many areas of computer science. Their influence in the field of BPM has already been profound, but it is anticipated that their increased acceptance will positively contribute to the maturation of the field. The development of new languages should not be done on an ad hoc basis, tool selection should be conducted in a structured and requirements-driven manner, and the modeling of complex business scenarios in a particular language should be guided by solid knowledge of the capabilities of that language and ways of dealing with its limitations. A deep understanding of pattern collections can greatly assist in these tasks, and we hope that by studying this book, the reader is armed with the knowledge to tackle them confidently.

References

[1] W.M.P. van der Aalst. The application of Petri nets to workflow management. *Journal of Circuits, Systems and Computers*, 8(1):21–66, 1998.

[2] W.M.P. van der Aalst. Business process simulation revisited. In J. Barjis, editor, *Enterprise and Organizational Modeling and Simulation - 6th International Workshop, EOMAS 2010, held at CAiSE 2010, Hammamet, Tunisia, June 7-8, 2010. Selected Papers*, volume 63 of *Lecture Notes in Business Information Processing*, pages 1–14. Springer, 2010.

[3] W.M.P. van der Aalst. *Process Mining: Discovery, Conformance and Enhancement of Business Processes*. Springer, 2011.

[4] W.M.P. van der Aalst. Business process management: A comprehensive survey. *ISRN Software Engineering*, pages 1–37, 2013.

[5] W.M.P. van der Aalst, A. Adriansyah, and B. van Dongen. Replaying history on process models for conformance checking and performance analysis. *WIREs Data Mining and Knowledge Discovery*, 2(2):182–192, 2012.

[6] W.M.P. van der Aalst, P. Barthelmess, C.A. Ellis, and J. Wainer. Proclets: A framework for lightweight interacting workflow processes. *International Journal of Cooperative Information Systems*, 10(4):443–482, 2001.

[7] W.M.P. van der Aalst and T. Basten. Inheritance of workflows: An approach to tackling problems related to change. *Theoretical Computer Science*, 270(1-2):125–203, 2002.

[8] W.M.P. van der Aalst, T. Basten, H.M.W. Verbeek, P.A.C. Verkoulen, and M. Voorhoeve. Adaptive workflow — on the interplay between flexibility and support. In J. Filipe and J. Cordeiro, editors, *Proceedings of the 1st International Conference on Enterprise Information Systems*, pages 353–360. Setubal, Portugal, 1999.

[9] W.M.P. van der Aalst, J. Desel, and E. Kindler. On the semantics of EPCs: A vicious circle. In M. Rump and F.J. Nüttgens, editors, *Proceedings of the EPK 2002: Business Process Management using EPCs*, pages 71–80. Gesellschaft fur Informatik, Trier, Germany, 2002.

[10] W.M.P van der Aalst and K.M. van Hee. *Workflow Management: Models, Methods and Systems*. MIT Press, Cambridge, MA, USA, 2002.

[11] W.M.P. van der Aalst, K.M. van Hee, A.H.M. ter Hofstede, H.M.W. Verbeek, M. Voorhoeve, and M.T. Wynn. Soundness of workflow nets: Classification, decidability, and analysis. *Formal Aspects of Computing*, 23(3):333–363, 2011.

[12] W.M.P. van der Aalst and A.H.M. ter Hofstede. YAWL: Yet another workflow language. *Information Systems*, 30(4):245–275, 2005.

[13] W.M.P. van der Aalst and A.H.M. ter Hofstede. Workflow patterns put into context. *Software and Systems Modeling*, 11(3):319–323, 2012.

[14] W.M.P. van der Aalst, A.H.M. ter Hofstede, B. Kiepuszewski, and A.P. Barros. Workflow patterns. *Distributed and Parallel Databases*, 14(3):5–51, 2003.

[15] W.M.P. van der Aalst and A. Kumar. Team-enabled workflow management systems. *Data and Knowledge Engineering*, 38(3):335–363, 2001.

[16] W.M.P. van der Aalst, A.J. Mooij, C. Stahl, and K. Wolf. Service interaction: Patterns, formalization, and analysis. In M. Bernardo, L. Padovani, and G. Zavattaro, editors, *Formal Methods for Web Services*, volume 5569 of *Lecture Notes in Computer Science*, pages 42–88. Springer-Verlag, Berlin, 2009.

[17] W.M.P. van der Aalst, M. Pesic, and H. Schonenberg. Declarative workflows: Balancing between flexibility and support. *Computer Science - Research and Development*, 23(2):99–113, 2009.

[18] W.M.P. van der Aalst, H.A. Reijers, A.J.M.M. Weitjers, B.F. van Dongen, A.K. Alves de Medeiros, M. Song, and H.M.W. Verbeek. Business process mining: An industrial application. *Information Systems*, 32(5):713–732, 2007.

[19] W.M.P. van der Aalst and C. Stahl. *Modeling Business Processes: A Petri Net Oriented Approach*. MIT Press, Cambridge, MA, 2011.

[20] W.M.P. van der Aalst, A.J.M.M. Weijters, and L. Maruster. Workflow mining: Discovering process models from event logs. *IEEE Transactions on Knowledge and Data Engineering*, 16(9):1128–1142, 2004.

[21] W.M.P. van der Aalst, M. Weske, and D. Grünbauer. Case handling: A new paradigm for business process support. *Data and Knowledge Engineering*, 53(2):129–162, 2005.

[22] M.J. Adams. *Facilitating Dynamic Flexibility and Exception Handling for Workflows*. PhD thesis, Queensland University of Technology, Brisbane, Australia, 2007.

[23] A. Agostini and G. De Michelis. Improving flexibility of workflow management systems. In W.M.P. van der Aalst, J. Desel, and A. Oberweis, editors, *Business Process Management: Models, Techniques, and Empirical Studies*, volume 1806 of *Lecture Notes in Computer Science*, pages 218–234. Springer-Verlag, Berlin, 2000.

[24] C. Alexander. *The Timeless Way of Building*. Oxford University Press, New York, 1979.

[25] C. Alexander, S. Ishikawa, and M. Silverstein. *A Pattern Language: Towns, Buildings, Construction*. Oxford University Press, New York, NY, 1977.

[26] G. Alonso and C. Mohan. Workflow management systems: The next generation of distributed processing tools. In S. Jajodia and L. Kerschberg, editors, *Advanced Transaction Models and Architectures*, pages 35–62. Kluwer Academic Publishers, 1997.

[27] J.C.M. Baeten and W.P. Weijland. *Process Algebra*. Cambridge Tracts in Theoretical Computer Science 18. Cambridge University Press, Cambridge, UK, 1990.

[28] A. Barros, M. Dumas, and A.H.M. ter Hofstede. Service interaction patterns. In W.M P. van der Aalst, B. Benatallah, F. Casati, and F. Curbera, editors, *Proceedings of the 3rd International Conference on Business Process Management (BPM'2005)*, pages 302–318. Springer Verlag, Nancy, France, 2005.

[29] A.P. Barros, G. Decker, M. Dumas, and F. Weber. Correlation patterns in service-oriented architectures. In M.B. Dwyer and A. Lopes, editors, *Fundamental Approaches to Software Engineering, 10th International Conference, FASE 2007, Held as Part of the Joint European Conferences, on Theory and Practice of Software, ETAPS 2007, Braga, Portugal, March 24 - April 1, 2007, Proceedings*, volume 4422 of *Lecture Notes in Computer Science*, pages 245–259. Springer, 2007.

[30] A. Bonifati, F. Casati, U. Dayal, and M.C. Shan. Warehousing workflow data: Challenges and opportunities. In P.M.G. Apers, P. Atzeni, S. Ceri, S. Paraboschi, K. Ramamohanarao, and R.T. Snodgrass, editors, *Proceedings of the 27th International Conference on Very Large Data Bases (VLDB 2001)*, pages 649–652. Morgan Kaufmann, Rome, Italy, 2001.

[31] E. Börger. Approaches to modeling business processes. a critical analysis of BPMN, workflow patterns and YAWL. *Software and Systems Modeling*, 11(3):305–318, 2012.

[32] J. Seely Brown and E.S. Gray. The people are the company: How to build your company around your people. *Fast Company*, November 1995.

[33] S. Ceri, P.W.P.J. Grefen, and G. Sanchez. WIDE: A distributed architecture for workflow management. In *Proceedings of the Seventh International Workshop on Research Issues in Data Engineering (RIDE'97)*. IEEE Computer Society Press, Birmingham, England, 1997.

[34] E.M. Clarke, O. Grumberg, and D.A. Peled. *Model Checking*. The MIT Press, Cambridge, Massachusetts and London, UK, 1999.

[35] D. Cohn and R. Hull. Business artifacts: A data-centric approach to modeling business operations and processes. *IEEE Data Engineering Bulletin*, 32(3):3–9, 2009.

[36] W.B. Croft and L. Lefkowitz. Task support in an office system. *ACM Transactions on Office Information Systems*, 2(3):197–212, 1984.

[37] P. Dadam and M. Reichert. The ADEPT project: A decade of research and development for robust and flexible process support. *Computer Science Research and Development*, 23(2):81–98, 2009.

[38] A. Dardenne, A. van Lamsweerde, and S. Fickas. Goal-directed requirements acquisition. *Science of Computer Programming*, 20(1-2):3–50, 1993.

[39] B. Depaire, J. Swinnen, M. Jans, and K. Vanhoof. A process deviation analysis framework. In M. La Rosa and P. Soffer, editors, *Business Process Management Workshops, International Workshop on Business Process Intelligence (BPI 2012)*, volume 132 of *Lecture Notes in Business Information Processing*, pages 701–706. Springer-Verlag, Berlin, 2013.

[40] J. Desel, A. Oberweis, W. Reisig, and G. Rozenberg. Petri nets and business process management. Technical report, Dagstuhl, Germany, 1998. http://www.dagstuhl.de/Reports/98/98271.pdf.

[41] W. Du and M.C. Shan. Enterprise workflow resource management. In *Proceedings of the Ninth International Workshop on Research Issues on Data Engineering: Information Technology for Virtual Enterprises (RIDE-VE'99)*, pages 108–115. IEEE Computer Society Press, Sydney, Australia, 1999.

[42] M. Dumas, W.M.P van der Aalst, and A.H.M ter Hofstede. *Process-Aware Information Systems: Bridging People and Software through Process Technology*. Wiley-Interscience, Hoboken, NJ, USA, 2005.

[43] M. Dumas, A. Großkopf, T. Hettel, and M.T. Wynn. Semantics of standard process models with or-joins. In *OTM Conferences (1)*, pages 41–58, 2007.

[44] M. Dumas and A.H.M. ter Hofstede. UML activity diagrams as a workflow specification language. In M. Gogolla and C. Kobryn, editors, *Proceedings of the Fourth International Conference on the Unified Modeling Language (UML 2001)*, volume 2185 of *Lecture Notes in Computer Science*, pages 76–90. Springer, Toronto, Canada, 2001.

[45] M. Dumas, M. La Rosa, J. Mendling, and H. Reijers. *Fundamentals of Business Process Management*. Springer, 2013.

[46] J. Eder and M. Lehmann. Synchronizing copies of external data in workflow management systems. In O. Pastor and J. Falcão e Cunha, editors, *Proceedings of the 17th International Conference on Advanced Information Systems Engineering (CAiSE 2005)*, volume 3520 of *Lecture Notes in Computer Science*, pages 248–261. Springer, Porto, Portugal, 2005.

[47] J. Eder and W. Liebhart. The workflow activity model (WAMO). In S. Laufmann, S. Spaccapietra, and T. Yokoi, editors, *Proceedings of the Third International Conference on Cooperative Information Systems (CoopIS-95)*, pages 87–98. University of Toronto Press, Vienna, Austria, 1995.

[48] J. Eder, G.E. Olivotto, and W. Gruber. A data warehouse for workflow logs. In Y. Han, S. Tai, and D. Wikarski, editors, *Proceedings of the First International Conference on Engineering and Deployment of Cooperative Information Systems (EDCIS 2002)*, volume 2480 of *Lecture Notes In Computer Science*, pages 1–15. Springer, Beijing, China, 2002.

[49] C. Ellis and G. Nutt. Workflow: The process spectrum. In *Proceedings of the NSF Workshop on Workflow and Process Automation in Information Systems*. Athens, GA, USA, 1996.

[50] C.A. Ellis and G.J. Nutt. Office information systems and computer science. *ACM Computing Surveys*, 12 (1):27–60, 1980.

[51] H.E. Eriksson and M. Penker. *Business Modeling with UML*. OMG Press, New York, NY, USA, 2000.

[52] D.F. Ferraiolo, R. Sandhu, S. Gavrila, D.R. Kuhn, and R. Chandramouli. Proposed NIST standard for role-based access control. *ACM Transactions on Information and System Security*, 4(3):224–274, 2001.

[53] M. Fowler. *Analysis Patterns: Reusable Object Models*. Addison-Wesley, Boston, MA, USA, 1996.

[54] E. Gamma, R. Helm, R. Johnson, and J. Vlissides. *Design Patterns: Elements of Reusable Object-Oriented Software*. Addison-Wesley, Boston, MA, USA, 1995.

[55] D. Georgakopoulos, M.F. Hornick, and A.P. Sheth. An overview of workflow management: From process modeling to workflow automation infrastructure. *Distributed and Parallel Databases*, 3(2):119–153, 1995.

[56] S. Gibbs and D. Tsichritzis. A data modelling approach for office information systems. *ACM Transactions on Office Information Systems*, 1(4):299–319, 1983.

[57] J. Gordijn, H. Akkermans, and H. van Vliet. Business modelling is not process modelling. In S.W. Liddle, H.C. Mayr, and B. Thalheim, editors, *Conceptual Modeling for E-Business and the Web, ER 2000 Workshops on Conceptual Modeling Approaches for E-Business and The World Wide Web and Conceptual Modeling, Salt Lake City, Utah, USA, October 9-12, 2000, Proceedings*, volume 1921 of *Lecture Notes In Computer Science*, pages 40–51. Springer, Salt Lake City, Utah, USA, 2000.

[58] F. Gottschalk, W.M.P. van der Aalst, M.H. Jansen-Vullers, and M. La Rosa. Configurable workflow models. *International Journal of Cooperative Information Systems*, 17(2):177–221, 2008.

[59] G. Governatori, Z. Milosevic, and S. Sadiq. Compliance checking between business processes and business contracts. In *10th International Enterprise Distributed Object Computing Conference (EDOC 2006)*, pages 221–232. IEEE Computing Society, 2006.

[60] C. Hagen and G. Alonso. Exception handling in workflow management systems. *IEEE Transactions on Software Engineering*, 26(10):943–958, 2000.

[61] T. Halpin. UML data models from an ORM perspective: Part 1. *Journal of Conceptual Modeling*, 1, 1998. www.inconcept.com.

[62] M. Hammer, W.G. Howe, V.J. Kruskal, and I. Wladawsky. A very high level programming language for data processing applications. *Communications of the ACM*, 20(11):832–840, 1977.

[63] M. Havey. *Essential Business Process Modeling*. O'Reilly Media, Inc., 2005.

[64] A.H.M. ter Hofstede, W.M.P. van der Aalst, M. Adams, and N. Russell, editors. *Modern Business Process Automation: YAWL and Its Support Environment*. Springer, 2009.

[65] G. Hohpe and B. Woolf. *Enterprise Integration Patterns: Designing, Building, and Deploying Messaging Solutions*. Addison-Wesley, Boston, MA, USA, 2004.

[66] A.W. Holt. Coordination technology and Petri nets. In G. Rozenberg, editor, *Advances in Petri Nets 1985*, volume 222 of *Lecture Notes in Computer Science*, pages 278–296. Springer, London, 1986.

[67] Y.N. Huang and M.C. Shan. Policies in a resource manager of workflow systems: Modeling, enforcement and management. Technical Report HPL-98-156, Hewlett-Packard Company, 1999. http://www.hpl.hp.com/techreports/98/HPL-98-156.pdf.

[68] S. Jablonski and C. Bussler. *Workflow Management: Modeling Concepts, Architecture and Implementation*. Thomson Computer Press, London, UK, 1996.

[69] K. Jensen and W M.P. van der Aalst, editors. *Transactions on Petri Nets and Other Models of Concurrency II, Special Issue on Concurrency in Process-Aware Information Systems*, volume 5460 of *Lecture Notes in Computer Science*. Springer, 2009.

[70] K. Jensen and L.M. Kristensen. *Coloured Petri Nets*. Springer, 2009.

[71] G. Keller, M. Nüttgens, and A.-W. Scheer. Semantische prozessmodellierung. *Veroffentlichungen des Instituts fur Wirtschaftinformatik, Nr 89, Saarbrucken, Germany*, 1992.

[72] B. Kiepuszewski. *Expressiveness and Suitability of Languages for Control Flow Modelling in Workflows*. PhD thesis, Queensland University of Technology, Brisbane, Australia, 2003.

[73] B. Kiepuszewski, A.H.M. ter Hofstede, and W.M.P. van der Aalst. Fundamentals of control flow in workflows. *Acta Informatica*, 39(3):143–209, 2003.

[74] B. Kiepuszewski, A.H.M. ter Hofstede, and C. Bussler. On structured workflow modelling. In B. Wangler and L. Bergman, editors, *Proceedings of the 12th International Conference on Advanced Information Systems Engineering CAiSE 2000*, volume 1789 of *Lecture Notes in Computer Science*, pages 431–445. Springer, Stockholm, Sweden, 2000.

[75] E. Kindler. On the semantics of EPCs: Resolving the vicious circle. *Data and Knowledge Engineering*, 56 (1):23–40, 2006.

[76] A. Lanz, B. Weber, and M. Reichert. Time patterns in process-aware information systems – a patterns-based analysis – revised version. Technical Report UIB-2009, University of Ulm, 2009.

[77] A. Lanz, B. Weber, and M. Reichert. Workflow time patterns for process-aware information systems. In I. Bider, T.A. Halpin, J. Krogstie, S. Nurcan, E. Proper, R. Schmidt, and R. Ukor, editors, *Enterprise, Business-Process and Information Systems Modeling - 11th International Workshop, BPMDS 2010, and 15th International Conference, EMMSAD 2010, held at CAiSE 2010, Hammamet, Tunisia, June 7-8, 2010. Proceedings*, volume 50 of *Lecture Notes in Business Information Processing*, pages 94–107. Springer, 2010.

[78] B.S. Lerner, A.G. Ninan, L.J. Osterweil, and R.M. Podorozhny. Modeling and managing resource utilization in process, workflow, and activity coordination. Technical Report UM-CS-2000-058, Department of Computer Science, University of Massachusetts, MA, USA, August 2000. http://laser.cs.umass.edu/publications/?category=PROC.

[79] F. Leymann and D. Roller. *Production Workflow: Concepts and Techniques*. Prentice Hall, Upper Saddle River, NJ, USA, 2000.

[80] C. Marshall. *Enterprise Modeling with UML*. Addison Wesley, Reading, MA, USA, 1999.

[81] J. Mendling, G. Neumann, and W.M.P. van der Aalst. Understanding the occurrence of errors in process models based on metrics. In F. Curbera, F. Leymann, and M. Weske, editors, *Proceedings of the OTM Conference on Cooperative information Systems (CoopIS 2007), Vilamoura, Portugal*, volume 4803 of *Lecture Notes in Computer Science*, pages 113–130. Springer-Verlag, Berlin, 2007.

[82] J. Mendling and W.M.P. van der Aalst. Formalization and verification of EPCs with or-joins based on state and context. In *CAiSE 2007*, pages 439–453, 2007.

[83] R. Milner. *Communicating and Mobile Systems: The Pi-Calculus*. Cambridge University Press, 1999.

[84] H.R. Montahari-Nezhad, R. Saint-Paul, F. Casati, and B. Benatallah. Event correlation for process discovery from web service interaction logs. *VLBD Journal*, 20(3):417–444, 2011.

[85] M. Montali, M. Pesic, W.M.P. van der Aalst, F. Chesani, P. Mello, and S. Storari. Declarative specification and verification of service choreographies. *ACM Transactions on the Web*, 4(1):1–62, 2010.

[86] M. zur Muehlen. Process-driven management information systems — combining data warehouses and workflow technology. In B. Gavish, editor, *Proceedings of the 4th International Conference on Electronic Commerce Research (ICECR-4)*, pages 550–566. IFIP, Dallas, TX, USA, 2001.

[87] M. zur Muehlen. Workflow-based process controlling — or: What you can measure you can control. In L. Fischer, editor, *Workflow Handbook 2001*. Future Strategies, 2001.

[88] M. zur Muehlen. *Workflow-based Process Controlling: Foundation, Design and Application of Workflow-driven Process Information Systems*. Logos, Berlin, Germany, 2004.

[89] N. Mulyar. *Patterns for Process-Aware Information Systems: An Approach Based on Colored Petri Nets*. PhD Thesis, Beta Research School for Operations Management and Logistics, Eindhoven University of Technology, 2009.

[90] N. Mulyar, W.M.P. van der Aalst, L. Aldred, and N. Russell. Service interaction patterns: A configurable framework. Technical report, BPM Center BPM-07-07, 2007. http://bpmcenter.org/wp-content/uploads/reports/2007/BPM-07-07.pdf.

[91] N.A. Mulyar, W.M.P. van der Aalst, and N.C. Russell. Process flexibility patterns. Technical Report Beta Working Papers No. 251, Eindhoven University of Technology, Eindhoven, Netherlands, 2004. http://cms.ieis.tue.nl/Beta/Files/WorkingPapers/Beta_wp251.pdf.

[92] C.C. Niculae. Time patterns in workflow management systems. Technical Report BPM-11-04, BPM Center Report, 2011. http://bpmcenter.org/wp-content/uploads/reports/2011/BPM-11-04.pdf.

[93] OASIS. Web Services Business Process Execution Language for Web Services version 2.0, 2007. http://docs.oasis-open.org/wsbpel/2.0/wsbpel-v2.0.pdf.

[94] OASIS. Web Services - Human Task (WS-HumanTask) Specification version 1.1, 2010. http://docs.oasis-open.org/bpel4people/ws-humantask-1.1-spec-cs-01.pdf.

[95] OASIS. WS-BPEL Extension for People (BPEL4People) Specification version 1.1, 2010. http://docs.oasis-open.org/bpel4people/bpel4people-1.1.pdf.

[96] OMG. OMG Unified Modeling Language (OMG UML), version 2.5, 2015. http://www.omg.org/spec/UML/2.5.

[97] OMG/BPMI. Business Process Model and Notation (BPMN) version 2.0.2, 2014. http://www.omg.org/spec/BPMN/2.0.2/.

[98] C. Ouyang, M.T. Wynn, C. Fidge, A.H.M. ter Hofstede, and J.C. Kuhr. Modelling complex resource requirements in business process management systems. In M. Rosemann, P. Green, and F. Rohde, editors, *Australasian Conference on Information Systems (ACIS 2010)*. AIS eLibrary, 2010.

[99] C. Ouyang, M.T. Wynn, J.C. Kuhr, M. Adams, T. Becker, A.H.M. ter Hofstede, and C.J. Fidge. Workflow support for scheduling in surgical care processes. In V.K. Tuunainen, M. Rossi, and J. Nandhakumar, editors, *19th European Conference on Information Systems, ECIS 2011, Helsinki, Finland, June 9-11, 2011*.

[100] G.A. Pall. *Quality Process Management*. Prentice-Hall, Englewood Cliffs, NJ, USA, 1987.

[101] J.L. Peterson. *Petri Net Theory and the Modelling of Systems*. Prentice-Hall, Upper Saddle River, NJ, USA, 1981.

[102]   C.A. Petri. *Kommunikation mit Automaten*. PhD thesis, Institut für Instrumentelle Mathematik, Bonn, Germany, 1962.

[103]   M. Reichert and B. Weber. *Enabling Flexibility in Process-Aware Information Systems: Challenges, Methods, Technologies*. Springer-Verlag, Berlin, 2012.

[104]   H.A. Reijers. Workflow flexibility: The forlorn promise. In *15th IEEE International Workshops on Enabling Technologies: Infrastructures for Collaborative Enterprises (WETICE 2006), 26-28 June 2006, Manchester, United Kingdom*, pages 271–272. IEEE Computer Society, 2006.

[105]   A. Reuter and F. Schwenkreis. ConTracts — a low-level mechanism for building general-purpose workflow management-systems. *IEEE Data Engineering Bulletin*, 18(1):4–10, 1995.

[106]   P. Rittgen. From process model to electronic business process. In D. Avison, E. Christiaanse, C.U. Ciborra, K. Kautz, J. Pries-Heje, and J. Valor, editors, *Proceedings of the European Conference on Information Systems (ECIS 1999)*, pages 616–625. Copenhagen, Denmark, 1999. http://www.adm.hb.se/~pri/ecis99.pdf.

[107]   C. Rolland, C. Souveyet, and C. Ben Achour. Guiding goal modelling using scenarios. *IEEE Transactions on Software Engineering*, 24(12):1055–1071, 1998.

[108]   M. La Rosa. *Managing Variability in Process-Aware Information Systems*. PhD thesis, Queensland University of Technology, Brisbane, Australia, 2009.

[109]   M. Rosemann and W.M.P. van der Aalst. A configurable reference modelling language. *Information Systems*, 32(1):1–23, 2007.

[110]   A. Rozinat and W.M.P. van der Aalst. Conformance checking of processes based on monitoring real behavior. *Information Systems*, 33(1):64–95, 2008.

[111]   N. Russell. *Foundations of Process-Aware Information Systems*. PhD thesis, Queensland University of Technology, 2007.

[112]   N. Russell, W.M.P. van der Aalst, and A.H.M. ter Hofstede. Workflow exception patterns. In E. Dubois and K. Pohl, editors, *Proceedings of the 18th International Conference on Advanced Information Systems Engineering (CAiSE'06)*, volume 4001 of *Lecture Notes in Computer Science*, pages 288–302. Springer, Luxembourg, Luxembourg, 2006.

[113]   N. Russell, W.M.P. van der Aalst, A.H.M. ter Hofstede, and D. Edmond. Workflow resource patterns: Identification, representation and tool support. In O. Pastor and J. Falcão e Cunha, editors, *Proceedings of the 17th Conference on Advanced Information Systems Engineering (CAiSE'05)*, volume 3520 of *Lecture Notes in Computer Science*, pages 216–232. Springer, Porto, Portugal, 2005.

[114]   N. Russell, W.M.P. van der Aalst, A.H.M. ter Hofstede, and P. Wohed. On the suitability of UML 2.0 activity diagrams for business process modelling. In M. Stumptner, S. Hartmann, and Y. Kiyoki, editors, *Proceedings of the Third Asia-Pacific Conference on Conceptual Modelling (APCCM2006)*, volume 53 of *CRPIT*, pages 95–104. ACS, Hobart, Australia, 2006.

[115]   N. Russell, A.H.M. ter Hofstede, W.M.P. van der Aalst, and N. Mulyar. Workflow control-flow patterns: A revised view. Technical Report BPM-06-22, BPMcenter.org, 2006. http://bpmcenter.org/wp-content/uploads/reports/2006/BPM-06-22.pdf.

[116]   N. Russell, A.H.M. ter Hofstede, D. Edmond, and W.M.P. van der Aalst. Workflow data patterns: Identification, representation and tool support. In L. Delcambre, C. Kop, H.C. Mayr, J. Mylopoulos, and O. Pastor, editors, *Proceedings of the 24th International Conference on Conceptual Modeling (ER 2005)*, volume 3716 of *Lecture Notes in Computer Science*, pages 353–368. Springer, Klagenfurt, Austria, 2005.

[117]   S. Sadiq, M. Orlowska, W. Sadiq, and C. Foulger. Data flow and validation in workflow modelling. In K.D. Schewe and H.E. Williams, editors, *Proceedings of the 5th Australasian Database Conference (ADC'04)*, volume 27 of *CRPIT*, pages 207–214. ACS, Dunedin, New Zealand, 2004.

[118]   P. Sarbanes and G. Oxley. Sarbanes-Oxley Act of 2002.

[119]   A.W. Scheer. *ARIS — Business Process Frameworks*. Springer, Berlin, Germany, 1999.

[120]   A.W. Scheer. *ARIS — Business Process Modelling*. Springer, Berlin, Germany, 2000.

[121]   H. Schonenberg, R. Mans, N. Russell, N. Mulyar, and W.M.P. van der Aalst. Process flexibility: A survey of contemporary approaches. In J.L.G. Dietz, A. Albani, and J. Barjis, editors, *Advances in Enterprise Engineering I, 4th International Workshop CIAO! and 4th International Workshop EOMAS, held at CAiSE*

2008, Montpellier, France, June 16-17, 2008. Proceedings, volume 10 of *Lecture Notes in Business Information Processing*, pages 16–30. Springer, 2008.

[122] A. Sheth. From contemporary workflow process automation to adaptive and dynamic work activity coordination and collaboration. In R. Wagner, editor, *Database and Expert Systems Applications, 8th. International Workshop, DEXA'97, Proceedings*, pages 24–27. IEEE Computer Society Press, Los Alamitos, California, 1997, Toulouse, France, September 1997.

[123] B. Silver. *BPMN Method and Style, Second Edition, with BPMN Implementer's Guide*. Cody-Cassidy Press, Aptos, CA, USA, 2012.

[124] R. van Stiphout, T.D. Meijler, A. Aerts, D. Hammer, and R. Le Comte. TREX: Workflow transaction by means of exceptions. In H.-J. Schek, F. Saltor, I. Ramos, and G. Alonso, editors, *Proceedings of the Sixth International Conference on Extending Database Technology (EDBT'98)*, pages 21–26. Valencia, Spain, 1998.

[125] L.H. Thom, M. Reichert, and C. Iochpe. Activity patterns in process-aware information systems: Basic concepts and empirical evidence. *International Journal of Business Process Integration and Management*, 4(2):93–110, 2009.

[126] N. Trcka, W.M.P. van der Aalst, and N. Sidorova. Data-flow anti-patterns: Discovering data-flow errors in workflows. In P. van Eck, J. Gordijn, and R. Wieringa, editors, *Advanced Information Systems Engineering, Proceedings of the 21st International Conference on Advanced Information Systems Engineering (CAiSE'09)*, volume 5565 of *Lecture Notes in Computer Science*, pages 425–439. Springer-Verlag, Berlin, 2009.

[127] H.M.W. Verbeek, T. Basten, and W.M.P. van der Aalst. Diagnosing workflow processes using Woflan. *The Computer Journal*, 44(4):246–279, 2001.

[128] F. Vernadat. UEML: Towards a unified enterprise modelling language. *International Journal of Production Research*, 40(17):4309–4321, 2002.

[129] F.B. Vernadat. *Enterprise Modeling and Integration*. Chapman and Hall, London, UK, 1996.

[130] H. Völzer. A new semantics for the inclusive converging gateway in safe processes. In *Business Process Management (BPM 2010)*, pages 294–309, 2010.

[131] K. de Vries and O. Ommert. Advanced workflow patterns in practice (1): Experiences based on pension processing (in Dutch). *Business Process Magazine*, 7(6):15–18, 2001.

[132] K. de Vries and O. Ommert. Advanced workflow patterns in practice (2): Experiences based on judicial processes (in Dutch). *Business Process Magazine*, 8(1):20–23, 2002.

[133] B. Weber, M. Reichert, and S. Rinderle-Ma. Change patterns and change support features: Enhancing flexibility in process-aware information systems. *Data and Knowledge Engineering*, 66(3):438–466, 2008.

[134] B. Weber, S. Rinderle, and M. Reichert. Change patterns and change support features in process-aware information systems. In J. Krogstie, A.L. Opdahl, and G. Sindre, editors, *Advanced Information Systems Engineering, 19th International Conference, CAiSE 2007, Trondheim, Norway, June 11-15, 2007, Proceedings*, volume 4495 of *Lecture Notes in Computer Science*, pages 574–588. Springer, 2007.

[135] G. Weikum and G. Vossen. *Transactional Information Systems: Theory, Algorithms, and the Practice of Concurrency Control and Recovery*. Morgan Kaufmann Publishers, San Francisco, CA, USA, 2002.

[136] M. Weske. *Business Process Management: Concepts, Languages, Architectures*. Springer, Berlin, Heidelberg, 2007.

[137] S. White. Process modeling notations and workflow patterns. In L. Fischer, editor, *Workflow Handbook 2004*, pages 265–294. Future Strategies Inc., Lighthouse Point, FL, USA, 2004.

[138] S.A. White and D. Miers. *BPMN Modeling and Reference Guide: Understanding and Using BPMN*. Future Strategies Inc., Lighthouse Pt, FL, USA, 2008.

[139] P. Wohed, W.M.P. van der Aalst, M. Dumas, and A.H.M. ter Hofstede. Analysis of web services composition languages: The case of BPEL4WS. In I.Y. Song, S.W. Liddle, T.W. Ling, and P. Scheuermann, editors, *Proceedings of the 22nd International Conference on Conceptual Modeling (ER'2003)*, volume 2813 of *Lecture Notes in Computer Science*, pages 200–215. Springer, Chicago, IL, USA, 2003.

[140] P. Wohed, W.M.P. van der Aalst, M. Dumas, A.H.M. ter Hofstede, and N. Russell. Pattern-based analysis of UML activity diagrams. In L. Delcambre, C. Kop, H.C. Mayr, J. Mylopoulos, and O. Pastor, editors,

Proceedings of the 25th International Conference on Conceptual Modeling (ER'2005), volume 3716 of *Lecture Notes in Computer Science*, pages 63–78. Springer, Klagenfurt, Austria, 2005.

[141] P. Wohed, E. Perjons, M. Dumas, and A.H.M. ter Hofstede. Pattern based analysis of EAI languages — the case of the Business Modeling Language. In O. Camp and M. Piattini, editors, *Proceedings of the 5th International Conference on Enterprise Information Systems (ICEIS 2003)*, volume 3, pages 174–184. Escola Superior de Tecnologia do Instituto Politécnico de Setúbal, Angers, France, 2003.

[142] P. Wohed, W.M.P. van der Aalst, M. Dumas, A.H.M. ter Hofstede, and N. Russell. On the suitability of BPMN for business process modelling. In *Business Process Management (BPM 2006)*, pages 161–176, 2006.

[143] Workflow Management Coalition. Reference model — the workflow reference model. Technical Report WFMC-TC-1003, 19-Jan-95, 1.1, wfmc.org, 1995. http://www.wfmc.org/standards/docs/tc003v11.pdf.

[144] Workflow Management Coalition. Terminology and glossary. Technical Report Document Number WFMC-TC-1011, Issue 3.0, wfmc.org, 1999. http://www.wfmc.org/standards/docs/TC-1011_term_glossary_v3.pdf.

[145] Workflow Management Coalition. Process definition interface — XML process definition language version 2.2. Technical Report WFMC-TC-1025, wfmc.org, 2012. http://www.xpdl.org/standards/xpdl-2.2/XPDL%202.2%20(2012-08-30).pdf.

[146] S. Wu, A.P. Sheth, J.A. Miller, and Z. Luo. Authorisation and access control of application data in workflow systems. *Journal of Intelligent Information Systems*, 18(1):71–94, 2002.

[147] M.T. Wynn, W.M.P. van der Aalst, A.H.M. ter Hofstede, and D. Edmond. Synchronization and cancellation in workflows based on reset nets. *International Journal of Cooperative Information Systems*, 18(1):63–114, 2009.

[148] M.T. Wynn, D. Edmond, W.M.P. van der Aalst, and A.H.M. ter Hofstede. Achieving a general, formal and decidable approach to the OR-join in workflow using Reset nets. In G. Ciardo and P. Darondeau, editors, *Proceedings of the 26th International Conference on Application and Theory of Petri nets and Other Models of Concurrency (Petri Nets 2005)*, volume 3536 of *Lecture Notes in Computer Science*, pages 423–443. Springer, Miami, FL, USA, 2005.

[149] U. Yildiz, A. Guabtni, and A.H.H. Ngu. Towards scientific workflow patterns. In *WORKS '09: Proceedings of the 4th Workshop on Workflows in Support of Large-Scale Science (2009)*, pages 1–10. ACM, New York, NY, USA, 2009.

[150] J.A. Zachman. A framework for information systems architecture. *IBM Systems Journal*, 26(3):276–292, 1987.

[151] M.D. Zisman. *Representation, Specification and Automation of Office Procedures*. PhD thesis, Wharton School of Business, University of Pennsylvania, Philadelphia, PA, USA, 1977.

Acronyms

A2A application-to-application. 69
ABC Activity Based Costing. 56
ACP Algebra of Communicating Processes. 40

BAM business activity monitoring. 71
BPEL Business Process Execution Language, also known as WS-BPEL. 18
BPM Business Process Management. 3
BPMI Business Process Modeling Initiative. 40
BPML Business Process Modelling Language. 18
BPMN Business Process Modeling and Notation. 7, 18
BPMS Business Process Management Systems. 15

CCS Calculus of Communicating Systems. 40
CIMOSA Computer aIded Manufacturing Open Source Architecture. 23
CPN Colored Petri Nets. 40
CRM Customer Relationship Management. 16
CSCW Computer Supported Cooperative Work. 69
CSP Communicating Sequential Processes. 40

DFD Data Flow Diagram. 38

ECA Event-Condition-Action. 68
EPC Event-Driven Process Chain. 18
ER Entity-Relationship. 6
ERP Enterprise Resource Planning. 15, 16

GUI Graphic User Interface. 61

HR Human Resource. 27

IE Information Engineering. 39
IT Information Technology. 3

JSD Jackson Structured Design. 39
JSP Jackson Structured Programming. 39

LDAP Lightweight Directory Access Protocol. 27
LTL Linear Temporal Logic. 96

OASIS Organization for the Advancement of Structured Information Standards. 71
OMG Object Management Group. 41
OOAD Object-Oriented Analysis and Design. 39

P2A person-to-application. 69
P2P person-to-person. 69
PAIS Process-Aware Information Systems. 15, 16

RCA Resource Consumption Accounting. 56
RDR Ripple Down Rule. 90

SADT Structured Analysis and Design Technique. 39
SSADM Structured System Analysis and Design Method. 39

TP Transaction Processing. 69

UML Unified Modelling Language. 18

WF Windows Workflow Foundation. 15
WFM Workflow Process Management. 16
WfMC Workflow Management Coalition. 23
WFMS Workflow Process Management Systems. 15
WPDL Workflow Process Definition Language. 65
WSCI Web Services Choreography Interface. 18

XML eXtensible Markup Language. 70
XOR eXclusive OR. 28
XPDL eXtensible Process Definition Language. 18

YAWL Yet Another Workflow Language. 18
YSM Yourdon Structured Method. 39

Index